PRAISE FOR DR. CHRISTINA HIBBERT'S

THIS IS HOW WE

GROW

"Through the authenticity of her words and the grace with which she lives each day, Dr. Hibbert has created a masterpiece she simply calls her life. *This is How We Grow* shows us there is great strength in being vulnerable as Hibbert opens her grieving heart to the restorative power of love and resilience. A truly inspirational book and a deeply profound tribute to her beloved sister."

—KAREN KLEIMAN, MSW, LCSW, Bestselling Postpartum Depression Author, *This Isn't What I Expected*, and Founder, The Postpartum Stress Center

"*This is How We Grow* is an honest and personal accounting of how Dr. Christina Hibbert and her family faced unthinkable tragedy and found the courage not just to overcome, but to thrive in spite of it. This beautiful, inspirational story will touch your heart and leave you with a renewed sense of gratitude and love of life."

—SUSAN CAMPBELL CROSS, Author, *The FabYOUList: List It, Live It, Love Your Life*, Lifestyle Editor, *SHAPE, OK!* and *Star* Magazines

"Dr. Christina Hibbert's memoir, *This is How We Grow*, is a true inspiration. As she chronicles the losses and additions she has experienced, her authenticity pulls you into the compelling and rich tapestry of her life. Dr. Hibbert shows us how to not just endure, but to overcome and grow. What a welcome relief to know that even a mental health expert can reveal her deepest fears, worries, and vulnerabilities, showing us that we are not alone. Simply a must-read book that will touch your heart and inspire your soul!"

—ELISA ALL, Founder/CEO, www.30SecondMom.com, a 30Second Mobile brand

"Dr. Hibbert doesn't just tell us, she shows us how to grow in this brave and heartwarming memoir. *This Is How We Grow* is a rare glimpse into grief and the triumph of the human spirit!"

—JULIE DE AZEVEDO HANKS, LCSW, Self and Relationship Expert, Author, *The Burnout Cure: An Emotional Survival Guide for Women.*

THIS IS HOW WE GROW

A PSYCHOLOGIST'S MEMOIR OF LOSS, MOTHERHOOD, & DISCOVERING SELF-WORTH & JOY, ONE SEASON AT A TIME

By
Christina G. Hibbert, Psy.D.

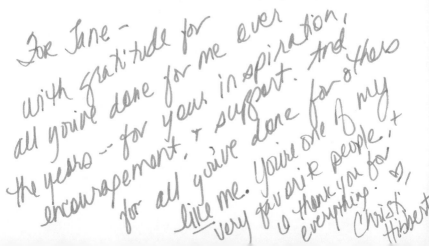

For Jane —
with gratitude for all you've done for me over the years — for your inspiration, encouragement, + support. And for all you've done for others like me. You're one of my very favorite people, + to thank you for everything. ♡,
Christi Hibbert

ISBN 978-0615918976 (Oracle Folio Books)

Author's Note
Some names, details, and circumstances have been changed to protect the privacy of those mentioned in this publication.
This publication is not intended as a substitute for the advice of health care professionals.

Cover design by Kristin McGuire Call
Author photo by Anna LaBenz Photography

~For Shannon and for our children.
May they read these pages and know how much they have always been loved.

CONTENTS

There is a great, cosmic ebb and flow—
energy pouring calmly, powerfully through all—
prompting change, nudging growth.
Telling us we cannot stay as we are.
Telling us we must become.

PROLOGUE

"She's dead, isn't she?" I asked, not feeling the words. My body was already erecting the wall that would hold back so many emotions for so many months. "OJ, just tell me," I pressed him, still holding the glimmer of hope that I was wrong.

Hesitation. Hesitation was a confirmation in itself. *He is my OJ—my husband and most steady supporter, my best friend.* He didn't want to drop this bomb. The moment before the truth comes out is so full of possibility; yet it was already determined.

"Yes," he said. "She died."

What do I say? When time stops and everything changes, what can possibly be said?

"Do you realize we just inherited two kids?" Half angry, half in shock, I laughed. My sister had just died, and I laughed.

Our family, before.

Shannon and Rob's family, before.

PART I:
FALL

Year of
PATIENCE

Fall is the jumping in, the beginning of learning, the end of the ease of summer.
Fall is the slowing down, the turning of the sun, sky, wind, and trees.
Fall is the surprise—
the hint of something coming,
the twists and turns signaling
that everything
is about to change.

ONE
Choose to Grow

"To everything there is a season, and a time to every purpose under heaven."
~ Ecclesiastes 31:1 (King James Version)

It was fall when my world came crashing to a halt. In that instant, everything changed. Life changes are to be expected, aren't they? Seasons change, years come and go, and so do we. Intellectually, I knew this, and as a clinical psychologist, I was an expert on this. My life and identity had been built around the study, the research, and the drive to help people adapt in the face of deep change. I had already lost many people close to me, and those losses had formed me into one who helped others through their grief and life trials. Now, here I was. The skilled doctor was to experience the role of the humbled patient. And I knew from working with so many other humbled patients how unyielding the work I was about to do was going to be. I was terrified. But I am getting ahead of myself.

A few years before this life-altering event, on January 1st, I had been reflecting on the nature of change. *What good is all this life change,* I asked myself, *if it doesn't change* me? I craved positive growth. Tired of too-often forgotten New Year's Resolutions, I came up with the idea of a yearly theme. This theme would serve as my one resolution for the entire year and give me focused, extended practice in mastering it. It would steer me in the direction of the person I wanted to become. It was time to choose to grow.

My first year's theme was "Carpe Diem"—a time in my life when I was ready to take on the world as a freshly licensed clinical psychologist, mother of three, and founder of a non-profit organization. I think I "Carpe'd" a little too much "Diem," if you catch my drift, and ended up completely burned out by the end of the year. But it was okay. It was the exact lesson I needed at that time and paved the way for my next year's theme, *Humility*. That is what I have found every year: my theme is always perfectly suited to help me grow.

There *is* a reason for every season of growth, you know, just like the scripture says. A "time to every purpose," "a time to break down," "a time to build up."[1] Like fall fades to winter and spring blooms to summer, we can choose to grow through the seasons of our life. There will be times in each of our lives when we will find ourselves falling. Our feet swept out from under us, we see the beautiful colors of the remaining leaves overhead on our way down to—smack!—the pile on the ground. We will then find our world shifting again. We will feel the isolation of winter—snow-packed, howling winds while we seek the safety of the burning fire within. We will feel the hope of spring—little green shoots pushing with all their might for even the smallest glimpse of the light. We will experience the rapture of the summer that follows the seasons of life, the seasons of growth.

As a wise person once said, "Life is change. Growth is optional. Choose wisely."[2] What will *your* choice be? *I* choose to grow. Take my year of Patience, for example. I could never have guessed how much patience I would actually require or how much growing I would have to choose to do, but somehow I knew—just like I always know—it was the direction to take. It was the precise thing I needed at that season of my life. In true cyclical fashion, my need for patience actually began the fall before, in my year of Charity. It was our first trip to Hawaii and we were in for, yep, you guessed it—change.

It all began with an earthquake.

Sunday, October 15

I came to Hawaii to decide if we should try for another baby. OJ thought I was just tagging along while he attended his dental seminar, but I admit, I had an ulterior motive. For the past three days, as he's been sitting in air-conditioned boardrooms, sipping mini-Sprite and eating chocolate chip cookies, I've been sitting on a beach towel, digging my toes into the grainy sand, watching the waves slip in and away and wondering when I should bring up the subject. We already have three beautiful, healthy children, so why have I been wondering about having one more?

I finally, casually, brought it up before bed last night. His reply? "We're good, hon. Why shake things up?" So OJ. And so *ironic*.

"Stop shaking the bed," I muttered, this morning, irritated. The clock read 7:07 a.m. OJ has a way of becoming annoying in the early hours when I want to sleep-in. I sat up, frustrated, and looked to my left, where he lay next to me. He was sound asleep, but the bed was definitely shaking. "OJ, wake up! Is this an earthquake?" I ran to the window and looked out from the 27th floor. The ocean and other tall hotels lining Waikiki beach seemed undisturbed, but *yes*, we were moving. In fact, we were swaying. The entire tower leaned side to side as I helplessly gazed at the tiny cars, people, and trees below.

Are we going to die? We don't have our will finished! Our kids! What would become of them? We'd never survive if this building should fall. Crushed. It would be quick. All these thoughts flashed through my brain in a dizzy moment.

I turned to OJ—sitting up, still in bed, as stunned as I was. "Should we run to the door frame?" Somehow I knew that would be pointless being so high up, so we stayed where we were. There was nothing else to do. We remained frozen and rode the vibrations of that eerie sound, like a buzzing wave rolling through every cell of the body.

And then…surrender. I stared out the floor-to-ceiling window, in the midst of a seven point zero magnitude earthquake. Our building rocked and swayed. Yet I saw below me…calm. Intense quiet. Peace. Peace found me. I submitted. A moment of beauty, surrendering to the power of nature, a moment experiencing nature's fury and absolute domination in such a calm and humbling way.

The vibration slowed. The building swayed to a halt. We were still, though our bodies had yet to recognize it was over. I looked at the clock: 7:08. It had only been one minute. It had only been one minute, and yet, something inside me knew that everything had changed.

Saturday, November 4

I keep thinking back to Hawaii. How different life feels, now, compared to then.

OJ's new Hawaiian habit of drinking endless pineapple juice and going to the bathroom umpteen times a night followed us home. He's been waking me up every night, and we're both exhausted. But *he* is more than exhausted. He seems unmotivated and maybe even depressed. Whereas he used to be the fun and helpful dad and husband, playing with the kids and pitching in around the house, he has, for weeks now, returned from work each night just to plop in front of the TV and fall asleep early on the couch. I was first annoyed, then offended, then downright furious with his newfound laziness, but I was put smack dab in my place tonight when, finally confronting him, I accused, "What is *wrong* with you? Do you have diabetes or something?"

"Yeah," he said. "Probably."

Having grown up the son of a diabetic father, he suspected this days ago. He even set up a doctor's appointment for this Tuesday, the first time he's called a doctor in eleven years of marriage. "I didn't want to worry you," he said. "At least not until I knew for sure." But I *am* worried, and it's clear he's worried, too.

OJ's dad was about his same age when he was first diagnosed with Diabetes. It was a good thing his parents were visiting this weekend; they understand what all this means better than we do. He told his parents about his symptoms tonight. I think they could see something wasn't right with him. He's just not his easy-going self. He's dragging. Even his face seems different—older, tired. He and his dad, Dave, spent the evening discussing what it is really like to live with Diabetes, while his mom, Lorri, buoyed me up, explaining what it's really like to *care for* someone living with Diabetes. Hard truth for both of us, but it was helpful. At least we're not alone.

So, we're in limbo until Tuesday's appointment. And then? We're probably in for a life change. I guess it's a good thing we decided not to have another baby. I couldn't explain why it felt wrong, why we both agreed we're most likely done having children. *This* explains it. That's one thing Hawaii did for me: made things clear. It reminded me to enjoy what is right in front of me, for I never know when it might rumble or disappear.

Monday, November 13
It's official. OJ has Diabetes—Type One, Insulin-Dependent, or Juvenile Diabetes. On top of that, he was also diagnosed with Hypothyroidism and Celiac disease—an allergy to gluten, a protein found in wheat, barley, rye, most processed foods, and a host of other products. I believe the doctors' words were, "You're such an *unusual* case," meaning he has so many autoimmune diseases at the same time, it's fascinating to the doctors. Well, good for them, but not so good for us. We definitely don't want to be called an "unusual case." OJ started insulin the day he was diagnosed,

narrowly avoiding hospitalization, and was put on medications to regulate his off-the-charts blood sugar and thyroid and, hopefully, bring back the man I married.

It's slow going, however, and he's been quite sick. This week, he's had flu on top of being weak from Diabetes and Celiac. We don't fully understand what we're supposed to be feeding him. All I know is pizza night is out the window, and pretty much all Italian food. He can no longer swing by the snack shack on the ninth hole during a golf game for a quick sandwich. Many of his favorite treats, like cookies 'n' cream ice cream, are no-nos. I'm doing my best to figure it out, but we're not there yet.

It's not just him. This changes *all* our lives, every meal together—what I need to buy and not buy, what I can or can't, should or shouldn't make. We've had to quit our dinner co-op, which consisted of four friends and I taking turns cooking for each other. I loved that co-op, but it's just too hard to feed him now. I'm learning that gluten is in store-bought chicken stock and most packaged foods. It's also in most sauces, including teriyaki and soy sauce, knocking out Chinese and Japanese meals. It's even in medicines, lotions, and shampoos! He has rashes on his arms from this gluten allergy, and we're doing our best to sort through and figure out which products are safe for his sensitive body. *Sensitive!* Even that sounds crazy for OJ. He's one of the toughest guys I know. All this doesn't even include the fact that he also needs to count carbs to make sure his insulin is right. For now, we're just trying to get and keep him stable. We're getting closer, I think. I hope.

Tonight, after a particularly long day at work, I came home, checked in with the kids, started making dinner, and found OJ lying on the couch, lethargic and weak. I asked what I could do. He sent me to the pharmacy to pick up his new medications. My legs were achy, wanting to buckle, as I stood in the never-ending line. Looking at the cheap toys, then the Thanksgiving-themed plates on the aisle end, and finally, the blood testers in front of the pharmacy window, I could hear the troubles of those in line before me—an anti-depressant for a middle-aged woman, a nicotine supplement for a rough-looking twenty-something, a beta-blocker for an older man—and that's when it hit me. *It's all changing. You have to be the strong one now.*

OJ has always been "the strong one" in my mind, the rock upon which I can roll in and out like the waves of the sea. He has been the one who doesn't change, the one who tempers my tempestuous emotions and makes up for the "nothing" parts of my all-or-nothing personality. He has been the one who is steady, even, positive, *content.*

But I knew in that moment: *It is my turn now.* I was exhausted. I already felt pushed to my limits from full days helping others—clients, my children, OJ, and my parents and siblings, who had struggled through crises of finances, mental health, and addictions. Yet, in that moment I could see, as I neared the end of my year of Charity—of service and love of the purest kind—I had been given the opportunity to *become* that love. I had been given the opportunity to really grow.

Just like that moment twenty-seven stories up in Hawaii as the world around me threatened to fall, I stood still, surrendered, and accepted what *was* before I even knew half of what *would be.* Taking a deep breath and exhaling slowly, I raised my head and shoulders a little taller as I settled into the voice repeating in my mind: *I am charity. I am love. I am the strong one now.*

TWO
Live Strong

"Live Strong. Love life. Don't ever let the chance to say 'I Love You' pass you by…"
~Lyrics from my song, Live Strong, *In Memory of Rob*

What does that mean anyway—strong? If we're going by outside appearances then it must mean muscles, might, and the ability to…oh, I don't know…pull a train, on a rope, with your teeth? But we all know muscles fade, and deep down, we all know that being strong really has nothing to do with might. Perhaps being truly strong simply means being vulnerable enough to allow our story to be written—to accept where we are, to learn the lessons we are taught—and to courageously *live* the story we are given, no matter how over- or under-whelming it may seem.

I do this for a living. I get to witness incredible strength as I hear some incredible stories. I get to see how the stories play out with the dramatic arc of the plot, the exposition, rising action, climax, falling action, and dénouement. Usually, I get to offer a little help for the character development and how the story will end. One constant I have seen, through each character's plot, is the story always has twists and turns no one could have predicted, but in the end, it's the twist that creates the hero and the turn that makes the story great.

We all have a story, but will it be a great one? Will we choose to allow ourselves to be created by the twists and strengthened by the turns? Will we slow down enough to participate in and be strengthened by the stories of the ones we love? Or, will we wait for tomorrow?

We mustn't wait; all stories come to an end someday. Sometimes that someday is much sooner than we could have known. My sister, Shannon, had a story—some chapters I know like they are my own while others I will never know. Her husband, Rob, had a story, too.

Sunday, July 29

We had such a hard time deciding to try for one more baby. OJ had been so sick for so long, and, even once he was better and we both began to feel that mysterious urge for "just one more," we still thought we might be crazy. But hearing "It's a girl," at my appointment, Friday morning, made everything suddenly right. *Two boys. Two girls. She'll be the perfect piece to complete our family puzzle.* We couldn't wait to tell Rob when we drove down to visit that afternoon.

"We just found out we're having a girl!" I exclaimed. "I hope you plan to stick around to meet your new niece."

Reality set in quickly as I noticed Rob's once-chiseled jawline, now thin and carved. He barely had the energy to smile and nod, and I realized I had no time to waste. *No time for false hope. Better to say it like it is.*

"Actually, you'll probably get to meet her before we do," I said, tears welling. "Tell her hello for us. And don't teach her any of your old tricks."

Only now do I realize that was probably the last time we'll see Rob in this life. I caught a glimpse, this morning, of a little photo of Rob with his son, Tre, which Tre carries in his pocket. I was once again reminded of the complete difference in Rob *then* versus *now.* After Friday's visit to Rob, my nephews, Tre and Brody, asked to come home with us to Flagstaff for a weekend of fun with their cousins. I sensed it was to take their minds away from their dad. We've been playing the part of the "normal," upbeat family all weekend, but seeing that photo in Tre's ten year-old hands put an end to my part in the charade, filling me with memories and nostalgia.

OJ had been in Boy Scouts with Rob when they

were young and had stories to tell, like how he could talk up a storm and always had "ideas" to stir up a little trouble. I'd met Rob during my freshman year of college. Muscular, dark-haired, and strikingly handsome, Rob could catch the attention of an entire room. OJ and I had doubled with him as he dated my close friend, and I found him funny and entertaining, but a little too attention-seeking and immature for my taste. Talking on the phone with him three years later, I surprised myself when I said, "You'd be perfect for my sister, Shannon. You're dark, hot, and a little wild. Exactly her type."

I remember the day OJ and I introduced Rob to Shannon—my college graduation day. He wore a suit and brought my pressed gown from the dry cleaners. Shannon told Mom, "He's cute, but he's too conservative. He's wearing a *suit!*" Well, that man in the suit proved irresistible. They eloped to Vegas a few months later. I remember Christmas Eve, our babies asleep, laughing 'til our insides hurt, seeing this "conservative" brother-in-law of mine strut around in his two year-old's Superman Underoos before shouting, "Dare me to jump in the pool naked?" We didn't even have time to object before his bare white bum plunged over the side.

I remember Rob's intensity—spouting passion or spitting fire—you certainly didn't want to be caught in the middle of either. Boy, could we get into it with our strong opinions. I remember him arguing relentlessly with me one time at a smoothie shop, over how "crazy" it was that I didn't like ginger. I remember the humor that tempered him, his ever-changing business ideas for energy drinks, mobile car detailing, modeling, and his dead-on Jim Carey impressions—always good for an honest laugh. I remember sitting along Lake Mary Road cheering him on in one of his first triathlons, expecting him to appear over the hill in the lead, instead seeing him carry his flat-tire bike as he jogged uphill way behind the others, never giving up.

I remember Shannon telling me they were considering divorce, Rob's "fun" side having become tiresome, and his fiery side having clashed too many times with her own. The "manic-depressive couple," OJ and I used to joke, so hot and cold were they. *It certainly doesn't seem funny anymore.* They loved each other. It was obvious. *They still love each other.* But somehow they couldn't figure it out together—too much frenetic energy between them, too much heat. I remember Shannon telling me they'd made their decision, how she thought it was the better way—the only way—and how she didn't listen when I told her she was wrong. "Try counseling," I suggested. But patience was never her strong suit—nor Rob's, for that matter. They lasted just longer than the seven-year itch. It's been almost four years now since they split.

Even since their divorce, I've loved having Rob around. Always the life of the party, every family event seems more eventful with Rob and Shannon there. Rob told Mom he still considers us his family, and I know we will always love him as a forever part of ours. In the past, I know this bothered Shannon. But I'm pretty sure she changed her tune. Until last week, Rob's hospice bed had been set up in Shannon's living room and he'd been living with her and their boys for a couple of months. Her loving nature has shone as she's taken care of and accepted him into their home so he could spend time with his children. Yes, I have to believe she regrets the divorce now, though she swears they are still "just friends."

I remember it was just last November when Rob broke the news that he had lumps everywhere, but was waiting for his new insurance to kick in before seeing a doctor. It was just after OJ was handed all his diagnoses when we pleaded with him to forget the insurance and get immediate help. Then, as OJ and I spent last

Thanksgiving afternoon in Rob's hospital room, he confirmed the news we already knew. His melanoma had returned. Did I pay attention to the knot in my stomach when I heard those words? Did I really believe *then* that it would come to *this*? After all, he'd made it through melanoma, and the long, sickening process of chemo, five years ago. *Wouldn't he make it again?*

Sunday is resurrection day; *if only Rob could be resurrected to his former self today.* Though I know he isn't gone yet, I miss Rob as we have known him. Perhaps it is only *now* that I'm seeing the *real* Rob as he calmly accepts his life's story. Strange how, the weaker his body has become, the stronger his spirit. This realization makes me miss him all the more, yet my feelings are accompanied by peace. His body may be fading, but *he* is not. It inspires *me* to want to follow Rob. It inspires me to want to be strong in spirit, too.

Tuesday, July 31

Shannon called and woke me first thing this morning, sobbing. "He died in the night." All I could do was cry with her—that's really all anyone should ever do—and all I could tell her was, "I'm coming." I then loaded up my boys in the car, called work to cancel my day, and headed down the mountains of Flagstaff to the sweltering heat of the valley.

We arrived earlier than planned and had time to spare while Shannon and her boys were at the gym— strange how routine can make a crisis feel somehow manageable—so we went to Target. I wanted to bring something for my nephews, something to console them in any small way. *They lost their dad today* kept repeating in my mind, the saddest part of this shared grief. *What do you buy for a child to tell him, "It will be all right"?*

My boys, ten and a half year-old Braxton and eight year-old Colton, and I rummaged through toys and treats and finally settled on two musical animals. For six year-old Brody, a warthog-rapper with a gold chain that sang, "I like to move it, move it," while apparently attempting to dance. For ten year-old Tre, an ape-dancer that played AC/DC's "You shook me all night long."

Presenting them to the boys, Shannon and I burst out laughing. "I know it's completely inappropriate for the occasion," I acknowledged. "But I thought we could use a little humor today." We laughed some more to the tune of dancing warthogs and apes.

How do you help someone heal from losing the one and only, the one she didn't even know was the "only" until after he was gone? We sat and shared memories; we laughed, we cried. I bought Rubio's tacos and Paradise Bakery cookies for lunch. I let her nap. We planned a memorial service for Friday, and I brought Tre and Brody home to Flagstaff with me to give Shannon space for her grief and to hopefully set the boys free from theirs, if only for a little while.

Friday, August 3
> *"…Love your children. Be a friend.*
> *Keep 'em laughing 'til the end.*
> *When we love, his legacy begins…so live strong."*[1]

I fear sometimes we don't recognize the good in others until after they are gone.

We had a beautiful memorial service for Rob at Lorri's and Dave's house tonight. They are OJ's parents. I know they loved Rob too, and it meant a lot to everyone that they would offer their home when Rob's parents said they didn't want to be involved. It seemed like something the parents should do—hold this memorial—but for whatever reason, they didn't want a memorial, even when Shannon mentioned how good it would be for the boys, for all of us. That didn't stop us. Shannon and I planned it all out, and Dave and Lorri stepped in as hosts. Robs parents showed up, last minute, and I hope it was good for them to see how loved Rob was. Playing music he loved, seeing his life in photos, and sharing his stories—it felt as if he should have been there, too. I wonder if he might have been.

Just as Rob would have wanted, this memorial was a *party*. A smile on every face, a laugh in every corner of the room, it was bittersweet as we remembered and celebrated Rob. "He was always interested in whomever he was talking to," one person said. "He sure loved his boys. They would play steamroller..." said another. "I remember when he threw a bowling ball into a toilet in college and shattered it!" was OJ's laugh-inducing contribution. "He really loved Shannon, too, didn't he?" I added, glancing at her across the room. In a fitted tank dress, her dark brown hair slicked back, smiling her magic smile, sharing her own stories and laughing, she looked as if she could have been at a mixer instead of a memorial. But I knew, underneath, she was less pulled together than she seemed. As we shared tales, the lessons of Rob's life seemed suddenly clear. *Take interest in others. Love your family. Love unconditionally. Live your life to the fullest.*

I wrote a song for Rob and sang it for everyone at the memorial. It seemed a crazy feat—to write a song in two short days and perform it in front of seventy-five people. I decided I would write the song not for *my* benefit but for *Rob's,* and only if I felt inspired. Last night, as I went to bed, I had just a few lines written with no real feel for the melody. But I prayed again for help, *Heavenly Father, if it's right for me to share this song tomorrow, please inspire me,* and somehow awoke in the early hours with the melody and lyrics floating in my head.

It was almost complete, but I knew I needed Dad to play the guitar for me if I had any shot at pulling it off. Luckily, Dad's good at winging it, too. Fifteen minutes before I was to perform, as Dad and I practiced for the first time, I found the words for the final verse, and it was only as I sang it for everyone that I knew it was exactly right—perfect—exactly Rob. The title? *Live Strong*. Not only is it a nod to Rob's hero, Lance Armstrong, and his cancer awareness campaign, but Rob was an example of living strong. He had "strength in spirit with the muscles to match. He ran through the obstacles and never looked back."[2]

At the end of the night, after all the guests had gone, as Shannon prepared to leave, we embraced. "Thank you," she whispered. "He would have loved this."

In my heart, I willed her all the strength she and her boys would need for the journey ahead, as her car pulled away. *How will she do this?* I wondered, and then committed to be there *for* and *with* her every step of the way. We may have been celebrating Rob all evening long, but it was Shannon's face I pictured as Rob's song chased me to sleep. *Live strong, Shannon,* I felt deep within. *Live strong.*

THREE
Appreciate Life

"If we have no peace it is because we have forgotten that we belong to each other."
~Mother Teresa

I remember teaching a class years ago at church. I was nineteen and speaking to a group of women my age and older. My message? "Appreciate life, and especially those in it, while you've got it." I walked around the room holding a picture of an eighteen year-old wearing a flowered dress and a slightly forced smile, posing next to an open casket. Her eight year-old sister had died three days before from kidney cancer. That picture was of me with my youngest sister, McLean, or Miki, as we called her.

Miki had been diagnosed with a Wilm's Tumor in April of my senior year of high school, when she was six and a half years old. I remember picking her up from a slumber party early Saturday morning as her friend's mother said with concern, "Miki didn't seem to be feeling well. She fell asleep early and didn't have any cake." Her usual spunky spirit seemed dampened as she looked up at me and forced a smile. "You're not feeling so great, huh?" I asked, hugging and kissing her gorgeous, natural, blond ringlets. "Yeah," she said, then lay down on the seat and, uncharacteristically, rode home without saying a word.

I brought Miki in the house and told Mom, though it didn't seem like a huge surprise to us since Miki had been home sick most of that week already. We thought she had a stomach flu. Mom and Dad decided to take her to the doctor, just to be safe, while I went to my best friend's house for a day of seventeen year-old hanging out and sleeping over. That evening, I was shocked right out of my teenage fun when Mom called and told me the doctor had found a tumor in my baby sister's kidney. They were doing tests to see if it was malignant or not.

The next morning, as I sat in church with my friend and her family, listening to a woman sing *How Great Thou Art*, one of my favorite hymns, I felt I might burst wondering what Miki's prognosis was. Watching the clock, I got up at the exact time Mom had told me to call, walked out in the middle of the song to the phone in the hallway, and dialed their number. They told me what we'd all feared: Miki's tumor was cancer. Stage *4* cancer. Stunned, I made my way back to my seat as the soloist finished the last chorus, "Then sings my soul, my Savior, God, to thee. How great thou art. How great thou art!"[1] The power of the words spoke straight to *my* soul, and I began to weep as I prayed that He, indeed, was great enough to give us a miracle.

We may not have received the miracle *I* was asking for. We lost Miki the beginning of the next fall. But many blessings and miracles came through Miki's youthful tenacity and acceptance of what her life's mission would be. Before her first surgery as a golden-haired six year-old when the odds were against her and she told us, "Either I'll wake up and see you or I'll wake up and see Jesus." Showing her bold personality as a bald seven year-old, making videos and joking, "I'm a boy! I'm a girl!" taking her wig off and on, Miki was a source of hope, courage, and wisdom that surpassed her eight years. Miki's life may have been short, but she lived—and loved—to the fullest.

Miki wasn't my only reminder that life is short. When I was ten, my Papa, my mom's dad, died of cancer. He was only sixty-two. When my dad told me he'd died, I hugged him, and then asked if my friend could spend the night. I didn't fully comprehend. A few weeks later, I had a dream. My grandfather had come back to be with me for the day. We went to a carnival, rode rides, played games, and laughed just like we used to. As the sun set, somebody shot him, and he died again. I woke up sobbing uncontrollably, and my mom let me miss school that day.

When I was fifteen, my mom was diagnosed with breast cancer for the first time. She became extremely sick from the chemo and radiation. I accepted the reality that, being the oldest, I would have to forego college to be there fore my siblings if Mom should die. She went into remission just in time for Miki's diagnosis. Only two years after Miki's death, right after my wedding, Mom was diagnosed with breast cancer again. She said, at one point, the stress of my wedding had made her sick. I don't think she meant for it to make me feel guilty, but it did. I took care of her through more chemo and sickness, being the mom while she could not—all of this, while I was pregnant with Braxton and becoming a mother myself.

Bottom line: We never know when life will turn like the weather. So I remind myself here of the lesson I gave that Sunday: *Appreciate life and those in it while you've got it.* We can all do a little better at appreciating the miracle of life and the lives of those we love. Starting right now, we can say, do, and *love* a little bit better. After all, a life full of love is a life fully lived, and a life fully lived is a miracle, no matter how long—or short—it may be.

Saturday, October 13

Fall cleaning is a tedious chore. I was, therefore, thrilled to be interrupted by a call from Shannon. Since Rob died, I've done my best to check in often and help with the boys, always calling and asking, "How *are* you?" and hoping for an honest answer.

Today it was Shannon who called and asked, "How are *you*?" stating *she* had been feeling terrific and thought it would be nice to call and check on *me* for a change. At a little over one month from my due date, I had plenty to say—swollen feet, sleepless nights, nesting—you know, the usual. But nothing seemed as important as knowing how *she* was doing. She couldn't escape my questioning. "I miss Rob, of course," she finally admitted, as I searched her voice and words for anything she might try to hide. "But I'm actually feeling a lot better this week," she said. And she *sounded* better—more…what was it? Hopeful. More at peace.

"Tre and Brody are doing as well as we could wish for," she added, anticipating my next question. "They're doing well in school, and they don't *seem* to be having any real trouble, although I know they miss their dad. I think we're all really excited about the move."

Shannon just signed the lease on a newer, bigger house. She sounded positive and excited about moving and said the boys were excited to have a new home, too. "It feels like a fresh start," she said. I agreed. It would be a welcome release for them to be out of the house where Rob had been so sick.

"I was planning on coming up to help you paint the baby's room sometime in the next couple of weeks," Shannon said. "What do you think?"

I was thrilled. I had wanted to ask her to come. She is the *only* one I want here, *need* here, to help me get ready for four kids and my last baby, but it felt selfish, considering all she's been going through. So, this was a real treat for me. I literally gasped and let out a "Yay!" I recalled how, when she met her first niece, baby Kennedy, she had burst into tears of love. I know she will love our second girl just as well. Not having girls of her own, mine are special to their Aunt Shanny, so it's perfect that she will be the one to help me get everything ready for our newest addition.

As we said our "I love yous," I told her how proud I was of her and how she was handling Rob's death. I hung up feeling hopeful for Shannon and her boys, feeling deep down that somehow this would all work out. It filled me with the desire to do more for them as a sister and aunt.

I realized, at the same time, it wasn't all about the doing. In this situation, it seemed to be more about the *loving. Patience says, "Just love them."* And so, I will.

Wednesday, October 17

I was waiting to turn left when I got the call. All week I'd been preparing for the two-day pregnancy and postpartum mood disorders conference I would ironically be teaching while eight months pregnant. Finally packed and on the road, I was sitting at the red light on Butler and Route 66, before turning toward the freeway for the two-hour drive south. Window down, sixty-three degree breeze tickling my skin, blissful silence speaking to me, I was feeling the freedom of getting away for a couple of days. *No one needing me. I'm on my own schedule,* I thought, and smiled. I had just decided to call Shannon and surprise her with a dinner invite, when my cell phone rang.

The caller ID said Indiana. Aunt Christina was calling. Unusual. Aunt Christina is my mother's only sister, the one I am named after—Christina Marie. She never calls me, especially not on my cell phone.

She spoke calmly and directly. "Christi—it's Aunt Christina."

"Hi," I replied, masking my surprise. "How are you?"

"I'm fine, honey. How are *you* doing?" she asked with the serene presence that let me know something was definitely not right.

"Fine," I hesitantly said. And then the pregnant pause.

"Honey, there's been an accident. We don't know what happened, but you need to go directly to your Mom's house."

Gripped with fear, I calmly said, "Okay."

"Something's happened with Shannon. The police called and told your Mom to come over to her house, but they won't tell her why." I felt my heart stop and my breath catch as I suspected the worst.

"Okay," I repeated, matter-of-factly.

"Just go to your Mom's. We will call you as soon as we know what's going on."

"Okay."

"Your Mom needs you, honey. I'm so sorry. Everything will be fine."

I was definitely not okay.

Have you ever experienced one of those moments—as if the world has stopped and all you feel is a powerful void? That was me as I took the I-17 onramp to Phoenix, but no longer to teach a class—to go and meet whatever unknown fate lay ahead of me.

I called OJ and recapped Aunt Christina's call. OJ was speechless. "Wh...what do you think happened?"

"I don't know," I replied. "Either she is seriously hurt or she's dead. I mean, those are the only options, right? The police don't just call and ask you to come without telling you why unless it's really bad."

I was hoping he would disagree, hoping he'd have a great explanation for why this might be happening, hoping he'd say, "It's nothing." But I knew he wouldn't say that. I knew like you know deep in your soul when something is really wrong—this was not "nothing."

We talked for a few more minutes, but what was there to say? "I'm scared?" That was unspoken, yet filled each space between our words. I finally said, "I'll call you when I hear something. I'm sorry to bother you at work like this."

"It's okay, honey," he consoled me. He was right. This was the kind of thing that makes work seem pointless—*everything* to seem pointless.

I called OJ's mom, Lorri, to talk, because I was so full of nervous energy I could barely sit still. Here I was, eight months pregnant, making the two-hour drive away from home, calm as possible on the outside, but inside I was a knot of anxiety. It helped to talk to Lorri. She is, after all, both a friend and a mother to me. She cares about my family and me just as much, it seems, as I do. She was in shock.

"Let's just talk about anything until they call me back, all right?" I suggested. We did, and it helped. For a few minutes.

I hung up with Lorri when OJ called back. He is my calm in any storm and it helped just to have him on the line. We were talking about mundane subjects when his phone beeped. "It's your uncle," he said in a way that mirrored my own nervous curiosity. Then, he clicked over, leaving me in silence. It was probably only a minute before he finally clicked back. I held my breath. "Okay. So where are you now?" he asked.

"Wait a minute. What did he *say*?" I questioned.

"Nothing. Don't worry," came his calm reply.

That made me worry all the more. "OJ, *what did he say*?"

"Nothing. We just want to get you there safely." He was trying to protect me. I knew they were all trying to protect me, but it was too late. There was no protection. I began to accept the truth I already knew: *My sister is gone.* I sighed, giving myself just a moment.

"She's dead, isn't she?" I asked, not feeling the words. My body was already erecting the wall that would hold back so many emotions for so many months. "OJ, just tell me," I pressed him, still holding the glimmer of hope that I was wrong.

Hesitation. Hesitation was a confirmation in itself. *He is my OJ—my husband and most steady supporter, my best friend.* He didn't want to drop this bomb. The moment before the truth comes out is so full of possibility; yet, it was already determined.

"Yes," he said. "She died."

What do I say? When time stops and everything changes, what can possibly be said?

"Do you realize we just inherited two kids?" Half angry, half in shock, I laughed. My sister had just died, and I laughed.

Somehow I made the rest of the drive and arrived safely at my parents' house. On the outside, this could have been any happy home, any happy day; no one would have guessed what was waiting inside. I moved purposefully, in slow motion, as I put the car in park, removed the keys from the ignition, carefully replaced my sunglasses in my purse, opened the car door, closed it, stood in view of the front door to the house—and breathed. As oldest child, I have been the caretaker, the one who eases others' suffering. It's been my role, my "assignment" in the family, an assignment I've turned into a career. As I stared, I inhaled as much air as I could carry, and prepared for the now seemingly endless walk to the front door. I was reminded of my assignment once more: *I am the relief person.*

I gently opened the heavy door and saw my mother, walking toward me, tears streaming down her face. Her short brown hair was half-combed, she had no makeup, and her clothes might have been pajamas, I wasn't sure. Two paramedics stood in the background with my sister, Ashley. "I'm sorry, Christi." Mom sobbed and embraced me, as if this were in any way her fault.

"It's okay, Mom," was all I could say, as I felt the release of my own soft tears but held them back so I could be the strong one.

I hugged Ashley, five years younger than I, who had been living with Shannon and her boys. Ashley was the first the police had called. Having gone to work early that morning, they'd told her over the phone that her sister had died and someone needed to be with the kids. Ashley had driven herself home and was playing with Tre and Brody when the police had called Mom, not telling *her* what had happened until she'd arrived. As we hugged, Ashley didn't say a word. Taller than I am and very shy, she simply nuzzled her head into my shoulder and quietly cried.

I then acknowledged the paramedics who were witnessing this intimate moment. How strange it must be to stand by and watch a family fresh in death—to be the awkward observers of cries and embraces. They had driven Mom, Ashley, and the boys home to Mom's house, not wanting anyone to have to drive after so much shock. Mom introduced me. I picked up that they'd been discussing how to help everyone cope.

"She's a psychologist," Mom told them.

They said something like, "Oh, great. So *you* know what to do." Relief overtook their expressions and they prepared to go.

"Uh, yes," I replied reflexively, wondering why they were leaving so quickly. Later, I would look back and hate this responsibility being handed to me because of my profession. After all, I was the victim as much as anyone else. It's like the day the Twin Towers fell. The entire nation—the entire world—was in shock, and as a clinical psychology intern, I was terrified, thinking, "I'm supposed to be the one to help others in crises like this, but I am a mess!" That was me today, internally a mess, but outwardly calm and collected. It's all I knew. *I'm the relief person.*

There was plenty of relief that needed to be found as I learned our next item of business was to tell the rest of the family—Dad, Bud, and Leighton—the news.

Dad was at work. "You haven't told him yet?" I asked Mom.

"I don't know how," she said. Our family had

already been torn up—fourteen years ago, when we lost Miki, and seventy-eight days ago, when Rob died. *How can we possibly take another loss?*

"We have to tell everyone, Mom," I gently encouraged and began to help her work out a plan. We still didn't know exactly what had happened. We knew Shannon had died very early in the morning, in her bed. We knew acetaminophen and alcohol had been found at the scene. We knew it appeared she had died by her own actions, but we didn't know much else. The police were doing an investigation, they said, and an autopsy. That word—autopsy. I couldn't believe it was being said about my sister, but perhaps it would give us some understanding, at some point. Today, however, we had to tell everyone what we did know: Shannon had died.

Mom arranged to have her brothers drive to Dad's office, break the news, and drive him home. Later that afternoon, as he pulled up, I ran to meet him. He looked heartbroken and in shock. Rubbing his face, exhausted and dazed, he shook his head. We embraced, and he whispered in my ear, "What is *happening* to our *family?*"

We waited to tell Carter Jr., seven years younger than I, whom we've always called "Bud," until after he got home from work, a couple hours later. He walked in the house looking surprised to see me, an uncertain smile on his face. Mom asked him to sit down and, nervously, he obeyed. "Shannon died," she told him. I watched this tall, handsome young man's smile shift from protective disbelief, almost a laugh, to stabbing reality, and pain. The look on his face will always be etched in my memory.

When Mom picked up the phone to call Leighton—the youngest in the family since Miki died— Ashley and I stood by. "Are you sitting down?" I heard Mom say, like people say in the movies. Leighton was at work in Los Angeles. "Well, you should sit down first."

She waited a moment, and then began. "Shannon died."
I pictured Leighton asking, "*What?*" as I heard Mom say,
slower and louder, "Shannon *died.*" At that exact
moment, ten year-old Tre walked through the living
room, where we were talking.

My heart gripped at the sight of him, thinking it
was probably too much for any boy to take, hearing
others discuss his barely deceased mother without
warning. Sitting completely still, I watched, but was
momentarily reassured as he kept walking and
disappeared into the family room. *He must not have heard
Mom*, I thought. He certainly showed no sign of it. But,
moments later he sprinted back through the living room
and into Mom's bedroom where he threw himself on
the bed and burst into sobs. Mom was consoling
Leighton, so Ashley and I ran to Tre.

"I didn't know! I didn't know she died!" he
cried.

I didn't know what to say. "Oh, honey." It was
all I could do to hold back my own tears and rub his
back. When Mom came in, I explained what had
happened, and she took over. I admit I felt relieved. I
didn't feel it was my place to be the one comforting Tre.
I'm not the mother; I'm not the grandmother; I'm just the aunt.
At least, for now. Plus, Mom is great in a crisis. She steps
in and gets the job done. In fact, Mom and Dad had
been like second parents to Tre and Brody, filling in
when it was too much for Shannon and Rob. Now OJ
and I would be the second parents, wouldn't we? This
gap was too huge for anyone to fill.

We looked at each other, stunned, while Mom
comforted Tre and I stepped back. We'd assumed the
boys knew their mother was dead. Brody, six, was there
when Tre had discovered their mother and called 911.
Even if they hadn't realized it at first, surely *somebody* had
told them later. Mom and Ashley had assumed the
police and paramedics had done it. I'd assumed Mom or

Ashley had done it, but nobody had. Tre had overheard the news that his mother was dead at the exact same moment Leighton was told. That meant Brody had yet to be told, too.

It now made sense why the boys had seemed so "fine" when I went in to see them after I arrived. Watching cartoons in the family room, they'd seemed a little too enthusiastic in their "Yeah!" when I'd tentatively asked, "Are you doin' okay, guys?" *They're handling this amazingly well,* I'd told myself, chalking it up to "Kids are so resilient." But, now, I understood, as Mom, Ashley, and I lay with Tre on Mom's bed, attempting to explain and console him. This little boy—who'd already been through so much—his parent's divorce, his father's death—how would he handle this, too? This little boy, whom I'd loved since I'd met him, minutes after he was born, who was best friends with my little boys—how would we *all* manage this? He poured out his tears and then looking to my mom—his Mimi—he finally spoke. "What's going to happen to us?"

"Well, you can live with Christi & OJ," Mom quickly and gently replied, both of them looking to me. Startled, I nodded and smiled, though really I felt awkward and unnatural. *I'm still not his mother—yet.* "Or *we* can take you," Mom continued. "Or your other grandparents. Whatever you want. You're going to be just fine." Even though I'd already known in my heart we would take the boys, and even though I echoed her words, it felt jarring to hear them spoken aloud without a single discussion. I deferred to Mom, going along with everything she said, needing this space before it was I who had to make the decisions—not ready to say a word, not ready take this on.

Later that night, I drove with Ashley and Bud over to Shannon's house. We figured someone needed to go check on things, to get clothes and toys for the boys, and to pick up Mom's car since she'd ridden home with the paramedics. As we pulled up, I saw flickering candles on the curb. Someone had set up a vigil with a sign that read, "Always in our hearts." Confronted with others' pain over my sister's death, the sentiment was heart wrenching, but I was also full of gratitude, for this was a reminder we were not alone.

We stepped out of the car and approached the dark walkway to the front door. There was absolutely no life there. I felt sick as we entered, my body swaying, head dizzy, and I was haunted, filled with an ache and fear of knowing that just hours ago this was where she had lost her life. *Get me outta here*, I thought, yet confidently led the way, turning on the lights, trying not to look around, not wanting to see—what? We quickly made our way to the boys' room and collected their things. It was so quiet. We talked to each other, trying to lighten the situation, perhaps, but I think also to ground us to each other, to calm our fears. I know none of us really *wanted* to, but we couldn't stop ourselves from looking into Shannon's room. Being in that house, seeing her bed lying vacant, sheets still ruffled, a few drops of blood on the floor, was too much. My mind flooded with thoughts I couldn't ignore. *Exactly what happened here last night? How did this happen? What did the boys see when they came to wake her up late for school? Why? Why?*

I can't wait to go away from here, I thought, turning toward the door. *I don't ever want to return.*

FOUR
Ask How

"I define myself more by my questions than by my answers."
~Elie Wiesel

Is it just me or does life seem to bring more questions than answers? I am an expert at asking questions—words make up the bulk of my professional work. It is my job to ask questions that help the woman, man, teen, child, couple, or family I am working with think, feel, and eventually discover the answers for the questions they bring to me.

One of the most common questions I hear is, "Why?" "Why do those we love have to die too soon?" "Why must we continually find ourselves falling?" "Why is all this growing so difficult?" I have been filled with an abundance of "whys" in my days. Some *can* be answered and provide deeper understanding, but many will *never* be answered in this life. Sometimes, in choosing to question "why," we choose to remain stagnant in our learning. We choose to stay in the dark—alone, frustrated, and even angry.

The question I find more helpful is *"How?"* *"How* do I carry on?" *"How* do I do what I'm being asked to do?" *"How* do I learn from this?" "How" is a question of commitment, a question of action, a question of faith. "How" is acceptance, willingness, and patience. Though we may not understand "why," the answer to "how" is always there, if we will simply ask.

Asking "how," listening, and then living the answers is the path of patience, learning, and growth. Patiently we listen, willingly we learn, and bit-by-bit we become the hows that we live. As we let go of "why" and center ourselves on "how," piece-by-piece, the puzzle of our life comes into focus. Lovingly, we rise from the fall as we stand, plant our feet, ask how, and get to work. This is *how* we learn; this is *how* we grow.

Friday, October 19

Today was OJ's and my twelfth wedding anniversary. *I* was in a mortuary.

I stood holding my sister's lifeless hair in my hands trying to form it into something that resembled her when she was living. The hair was wiry and difficult to mold. *Has it always been this way or has it somehow stiffened like her body?* I made my finger touch her scalp. It was hard, swollen, cool. I made myself look closely at her face. It resembled her, but more like a caricature in a wax museum—not exactly her. *How* could *it with no life in her body now?*

It was hard to believe only an hour ago I'd been teaching a room full of doctors, nurses, and therapists about postpartum psychotherapy. Hard to believe I actually made myself do that; it's only been two days since Shannon died. I wasn't sure what made me go. Certainly it wasn't the pressure of commitment. My co-presenters and dear friends, Carole and Michelle, had assured me they would take care of everything. I knew they would, but I woke up this morning needing to do something. Something to take my mind off everything. Something I am good at. I called and let them know I would be there for that two-hour portion of the two-day event. "Are you sure?" they asked. I was. I must have looked crazy, sitting in front of the room, swollen belly propped on my lap, swollen feet resting on a chair in front of me, as I lectured about postpartum depression treatment. Maybe I was. I could tell by the way everyone was looking at me—that mixture of shock and awe—that it wasn't a "normal" thing to do.

Now, here I stood, doing something even more abnormal. Ashley and Leighton stood nearby, noticeably nervous. I felt their tension in the air, and my own. When the funeral director asked if we would like to do her hair, I wanted to scream, "No! Are you kidding? Do people actually *do* that?" Instead I heard myself say, "Oh? We can *do* that?" then listened to her explain how some family members prefer to do it themselves so their loved one's hair looks more like it did when they were alive. *"But she's not alive! She's dead!"* coursed through my body, pulsed through my living blood.

I heard myself say, "Okay. Yeah. Sure. We'll do it…right?" Looking to my younger sisters, I saw the trepidation etched in their expressions, like my own, yet I heard us all say, "Sure, yes," as if it were natural.

We were led back to the viewing room, the room in which, just minutes before, we had "viewed" her dead body for the first time. We were given styling tools—a hairbrush, comb, pins, curling iron, blow dryer—tools of the living. *Superficial* tools of the living. I'd used those same tools to make myself look beautiful today—my hair smoothed into a stylish double-twist, still wearing the white cap-sleeved tee and sunflower tank dress that showed off my baby belly and made me feel like summer. Somehow, looking perfect didn't seem important in that setting. *Would it ever feel important again?*

I stared and wondered, *how do I do this?* In true oldest child fashion, I took the lead, stepped confidently forward and touched her hair. I allowed the strands to fall through my fingers like my hairdresser does while I tell her what style I'd like, and my sisters followed. We combed her hair. We commented on the small cut on her forehead and wondered how it had gotten there. We didn't know—had she fallen, perhaps? We decided to sweep the hair into a twist on the back of her head so her beautiful face could show. *She had such a beautiful face. This face right here.* But this—this was just a shell—a waxy model of the one I so dearly loved.

In an eerie way, it felt almost like getting someone ready for a wedding, and even more so when we were asked to run one final errand. The dress Mom had selected for Shannon was too low-cut and would expose the incisions from her autopsy. The mortician kindly asked us to go buy a tank that would compliment the dress and cover her scars a little better. I got in my car and drove to Wal-Mart, of all places, and my sisters followed behind. As we walked in and toward the women's clothing section, my sisters and I looked at each other. If we'd thought doing a dead person's hair seemed surreally superficial, how do you think it felt to walk into Wal-Mart and "shop" for the dead? All I could do was shake my head in a nervous laugh—and sigh.

We successfully completed our errand, my sisters offered to deliver the undershirt to the mortuary, and I finally began the two-hour drive home. I'd spent countless cell phone minutes over the past two days recounting to friends and family the details of what had happened, and I was sure I'd have the cell phone bill to prove it, although shouldn't those minutes be free? Yet, I still had to tell my own children. They thought I was teaching a class in Phoenix all this time. OJ and I had decided it would be better to tell them in person after I returned. I drove home in silence wondering how to again break the news I'd already broken too many times.

It was clear the kids had no idea what was going on as they showered me with kisses and detailed descriptions of their week without Mom. OJ gave me a knowing glance and a long embrace; *Happy Anniversary,* we wanted to say, but how could we? So we didn't. Instead we listened intently to the kids. After their report, it was time to give them mine. Four year-old Kennedy was playing in the other room with her dolls. She was too young to understand, so we would tell her later. I already had the attention of eight year-old Colton and eleven year-old Braxton.

"Something has happened and I need to tell you guys about it," I said, pausing momentarily to take in their still faces. "Shannon died," I choked out, my tear-filled gaze holding theirs' deeply, searching for their level of comprehension.

"Shannon? *Aunt* Shannon?" they asked.

"Yes, honey," I replied.

"But Rob just died," said Braxton, concern spilling into the pieces he had quickly put together.

"What will happen to Tre and Brody?" Colton quickly filled in the blank.

"They are going to come and live with us now. They're going to be part of our family."

I held their gaze and saw them want to smile, but instead the tears began. Colton came to me and poured his heart out openly. Braxton was stone-like. A deep thinker, he was taking it all in—a mixture of confusion, hurt, excitement, and…anger spreading across his young face. "What if we were brothers?" they'd often dreamed. Now their dream was coming true, *but* I could see their young minds struggling with the question, *at what cost?*

Tears, smiles, and hugs intertwined this night as I assured my children everything will be okay. Now I lay awake, flooded with a million questions of my own. *How will I do this? And I'm having a baby so soon!* Oh, the baby. *I haven't thought about my little baby for far too many days. We are going to have six kids! How can I find twice as much love for twice as many children? How will they heal from these unspeakable wounds? How will any of us heal?*

My body and mind were exhausted. I'd sleep solidly despite knowing that, even though it felt like the *end* of the hardest part, it was really just the beginning.

Sunday, October 21

In my bed, sometime between two or three a.m., I couldn't sleep. My pregnant abdomen stretched to capacity, back achy, feet the size of footballs, I'd been wrestling with pillows for an hour, trying to find relief. But it was the struggle in my head that was really keeping me awake. I was flooded with a million questions: "Why…" *no. Not yet. Don't think about it. Get up. Go to the bathroom. Get some water. Go back to sleep.* Thirty minutes, one hour, two hours later, it wasn't working.

Take a bath, read—anything to occupy your mind. Write a song? Oh, yes, I need a song about Shannon for later, tomorr- no, tonight. It's already today and the memorial is tonight. The "memorial"—a bunch of people, one dead body, food and music—it's like a party, but's not a party. It's a memorial service, but not like Rob's memorial. This is a tragedy. A funeral. *Dead. Shannon.*

Here it comes…just give in. I searched my music for comfort and companionship in my lonely bed. OJ was sleeping upstairs again. Between my pregnancy and his Diabetes, we never get any sleep together anymore. My iPod found The Mormon Tabernacle Choir, *Abide With Me, 'Tis Eventide,* and I set it to repeat. It sang to me, over and over, "Oh, Savior, stay this night with me. Behold, 'tis eventide."[1]

Pain, sorrow, and more…fear. Dreadful fear. These horrible questions, screaming at me, all boiled down to fear. *Someday they'll hate me. They'll think I'm trying to replace their Mom. They'll blame me for ruining their lives. How will this change us—the kids, our family? Me?*

"The darkness of the evening falls, the night is coming on,"[2] the choir's voices were building. The words echoed the clouds in my head. Tears trickled, then flooded. After days, I finally cried. I pleaded in prayer, "Father, if thou be willing, remove this cup…"[3] Fearful I couldn't do this, I questioned again. *Me? I'm not an incredible mom! I have so many faults! Why is this being asked of me?*

The choir quieted. "Savior, stay this night with me…." I prayed. I cried. And then, I felt it: arms. Warm, embracing, enfolding arms.

I knew now, I could do this. I knew I was not alone. *He is with me always. Here. Now.*

I turned off the music, closed my eyes, and drifted into dreamless sleep.

Later tonight...

All eyes were on me as I entered Mom and Dad's crowded living room for Shannon's memorial tonight. I'd spent ample time styling the light brown curls hugging my shoulders and selecting the plum knit dress that now clung to my eight-month pregnant (and proud of it) body, tied with a big satin bow at the top of my belly, framing it like the gift it was. My hazel eyes were especially green, as they usually are when I'm either sick or way too tired. I felt glowing, even if I was near the end of my pregnancy and the third trimester is not known for the "glow" anymore.

I spent all that time getting ready, but for what? To look "the part" I will be playing—the devoted, pulled-together mother? Or perhaps to delay that very moment—all eyes on me and that look that said, "You're a saint," and "Poor thing," all at once? Perhaps looking great was the only thing I could control as my world spun and crashed around me.

OJ and I had driven two hours from Flagstaff this morning, dropped the kids at Mom's house, then driven another forty-five minutes to meet with Tre and Brody's grandparents, Bill and Kay Cutler, at their request. Neither OJ nor I wanted to be there. Not today. Besides, I'd already had a "meeting" about what would happen to the boys, with them and my own parents. They had decided, along with everyone, this was best. We'd agreed to come today, knowing it was important for them to know our plans for their only grandsons, to know what we are like as parents and as a family, and important to help them feel right about us raising the boys. There hadn't been much peace between Shannon and the Cutlers, not even between Rob and his parents, but OJ and I were determined to make this work.

"We hope you will be grandparents to all six of our children," I told them. "And we hope they will be grandchildren to you. We really think it's the best way, for everyone. You're not losing two grandkids; you're gaining four. And the kids are gaining another set of grandparents." Tre and Brody being their only grandchildren, this idea seemed to make Kay light up. Bill didn't seem so sure. He started in on the questions. "Will you put the boys in Scouts?" "What kind of family routines do you have?" "Will you take them to church with you?" Bill and Kay wanted these things for the boys, and so did we. "We're going to take really good care of them," I assured them. "We love them."

"Shannon told her friends that she wanted *them* to raise the kids if she ever died. Did you know that?" Kay said. I was surprised—not at what she said; I'd heard that mentioned somewhere before. I was surprised she would bring it up. I wasn't sure if it was a threat or a "by the way," or what, but it made me uneasy.

"Yes," I said. "I've heard that. But Shannon didn't have a will, and everyone knows this is where they should be, including the kids. I would hope you could see that, too."

"Oh, yes. I agree," she replied. "The kids need to be here, in Arizona, with family." Older than my parents, Rob's parents had always seemed a little confusing to me. I wasn't sure if it was the grief, or just they way they were, but I was confused today. OJ and I were glad when we finally got their "seal of approval" and drove away, back to the memorial. The Cutlers would not be attending, they'd said, although I hadn't exactly understood why.

Now, I made my way through the crowd of friends, family, and strangers who loved Shannon or Rob or the boys or someone in my family. Mom's living room was already packed with people. "Hello," "Thank you so much for coming," "Yes, it is very tragic," "Yes, the boys are going to live with me," "Oh, thank you. I don't *feel* amazing," "Yes, the boys are doing well so far." It was a constant stream of questions, all night long.

At sunset, we made our way to the small, fenced backyard. That time of day, in October, in Phoenix, was beautiful—the desert breeze and rosy glow fit the respectful silence the hundred or more people observed. My dad briefly thanked everyone for coming, and my mom stared at the ground, teary, by his side. Then, my siblings and I each shared a song. It's what we do in our family. Thanks to our Dad, who always sang to us growing up, music is our language.

I wrote a song for Shannon. Putting the unspeakable into words and music has a way of calming me and giving me meaning in meaningless situations. "…Her laughter fills my soul 'til we're both rolling on the floor. Her heart—so tender and so true— she's always coming back to you. But it's her smile her soul shines through…"[4] As I sat on the back patio at dusk and sang, Colton, Braxton, Brody, Tre, and Tre's school friends sat cross-legged at my feet. Hugging one another, they sobbed heart-rending tears for all that had been lost. Everyone sobbed, even me, as my voice broke in song—to Shannon, and to the children at my feet. Barely singing, I finished the last words, "…and I can see her smile any time I close my eyes." I wanted to say something. Something to calm everyone. *Something to calm me.*

"It's okay," I said, eyes overflowing, barely able to speak, reaching for the kids in front of me. I comforted Tre and Brody, Colton and Braxton. *I'm the mother now. I'm the one who comforts their pain.* "I'm lucky," I said, looking up at the crowd, then back to the kids. "Because I get to be your Mom now. We are *all* lucky," I said, looking to OJ and my boys, "because we get to be your family." All four boys hugged me at once, and, in that moment, they were all I could see. I barely noticed the sobs of the audience, growing louder, or the tears being wiped away.

Though my voice was cracked and broken and each note filled with pain, it felt right as I sang tonight. The song was for all my boys, to help them remember their mom and aunt. It's called "Her Smile," for that is what *I* will remember most.

Monday, October 22

It's a lonely habit, early morning awakening. It's 5:30 a.m. and I'm in bed writing. Last night I couldn't get comfortable. My huge belly makes it tough to move or roll over, and I had to go to the bathroom umpteen times. But mostly, no matter how hard I tried, my mind would not turn off. I finally gave up, and here I am— awake but still in bed, because I know I need the physical rest and mental break of being alone.

Today, we buried Shannon, in the plot right next to Miki. We put some of Rob's ashes there, with her, so they could rest together. It was out-of-body, the whole thing. I actually made the kids pose on the chairs set up in front of the casket and smile for my camera. Why did I do that? Why did I feel the need to capture all five new siblings, together, smiling, today? Why did I feel like I had to be "on," to be "fine," to make everyone else feel okay about burying my sister?

There was so much more I wish I'd shared last night at Shannon's memorial, but the emotions took over, and I couldn't remember what to say. Now, I am letting myself remember her once more. I am letting the memories flood me one last time before I pack them away.

I remember how Shannon supported me when I was in Graduate School and stressing about how I could possibly complete my doctoral dissertation, a half-time

internship, a part-time job as an aerobics instructor, and
still be considered any kind of wife and mother. She
baked me oatmeal chocolate chip cookies, my favorite,
and mailed them to me in California with a note that
read, "You are amazing. I'm so proud you're my sister. I
love you!" I remember her massages. I'd been one of her
first clients at the massage school, while pregnant with
Kennedy, and, once she was licensed, I was a regular on
the blue table she had set up at home. Her hands were
strong. She had a gift for healing. She'd give me massage
coupons for birthdays and holidays. They were my
favorite gifts.

I remember our childhood—how, only sixteen
months apart, she was my shadow. I smile and cringe
thinking of the time when I was seven and dared six
year-old Shannon to dunk herself in the freezing ocean
only to say, "I don't feel like it," when she told me it was
my turn. *Typical older sister.* I could sure be mean when I
wanted to. I remember, in elementary school, begging
my mom to "make Shannon leave my friends and me
alone!" It seemed she was always trying to tag along. I
remember dancing on stage in matching white gowns,
singing, "Sisters," in the middle school play. I recall her
resenting me in high school, taking me to the top of the
hill behind our house just to tell me, "I'm not *like* you!
And I *don't* need your *advice!*" I withheld that advice for
years after.

I remember college, calling her first when I
heard Miki had died, picking her up from her dorm and
going to lunch together, to share memories, before our
flight left later the next day. I remember standing belly-
to-belly for a photo just before giving birth to our first
little boys, only four months apart. I remember
Halloween when our boys were twenty-five and twenty-
one months, how we hand-made their costumes.
Braxton was Hercules and Tre was the most adorable
little pig. I was an incredible Michael Jackson, and

Shannon shocked us all by shaving her head, to be G.I. Jane. Gorgeous—she was one of the few who could actually pull it off. I remember visiting Mom's three years later, home from graduate school, when Shannon ran into the house crying, "There were no heartbeats! They both died!" The day she found out she was having twins was the day she had lost them. I remember a year later getting the phone call that Brody was coming. I dropped everything and rushed to be at the birth, but only arrived in time to hear his newborn cry. Her labor progressed so quickly, I missed it all.

I remember the past several years—her adventurous side taking over as she traveled to China to study acupuncture and Traditional Chinese Medicine, to Hawaii with her boyfriend and the boys for a vacation not long after Rob got sick, and to Costa Rica, twice, all by herself. Searching. She always seemed to be searching for something. I remember the rockiness of her emotional struggles—her highs and her lows—and how she always seemed triggered by me. Our last big blowout was two years ago on Christmas Eve. With her screaming at me in the doorway while everyone watched, it was the first time I truly felt assertive, calmer by the minute, as I told her, "You can't blame *me* for your problems anymore. This is *not about me*. Perhaps you need some time alone to sort it all out." She slammed the door on the way to her "alone time." She *did* sort it out. Over and again, we sorted things out. *Thank goodness we sorted things out.*

I remember last Christmas, Shannon sitting our whole family down and saying the words, "I can finally admit it. I am an alcoholic." It came as a shock to me. Though I knew she liked to drink, and could be a mean drunk, I had no idea how bad it really was. "I've been going to AA," she said. "I'm working the steps, and I'm getting better." I realized in that moment, that because I didn't drink and didn't party and didn't live the same lifestyle, there was a whole part of Shannon's life she always hid from me. It broke my heart. I pulled her aside, hugged her, and offered my full support and listening ear, any time.

I'm not ready to admit the truth—that, besides OJ, Shannon was the best friend I've ever had and probably ever will. She was the one who could make me laugh so easily; anytime we were together we were rolling. She always said, "I love you," at the end of every phone conversation. I felt it was overused to say it every time, but now this is what I remember, with relief—that thanks to her, I know she loved me and she knew I loved her.

Between preparing the house and myself for the three new children who are about to join our family, there is so much to do, I can't think, and that is exactly what I want, at least on some level. Soon enough the hustle and busyness will be gone, and I'll be left alone with six children and my thoughts. That is the time I fear most.

Friday, October 26

We spent the day in Cave Creek at Shannon's house. As little as I wanted to return, it was my responsibility. Though eight months pregnant and grieving, I was still the only one in my family who could cope. I'd hoped my parents and siblings might show, but as we pulled up, I saw it was just OJ, Aunt Christina, OJ's parents, and me.

Stepping out of the car, it was 103 degrees, and even at eight o'clock in the morning, sweat was beginning to drip. I opened the front door, walked in, and drew a deep breath. It smelled like Shannon's laundry detergent and incense, and it was musty and warm—like it needed someone's attention, someone to come back and open things up. *I don't want to be here,* I heard in my head. I didn't. I didn't want to see the circular white IKEA bed lying so still and imagine her lying there still, too. I didn't want to walk past the little drops of blood on the carpet again. I didn't want to envision what must have happened that night, that morning. So, instead, I got to work.

Despite the heaviness of my stretched-out tummy, it felt good to work hard. I started in her closet, sorting clothes—"Keep? Donate? Who wants this? Anyone?" *I sure don't.* So many *things*—jewelry, shoes, coats, dresses, underwear, exercise bras, belts, drawers full of fabric, elastic, knick-knacks, racks full of hangers full of *stuff.* And this was only her closet. There was still an entire three-bedroom house to sort through.

Have you ever gone through someone's personal belongings? It felt like I was an intruder, yet, I knew it was my duty. All the while, though I told myself I wasn't, I was desperately searching. For what? Evidence? Understanding? Some clue as to how this could have happened?

The perfectly laid-out gear near the couch in her bedroom told one story: brand new lantern still in its box, sleeping bag, foam pad, ready to go away to the woods with her boyfriend, for the weekend. From Shannon's texts, we knew they'd gotten in a fight that night. Perhaps even broken up. *Was that what made her drink so much, and take too many pills?* The last text of her life was to him, and it said, "See you in hell!"

The still white bed, spots of blood, empty wine bottle, and lone acetaminophen pill found under the nightstand told another story. Just one week ago, *what transpired here?* I ached to know but was gripped by fear. My mind ran screaming as my body kept to the task at hand—sorting, clearing bits and pieces of the stories of Shannon's life. Some bits told stories of the life I never knew.

We pushed through the bedroom, the family room, the boys' room. The boys' room, toys everywhere—piles of Legos, action figures, dinosaurs, cars—most already outgrown. *What should come home with us? What should be given away?* "Christi, can you come help me...?" "Christi, do you think...?" "Christi, do you want...?" *Yes, I want. I want to be at home, covered in my bed, sleeping into another dream, another world.* Everyone needed me because I was the "successor". *I am the new mother, I know.* But it didn't feel like it yet.

Mom and Dad had said they were coming when I'd called to ask, but it was nearly eleven, and there was no sign of them. My siblings weren't there yet, either. We needed help. Cleaning out an entire house, under such circumstances, was too much for just OJ, Aunt Christina, OJ's parents, and me. After eleven, Dad finally showed up with Ashley, Leighton, and Bud, and I could see it all over their faces: *We don't want to be here.* I felt the same.

Mom didn't come at all. It was too much for her, I knew. I couldn't really blame her; it was too much for any of us. But somehow I felt resentful she wasn't there. *She should be here, then maybe it would feel like we are actually still a family.* It's not fair we mothers carry this burden, but it's the way it is. A family *turns* around the mother; the mother is the center. *Maybe if my mother were here then I wouldn't have to be the center today.*

It was after noon now, and I hadn't stopped sorting, boxing, and cleaning, except for a brief lunch break. Propped in a black office chair, its stiff back sat me straight up as I sorted through books—novels, self-help, and several on Eastern Chinese Medicine, the goddess within, spirituality, and new age wisdom. Searching. She was always searching. *I hope she's found what she was searching for.* Sorting through piles of papers—documents that remained even after the one documented no longer existed—I found *myself* again searching. For what? Items I would need—birth certificates, school and medical records for the kids—

and anything we might need to start our new family—photos of the kids, old report cards, and artwork—anything to help them retain some sense of their past. Mostly it was Shannon's papers. *Do I throw these away? Or do I keep them...for what? For the boys someday?* It was too hard to know what to do right then and there. My energy was fading as adrenaline gave way to complete exhaustion.

It was two p.m. now. I looked around and saw that the bedrooms were empty, their contents having already been distributed outside to the sell, donate, or the trash sections of the garage. The most daunting pile at this point was the "move to Flagstaff" section being loaded bit by bit from the garage into the full-sized U-Haul truck OJ and I rented to carry these *things* back to our home. Overwhelmed at the sight and the heat outside, I returned to the air-conditioned office chair, sat my aching belly on my lap and my swollen feet on an ottoman, picked up another pile of papers, and began to sort.

Throw away...throw away...throw away...wait. My heart stopped as I stared at the small, rectangular scrap before me and recognized Shannon's handwriting. It had been in the middle of her desk, in the middle of her house, far from where she had died. It had been off to the side, next to piles of papers. *Was it written that night?* As I read it, I was convinced it must have been, or from a dangerously similar night, at least. The tight writing described her many failures, "I feel worthless," it said. As the writing loosened into loopy scribbles, it was clear she was drunk as she wrote of Rob, or *to* Rob? "They will be better off" was barely legible as the loops expanded and became curly-cues, ending, what looked like, mid-sentence.

I looked left and saw Aunt Christina stacking books into a box. "Will you come here, please?" I asked, and she came. "Look at this." She read in silence while I waited. When she was done, she looked up and we stared at one another.

"What should we do with it?" I asked, worn out.

"Do you think your Mom should see this?" she questioned.

"No." This was easy to answer. "She couldn't even handle coming here today. She definitely can't handle this." *I barely can.*

"Yeah, you're probably right. What do you want to do then?" she asked.

I was so tired of that question. *Why am I making all these decisions? It doesn't feel right. I'm neither the parent nor the spouse. I'm just...I'm just worn out emotionally and physically to the core.*

"I don't want it." I turned my head away and held the scrap of paper out for her to take.

"I'll keep it. So if you ever want it back, just ask." Aunt Christina paused and then resumed her work.

I will never see the paper again.

FIVE
Accept What Is

"God grant us the serenity to accept the things we cannot change,
courage to change the things we can,
and wisdom to know the difference."
~The Serenity Prayer, *adapted by Alcoholics Anonymous*

How many times do we needlessly struggle with ourselves to prevent, stop, or ignore the very thing that is already done? We waste our energy. We waste our time. We are always the loser in this battle. The key to learning patience is learning to accept what *is*. Instead of the struggle, we find peaceful surrender. Instead of wasted time and energy, we find a self-renewing source of strength. Instead of losing, we win. Learning to accept what *is—is* the only way.

The struggle to accept what *is* usually comes in times of trial, challenge, or pain. We fight painful emotions; we fight the behavior we're engaging in; we fight the truth about ourselves, life, and the way it is. We find ourselves in denial, pretending things are different, or ignoring the very circumstances staring us in the face. The longer we deny or pretend or ignore, the more we suffer.

It's ironic, I know. We think if we give in to how things are that we are "giving up" or handing ourselves over to even greater suffering. It's just not true. In failing to accept, we keep ourselves stuck—full of tension and internal warfare that actually makes us feel worse. Acceptance doesn't mean we always *like* how things are or even that we *agree* with how they are. It simply means we are no longer willing to engage in a war with ourselves over *how* things are.

"But *how* do I accept what *is*?" That's the question I hear over and over from others and from myself, and the answer I give is, "Make space to let yourself feel, process, understand, cry—do whatever you need to do. Then, *choose* to accept what *is*." Letting ourselves get in touch with what is really happening helps us accept it. Acceptance allows us to really *feel* the emotions, helping them dissipate like air seeping out of a hole in a balloon. That is accepting what *is*.

Saturday, October 27

Today our family changed forever. Tre and Brody spent the week with their paternal grandparents, made their goodbyes to friends and school, and this afternoon, their paternal grandparents drove them up to Flagstaff, to their new home, to our home.

Yesterday, we spent eight hours moving the bulk of *Shannon's* house into *ours*. I'd rescued the toys and memorabilia the boys love most, and, this morning, I tucked them into their new bedrooms. I'd already bought matching flannel sheets and, with the help of friends, had made up all four boys' bunk beds, done their laundry, and organized their rooms. This morning, we hung up the banner some friends brought last night, signed by dozens of kids after school yesterday, that says "Welcome, Tre and Brody!"

It's the family photos on the wall that had been bothering me, though. Seeing our happy family everywhere, without Tre and Brody in it, seemed unfair to them. So, I blew up pictures of each of them and one of all five kids at my grandpa's funeral last summer and hung them up, too. I also enlarged a photo of Shannon, Rob, Tre, and Brody, and put it on the shelf in the family room next to *our* family photo, as a reminder we are all one family now and as a sign that it's okay to talk about it. I wanted to make everything perfect, to say to them, "Welcome home."

When the boys finally pulled up to the driveway, OJ and the kids rushed out to greet them, but I took a moment to myself. It's one thing to raise one's own children. It's another to raise someone else's. Not knowing if Shannon and Rob would even have *wanted* us to raise their kids felt like the hardest part. *No matter what they would or wouldn't have wanted*, I reassured myself, I *know this is right.*

In my heart I made a vow. *These boys will feel important. They will find joy and success and peace. I will give it all I've got to build them a home and to make sure they know love.* I looked at the photo of Shannon, Rob, and their family that was no more, and hoped someday they would simply say, "Thank you." Then, I put on my smile and went to welcome my new sons.

Wednesday, October 31

Day five, and so far so good. The boys are adjusting smoothly. At least, I *think* they are. They say they enjoy school, are making friends, and that they "love" their new home. Emotionally, they *seem* healthy, but honestly, it's hard to tell. *My* three children seem to be doing well, too. All five are getting along and definitely excited—if not over-excited—about this change. I'm guessing there will come a point when everyone feels like this is our permanent family, but right now it feels new and temporary. We are all adjusting. Thank goodness we start counseling tomorrow. I look forward to someone else's perspective on how the kids are doing and welcome any help in identifying exactly what they need from me.

As for OJ, he's been pretty incredible. He has stepped up his fathering in remarkable ways. He plays with the kids and helps with their homework. He interacts more with them and helps me as much as he can. Most of all, I've been impressed with his 'get to work' attitude and lack of complaining. In fact, I haven't heard a single complaint from him, which is pretty inspiring.

And me? I'm hanging in there. This family doesn't yet seem real, though I keep trying to make it so.

There's so much to do, day and night, that I don't have time to process, and my body is paying the price. There's definitely more housework involved with four rowdy boys and a little princess at home, and we still have boxes upon boxes to sort through from Shannon's house. We just piled them in the basement—too much to even think about right now. Oh, yeah, and tonight is Halloween. I've managed to scrounge up costumes for everyone, but it's definitely not my best work.

Everyone keeps saying, "If anyone can do this, you can." To which I reply, "I guess we'll see." While I appreciate the vote of confidence, it's going to be tough. All I can say is I'll give it my best. Though I don't know what the future holds, I *can* see the future for my six children—and it is bright. They will be loved. This I can see. *This* is real.

Friday, November 2

I was dreaming of Shannon when I awoke, unwillingly, at five a.m. She came to me, carefree and mischievous, and told me this is all pretend. I was trying to listen, feeling curious and blank, when I was ripped back to real life. I wonder if this is my mind's way of explaining why things have felt so "easy." I wonder if part of me still feels this is all pretend?

Wondering "why," my "Dr. Hibbert" brain kicks in and tells me I'm in shock. This may be one answer, yet I sense there's another. I can't help but envision the famous "Footsteps" poem, how there were always two sets of footprints in the sand, one for the dreamer and one for the Lord, but when times got tough there was only *one* set of footprints. That is me, right now…being carried.

Our first family counseling session, yesterday, was a big help. I'd called Dr. Hale the day after Shannon's funeral. Having known him, professionally, I knew he was good with kids and especially boys. I knew he did family therapy, and he'd already helped me once before, when I was looking for post-doctoral clinical hours. He seemed like the perfect fit for our family. "Let's set up an appointment for the boys and me, together, first," I'd told him. "I know I'll need my own therapy, too, after the baby comes. I usually get postpartum depression, and this time? Well, who knows what kind of mess I will be."

I showed up with Braxton, Colton, Tre, and Brody yesterday afternoon, asking Dr. Hale to help me know how they were *really* doing. "They seem to be doing very well at this point," he agreed. "And it's okay if you don't feel like you can read them yet," he added. "It's only been one week."

I *can't* read them the way I can my own children, and it's been nagging me. *It's because you haven't spent as much time with them*, I've been trying to reassure myself. But I didn't really believe it until Dr. Hale said so yesterday. It *has* only been one week. And I'm already feeling closer to Tre and Brody. They are doing well and seem to be feeling closer to us, too. Perhaps, they're also being carried? Perhaps, we all are.

They started calling us "Mom and Dad." I knew it would come eventually, and *should* come, but this seems quick. I admit, it feels a little awkward, having been "Aunt and Uncle" only days ago. It's also a little guilt-producing, like we've stolen Rob and Shannon's place, but it means Tre and Brody are feeling comfortable. It means they're feeling like part of this family, and *that* I find beautiful.

So, how has it been with five children? Louder and more chaotic, for sure. We're having problems getting them to listen and act responsibly. I know, big surprise. Tre and Brody aren't used to a structured environment. Shannon and Rob always let them stay up late and sleep in 'til one, like teenagers. We're an early to bed, early to rise family. They're adjusting. Also, all the kids are just too busy having fun. They've been late to school two days in a row. We've never been late before. OJ and I know we need a whole new system. They need order and structure. Eventually we'll adapt; we'll have a solid routine and understand each other better. The newness will wear off, and it will feel less like a slumber party, but in the meantime, we have much work to do and much patience to practice with all of them and with ourselves.

I've been able to think a little about this baby coming soon. It's hard to believe I have only a couple of weeks. There are many things I wanted to do to feel "ready," the biggest of which was to become as emotionally prepared as possible. That has not come, due to everything that's happened. I'm pretty sure it can't come now. I feel like I'm on a speeding train, trying to see the sights, but we're moving so fast, it's just a big blur. I can't slow it down. I can't stop. Before I know, it will be months from now and I'll be trying to figure out where all the time went. I can only hope to enjoy the ride as much as possible in the meantime.

When people ask, "How are you?" I shrug my shoulders and say, "Fine, I think." I know someday I'll have to be set back down, but, for now, I am carrying on and also being carried. I think I *am* fine. Right now, I don't really know how else to be.

Sunday, November 11

It's a strange truth that we are often prepared for the unexpected circumstances thrown our way. How can this *be*? We don't know what is coming. We have no way to know, and yet, on some level, I think we know.

I knew. I didn't *know* what I knew, but, thinking back, I *knew*. The feeling was "be prepared." I thought it was for the baby to come, for leaving full-time work, for being a more focused mother. Yes, these were all part of my plan, but it is so much more. I remember thinking, as we bought our house this past April, *It's too big for us; if we had six kids, it wouldn't be too big, but we don't.* We didn't. Yet. Then there was work. I'll admit that I was ready to be free from the job I'd had for nearly three years. It wasn't the right setting for me—way too stressful. Yet how could it have been so perfectly timed—to have seen almost all of my last counseling clients the day before Shannon died? Sitting on the driveway with my friend, Kathy, just two days before, I'd said, "I don't know what's coming, but it's something. I feel like I need to be home, focus on my family, and become the mother I am meant to be." How could I have known *then* what that would possibly mean days after?

Yes, *we* were prepared. Somehow, I think we are *all* prepared for whatever life brings. It might take time and perspective to see, but we *are* prepared.

Tuesday, November 13

"Overwhelmed" doesn't quite describe my reaction when my OB called this morning and asked if I'd be willing to be induced tomorrow instead of the day after. Apparently, she has a "date" with her daughter on Thursday that she would like to keep. Therefore, *I* have a date with childbirth tomorrow.

The usual fears are all here. *Will everything go smoothly? Will I be okay? Will she?* Part of me feels like nothing can go wrong, considering all we've just been through. *We couldn't possibly handle any more.* The other part knows just how wrong things *can* go.

But I choose to believe all will be well. I co-created this little life I am about to meet, but this part is beyond my control. It is in the hands of the true Creator, and I know that in those hands, all is always well.

Thursday, November 15

Yesterday, I got the kids off to school and then

got myself dolled up for baby girl's birthday. I curled my hair, chose my favorite maternity clothes—jeans and a stylish t-shirt that showed off my belly for the last time—and took a few self-timed photos before I headed out the door. *This is my last baby*, kept running through my mind, filling me with a strange mix of sadness, relief, and bitterness, which I continually ignored.

After driving myself to the hospital, checking in, and putting on the flapping gown, I took my place in the clean, cool sheets and relaxed into the building contractions. I had done this a few times—a "veteran," the nurses called me—so they pretty much left me alone, which was perfect.

OJ eventually showed up, after working a few hours, and later, Mom and Dad. It seemed easiest to just let them be there. Perhaps this would be healing for us all. I had my epidural early so I could save my energy, and I was able to lie down, listen to a relaxation CD, and take a little nap. This time felt different, and not only because I was allowed to eat whatever I wanted during labor. There was something peaceful about this, something at peace in me.

Hours later, OJ, Mom, and Dad seemed anxious for me to "be done." This was the only downside to the labor, for I wanted to savor this experience—*my last baby*. I tried to ignore their haste. I let things progress. The epidural wore off right as I transitioned to pushing. I felt the pain and dug in. It felt good to have to work for this baby; I welcomed the work of bringing her into the world.

And then, she was here, crying the sweetest cry and placed right up on my jelly-like tummy. On our first face-to-face meeting, she was perfect, beautiful. "Oh." My heart leapt. "Look at you." She moved her head toward my voice. She knew me already—incredible, considering I felt as if we'd just met. I watched her in awe, submerged in gratitude. OJ kissed me on the forehead, and we turned to each other. Though neither of us spoke, I could see we both felt the same. *Thank you.*

I was moved to a recovery room shortly after. It was getting late by then. OJ tucked me in, kissed us both, and headed home to sleep. I didn't sleep much. That's one myth of childbirth—that you'll actually *sleep* in the hospital. Drifting off around midnight, I had to use the bathroom two hours later. Only half awake, I stumbled back to bed, glancing just for a moment at our unnamed baby girl, wrapped like a cocoon in her bassinet. Still as a stone, she was awake, her tiny almond eyes slowly scanning her new world.

I scooped her into my bed. As I pressed her to me, her eyes held me with their gaze. "What do you know?" I whispered. So pure and fresh from the other side. *How I wish you could tell me before you grow up and forget.* I sensed a wise soul in this little body, sent here with a divine purpose—as we all are—but I could actually *see* it in her eyes. This wise baby. The final adorable piece to our family puzzle.

OJ came back early this morning, and, though I'd been trying on names in the early hours, "baby girl" was still unnamed. I had been leaning toward McLean, after Miki, to remind us of the bravest little girl I ever knew. As OJ and I looked into her eyes and tried the name "Sydney," it fit perfectly the sweet, knowing nature of that little one. Remembering all we'd been going through, we gave her "Leigh," Shannon's middle name, and just like that, "baby girl" became Sydney Leigh Hibbert, our sixth child.

Friday, November 16

Pulling up to our house last night, we could see the kids through the window, busy with excitement, helping their grandmothers make everything perfect, bursting to meet their new little sister. OJ and I sat in the calm, warm car for just a moment—a breath before diving in. We looked at each other. He held out his hand. I took it. We both inhaled slowly, and sighed. "Well, here we go," I said, and we got out of the car and entered the house.

It was almost bedtime, but the kids could barely contain their enthusiasm. Gently taking turns holding Sydney, breathing her in, they couldn't get enough of her.

"She's *so lovely*," four year-old Kennedy kept saying, absolutely entranced.

"Let me hold her," one boy would say. "Mom, it's my turn!"

I would mediate, "Okay, give her to your brother." Then, "Stand back, guys, give her some space," over and again. They crowded as they cooed.

It was definitely loud—a distinct contrast from the hospital, but it was also still, reverent, and right. I think we could all see just how much little Sydney was going to be loved.

As I stood back and took it all in, I could sense *her* sense of her place in this family. Calmly allowing herself to be passed and shared, it was as if she delighted in it. We delighted, too—a welcome relief to weeks past.

I'd been concerned about how this baby would affect everyone. It didn't make sense, adding another child in the midst of so much trial, but after seeing the joy on everyone's faces last night, I knew I was wrong. Born a sister to all five kids equally, *I think this baby is* exactly *what we need.*

SIX
Live in the Paradox
"A time to be born, and a time to die...."
~Ecclesiastes 3:2, KJV

The juxtaposition of life and death is one of many reminders that this world is full of paradoxes. The word paradox means "something absurd or contradictory." [1] Life and death are definitely contradictory. And at times—let's face it—they can seem rather absurd.

Feelings and thoughts are the same way. Our thoughts say, "This is absurd," while something inside tells us, "This makes complete sense." Our feelings contradict one another—we feel elevated joy and deepest sorrow all at the same time. This is just the way mortality is, and I have come to understand that it is okay to live in the absurd contradiction of paradox.

Human brains don't do so well with paradoxes, though. When faced with two contradicting beliefs, feelings, or behaviors, the brain tends to feel stressed, unable to handle the tension of the opposing forces. Psychologists call this "cognitive dissonance." Cognitive dissonance is usually relieved by changing a belief or behavior. For example, if I believe I am a good *person* but I do a bad *thing*, I either have to change my *behavior* and not do that thing again, to remain a good person, or I have to change my *belief* of what a good person does by maybe telling myself, "I'm good in *most* ways, but I do have my *devilish* side" (then grin and laugh, evilly). By making devilish seem good, I relieve the cognitive dissonance and feel at ease again. However, although cognitive dissonance has its upside, often prompting positive change, it also has a distinct downside. When under the influence of cognitive dissonance, our magnificent brains have a heck of a time comprehending that we may not *need* to change a behavior or belief, and that in fact, *both* may be true.

Paradox is part of the cyclical nature of things. As we die, so are we born. As we love, so are we left. As we do, so are we undone. Sometimes these cycles happen simultaneously, which can feel against nature. But we can choose to let it be. Life and death can and do coexist. I can be a good person and still make mistakes. I can feel many emotions all at the same time. I don't have to get rid of one thing to make the other true. Sometimes, many times, they are *both* true. It is okay to tell my brain, "No. I don't need your help on this one. I am keeping both."

Learning to live in the paradox is to appreciate the duality of nature, the complexity of emotion, the abundance of cognition. It is understanding the season, the "time to every purpose," the richness that only a paradox can offer. Paradox is the ultimate soil for patience and personal growth, for it forces us to choose. When we choose to plant ourselves, we find that the wealth of the soil of paradox somehow makes the absurd contradictions of life all worthwhile.

Saturday, November 17

I felt like an overachiever yesterday morning when I put on my "perfectly fine" face, made my way to the driveway, and plunked my postpartum self in a camp chair to cheer on OJ. He was working in the garage all day and cleaned it out enough for two cars to again fit. Yippee—a good old-fashioned American miracle! I was honored to witness it.

It was nice to sit outside, to have a little adult conversation with OJ and his mom while I nursed Sydney. This isn't my first "rodeo," as they say, and I know better than to be up-'n-at-'em too soon, so my goals for the day—nursing and resting and nursing some more—were easily met, and happily exceeded. A great first day home, by my standards.

But today, my "fine" face is strained, and I'm feeling a little smothered.

Mom, Dad, and Lorri are all here for the weekend. Also, Grandpa and Grandma Cutler, Rob's parents—or as I affectionately refer to them in my head, our "*out*-laws," since they're not exactly *in*-laws—have come to meet Sydney, too. When they "interviewed" us about taking Tre and Brody, we shared our vision, that, despite the tumultuous past they had with Shannon and Rob, we wanted to start fresh and hoped that all six kids would become their grandkids. It's therefore heartwarming to see them welcoming Sydney as their newest grandbaby. My kids have even started calling them "Grandma" and "Grandpa." It's awkward, suddenly having "out-laws" and another set of grandparents, but it gives me great hope for our future with the Cutlers.

Hopeful as I may be, it's still exhausting having so many houseguests when all I really want to do is be alone with my husband and baby. I tell myself, *though I am feeling smothered, at least I am smothered in love.* And, *though I want to be alone, I appreciate the help I am receiving right now.* I do. I need it. I can't imagine managing this home, five young children, and a baby on my own.

I'm reminded of my theme for the year…patience. One foot in front of the other, one day at a time, one weepy moment, one joyful one.

Tuesday, November 20

You know that "emotional rollercoaster" thing I'm always teaching about in my Postpartum Mood Disorders courses? Yeah, that's what I'm on.

It started in the midst of postpartum day four and, unfortunately, in the midst of engorgement. This is the part I always tell mothers about because, in my opinion, it's the most miserable time of pregnancy and postpartum. No one warns you beforehand. My boobs are swollen as hard as rocks, and my bottom is sore from stitches and all the drama it has endured. My energy is drained, and I'm plain old tired. Add that together with a desire to be left alone and a house full of five noisy children, one newborn, one trying-to-be-helpful mother-in-law, Lorri, and a husband who has been focused on housecleaning and kids (a good thing, but I miss him), and you have many, many tears.

Sensing a major meltdown, I curled up while Sydney was sleeping and took a nap—because everything looks better after a nap. I woke up and curled my hair. It sounds silly, I know, but having one thing that felt put together, that felt "done," helped more than I could say. I tried to talk to OJ, but he was helping kids finish homework and then playing pool with them. *I'm so grateful he's taking care of them while I heal,* I kept thinking. *But I wish he could take care of me.* I didn't want to bother Lorri either, who was busy doing laundry, organizing bedrooms, cleaning out the kitchen, and entertaining kids. Everyone was here to help so I could rest. *But I wish I didn't need it,* I thought. *I don't want to have to rest. I don't want to need help. I don't know how to accept it.*

Starving, I went to see what might be for dinner. Everyone had been so busy, it had been overlooked. Lorri offered to make something. I politely declined. Then, OJ offered, but I was so distraught, I found myself boycotting eating all together. "Just do whatever," I told OJ. "I'm not hungry anymore, anyway," I lied. "If you make me anything, I won't eat it, so don't worry about me." I walked calmly to my room, closed the door, and cried. Why was I pushing help away?

While OJ and Lorri pulled together food for the kids, I tried to sneak out and go for a drive. OJ caught me and tried to intervene. I was too upset. When he tried to stop me with a "Honey, come back. Let me take care of you," I wiggled away and told him "No!" I then drove for twenty minutes and came back feeling even more frustrated. I'm sure he's frustrated, too.

I'm tearful one minute, fine the next. I'm not really *happy,* but at least I'm content at points throughout the day. Back and forth, back and forth, my paradoxical emotions tug like a war. So, here's the question: Is this my life now? I know it's not, at least not permanently, but maybe temporarily? I keep trying to remind myself that I am hormonal, that I am sleep-deprived, that I just had a baby!

Welcome to the Baby Blues! I hear in my head. Whether it's Dr. Hibbert gently reminding me or my brain sarcastically taunting me, I can't say, but I am listening. Dr. Hibbert is an expert on postpartum mental health, after all. *I should listen to her.* "This is the Baby Blues, *remember?* Up to eighty percent of moms feel this way after the baby's born? It's normal to feel like you're on a roller coaster—crying, exhaustion, irritability, elation, feeling lost and overwhelmed—and it all peaks around day seven to ten postpartum. This isn't 'life' now; it's the Baby Blues. It will get better—you know it will. Be patient."[2]

Well, today is day seven. *So, I'm "normal?" Can that be?* At least one professional opinion thinks so. "Patience." I hope Dr. Hibbert is right.

Thursday, November 22

Today was Thanksgiving—and my birthday. It never seems to go well when my birthday's on Thanksgiving, and considering I just had a baby last week, I was careful to keep my expectations low. I didn't sleep much last night, however, thanks to Sydney's voracious appetite, and waking up to a house full of Thanksgiving guests was not exactly encouraging.

It was *my* idea to have everyone come to our house for Thanksgiving, and therefore, my *fault.* Knowing we wouldn't want to travel to Phoenix so soon after Syd was born, and believing the best thing to do was to have everyone together, I invited my family, OJ's family, and Rob's parents, the Cutlers. I'm not *completely* crazy. I only invited everyone with the stipulation that I would not be cooking a single thing. Everyone agreed. But, as these things go, cooking ended up only a fraction of the work. Not only was it the first time several of our family members met Sydney, but our nephew, OJ's brother's son, unexpectedly arrived home from fighting in Iraq, so my little plan to host around nine extra people ended up with nearly thirty guests come Turkey Day.

As everyone was arriving, *I* was attempting to find something to wear that I could actually fit in. I had finally gotten Sydney back to sleep and was in my bathroom, forcing myself into stretchy pants, when I caught a glimpse of something in the mirror. It was Mom, creeping past me into my bedroom. I quietly followed and observed. Just as her hands were reaching into the bedside crib to pick up Syd from her slumber, I loudly whispered, "Don't sneak her away! I just finally got her to sleep!"

I startled Mom, without meaning to. She just stared at me, looking heartbroken, then tearful, and stormed out of the room. I collapsed on my bed, not knowing exactly what had happened. I had no clue what to do next.

I finally opted to finish getting dressed so I could make my "hellos." Then, I snuck up to handle the situation with Mom. As I opened her door, I could tell—she was broken. "I'm sorry, Mom," I said. "But you were sneaking her away, and I've been up all night, and I just needed her to sleep for a while so I can actually eat Thanksgiving dinner without her crying."

It took her a moment to compose herself. "I'm just so sad today," she forced out between sobs. "I can't stop thinking of Shannon. She should be here. I miss her so much my heart is broken."

Tears of empathy welled in my eyes. *My heart is broken, too.*

She went on. "But then, I thought of Sydney. I thought if I could hold her maybe I would feel a little less pain."

Well, I felt like a monster. Sometimes I'm so caught up in my own drama I can't even see how it's affecting everyone else. This isn't the only holiday that's been way too hard for Mom. I apologized and hugged her. "I love you, Mom." I meant it. But, as I learned years ago with the death of Miki, at least for *my* mom, the love of one child can't replace the loss of another. The damage was done, and I could see she wanted to hide away even more than I did today.

Sitting down to Thanksgiving dinner didn't seem to help much either. I was trying to have OJ, the kids, their three sets of grandparents, and me, all at the big table in the dining room. It ended up being half of our kids, OJ's parents, Rob's parents and my siblings at the big table, Mom and Dad with two of our little kids at a smaller card table in the nearby entryway, and OJ's sisters, brothers, and their families chatting away and taking turns sitting at the table in the kitchen. Not only were we split up all throughout the house, but the Cutlers had made it clear, long before today, that they didn't like Mom and Dad. Mom and Dad had never liked the way the Cutlers treated Shannon and Rob. OJ's parents didn't know the Cutlers very well and had little in common. OJ's siblings didn't know my parents and siblings well. Everyone was trying to be polite, but the whole thing was *very awkward*. Although my hope to show the kids how much love and unity we had for them was not quite the master plan I'd envisioned, we *were* all there, and that was good enough.

I hardly remember getting to visit with anyone. I crashed after dinner and slept through the family picture. I figured they'd at least wake me up for that. OJ didn't get me a birthday gift, and it really didn't feel like my birthday at all, but at least we made a first Thanksgiving memory for our kids. I guess that's the best gift I could ask for and the thing for which I give thanks tonight. We made it through, and I won't have to have another Thanksgiving or birthday for 365 more days.

SEVEN
Fake It 'Til You Make It

"I love every moment of being a mother. I even love the moments I don't love."
~Me

We've all heard the advice "Fake it 'til you make it." Although I'm no proponent of fake-ness, I agree it can help from time to time. It's a great tool for learning patience.

For example, if I'm about to lose it on the loved one nearest me, it's obviously a better option to "fake it" instead. I've learned to do this with OJ sometimes. When I'm at a point where it feels like the only options are to fall into sobs or maim someone, I choose the secret third option: to engage in an obviously fake, deep belly laugh. Like Santa might do if he said, "Huh, huh, huh," instead of "Ho, ho, ho." It sounds so ridiculous I end up laughing for real, and so does OJ. It is our little sign that we are at a cliff's edge and doing our best not to fall, get pushed off, or voluntarily leap to our demise. Somehow, laughing together, fake as it may start, helps the cliff disappear altogether. By "faking it" we can "make it" patiently through the rough moment in front of us to the next, which is usually easier to manage.

Faking it can involve putting on a smile, remaining silent, even pretending we feel differently. Don't misunderstand me—it's not about *being* fake. "Faking it" is about giving ourselves *time*—time to patiently choose the best way to think, feel and behave. Often, in faking that smile or laugh, we actually end up feeling a little better.

The trick comes in knowing when it isn't helpful to fake anymore. Faking is a great *temporary* tool, but for extended periods of time faking is a shaky path, leading to greater psychological distress and psychosomatic problems like headaches, back pain and toothaches.

Keeping up, indefinitely, the temporary walls that protect us in times of stress builds enormous pressure—like a soda that keeps getting shaken, but remains bottled up. Eventually, something's gotta give.

So, "fake it 'til *you* make it," but not for too long. Fake a smile, a laugh, a look, but we mustn't fake who we are or what's really going on inside. Instead, we can patiently get honest with ourselves and release the pressure within. Slowly turn the churning soda's lid—there is no bubbling over, there is no sudden explosion. It will *make it* so much better.

Wednesday, November 28

This seemed like a great idea an hour ago. Taking six kids shopping for school clothes. How tough could it be?

I awoke this morning feeling magically rested. Sydney's only two weeks old, but for some reason I felt on top of the world and figured, *it's a good day for an adventure*. Now, in the parking lot, I swaddled Syd into her baby sling, grabbed four year-old Kennedy by the hand, and just tried to keep up. With four kids bounding to the nether realms of Old Navy, it felt like a giant Labrador on a leash, dragging me behind. Pulling me from one "awesome" t-shirt to the next "lovely" skirt, I was just trying to keep up. Without waking the sleeping baby. I was pretty sure we didn't have a dog; it was just the energy of six kids, and I'd better get used to it.

Finally at the checkout counter, I was struggling to add it up in my head, "Six kids times three shirts, two pants, one jacket, one pack of socks each…" *It's best not to figure it out.* The kids were still seeking my attention. "Mom, look how cool this is!" To which I replied, "It *is* cool. But we're *not getting it.*" *Just get me through the checkout line and we're on our way home!*

"Wow!" I heard, coming from the adorable cashier. A look of disbelief—or chastisement—was on her face; I wasn't sure which. "Are these *all* your children? How many do you *have?*"

It was the first time I'd been confronted with this question. *Do I say, "Well, these four are mine and the other two are my nephews and their parents just died?" No, that's probably too much information.* Or perhaps, *"I've only given birth to four. The other two are adopted?"* Or, do I just say, *"I have four children"* and leave it at that?

"Yes," I said. "They are all mine. I have six." I shrugged with a grin and a lift of my brow that said, "I know, it's crazy." Then added to myself, *you don't know the half of it.*

Wednesday, December 5

I don't know the half of it. There's a wall in my brain preventing me from processing any of this. I'm simply floating along, working to keep pace with everyone's needs, and trying not to overdo it, but the truth is, I'm also staying busy so the wall can remain in place. I know it's protecting me, and I *need* some protection, but I worry I'll end up stuck behind that wall if I don't do something. I worry about a lot of things.

Thus, I started my own therapy on Monday. I'm a believer in the power of therapy—as a psychologist, I'd better be. It's more my *personal* than my *professional* experiences in therapy, however, that really make me believe.

My first therapy experience was after Miki died. An eighteen year-old sophomore at BYU, I lost my littlest sister the opening week of fall semester. I walked the campus, explaining to my professors what had happened, and wore dark sunglasses to hide my tears. *Why hasn't the world stopped?* I wondered. *Don't they know my sister just died?* I remember returning to school after the funeral, pushing myself, studying and succeeding— *until* the toothache that wouldn't quit. I figured I needed a root canal and went to the dentist only to be asked,

"Are you currently under any stress?"

"Well…my sister died two months ago, if that counts," I replied.

It counted all right. He kindly suggested that holding in the pain of losing my sister was making me clench my jaw, causing my tooth to ache. In other words, I was experiencing a psychosomatic reaction. That explained why my hair had been falling out, too. What started as a *dental* issue was really a *mental* issue. I called and made a counseling appointment that day.

My second stretch of therapy came as part of my doctoral requirements. Each student had to do one year of therapy—to give us the experience of being the client, but also, no doubt, to ensure our *personal* issues were resolved before they set us free on others. I was in my second year—a full-time student with four year-old Braxton and one year-old Colton at home, doing a fifteen hour-a-week practicum and working as a Group Fitness Manager and Instructor and as a Teacher's Assistant for a psychological testing lab, all while OJ was in dental school. Whew! Looking back, it sounds crazy. What better time to seek help?

I attempted to get a therapist referral from my doctor, explaining all the stress I'd been under. His reply? "Just talk to your husband about your problems." He then proceeded to ask me why I have a wrinkly forehead, commenting, "You are too young to have wrinkles! You need to relax!" *Now* I needed not only a *therapist,* but also a new *doctor*! I finally found the psychologist that fit me best. Through my year and a half of therapy, I learned about my own nature, how to manage stress, challenge thoughts and emotions, and improve relationships—just what I needed at that time.

These experiences were in the back of my mind as I started therapy, round three, on Monday. This has inarguably been the most stressful and complex time of my life. I know I can't do it on my own. I need that outside, expert view of things to help put my insides back together. Meeting with Dr. Hale was a relief, and I was able to take several valuable ideas home.

For one, he gave me permission to feel tired and resentful. The truth is I *do* have resentment. It does me no good to pretend it isn't there. As usually happens, once I was granted this "permission," many of the resentments simply went away or became less powerful. As I often preach: Acknowledging and feeling emotions decreases their power.

Dr. Hale also asked me a question that, I must say, left me speechless. "What do *you need*?" I hadn't given much thought to what *I* need. I guess I didn't feel a right to need *anything*. It was hard to form an answer.

"I need...a nap everyday. And time alone." Beyond these I couldn't say, because I don't have time or space for my needs right now. He used the effective therapy technique of silence. I gave it more thought. "I need to talk out how I'm feeling with others." I told him I've been overwhelmed—in a *good* way—by the support and love we've received from others. "It's been humbling to see how much people care about us," I said. "There are many people I could call and talk to anytime. But I *don't*. And I'm not sure why. I think I need to allow myself to reach out and receive help right now."

That brought me to tears. Perhaps the reason I haven't been willing or able to reach out has something to do with the pile of emotion inside of me. I'm not sure what to do with that pile, and I certainly don't feel I should dump it on anyone else. "I know it's there," I confessed to Dr. Hale. "But I'm not in touch with my emotions. I don't have the freedom to feel and process things right now, so it ends up coming out in random little spurts I don't understand."

"You're definitely in touch with your emotions," he replied. "It's just, there are so many, it's hard for you to decide where to begin."

That hit me. *I'm not sure where to begin.* So much loss. So much change. A new life, really—new family, new baby, new lifestyle. No more career. No time for me. Being a mother to the fullest degree—a gift, but also a challenge. *Where do I begin?*

That's where I am tonight, as I write out my worries and peer over the wall inside me just a bit. I'm trying to understand where to begin. Yet, when I slow my thoughts and patiently listen, I sense an answer: *You have already begun.*

Hmm. I guess I have.

Sunday, December 9

I was sitting in sacrament meeting at church with my six children and husband. Our first time here together, I did a double take as I followed the line down the row, from OJ to me to six perfectly dressed children lined up in order, oldest to youngest: blond boy, brunette boy, blond boy, brunette boy, blond girl, baby in carrier. *Wow.* This *is* my *family.* Surreal.

The sacrament tray came, and I watched as it was passed down the aisle, each child taking a piece of bread. Silently, respectfully we partook: Dad, Mom, Braxton, Tre, Colton. When the tray found six year-old Brody, he was distracted by something on the floor. Eight year-old Colton nudged him and he looked up, bewildered, and reached for a piece of bread, dumping the contents of his little hand—*pencil shavings*—into the tray. I tried to intervene, but was too late. The tray was picked up and whisked away to the next poor soul.

Next, it was time to take the water. Again, I watched as it passed carefully and quietly: Dad, Mom, Braxton, Tre, Colton. Brody's little hand grasped the tray, and just as it did, he sneezed violently, and then calmly reached for the tiny cup. It's never a good idea to sneeze over someone else's water, but again, what could

I do? The giggling started, and I looked over to see a long string of boogers hanging out of Brody's nose, perilously hovering over the tray. "Hurry, pass the tray!" I said, but he was laughing too hard to hear, egged on by his now laughing brothers. Luckily, our friend who was helping pass the trays saw the problem, and, repressing a laugh himself, intervened, removing the tray out of harm's way. As I wiped Brody's nose and sat him back down, I shook my head and sighed, wondering if our poor church members would either come down with a cold or lead poisoning on account of us. I may have looked like the pulled-together mom of six, but all I kept hearing inside was, *I don't know* what *I am doing!*

After the meeting ended, a friend, who's raised six children of her own and was sitting in front of us, turned around and gave me that look—the one that said, "Oh, dear, you really *do* have your hands full, *don't* you?" "How are you?" she asked.

I told her the unfortunate news of the sacrament trays and couldn't help but burst out laughing. It seemed the only available option. After all, *I don't know what I'm doing!* Luckily for her, she'd received the bread and water before it had gotten to us. She laughed, too. Humor is a must when you're raising children. I could tell she could relate, which somehow made me feel a little less inept.

"Oh, Christi." She chuckled and shook her head. "You're going to have to write a book someday."

And I thought, *I just might.*

Tuesday, December 11

I was frozen with anxiety the moment I awoke and saw the snow-covered ground. My anxiety intensified as I checked the school website, and completely iced over as I read, *School is Cancelled*—again.

Having all the kids inside for four days had lead to an increasing level of messiness and diminishing level of food, and, for me, to an increasing level of frustration and diminishing level of patience, especially since I reached a new level of sleep deprivation over the weekend. I certainly wouldn't be writing any books anytime soon. How was I supposed to survive when I kept getting thrown curveballs?

After the kids awoke, elated, of course, I could feel it bubbling to the surface. I didn't want to lose it, so, I did the only thing I could think to do: force myself to my knees in a pleading prayer for patience and strength. Then, I got up and acted as if I were fine. I made breakfast, nursed Sydney, and shoveled the walkway while the kids scattered gloves and scarves on the floor and argued about whose snow pants were whose. Just when I needed it, the patience arrived. We made a snowman, drank hot chocolate, and watched a movie. I even stole a short nap. Somehow I was able to get a little work done and enjoy the kids. Believe it or not, I never lost my temper!

Then, this evening I had a moment. We were all in Kennedy's room, the kids and I. Four year-old Kennedy was performing a ballet "'cital," as she called it, and the boys were doing a magic show. We were clapping and cheering each other on, when I had this moment of clarity as I caught our reflection in the window. Five laughing children, a sweet baby, and tired ol' me. I thought, *these are my children. All of them. This is real.*

It brought tears to my eyes, for in that moment, I believed it. In that moment, we felt like a family and, for the first time, I really felt like their mother.

Monday, December 17

It's been two months since my fall, since Shannon died. It still seems weird. I had a brief moment of sadness this morning when I heard the Indigo Girls' song, *Closer to Fine*, which we used to sing in two-part harmony while I played the guitar. One moment of sadness, and then my brain flipped off my thoughts like a switch. It must be protective. But I'm not sure it leads *me* any closer to fine, for someday that switch will no longer flip.

Today was rougher than usual. I'm sure it had to do with the fact that between Sydney's eating schedule and Brody's coughing schedule, I barely slept a wink. I was, nonetheless, up-n-at-em, wrangling kids, and grateful today was a regular school day, when before I knew, it was two p.m. I wondered what I'd done all day, and listed it in my head. *I fed Sydney. A lot. And took care of Brody, giving him chicken soup and ice cream, to ease his sore throat. I did two loads of laundry, even if they're not folded. And got dinner started in the crockpot. I walked on the treadmill for twenty minutes, and took a shower.* It felt like I'd been working on amazing feats, but with nothing to show for it in the end.

By the time OJ got home, I was worn out, and when a spark of hot grease burned me while making dinner, it made me cry! I held it together and didn't unload on OJ, remembering I was too tired, trying to force myself to be fine. OJ was great. He listened while I vented. Then, he traded me places for the evening, letting me stay home with Sydney while he took all the other kids to board the Polar Express train, bound for the North Pole and Santa. *What a guy! He is riding the speeding train tonight so I can get off for a little while and rest.*

I needed those couple of hours more than I realized—to slow down, take a nap and a hot bath and, well, to just be "me." I've been so lost. My brain is mush; I'm dragging all the time; and simply trying to hold myself together. But tonight, I started to feel just a *little* of something. I can't explain except to say I felt the urge to sing and write a song. Even if it was immediately followed by disappointing thoughts. *How will I ever write a song again? I can barely get the grocery shopping done! At least the desire is there.*

Whew. That means I am somewhere in there, too.

EIGHT
Slow Down and See
"Beware the barrenness of a busy life."
~Socrates

Living life in the fast lane may get us where we think we want to be in a hurry. But how much do we miss as we fly on by?

Everyone I know is busy, including me. There are mouths to feed, bills to pay, things to get done, and, hopefully, some fun added into the mix. It's not a bad thing to be busy; it's part of life. But how often do we fail to see life's beauty and richness simply because we're going too fast? The slower path is the path of patience, and the gift of the path of patience is the opportunity to *see*. Slowing down, getting still, breathing deeply, and taking a good, long look enables us to see our gifts, lessons, weaknesses, and strengths, and to choose to appreciate and learn from them.

Sometimes, life's circumstances knock us out of our fast lane, but more often than not, slowing down is a choice we make with conscious effort. As psychiatrist and bestselling author, Judith Orloff, writes, "…calm is something you must go after, whereas stress comes after you."[1] It is precisely when stress is coming after us that we most need to slow down and see. Seeing involves all the senses—hearing a bird's song, smelling the love in the dinner on the stove, tasting the salt of a falling tear. By noticing the beauty of the world, we begin to actually *see* our world. Seeing opens our eyes to what really matters.

As we exit the speeding highway and opt for the slower, scenic route, we find a richness to life and we wonder how we've missed it all this time. We catch the beautiful moments shining right in front of us. We see our life. We see where we have been. We see where we are headed and have an opportunity to decide if we need to alter our course. We see one another. When we see, we are filled with gratitude and peace, for we no longer miss the blessed gifts sparkling in the gutters that seem to be our lives. We bend down, see the jewel, and choose to pick it up. We become a little bit richer each time we slow down and choose to see.

Thursday, December 20

It's the middle of the night. Feeding Sydney, I started to focus on the beauty of a newborn baby.

From the soft skin of her cheeks to the tight grip of her tiny hands, *I adore this little one.* I love the way she bobs her head when she's hungry, like a baby chick pecking for seed. I love how she opens her palms after she eats when she's full and sleepy. Or how she smacks her lips as if to say, "Great meal, Mom. You've really outdone yourself."

When she's drifting to sleep, her mouth sighs and moans and makes random smiles. Her lack of eye control leaves her cross-eyed at times, which always gets the kids laughing and commenting how "weird" she is. As Kennedy said just yesterday, "Oh. She is so smart and beautiful, mom! But she does have crossed eyes a lot." Kennedy is especially infatuated, calling her "Heart," and "Twinkle," and "Ring-Diamond"— anything but Sydney. I love how much she loves her baby sister. I love how much this baby brings out the best in all of us.

When she's awake, I love her intense stare. I feel as if she knows me, like she's trying to communicate the mysteries of life and beyond. I try to listen; I can't turn away. Of course, there's the baby smell, which someone should bottle, for it's far better than any cologne or perfume. But when she is soundly asleep, that is the best. The weight of her warm, nine-pound body on my chest has a way of slowing my heart and calming my crazy mind. I feel her rise and fall with my breath and imagine she loves to hear the familiar sound of my beating heart. It's as if we are one again, and oh, it is a small slice of heaven.

She is my refuge from the storms. *Such a relief. Such a happy surprise.* I have definitely fallen for this baby girl.

Sunday, December 23

It's two days before Christmas, and I'm extremely busy making everything perfect. Last Sunday, we took care of our Christmas card photo. Since everyone was looking sharp for church, I got dressed up, too, even though I wasn't going. I posed us, and snapped the shot before they left. If you look closely enough at the photo, you can see my sweat pants beneath their ties and dresses, and the terrified look in my eye behind the perfect smile.

The perfect balance of gifts for the children is coming together. The woodcarvings of each child's name—so they can make their rooms their own—just arrived. One-upping Santa, *my* detailed list *I've* been checking *more* than twice to ensure everything is fair and no one will be disappointed. I've also spent way too many hours fussing over the perfect way to decorate the house, to help everyone feel at home.

I realize the pressure to make Christmas perfect is unreasonable and self-inflicted. I don't even believe in perfection, but it's been such a hard year that I want the gift I give to be a peaceful Christmas for our family. I've already agreed we'll do Christmas Eve and morning with Mom, Dad and my siblings here at our house, then drive two hours to OJ's family in Phoenix for the remainder of Christmas day, and wrap it up at Grandpa and Grandma Cutler's to have dinner and sleep over. It sounds insane, I know, especially with kids in tow, one being a newborn. Truth be told, I'd much rather just stay home with my own little family, but again, I want everyone to enjoy this holiday. While I may not believe in perfection, I *do* believe in sacrifice. I will do what it takes for us to find some meaning, some hope, some peace.

Grief is already mixed in with the excitement. I already know I will miss Shannon—the way we laughed, the way she made everything just a little more exciting. And Rob—he was pure entertainment at Christmas time. I let myself think of them and cry a couple of times this week, just a little. It felt good to be able to grieve.

I have a lot more grieving to do in the days, weeks, and months to come, but, for now, I will put on my smile. I have a Christmas to make perfect.

Thursday, December 27

I'm exhausted, but mission accomplished. The kids claimed it was "the best Christmas ever!" They were ecstatic about their gifts, especially the half-pipe OJ secretly built in our friend's garage and Santa secretly dropped off in ours. Combine that with their new skateboards and helmets, and there was non-stop "dropping in" all morning.

We had breakfast with my family in Flagstaff, lunch with OJ's family in Paradise Valley, and dinner with the new grandparents in Scottsdale. Even though it felt strange sleeping over with Rob's parents, whom we barely know outside of the tales Rob used to tell, it was the right thing to do. I think everyone was happy.

Now, we're skiing and boarding in Telluride, or, rather, OJ, Colton, & Braxton are skiing and boarding. I am sitting in a hotel room, nursing the baby. It was a last minute decision to get away for a few days. After the "perfect Christmas," we all needed a vacation. Kennedy is staying with OJ's parents, and Tre and Brody are with their grandparents in Pennsylvania, where the Cutlers are from. They want trips and visits, alone, with their grandsons, and I get that. Still, it's awkward for the other kids, and it's awkward for Tre and Brody. The first time their grandparents took them on a trip alone, last month, they were supposed to be gone for two days at the Grand Canyon, but less than twelve hours later, they showed up back home, their grandparents dropping them off with no explanation. The Cutlers are confusing to me, and they must be confusing to Tre and Brody. They called us, crying and begging to come home, while my other boys felt neglected and wished they could be traveling with their brothers. This trip to Telluride felt like the best solution for the tense situation. But it's hard.

I know their grandparents want time alone with them; I *do* understand that. Still, I don't know that anyone has considered what it feels like for all of us—to have them suddenly removed, to have to explain *why* to the other kids, to feel this guilt that we're on a "family vacation" without two of our children. It's like slamming into an alternate universe, and then wondering if that universe is actually the real one. Having "our" children here alone feels almost like it used to be. I restrain myself from thinking about how it used to be because *that's not how it is anymore.*

I recognize we're all just trying to figure this out. There's no perfect way right now, and honestly, I'm not after perfection. *I* am after patience. So, I breathe and pray and put one foot in front of the other, and I'm now beginning to see that I am somehow altered. I am calm. The baby's cries, chaos with kids, learning to work together with new family members, being stuck in this small hotel room while my family's off having fun— these are situations that would have sent me reeling before. Yet now, I sit calmly and try to enjoy what I can and make the best of the rest of it. Not that I am *always* calm—but there's a dramatic shift inside.

It's almost the end of the year. It seems I've

learned a little patience after all.

Saturday, December 29

I snuck away to my first voice lesson since July. I had actually been planning to take a lesson the day Shannon died. In fact, I haven't sung a single note since, but back in Phoenix, picking up the other kids after our Telluride trip, I escaped the busy mom life for an hour to discover my voice again.

When I first started singing—I mean *really* trying to learn to sing—I had it all wrong. I thought, like many others, that you've either "got it" or you haven't. I thought the point of singing was to shape and mold the voice to sound the way a voice is *supposed* to sound—like the other beautiful voices out there. I had taken voice classes in high school and college and been taught basic principles: "It's about breathing from the diaphragm, supporting the voice." I'd been given homework assignments to draw pictures of the diaphragm and to listen to opera singers to get a feel for how they sound. I pushed my voice to sound more melodious, with more vibrato, more power, more softness. Sure, I had a *decent* voice. I could carry a tune. I could sound nice singing a nice song with another person—duets, trios—that was my thing. I loved harmonies. I loved to blend. I wasn't confident enough in my own voice to sing alone. So, my decent duet voice remained through college, into marriage, and that's when I met John.

I was pregnant with Braxton and needed to do something just for me. Since I loved to sing, what I really wanted was to work on improving my voice. I found Bel Canto Studio and its owner, John, through the phonebook. It turned out John was not only a former opera singer, but he'd grown up with OJ's uncle and was just like a Hibbert—ready with a friendly word, quick wit, and a laugh. I worked hard at voice for over a year. Even after Braxton was born, I would bring him along in his carrier, but life changed. We moved away, had another baby, and went off to LA for graduate school. I left my voice in Phoenix.

I didn't sing at all the first three years of graduate school. I thought I was done with singing. My voice was "terrible" and my guitar and piano playing even worse. I was no longer a *singer,* but rather someone who *liked to sing.* There is a difference, you know. Near the end of graduate school, however, I had the opportunity to choose any type of project for the final in my History of Psychology class. I hadn't written a song since my last semester of BYU, for a final in a similar class; my song-writing talents, too, apparently lost by the wayside. Still, I had something to say, and it wanted to be said through music. I worked tirelessly on that song, but it never felt right. I finished on a Saturday, and, disappointed, went to sing it for OJ—my safe audience—before embarrassing myself in front of my classmates.

The title was *Surrender.* It told of a woman's struggle through doubt. It told of her search for truth and love. She finally learns to surrender to her heart and soul, to stop relying on her head. Though my voice cracked and my guitar kept finding mixed up chords, I sang for OJ that afternoon, and I felt a wave of gratitude, because it was perfect. I had no idea how perfect until I was singing. The process of writing the song ended up reflecting exactly the words written. Trusting in one's soul—putting aside those thoughts that whisper doubt—I had found meaning. A renewed desire to make music part of my life was born with that song.

As I resumed lessons with John after graduate school, I began to finally see that singing isn't about turning your voice into something else. It's about getting in touch with your *authentic* voice. It's a process of *un*covering the true voice, of gently polishing it, of putting away each note in exactly the right place so it will function perfectly. The upper and lower registers must become united for strong singing. Once united, they form a sturdy staircase that is able to support any power given them. Singing is uncovering what already exists. It is relaxing and trusting what cannot be seen, but only felt. In fact, great singing relies mostly on feel, not sound. Each note has a feel that guides it to where it should be. I can't force my voice to sound this way or that; it simply is what it is. But I *can* polish and refine it into something a little stronger and a little sweeter.

That's a perfect metaphor for me. Just getting away for a voice lesson was part of me uncovering, polishing, and strengthening myself. A little reminder of who I really am. Today, I was feeling very *un*refined and hoping for a little strength and sweetness. John told me how sorry he and his wife were about Shannon, asked how I'd been managing, and after a little pat on the back said, "Well, are you ready?"

I stood, inhaled, and took my place near the piano. "I'm ready." Then, I added, "I have to admit, I'm hoping that, considering all I've been given to cope with lately, I'll be blessed with an increased talent for singing and writing music, as a little favor in return." He sort of laughed and shook his head, as did I, and we went about our lesson.

I gave it my all—slowing myself enough to listen to instructions, breathing into my deepest parts, then relaxing into each note. I'd forgotten how I needed to sing. It's been part of my life as long as I can remember. As a child, singing Kenny Loggins' "Return to Pooh Corner," with my Dad, while he played guitar; as a teenager, in three part-harmony with my friends, entertaining our dates while I played guitar; performing my first solo in the Messiah; singing personalized messages of love at weddings and funerals; sharing my own songs to anyone who'll listen; singing is my heart.

As I prepared to leave, the air was still. John

looked me straight in the eye, and, with a hint of emotion, said, "I need to tell you something. When you said that earlier, it stuck in my mind. I can tell you, that's exactly what has happened today. You've never been able to sing like that before."

Even though I hadn't sung in a long time, I believed him. Emotion filled me as I walked to my car—emotion for singing again, even if singing reminds me of Shannon's death, and also, emotion for this small gift of finding my voice. I left the studio, and as I drove back to my family, I sobbed.

Monday, December 31

As difficult as times have been this year, I've been busy and things are still "new." But this next year is when I will have to actually *do* what I've been asked to do and *see* of what I am made. The talk had been talked; now, the walk must be walked. It is terrifying.

The only thing I can put my finger on, as I write my year-end review tonight, is this truly has been a year of patience. I've learned to let go of control, or rather, I've learned I never really had control in the first place. I feel more capable of seeing God's plan for me instead of only seeing my own. The true test of my life is how I respond to this plan.

I feel more peace than I ever have in a time when things are most chaotic, because, hard as things are, I have meaning and purpose in my life. Perhaps Viktor Frankl was right when he postulated that we shouldn't be seeking a peaceful life anyway. "What man actually needs is not the discharge of tension at any cost, but the call of a potential meaning waiting to be fulfilled by him."[2] That is where I am. There is a meaning waiting to be fulfilled by me.

As Frankl said, "When we are no longer able to change a situation—we are challenged to change ourselves."[3] That's what I feel. I am fundamentally changed from who I used to be. I have a big journey ahead of me. I wouldn't dare hypothesize what it will entail. But, I love a good adventure. I love a life full of meaning. I love learning. I crave growth. And I'm about to be given each of these.

I'm ready. The year of patience is over. Let the year of Gratitude begin.

The kids, meeting Sydney for the first time.

PART II:
WINTER

Year of
GRATITUDE

Winter is the chill—slipping,
sloping away from the length of light
into the shrinking dark.
It is the heart's deep knowing through a frozen night.
Winter is the mystery. The stillness, slowing down.
And the soft, courageous singing
of the blanketed,
emerging soul.

NINE
Yield Control

"Everything can be taken from a man but...the last of the human freedoms—to choose one's attitude in any given set of circumstances, to choose one's own way."
~*Viktor Frankl,* Man's Search for Meaning[1]

There's really not much in life that we can control. We attempt to control everything—using the remote control, birth control, air traffic control, wearing control top pantyhose. Control your temper. It's under control, self-control, mind-control. You're losing control!

Most of the time we have little *actual* control. We can't control what happens to us, how people treat us, what they say to us, or how they feel about us. We can't control what others do—even our own children, much to every parent's dismay. We can't control the weather, the passage of time, or the seasons. We often can't even control what we think or feel in response to this out of control world.

Yet we go through life thinking we are calling the shots. Thinking we are making the plays, and orchestrating the people around us. We think we are spinning our world, until, one harsh day, our illusion vanishes. Like a baby losing its favorite toy, we cry, kick, and scream. We desperately scramble to regain control only to discover we never really had it in the first place.

I once heard an interview with author Byron Katie that helped me understand just what is in my control and what is not. She said there are three kinds of business in the world: my business, everyone else's business, and God's business. God's business is big. He deals in huge issues, like natural disasters, weather, and the cosmic order of things. We certainly have no control there, so we must let it go. Then, there is other people's business, which means just what it says—it is their business and not mine. I can't control other people and shouldn't even try. Let them handle their own business.

Then, there is my business, which is the only thing I should ever attempt to control. Yet much of it is ultimately outside my control. Thus, my only true business is self-control. I can work to improve my temper, to communicate more effectively, to be a hard worker. I can strive to do what is right, to make choices that lead to a better environment, better relationships, a better life. I can recognize that, sometimes, no matter what choices I make, the circumstances are simply provided *for* me, like them or not.

The truth is most of what we believe is ours to control is really God's. He makes it His business to take care of the million little pieces that, from our limited perspective, seem so out of control. Once we know this, we can choose to use our self-control to yield control to that Being who loves us most. We can let go of the handle we thought was spinning our world and finally be free. The world truly does keep spinning without us.

Wednesday, January 2

I completed my piddly twenty-five-minute power yoga, and placed myself in lotus pose in front of my huge bedroom window. Sun warmed my skin as I sat quietly, sound machine tuned to "Oceanside" in an attempt to drown out Guitar Hero downstairs and Eminem's "Lose Yourself" upstairs.

Five minutes was my goal today. My eyes were closed. I felt relaxed. I cleared my mind and focused on deep breathing. *Inhale slowly, deeply…exhale, three breaths.* Already I noticed my back was straightening, chest expanding, light filling my head as though a tiny string was pulling it heavenward.

Wow, this is kinda working. I shushed my mind and told it to be quiet. *I'm not supposed to be thinking,* I said. *Breathe in, out.* Stillness came again.

This is so peaceful. But my room isn't as relaxing as I'd like it to be. How could I rearrange the furniture so it would feel more peaceful? The treadmill would have to go, but where? Oh, and Tre's birthday. He wants a slumber party. Ugh. That means a night of no sleep and an early morning to go along with it. Perhaps I could persuade him into something easier—Peter Piper Pizza for an hour?

Stop! I said no thinking! Inhale, exhale, string pulled heavenward.

Dr. Hibbert's voice chimed in. "Our tendency is to avoid the present moment, to focus instead on the past or the future. This means we too often miss what's right in front of us. It's a habit that can lead to increased worry, fear, anxiety, depression, and so many stressful experiences we could otherwise avoid." *I know I should listen to her more.*

Not now, Dr. Hibbert. I'm trying not to think. I'm trying to be still. Breathe in, out, string's pulling heavenward.

What was that quote I read in Eat, Pray, Love *the other day? "Zen masters always say that you cannot see your reflection in running water, only in still water."*[2]

"Letting go, of course, is a scary enterprise for those of us who believe that the world revolves only because it has a handle on the top of it which we personally turn and that if we were to drop this handle even for a moment, well, that would be the end of the universe."[3]

I am getting better at this, aren't I?

"Sit quietly for now and cease your relentless participation. Watch what happens… Life continues to go on."[4]

Interesting idea when I'm trying to keep six kids, a husband and a home revolving. If I "let go" too much, what will happen is piles and stinky diapers.

The deeper question is, "Am I really revolving this family?" It sure feels that way. Yet something within says perhaps

I could let go for just a little bit. Perhaps this meditation can instead revolve me.

Breathe in. Breathe out. Sit. Still. Watch. See.

Saturday, January 5

"A mother's work is never done." That's what they say, and guess what? "They" are right. I'm surviving by making and checking off lists in my mind.

Feed Sydney. Begin chicken for dinner tonight. Make grocery list. Feed Sydney. Eat banana. Run, no, walk on treadmill for measly twenty minutes. Feed Sydney. Write a thought in journal before I forget. Help Kennedy get a movie and a drink. Grab muffin and head out in snowstorm to take Brody to birthday party. Go grocery shopping, come home, unload, and put away groceries. Feed Sydney, change, and dress her. Begin salsa and tomatillo dressing for gourmet fresh-Mex dinner. Be a good hostess, spending time with Lorri and Dave who are visiting for Sydney's baby blessing tomorrow. Begin making pink satin slip for Sydney to wear under her hand-knitted white blessing gown knitted by Mom. Feed Sydney. Start gourmet rice for dinner. Talk with Cory, OJ's brother, and Emilie, Cory's wife, who are also visiting until tomorrow. Straighten kitchen. Supervise laundry. Feel grateful that Lorri is actually doing said laundry. Help boys find various items they apparently "need" and have lost. Begin to sew slip (first time making any baby clothing and with no pattern). Supervise boys skateboarding, Lorri helping with baby, Emilie helping with Kennedy, and OJ and Cory painting newly built kitchen pantry (hopefully big enough now for all the food our family is eating). Finish gourmet dinner and serve (utter satisfaction on everyone's faces but also a hint they think I'm crazy for taking the time to make *a gourmet dinner). Inhale food because baby is crying. Leave to go feed Sydney. Come back. Everyone has finished eating and gone downstairs to play Wii "Guitar Hero." Finish dinner alone (it is delicious). Feed Sydney once more and put her down in bed. Turn on water for a quick shower, but get greedy and run hot bath instead. Get in, soak, ahhh…Kennedy comes in and wakes baby up! Baby crying. Get out, throw on towel, feed Sydney. Ask Lorri to hold Sydney so I can quickly finish bath. Get all church clothes ironed and laid out for tomorrow. Supervise boys doing chores. Feed Sydney. Brush my teeth. Feed Sydney. Put Kennedy to bed. Make Cory and Emilie a place to sleep. Finish sewing slip for Sydney's blessing dress, which ends up looking like a long pink satin prom gown, but oh, well! Feed Sydney.*

Somewhere around nine p.m. I felt a sense of accomplishment. *I am the complete mother—nursing, cleaning, nursing, cooking gourmet meals, nursing, sewing, supervising, and nursing!* Like I'm the conductor of a fantastic symphony! It starts with one instrument—the violin. Then, the oboe and French horns are added. Percussion. Harp. Cymbals! And I was keeping time perfectly, ensuring it all harmonized and came out sounding beautiful. Now for the dramatic finale (imagine the crescendo).

Put boys to bed. Sydney still won't sleep! Not quite two months old, and the hardest kid in the house. At least, right now. Feed Sydney more and more. Put her in her cradle at eleven and crawl in bed. Finally lay my head down and Bang! Click! Slam! Stomp past the pencil drawings OJ made of Braxton, Colton, Kennedy, and me, as I head to the basement, fuming. Every light is on in the too-beige room, and all boys are laughing, obviously not in bed. Tre is playing video games. Braxton and Brody, Nerf basketball. Colton is organizing his room, again, *which is normally wonderful but I told him an hour ago not to clean tonight!*

"Go to bed! You're all grounded!" is what came out.

"From what?" they asked.

"I don't know! Whatever you love most! I'll tell you tomorrow!" I was so exhausted.

Colton was crying. *Soothe him.* "Goodnight, boys. Even if you're not minding me, I still love you very much."

"Thanks, Mom. Goodnight."

Drag my tired bones upstairs. All other adults are asleep.

The symphony needs to end! But, Sydney is crying. Again. I hold her and start to cry. Not letting myself think too much for fear I won't be able to shut the tears off, I cry as a loving release, a moment to feel sad for myself, my one break today.

Feed Sydney. Try her in bed one more time…no luck. Bring her to my bed. Wedge her between pillows and begin writing in my journal. She is sort of asleep. Should I move her? Or sleep with her on my chest? I'll try her in bed once more.

Symphony complete, 12:07 a.m. It's stormy out. Windy. Loud windy. I hope it doesn't keep me awake.

I love being a mother (not sarcastic).

Tuesday, January 8

I've been reading all kinds of parenting books—how to teach kids values and responsibility, how to get organized, how to increase order, structure, and love. Braxton keeps reminding me, "We have way more rules now than ever before!" He is right. Before, we were floating by, and because the kids were relatively problem-free, it worked okay, but now, my full-time job is being Mom, and I feel a deep need to do my best. For now, that means getting us organized.

I've heard it said that, "Anything over four kids is all the same." Well, I don't know about four, but let me just say that six kids is far more than three. It's almost like a synergistic effect—the whole does not equal the sum of its parts. The whole feels so much bigger than the parts. Thus, we must become a well-oiled machine lest we fall prey to noise, chaos, and mess.

I'm also grasping how much more I need to teach my children. I mean a *concerted effort* to teach them, not just a lesson here or there. We're working on values, therefore, and this month is Honesty. I need them to understand it's okay to tell me how they really feel—to own up to mistakes, to speak the truth. Even if they're afraid it will upset OJ or me, they need to be honest. "If you break the rules, you're far better off being honest about it," I keep saying. "You'll get in worse trouble for lying." I printed off HONESTY in an encouraging font and stuck it on the fridge, along with this quote from Spencer Johnson: "Integrity is telling myself the truth. And honesty is telling the truth to other people." We'll broach integrity another month, but for now, I've asked them to report back on their honest progress at Family Home Evening each Monday.

I'm also developing "Family Laws" to replace our old rules, and a new system of responsibility and payment. We have so much work to do, and I would feel miserable if I didn't do everything possible to help my children become incredible adults. I would feel like a failure. I realize they will make mistakes. I realize they may not choose to embrace the values I hope they will. All I can do is give my all. That's why I cannot rest. Now is the time to teach and be vigilant in my role as a mother, as caretaker and leader of this family and home. I feel passionate about this work. It is the most important work I have ever undertaken.

The incredible thing is how much I am enjoying the "job." Even today, with a second snow day following winter break, I managed to keep a smile—a real one—and feel happy. I admit, I had a tear for a moment when I found out it was another snow day, after a long and sleepless night with Syd, but I am enjoying my work and really loving my children.

Monday, January 14
A web of thoughts and emotions has built itself into the corners of my mind and body, settling in for the winter. I see my insides, looking like an abandoned attic in a beautiful home. Outside, the home looks strong, graceful, and cozy. But inside it is cold, dark, and filled with cobwebs. A small stream of light breaks in through the tiny, round attic window above, so there is hope for this place. It just needs some cleaning, a comfy chair, a

flannel blanket, and someone wishing to sit and read a good book. I want to be that someone, but first, I've got a lot of emotional cleansing to do.

It's like I've been holding my breath for a terribly long time, and now that the kids are more settled, I'm able to exhale. But only a little. As soon as I begin to feel, I suck it back up because, inevitably, someone needs me.

Last night, OJ and I escaped for twenty minutes when we went to pick up dinner. Twenty minutes to talk to each other—a luxury these days, thanks to the busyness of our new family. I deeply miss it. We hadn't even turned the corner before I was in silent tears, finally releasing the boxed up emotion.

As we pulled up to the take-out window, OJ took my hand and looked into my eyes. "Honey," he said. "What are you feeling?" This was OJ at his finest. Not a touchy-feely guy at all, he knew how much I need to talk, to let it out. It reminded me of his love; it reminded me I wasn't alone.

All I could do was cry and shake my head. *The kids. The baby. You. The house. The pain. Me.* "It's just so much."

He nodded and hugged me. We talked about how hard it is for all of us. It was strangely comforting to hear OJ affirm that it still feels like a made-for-TV movie, not our real lives. I cried the whole way home, freeing as much as I could.

Then we were back, and I was blowing air up to my eyes so they might dry and I could face the kids. It's not that I'm ashamed to cry in front of them. I believe in expressing emotion and modeling healthy ways to cope, but they don't need to see my grief right now. They're doing well, and I don't want them worrying about me. This isn't something they should have to take on. *They have had enough to take on.* They just need to be kids.

When I slow down, like last night in the car, I feel like a jumbled mess. I feel like I need help, but I don't know where to turn or how to ask. So, instead, I just keep busy. When I ask Dr. Hibbert, she says, "You're beginning to grieve. It makes sense you would start to feel these emotions now that your life is settling into a more 'normal' routine. You're also sleep-deprived," she adds, "which never helps."

Yes. I know she's right. Still, I feel weak, just when I thought I was amazingly so strong. I have been trying to be tough, to give my all, to make a concerted effort to function perfectly as a mother, wife, homemaker, human being, and to make everything better for everyone. But it's not better for me.

The sad truth is I can't make everyone better. I will fall apart if I try. I *am* falling apart. I have to take care of myself, too. I must be realistic. So, I check in again with Dr. Hibbert: "Letting yourself feel weak and vulnerable is at the core of being strong."

Friday, January 18

I rose early, fed Sydney, and set her up with a babysitter before driving myself to the outpatient wing of the hospital. Although I'd been bleeding for nine weeks, I never expected, when I went in for my post-baby checkup on Monday, that I still had placenta inside, requiring a D&C, the Dilation and Curettage procedure most common after a miscarriage. I robed up and waited on the cold exam table, thinking up song lyrics inspired by a poster on the wall. "Eternal Rhythm," it said, with a picture of a majestic red rock view. *"Eternal Rhythm, beating like a still, small drum."* Yeah. *I like that. "Whispering why I was sent here, reminding me where I am from." Yes. Love it.*

The nurse interrupted my songwriting by having me move to a wheelchair so she could push me into the operating room. I greeted my doctor, anesthesiologist, and nurses, lay down on the warm surgery table, and tried to say something witty to cover my nerves. Next thing I knew, it was post-procedure and I barely knew where I was. All I remember is I was shivering so much I could hear my teeth chattering and a gruff old nurse was telling me, "Everything went fine, but you've been bleeding more than normal and your body temperature has dropped." I was weak and out of it. She tried to warm me with those microwaved blankets I love after having a baby, but it didn't seem to work. In and out of reality, I dozed, then woke shivering to another nurse administering more medication, rectally, and another warm blanket. They were doing their duty, dutifully, but it made me feel even colder.

Four hours after I checked in, I was still not warm, but they said my body temperature was "normal" and I could be released into OJ's care. He had been there the last hour or so, with Sydney, and was ready to leave, though I wasn't sure I could stand without collapsing.

We arrived home in what felt like seconds. Still heavy with anesthesia, I had slept the entire way. OJ helped me to my turned-down bed, waiting, luring me to crash. But first, I had to pump. "Pump and dump," for twenty-four hours, my first stint without breastfeeding Sydney. I made sure OJ had a bottle ready and pumped while he changed her diaper. Luckily, the other kids were still at school, Kennedy was at a babysitter, and I was going to finally get to sleep.

OJ was acting strange—rolling and hanging his head, and walking like a drunk. My mind might have been fuzzy, but he was definitely acting low, as in low blood sugar. I asked if he'd eaten in a while. After all, he'd ended up waiting far longer for me than intended. He told me not to worry. "I have it all under control," he said with a smirk, as he let his head spin and drop.

People say OJ looks like Matt Damon or Jason Bateman, but that face he was making, the one where he raises his eyebrows into points, eyes wide as he grins, looks more like Jack Nicolson, playing one of his *crazy* roles. It always spells trouble.

"What is your blood sugar?" I demanded.

"Don't worry about it," his cheeky reply.

"I *am* worried about it," I said, growing frustrated. "Because I'm about to fall asleep for who knows how long and you're supposed to be watching Sydney. Just eat something, and I'll be satisfied. *Here.* Here's a candy," I pleaded, handing him a caramel I'd been saving for better days.

"I don't need that. I'm fine," he said. "*You're* the one on drugs. You just don't know what's really going on."

What? Me, on drugs? Well, yes, technically I was on drugs, but my head was clear enough to know that he was not acting normal and that my blood pressure was rising.

"Honey, *please*, just eat something. Or, test your blood sugar in front of me so I can be sure you're not super low. I can't go to sleep worried about you like this. And I'm *so* tired." The anesthesia was calling me like a siren.

"Sleep, sleep, just go to sleep" he teased, placing his hands over my eyes, trying to close them.

"Cut it out!" I yelled, frustration turning to upset as he continued to laugh. I wasn't sure what to do. He was right. I was in no position to be caring for him, but I couldn't rest until I was sure he and our baby were out of harm's way.

Desperate, I called his mother. "Let me talk to him," she said, in that voice only a mother can use. Lorri's had years of experience dealing with this sort of thing. The stories of OJ's dad being low are infamous. Some scary, like seeming drunk and refusing to get out of the driver's seat, and some hilarious, like doing, as OJ says, "Impressive gymnastics, like handstands or one-handed push-ups—things you wouldn't expect a man that old to be able to do." Diabetes can really mess with one's reason. "Owen, what are you doing?" his mom demanded. "Go and eat something. I am your mother and I demand you go and eat."

He was laughing by now and telling his mom how *I* was on drugs and making way too much out of this.

Seeing how OJ was responding to his chat with his mother, I found my cell phone and called my friend, Terri. "Can you please come over?" I asked. "OJ has low blood sugar, and he won't eat, and he won't test, and I just had my D&C, and I am so tired, and he's supposed to be taking care of the baby. Can you just come and make sure he eats so I can go to sleep?"

"I'll be right there," she said.

In a few minutes, she was. Pushing him into the kitchen while he laughed all the way. I was finally able to crash into anesthesia-induced sleep knowing that everyone, for the moment, was taken care of. A welcomed break. Too bad I had to have surgery to get it.

I can't say for certain I was completely in my right mind today, but I am certainly right when I say OJ was not. Thank goodness we have each other. Thank goodness usually one of us is well enough to help the other through.

Monday, January 28

Today we were granted guardianship of the boys. Despite my fears about what might happen since Shannon didn't have a will, within twenty minutes, the kind judge granted OJ and me "Legal Guardians" of Tre and Brody. Mom and Grandpa Cutler were both there to offer their support—literally, to the judge, but also to us. I was flooded with gratitude for their confidence in us to raise these boys. Tears welled in my eyes as the judge made the pronouncement, because this is the *official* beginning of becoming the family we have *unofficially* been working on for over three months. Somehow, it gave me a little extra boost I didn't even know I needed.

I came home and told the kids the news and couldn't help hugging and kissing each one. My heart was so full of love. It's just another example that I *can* let go, that everything will work out fine, just as it is meant to be. Kennedy came home the other day from her Christian preschool and said, eyes wide with wonder, "Mom, did you know Jesus has the *whole* world in His hands? He has the mommies and the daddies, the brothers and the sisters, and the babies. He has everyone in His hands!"

How true.

Wednesday, January 30

"How are you doing?" A simple enough question, or so it would seem. Yet, there appear to be only two acceptable answers: either I'm fine or I'm not fine. Most people don't expect or even want elaboration on "How are you doing?" so, when asked, I say, "Fine," because I'm not *not* fine.

I'm not exactly fine either. I wish someone would ask for my highs and lows, like I do with the kids, instead of a one-word summary of my current existence. I wish there were a way that, when asked, "How are you doing?" I could succinctly say, "Each day has many challenges. Some days feel like too many challenges, but most days I manage, and some days I even grow. Some days I cry. Some days I scream into my pillow. Most days I feel content and even have joyful moments. It's hard. Many days, it feels very hard. Some days, there is lightness amidst the hardness and I know I have divine help. In fact, I know I haven't even scratched the surface of how I'm really doing because there's too much to take care of, so I can't yet take care of me. I know the coldest days are still to come, and that scares me. All these experiences are changing me—fundamentally changing my very being. So, overall, I feel...grateful, and...fine."

TEN
Seek the Sun

"In the depth of winter, I finally learned that within me there lay an invincible summer."
~Albert Camus

Things aren't always fine. I'm sure you know that by now. Sometimes the wind howls—raining, hailing, snowing, flooding, freezing—and the next day, it happens all over again. That's the hard part of winter. The cold can feel relentless. Yet, we have a choice, even in that cold. We can choose to embrace the season we're in. We can seek the warmth that feels absent and, with gratitude, recognize it's really not.

My young daughter, Kennedy, says winter is her favorite season. She loves the snow, sledding, snowman-building, hot chocolate, and, of course, the snow days, when school is cancelled. I, however, cannot echo Kennedy's sentiments. I do love the beauty of winter—the coral pink reflection of the rising sun off the snow-covered mountains out my bedroom window, the quiet that comes after a snowstorm, the cozying up with my family next to the fire to keep warm. But, I do *not* love dark mornings and early nights, going for days without feeling the warmth of the sun, the isolation that can result from staying so often indoors, and waking up to yet another day of "no school" with six bored children piling mess upon mess.

We all have winters in our lives, times when things feel cold, isolated, frozen over, times when everything seems "cancelled," from school, to warmth, to life itself. But that's just winter. And, like every season, winter must be experienced before it moves on; we can't skip it, much as we might wish. Instead, we submit to winter. We pay more attention to internal needs; we slow down, sleep longer, stay indoors, and focus on what's right in front of us. This is the gift of winter—the time to turn inward, synthesize, and understand seasons past. Yes, even in the coldest winter, when the ground outside looks frozen with no life to be found, deep under the surface the seeds are working, preparing to grow. When we take time to look within, to feel deeply, to understand the seeds that have been planted, we rise and bloom once the soil thaws in the spring—and the spring always comes.

It is in winter that we most need the companionship of a grateful heart. As we gratefully submit to the chill of winter and seek the warmth of the fire within, we are able to look around and see the beauty and the peace—to experience the wonder of a snow-filled sky, to appreciate the slowing down that has to follow shorter days, or the extra time spent with the ones we love on a blizzard night. Practicing gratitude reminds us, no matter how dark or cold the skies may be, there is always sunshine within, if we will but look and gratefully see.

I learned this back in college at BYU, during those dreadful winter days the residents of Provo, Utah, call "inversion." Provo is typically a picturesque valley surrounded by immense mountains that leave you with a sense of wonder, but on inversion days, those mountains, like a barrier, catch the clouds, leaving the poor inhabitants of the valley below socked in with darkness and snow. After weeks of cold, grey skies, I'd begin to find the dreariness overwhelming. So, I learned to hop in my car and head south, like a bird flying to warmer weather. A short thirty-minute drive later and "Ta-da!" there would be the sun. I'd pull off the freeway to the frontage road, park my car, and wrap myself in a blanket as I sat on the roof, basking in the sunlight. Gazing north, to the blanket of darkness, now an obvious ball of clouds, I would gratefully remind myself again, "See, the sun is still here. No matter how dark things seem, it's always here."

Yes, the sun is always there, behind the storm, constant and sure, and we can choose to seek it. We can submit to our winters, feel what we need to feel, and learn what we need to learn. We can seek the sunny moments or even get in the car and drive to warmer weather. It's not easy, I know, but practicing gratitude gets us through. After all, "We can only be said to be alive in those moments when our hearts are conscious of our treasures."[1] Winter may not be our choice, but experiencing winter with gratitude *is*.

Thursday, January 31

Last night, I dreamt of Shannon again.

I'm in Mom's and Dad's family room, trying to watch TV and relax. It's a holiday, like Thanksgiving, but all these teenage boys are here, laughing, eating pizza and popcorn, and daring each other with loud, crazy stunts. I don't know who they are, and I want them to leave. I move into the back bedroom, to get away from the noise, and just as I'm settling on the bed, Bud comes in. He's much younger than the twenty-something brother I know today—probably only eleven or twelve—and wrapped in a blanket.

"Shannon's here," he says, eagerly.

"That's impossible," I reply.

But he insists. "No, really, she's in the bathroom. She's here!"

"I don't believe you," I say. "She's dead."

And then, there she is, in the doorway, looking disheveled, yet calm, and saying, "I am here."

I feel shock and, disbelieving, yell, "No! You're not real! This is a dream!" I fall crying to the floor as she tries to reassure me I am wrong, that she is actually alive. But I keep saying, "This is a dream! This is a dream!" until I wake up enough to fall back asleep and into another dream.

It still doesn't seem real. Shannon is dead. *Will it ever?* I have these snapshots in my mind, etched in stone. Waking at Lorri and Dave's at two or three a.m., almost exactly twenty-four hours after she died, and seeing these blinking rubber ducks in the bathroom, now lighting up. Wondering if it were her spirit, trying to say goodbye. Running back to my bed, wanting to see her, but afraid. Repeating, "Oh, Shannon! What did you do? What did you do? It's all so stupid, it's all so stupid," and letting myself cry just a little before sucking it back up. Being the strong one—for my sisters, at the mortuary, for my boys, as I told them she had died and absorbed their hurt, for my family, cleaning out her house.

Dr. Hibbert is trying to remind me to be gentle with myself. "Feel what you feel," she says. "Feel overwhelmed, tired, frustrated, sad, grief-stricken, angry, whatever. Let yourself feel like you're never going to get out of bed again, like you won't be able to manage the many responsibilities awaiting you. Let yourself cry. Let yourself curl into a fetal position. Then, get up and get moving again."

It's hard to let myself feel these things. I've seen how difficult it's been for my mother to get out of grief these many years. I can't afford to get lost in it, too. But, today, I did exactly that. I cried. I missed Shannon. I thought, "I'll just let things go." I feared I'd never get out of bed.

Then, I got up and started walking on the treadmill. I said a prayer. I am going again.

Tuesday, February 5

Waking up each day feeling like I'm going to cry can't be good.

Last night, I was so tired as I turned out the light at twelve, with Sydney in my arms, that next thing I knew, it was 1:30 a.m. and she had spit up all over me and fallen back asleep. She didn't wake until 8:15 this morning—the longest stretch yet. Unfortunately, I awoke just before seven to the other kids and OJ getting ready for school and work. Only after we were all awake did we learn that today was a snow delay. *Oh, well.*

I tried to go back to sleep and enjoy the extra two hours before shuttling kids to school, but mostly, I just lay in bed—gazing out the window, my body dead weight—and let my mind turn on. Sometimes, I wish I could go back to the first week after Shannon died. I know it sounds crazy, but my mind keeps revisiting moments of pain, curiosity, sadness, fear, worry, and I wish I were there again. It's like, if I could just witness it again, with seasoned eyes, I might, perhaps, be able to take more in, or find new understanding. "Then" was, in many ways, easier than here and now. For one, everyone *expected* us to just be sad, confused, afraid, and grieving. Now, it's as if everyone has forgotten. It makes me feel like something's wrong, because I have *not* forgotten. I'm not "over it." Not *yet.* Not *still.* Not even four months later. Though I often wonder if I should be.

I know. I hear it, too. *Of course* "these things" are affecting me. Four months is a speck. I'm pretty sure the "affecting" has barely even begun. I'm aware of how I feel, what I think, and what is happening around me, but I feel like a passive observer—seeing us go through this, but not feeling connected. I have moments of connection—with OJ, with my children, with my former identity as a psychologist, with my life's meaning and purpose. The days are like unconnected dots, waiting for a line to be drawn that will bring the picture to life.

I can definitely hear my inner judge, loud and clear. *You "should" have finished that already,* is a common theme, whether it's referring to work for my Postpartum Coalition, slides for the *Women's Emotional Health Across the Lifespan* talk I'm supposed to do in March, booking our rooms for the boys' All-Stars basketball tournament in California, cleaning out my bathroom closet, doing laundry, grocery shopping, tidying up, talking with kids to see how they're *really* doing, teaching them values, cooking, creating my weekly and yearly calendars, organizing each room in the house, decorating, or calling friends or Mom and Dad to check in on them, or working out more... I've already had all these "shoulds" this morning, and it's barely 11:00 a.m.

The only tasks I've been able to do so far today have been to get the kids ready and dropped off at school, change the baby, put her to sleep, do a half-hour workout because the baby was crying, finally eat a little breakfast, start two loads of laundry, and now, to write in my journal, for therapeutic purposes. *Ha! Only!*

Thursday, February 7

Driving out of the snowy mountains, down to the summer-like temperatures of Phoenix this morning, was a welcome relief. Oh, how the sun warms my soul. Unfortunately, attending court does not warm my soul, and that is why I was there.

I walked into the dimly lit building, followed the silver-flecked white linoleum floors, and met Grandpa Cutler in the hallway outside the courtroom, thirty minutes early, as planned. He is now Conservator, responsible for the boys' inherited monies from Rob's life insurance policy. All this legal stuff is trickier than it should be, since Shannon had no will, and thus every decision has to be approved by the court.

I was nervous, waiting to enter the courtroom. OJ was back in Flagstaff, working, so it was just Grandpa Cutler and me. Though he seems like he's on our side, I know, from his past with Shannon and Rob, he can flip in a moment. He's done it a few times already with me. He can make me feel more judged than the judge himself. I couldn't wait to just be done with this. We entered the courtroom with a dozen other people, sat in the back, and waited for our case to be called. We were second.

I was there to ask the judge to grant us funds from the money Shannon inherited from Rob, that the boys will eventually inherit, to help raise them. Grandpa Cutler was there as conservator, and in support of us. I first explained our story, how Rob and Shannon had died. How we'd inherited the kids. How we'd had a baby and now had six total. How we were trying to heal. A collective sigh and headshake came from the onlookers in the back as they awaited their turn for justice. Pity. That's what it felt like to me. *I don't want these strangers knowing my business, let alone feeling sorry for me.* It felt embarrassing.

But pity turned to judgment as I spelled out our reasons for requesting monies—what our budget was, and how we would use the extra money to help pay for braces and vacations and supplies and school. It felt too personal to have all these strangers listening to these financial details and judging me, and I was grateful when it was finally over. The judge awarded us a small amount of money each month—much less than we'd hoped. A disappointment, but I was burning to get out of there.

Part of me felt relieved the judge awarded anything, and all of me felt relieved to tell Grandpa Cutler goodbye and get back to the solace of my car and the long drive home. I called and told OJ what had happened. "Are you kidding me?" he said. "That's ridiculous." I tried to explain how awkward it had been pleading our case with these other people looking on, but he just kept saying how the judge doesn't understand how much extra income it will take to raise two additional kids.

"I know, honey. I agree. But you don't know what it was like in there. I was grateful they at least gave us something," I said, a little defensively. OJ's already been stressed, financially, since we are spending more—we even had to buy a bigger car to fit all eight of us—and business has been slower lately. I understand where he's coming from and feel for him, but I felt very alone today.

In fact, all of this court stuff makes me feel alone. I've made it my job to deal with Bill Cutler regarding settling Shannon's estate, because OJ has enough to deal with at work. Bill is older than Mom and Dad, in his late sixties, I think, with slicked dark hair and large-rimmed glasses. Barely taller than I am, with a bit of a potbelly, his outward appearance is unassuming. His personality? Quite the opposite. I've been on the phone with him way too much lately, trying to manage not only his unfounded accusations about us and Mom and Dad, but also his attempts to tell me how we need to parent the kids. He pays way more attention to Tre, hardly ever asks about Brody, and the other kids? I'm not sure he even remembers their names. "You need to send me a copy of Tre's report card," he says, "so I can make sure he's doing well enough in school." To me, his voice seems whiny and unassuming, but his words are absolutes, sly insults, and subtle threats. I'm not a dummy; I hear it. I just choose to ignore it, and try to keep the peace. OJ says his voice is like a chainsaw. The more upset he gets, the more high-pitched and angry he sounds. He certainly does get angry easily. He says we stole property from Shannon and Rob—their wedding rings—even though we've got them in the safe for the boys, and all their property belongs to the boys anyway. He says I need to be more on top of their scouting activities. He says a lot of things.

I listen and try to calm him down, my psychology skills coming in very handy, but really, I don't want to deal with any of this. I don't care about any money or property. I just want the kids to be safe and well. I just want everyone to get along and leave us out of the drama.

For now, they finally are. A moment of peace. I hope it lasts.

Saturday, February 9

OJ took the kids away to play basketball at the park while Sydney was napping. That left me with a lovely nugget of quiet time. I opted to spend it in my favorite place these days, the place I go to drown my worries and cleanse my soul—the bath. The water was perfect, just hot enough to make me slow down and adjust my way in. As the heat released the tension in my body, the quiet released the tension in my mind.

I was able to actually *ponder* rather than simply holding back the flood of the past—a gift I welcomed wholeheartedly. I reflected on all the instances when I think, *I should do something,* then second-guess myself. It can be as small as thinking, *I should grab my cell phone and put it by the tub before I get in.* Which I heard today, and which I chose to obey. Not a big deal, but OJ called as soon as I settled into the water, and it saved me the hassle of getting out to answer.

Then, minutes after, Syd started crying. My immediate thoughts were, *Hurry and wash your body. She's crying! You need to go get her now!* But something else said, *Just soak for a moment. That's why you're here.* I sat back, took a deep breath, and decided to calmly wash my hair and body, reminding myself that Sydney could wait a few minutes. By the time I'd finished washing, she had fallen back asleep. This allowed time to submerge my body and head and make that humming sound I love so much—the one that vibrates through the water, detoxifying my body, mind, and spirit.

Rejuvenated, I was ready for a lovely evening with my family. I could feel the joy of watching Sydney sleep on my arm, of seeing Kennedy's eyes shine as she told me all about her "fun day," in hearing about the boys' "sweet shots" from their basketball games and watching Transformers together, in spending time with OJ.

Now, it's 10:00 and I'm hearing: *Sydney's asleep.*

Go to bed. Life is simple and brilliant when I listen to that still, small voice.

Sunday, February 10

Something hit me this evening, an unexpected truth: I am more disrupted than I realized. I'm in a winter of my life. I feel isolated, buried. I've been surviving by living moment to moment. I've always thought living "in the moment" was a good thing, and I guess it can be. I know that the tough moments are just that—moments—and they do pass. The "good" moments are good, but again, they pass. Knowing this helps me get through the hard times and makes sure I don't miss the good stuff.

But then there are all these mindless moments when I feel like I'm in auto-mode—getting through, carrying on, doing what must be done. Driving, cooking, cleaning, tucking in, kissing goodnight. These are the bulk of my moments since October 17th. I see what must be done and do it. Like a robot. Strange how quickly we adjust to our given path. What seems at the outset an impossible journey quickly becomes "simply the way it is."

The mind is harder to change. My mind wants to keep reminding me that this *is* an impossible journey, though my body can't remember what it was even like before. It wants to remind me how hard my days are and how much grief I still have to feel. It wants to shout that I'm a different person, that I might even be lost, and truthfully, I'm grateful for those reminders, and for the empathy. Because I can't escape the nagging feeling that the life and existence I knew *did* stop the moment I said the words, "She died, didn't she?" and OJ said, "Yes."

Thursday, February 14

It didn't feel like Valentine's Day today, but then again, I'm not a huge fan of having the calendar tell me when I need to express my love to my O.

It snowed all day. The bus forgot to pick up the kids. Tre remembered at the bus stop he had a project due today. Kennedy was sick with the flu and earaches. Colton had a birthday party and forgot he needed a gift. The busses couldn't bring the kids home from school because of the snow. Mom, Dad, and Grandpa Cutler were in disagreement about getting Shannon's estate settled and kept calling me with their arguments. Kennedy threw up—three times. OJ had to work late, and then plow snow when he got home. I felt so run down, with a sore throat and headache, I only made it through the day courtesy of numerous prayers. Now, I'm writing just a little before I collapse into bed.

I've been expecting the days to be "normal" for a while now, but they're not. Who's to say what "normal" is anyway? It's as if normal is nothing and nothing is normal anymore. Every day just feels hard. I have easier days and even some good and fun days. I guess these easier days used to be the norm. Today, I'm wondering if the hard days are the normal days and the easier ones are just the candy sprinklings to keep me going—the "little wonders," as I call them, and as Rob Thomas, lead singer of Matchbox Twenty, sings in his beautiful song of the same name.

It's true. Life *is* made from moments. Somewhere along the way, I've realized that, amidst the big twists of life, the little things are what make it great. I often flash forward to the day this house is empty and silent. It makes me appreciate the chaotic times and helps me feel grateful that our home is so full of noise— laughing, playing, singing, bouncing, piano, guitar, TV, whatever. It's full of love. So, no matter what normal turns out to be, I will continue to seek the little wonders, the sprinklings that keep me grateful.

I actually started keeping a "little wonders" section in the back of my journal a few months ago. I write the magical moments I don't want to miss: Sydney sleeping through the night last night and smiling today; Kennedy's enthusiasm and how my friend, Barb, calls her "The exclamation point!"; the boys' willingness to work hard at making this family; laughing with the kids at the dinner table as we discuss our "highs and lows"; a sudden moment alone with OJ; our safe-haven home; my talents; unexpected quiet; *Canon in D*. I love that song. It moves me.

Monday, February 18

Cynthia called this morning, to see how I'm doing. We haven't spoken much since graduate school, but there's something about doing your dissertation and producing a *Postpartum Couples* video together that bonds you for life.

It actually caught me off-guard. My cell rang just as I was sinking into yet another hot bath, while Sydney napped and Kennedy was at preschool. I wondered why she was calling at first and felt guilty she was checking up on me. *I don't want people to feel like they have to be concerned about me*, I thought, but quickly admitted how grateful I was that she *was* concerned. I'm not used to people taking care of *me*. But I need it.

"How are you?" she asked. Her Boston accent turned "are" into "ah".

"Fine. Pretty good. For the most part," I said.

She could read right through me. "You don't sound so good. What's really going on?" *Cynthia's a psychologist too, of course,* I reminded myself. It made me feel as if I could safely relinquish myself to her care for just a bit.

"It's hard to put into words," I said. "I just feel so many things. It's like a ball of emotion. I try to feel and understand, but then have to shut it off because I need to be there for everyone else. It's all stuck inside, I know. I don't want it to be, but I don't think I have the luxury of processing things right now. All I can really feel is…exhausted."

"Lady, you are doing so much," she said. "And such a great job loving those kids. You know, you're shouldering the weight of everyone else's emotions, too." This was new to me. "No wonder you're exhausted. It's too much for anyone."

She's right. I am and it is. Tears began to drop as the truth sank in. I took a moment to collect myself.

"It isn't the big things that make life hard," I said. "The deaths and traumas and losses. I used to think it was, but it isn't. It's the carrying on, day-to-day, *after* the big things—or, in-between them."

That sums it up. I can see the plusses and minuses. I can feel grateful, see profound growth, think positively about my future and present most of the time. It isn't fake. It's really how I feel. Paradoxically, I feel so many other things, all at the same time. I feel worn-out, drained, overwhelmed, and frustrated. Sad about Shannon and all the loss. I feel grief, self-doubt, and fear. I feel anger. The difference is, I'm no longer all-or-nothing, as I've existed for so long. I'm more like all and everything at once. There is no nothing.

Talking with Cynthia helped me get in touch with the myriad emotions shoved inside, and it struck me, by the end of the conversation, how much I actually had to say. "I'm just surprised by all of this," I confessed, having trouble getting my words out. It felt as good to cry as it did to talk, like finally taking a breath after drowning. And talk, I did. "I'm obviously not doing as well as I like to think I am. For the past few months I felt like, 'Wow! I am doing way better than I thought I would be!' But now, it's like I'm trying to force myself to keep 'carrying on' when I'm clearly burning out. I've been having crazy dreams," I continued. "Nightmares. I've never had nightmares like this before. I know there's more inside than I have yet been able to grasp. Yet, part of me feels like I should be settled into everything by now. It shouldn't be a big deal. I should be over it."

"How *could* you be?" Cynthia replied. "What you've been through is unimaginable."

I heard her. I tried to believe her. I have no perspective anymore. How can I? Unimaginable? It used to feel that way. Now it just seems like the way it is. It helps to hear someone else's perspective. In that one phone call, she helped me turn a few puzzle pieces over and at least get a glimpse of what they look like.

It helps to be shown the puzzle is far from complete. It helps to be reminded, I don't have to be whole yet either.

ELEVEN
Dream

"A dream is a microscope through which we look at the hidden occurrences in our soul."
~ Erich Fromm

I have always been good at remembering my dreams. When I was growing up, I would write them in my journal the morning after. It's a habit I continue when those powerful, "learn from me" dreams come my way. I've had dreams in French, when I was studying it in college, dreams where I know I'm dreaming, dreams where I wake up with tears on my face, and even a dream that was a cartoon.

Dreams are the gateway to the subconscious. That which we can neither see with the eye nor comprehend with the brain becomes clear when unfettered in the story of a dream. What we glean from our dreams is as priceless as gold to our emotional development, if we stop and pay attention.

I recall a dream I had in graduate school. I was driving a short, yellow school bus when there appeared, suddenly, on the road before me, a man in a Superman shirt, wearing a red rubber nose, curly clown wig, and overgrown plastic shoes. His red clown mouth was smiling, his hand was waving hello, even as I kept driving and plowed him down! Quickly realizing my mistake, yet unable to stop the bus, I panicked and checked my rearview mirror, expecting the worst. There he was, still smiling and waving, having bounced back up, like one of those toy punching bags.

The day after I had this dream just happened to be "dream therapy" class in grad school. Volunteers were solicited. I raised my hand, described my Superman Clown dream to the class and teacher, and they set about helping me decipher it. The key to understanding dreams is that they are a figurative representation of the literal happenings of life. The class asked questions like, "Who might the clown represent?" "What emotions were triggered in the dream?" and, "How did you feel when you woke up?" The main point was, "It's ultimately about what you, the dreamer, believe it to mean." Though my classmates had some interesting ideas, I was the only one who could give my dream any real meaning, and it wasn't until the class was over that I knew exactly what it meant.

The Superman Clown was OJ, since I see him as a manly thirteen year-old with the heart of a hero. I plowed him down with all my ambitions and ideas—which, at that time of life, felt like a speeding bus, and a "short bus" at that! Yet there he was, unscathed and standing, ready to love me. Understanding this dream helped me recognize how terrific OJ had been, supporting me in my dream to become a psychologist even while he was pursuing his dream of becoming a dentist—and apparently, a semi-pro golfer too. I could see I hadn't fully appreciated him for years; I had taken him for granted. What, at the outset, seemed like a random dream, through dream work, led me to make changes I didn't even know I needed. I worked on ways to slow down and stop for my Superman Clown, and our relationship improved.

This is the beauty of dreams. When we work to remember, to write them down, to ponder and reflect on their meaning, the lessons learned from dreams can give direction to improve our lives. Even if we don't know we need it. Dreams, both "good" and "bad," are the mind's way of processing the endless information we acquire through life, a way of sorting it all out and forming it into something useful. Dreams are also connected to our emotions. They validate losses and express feelings we may have neglected or buried. They help us see what is hidden.

Dreams take us deeper into our authentic self,

into what is real. As psychiatrist and author Judith Orloff writes of dreams, "The memories that surface are stunning. You'll remember things about your childhood and your past, about your present and your future. You may even remember God. What this all adds up to is remembering your whole self, your essence."[1] If we want to know what is really happening in life, what we really feel and think, what we really need, and ultimately who we really are, perhaps we should search our dreams. It is in dreams that we are most free to simply be.

Wednesday, February 20

Tre had a dream last night that he woke up on the day his mom died and "just went to school and had a regular day." He dreamt his mom and dad were alive again, then woke up, and cried himself back to sleep.

This morning, he was fighting with Braxton. I heard their yelling and ran down to the room they shared to find Tre had locked himself in a closet, sobbing. Though they used to be best friends, those two have had the hardest time adjusting. They argue. They bug each other. They compete. Both born oldest children, Tre is now the second, and being only four months younger than Braxton, it's tough for them both to find their place in the family.

"What is going on?" I asked him, concerned at what could possibly have made him this upset. He told me about the dream. We held each other and cried.

"I thought I would like it so much here that I would just forget about everything," he said, and held me tighter.

"I think we all wish we could forget, honey," I said. "But we can't. And we won't. That's just not how it works. But we love you very much. And life will get easier. But probably not for a while. Someday, we'll be grateful that we don't forget."

This set off a chain reaction. A snowy day,

school was delayed, and the time was filled with one incident after another. First, Braxton came in crying about how hard everything is, how he hates fighting with Tre and wishes things could be like they were before, when they were just cousins, and didn't fight. Though he seems older these past months, in that moment, I was grateful he could be a crying child, grateful he could let me be his mom, drying his tears. His voice still sounded like a little boy as he shared his heartache, his questioning. "When we were out to dinner last weekend with Grandma and Grandpa Cutler, on our 'boys' sleepover,'" he said, "Grandma Cutler pointed to Tre and Brody and told the waiter, 'These are my grandsons.' Then she pointed to Colton and me and said, 'and these are their brothers.' It made me feel bad, and I'm sick of all this stuff." He wiped his eyes and looked at me, back to being the tough young man again.

I told him I understood how this would make him upset, gave him a long hug with my whole heart, then gently reminded him that we are *all* still adjusting. "We all have times when we wish things were as they used to be," I said. "It's hard, you're right. And it's okay to feel sad about it. I sure do love you."

Then, Colton became frustrated and cried because he feels left out and wishes "Braxton could be as kind to him as he is to Tre and Brody," that their relationship could be just like it used to be. I explained that Braxton does love him, although it might not be like it used to be right now. "You will always be brothers, with a special bond. Trust me," I said, and kissed him on the forehead.

The tension built, in them and me, until it was time for school. Even with the two-hour delay, they weren't ready on time, and my frustration was seeping out in my voice. "You have to leave *now* or you will miss the bus," I said. They wouldn't wear snow clothes, even though it was coming down, and they slammed the door when I said, "Just try to make a good day!"

I was able to cry a few tears after they left, but not enough. I wanted to scream, "I don't know how to do this!" But instead, I clenched my fists, sat on the couch, and opened my scriptures to the first verse I could see. "And all thy children shall be taught of the Lord; and great shall be the peace of thy children."[2] A message of comfort I swear was written just for me. *Now* I could cry, and did.

After school, Brody and Colton were arguing, and Brody broke down. I found him lying on the mattress in his makeshift room under the stairs. It is really a closet—a "Harry Potter" closet, the kids call it. When he'd asked if he could move in, I hadn't been so sure, but now, I understood. It was just his size, and he loved having his own space. Formerly the baby of the family, now the fourth of six, Brody needed something that was only for him. I crawled back to where he lay, looking at the photo album of his Mom and Dad. He was barely seven now and had already been through so much.

"It's okay to miss them," I said, pushing his dark, gently curling hair from his sweaty forehead. "I miss them, too." He kept crying, quietly, now staring at the wall. "If you're sad, honey, I want you to know you can talk to me about it. Talking about things helps so it doesn't turn into anger and fighting with your brothers." He let me comfort him. He let me hug him, something that still feels awkward, for both of us, at times. Today, it felt just right. *Days like this remind me how real this is for everyone.*

Tonight, Braxton came and talked to me for a long while. He is eleven and a half years old, and this has hit him in a more existential way. We talked of death and dying and what happens after this life. OJ and I had made it a point, early on, to teach the kids all we know of death, eternal families, and life beyond. Tonight, we talked of deeper truths—things I know and he has yet to discover. I told him he's getting old enough to start the process of coming to the truth on his own.

"Just be careful not to rely too much on thinking," I said. "Learn to listen to your heart—to your spirit—for that is where truth is found." I encouraged him to be patient and to pray for guidance. I told him how grateful I am that he comes to talk with me. I told him I love him, no matter what, and I am here to support and help him with his journey.

I felt panicked throughout the conversation. I wanted to make it all better. I wanted him to be little again so I could kiss his booboos and make it all right. So much these kids are bearing. So much I try to bear for them, but can't. Tre and Brody wish they had their parents back. Braxton and Colton wish they had their old family back. Mom, Dad, and the Cutlers wish they had their children back. I wish I had my sister back. Everyone wishes this. But we won't. Ever.

They are learning at such a young age that we have little control over what happens in our lives. All I can do is teach them what I know, love them, and then pray I have done the right thing. If we have to learn these lessons, I guess the best we can ask for is that we learn them together.

Friday, February 22

I'm walking in a lush, green park, sunshine warming my hands as I bend to smell the bright flowers beside the path. A spirit appears, bearing a message for me. I am interested to hear the message and joyful when I realize the spirit is Shannon. Miki is here too, a little girl with golden ringlets, playing with other children in the background.

"Rob didn't want to scare you, so he didn't come," Shannon says. "But he's thinking about you. We all are."

She says she came because they are worried about the boys and how everyone is doing. I can feel the love they have for the kids, and for me. I start to reply, "It's a rough road," but notice people gathering around me as I speak, looking at me like I'm crazy because they can't see the spirits. I appear to be talking to myself. I try to explain to the crowd. "I know this looks crazy, but they are really here." No one believes me. I feel desperate for someone to understand. Only OJ takes my hand and gives a knowing smile and nod of his head.

Monday, February 25

My night was filled with more crazy Shannon dreams.

I am boogie boarding in a beautiful ocean with Shannon when we see a Tsunami rolling in on the horizon. It is pointless to try and out-swim the wave, so we wait, and somehow survive as we float over the wall of water and fearfully watch it overtake the shore. "The babies!" I scream. Both our babies are in the high-rise hotel, on the island. We paddle back, watching the wave cover everything, reaching twenty stories or more. I hope the hotel withstood it, but don't see how it could be possible. Next, we're searching from room to room in upper floors of the hotel, desperate to know if our babies have survived. We open door after door but still haven't found them, when we look out the high window and see another giant wave coming right at us. We attempt to outrun it by climbing higher up the stairs. I wonder if any of us will survive this next blow.

Then, I am at home, and Shannon is there. It feels like our home growing up, although everything looks changed. We are talking, and she is laughing. She is fun and beautiful. Watching her, I start to cry and say, "I miss you so much. I'm sad you are dead." She says, "I know," and reaches her arms to comfort me, but before I receive her comfort, I ask her to stand in front of a floor-length mirror while she holds a book. She does so with a sorrowful look on her face, because there is no reflection. In the mirror, the book is floating in the air. I know she is just a spirit vision and must soon leave, and then, she is gone, and only the book remains.

Thursday February 28

I feel the pit in my stomach. It is finally sinking in that Shannon is gone.

Over the weekend, we went to Phoenix for the boys' basketball tournaments and to get out of the cold. It was good to just watch them play, and play they did. Colton's team placed third and Braxton's took first! They had the biggest smiles as they were presented with their trophies, and we all warmed as we cheered them on. After the ceremony, we piled in the car and decided to stop and see Mom and Dad—Mimi and Pop—for a while before heading home.

Dad greeted us at the front door, gave us each a hug hello, and the little kids, big kids, and OJ, made their way to the toy, band, and TV rooms, respectively. Sydney was asleep in her carrier, so I set her by the front door, and followed Dad into the kitchen, where he was throwing hamburgers on the grill.

For as long as I can remember, Dad's done the cooking in our family. When I was young, people used to say, "You're just like your mother." Now, I feel Dad and I might have more in common. I may not be as quiet and keep-to-myself as he is, but I admire and emulate his work ethic. I've always looked more like Dad, which is another compliment, because people have always told me how handsome he is. Tall, with dark hair, he's always looked younger than his age. Now that I'm older, people think we're a couple when we're out together, instead of father and daughter. I inherited my love and talent for music from Dad. Growing up, he was always playing his guitar and singing to us. In fact, my earliest memory is of going to Dad's band practice, watching him sing and play the drums. He says I couldn't have been more than two.

Dad said he had the cooking under control, so I went to look for Mom. I found her in her pajamas, in their bedroom, as usual. Like I said, everyone used to tell me I was just like my mom, which I took as a compliment, because that meant I was outgoing, friendly, and fun. I took pride in having a "cool" mom, and especially loved raiding her closet. High-top Reeboks in every color of the rainbow? An '80s high school student's dream—at least, until my feet outgrew hers. But sometime after Miki died, her outgoing side seemed harder to find. She'd been struggling through grief and depression for years, and it had impacted our relationship just as much as my teenaged attitude had back in high school.

I know they've both been through more than I can imagine, but I miss having a "Mom" and "Dad." If only things hadn't changed when Miki died, my fun mom might still be outgoing, my handsome dad might not have escaped and isolated himself through work and other things. They might call just to see how I'm doing and offer wisdom and support, instead of me feeling like I always have to solicit it or just let that need go. I might not feel so awkward with them. Our family might not feel so disconnected.

Mom was sitting on her bed, holding Sydney, a contented look on her face, which made me happy, too. Kennedy had made her way in there, toys in hand, and was requesting "Dora." Though Mom always says, "I don't think the kids like me much. I'm not much fun," she's wrong. They adore her. I bent to kiss her hello, and that's when I saw it: Shannon's autopsy report sitting on the nightstand by their bed. I didn't even know they'd gotten it back yet. I'd been waiting for that report to see if it could give me some answers.

I equally wanted and did *not* want to know what it said. Fear and curiosity battled it out. Curiosity finally won. I carefully picked it up and looked to Mom. "So, what does it say?" I asked. "Can I read it?" I don't know why I felt the need to ask; something just felt odd about it all.

Without a word, Mom turned to the paragraph titled, "Cause of Death," and left me to read while she cooed at Sydney. "Heart failure, due to acetaminophen and alcohol." Those words, "heart failure," made my heart stop, flooded with sorrow and a piercing pain. It was all I could take for now. I gave the report back. "Can you please make me a copy of that report sometime, Mom? So I can really read it." She nodded and said she would, but, like I said, something felt off about it, about her. I wasn't sure if I'd imagined it or not.

That night, after I woke to feed Syd, I couldn't fall back asleep because of pain in my abdomen. When I did sleep, I was haunted by chasing, grasping, falling dreams. I'm still haunted. Like a stone in my chest, all week, it has surprised me; it has stopped me.

I've taken comfort in the snowy days, having a reason to stay home, in slouchy clothes, and do way less than what my mind tells me I "should." I've been doing the minimum with the kids and been focused only on taking care of Sydney. She has provided me with relief in this way—she's my savior. Strange, I know, but she has graced me with a whole new way to cope. I focus on her. I feed her. I get up with her at night. I hug and love her. I feel successful in at least that one way. I also get a healthy distraction from everything else, and I get a very good reason to say "no" and do less.

It's ironic that having a baby is turning out to be my healthy coping tool. It's always felt so hard before. Not that I didn't love my other babies, but just that I resented feeling so emotionally distraught and tied down with a newborn. Even this time, I'm still sleep-deprived and on that emotional rollercoaster, and anxious at times, and maybe even depressed. Perhaps, because everything else is so hard, this is the one straightforward thing in my life. It's simple, though not easy. I can take care of her, and it helps me feel like a good mother. It helps me feel better. Still, part of me grieves the postpartum experience I'd been hoping for—a calm time to get to know my little one, to rest from other labors, to just love my family. I have grief for my new life and missing my old. I have grief for my lost identity and sense of self. And I have grief for my sister.

I also feel for Mom and Dad in their many losses. I still can't fathom losing one child, let alone two, or rather, three, since Rob was such a tight member of our family. I remember, not long after Braxton was born, when I was in the depths of my first postpartum depression. OJ and I had been staying with Mom and Dad so Mom could help me while OJ went to work and school. One afternoon, I woke from a nap Mom had forced upon me. I had such a hard time letting anyone help me, and I was crazy-making tired, so thank goodness she made me get some rest. Mom brought Braxton to me so I could nurse him. I was overcome with love for him, again. I may have been depressed, but I adored him. I literally fell asleep dreaming of him, like I used to do with OJ when we were dating. Sitting there, in that room, the room where Miki had died just three years before, it hit me—a tiny fraction of what it must have felt like for Mom to lose *her* baby.

"I'm so sorry, Mom," I told her. "I get it now, how much you love your kids. I never realized how much I would love mine. I'm so sorry you had to lose Miki. I never really got what that must have been like for you until this moment." We embraced, and cried together—for Miki, and for my fears of losing my baby, and for all the mothers and fathers who lose their babies. I still think about that. I don't ever want to forget.

I dreamt last night that Mom and Dad were being robbed and someone was trying to kill all of Mom's dogs. I was trying to stop the robbers when I saw them grab Kennedy and drag her out an upstairs window. I screamed like a madwoman. "You can't take her! You can't do this! Don't you know what they've already lost? What we've *all* already lost? How could you do this to them—to *us*? Don't you know?" They let Kennedy go, although she was bleeding because they'd hit her head on a window. Very scary.

It's strange to live such a paradox each day— pain *and* gratitude. Cognitive dissonance, again, makes me want to choose. But I believe it all. I'm trying to make room for all these feelings so they can teach and grow me into something amazing. I'm thinking of the quote, by F. Scott Fitzgerald, "Show me a hero and I'll write you a tragedy."[3] Will I become the hero of *my* tragedy? I guess that is to be determined.

Monday, March 3

I've been keeping a log of my thoughts and feelings today—a "Thought Record,"[4] like I used to teach my clients to do. I want to understand who I am now, or rather, who I'm supposed to be and what I'm supposed to do.

I'm still trying to be strong—to carry on. But a wide range of emotions are battling it out in my heart. Frustration, sadness, joy, satisfaction, gratitude, anxiety, fear, worry, anger, confusion, feeling lost. You name it, I seem to be experiencing it. No wonder I feel so uncertain. Underneath the uncertainty are some pretty intense thoughts I'm only beginning to hear. Dreaming thoughts. Escaping thoughts. Criticizing thoughts. Condemning thoughts.

Tonight, I spent some time talking with the boys about life while I made dinner and helped them do chores and finish homework. We had our family home evening, and I introduced our family theme for March, "Courage," something we all need a little of right now. It was a nice evening. My mind gets quieter when I push myself to fulfill my responsibilities as a mother, because

I know how important it is, and I know I'll feel sorry if I don't give it my all. Perhaps *also* because working hard lessens the ammo available to aim at myself when mommy self-doubt begins to flame.

I remember reading an article a couple of years ago about a woman named "Mother of the Year." She had seven children, looked fabulous, and seemed remarkably happy. As I read the article about how wonderful she was, I thought, *I wish I could be a mother like that.* But the voice in my head reminded me, *you never will be. There are so many things you feel called to do in this life, in addition to being a mother. You'll never have a big family. Being mother of the year is not in the cards for you.* It wasn't that I didn't feel like I was a good enough mom, just not "mother of the year" material.

Now, I do have a big family, and I'm given the opportunity to feel like a "mother of the year." I'm given the opportunity to rise to a great challenge and become so much more than I ever imagined for little old me. I take this challenge seriously. There is no easy way to measure what I do with my kids. It's not like writing a report, in which there is a final product and a grade. It's a challenge to keep motivated, because it can feel like "I did nothing today," when in reality, as a mom, I do so much that can't be quantified. A friend once explained it to her lawyer husband this way, "It's like you, going to work, and spending all day writing your briefs and arguments. Then, at the end of the day, someone hits delete, and poof! It's all gone." That's the job of being a mom, all right.

I think it's one of the adversary's greatest tools—to make mothers feel inadequate, to make us want to give up, to go find something that gives us that result, instead. Sometimes I, too, want to "quit my day job" and head back to work, where I actually feel good at what I do and receive positive feedback. But I am needed here. The role of a mother is the greatest, holiest responsibility a human being can experience, whether a birth mother or other. I believe that. I am deeply grateful to be entrusted as a mother to these six children. Still, it's hard to get to "mother of the year" status when my moods keep pulling me down. I remind myself to be patient, to be grateful for where I am and the opportunities with which I've been blessed. To give myself time to receive clarity, and to allow God to gently unfold my life to me.

I carry Sydney around all the time, probably because she's my favorite coping tool, but also because she's my last baby and I want to hold her as much as possible. Because I carry her so much, she hasn't had a chance to practice pushing up on her arms, strengthening her neck, holding her head up, and rolling over. In holding her, I've been holding her back. I need to put her down on her belly more, so she can grow stronger and progress.

The same goes for me. I've been carried through these first four and a half months. I now see that I need to be put down, that I *am* being put gently down. It's hard, but I'm grateful to see what I need and to let it happen. It's the only way. I'm learning to lift my head up, roll over, crawl, walk, and hopefully someday, run. Just like a baby.

TWELVE
Grieve

"Grief is the price we pay for love."
~Queen Elizabeth II

Grief can make a baby of any of us—sensitive, unsure of what's happening, and with limited ability to communicate it to others. There's a lot of growing up done through grief work.[1]

As one grief expert so aptly put it, "Grief can only be described as a time of craziness when all the rules that govern life are suspended, when coping mechanisms that used to work no longer do, when the foundation and rhythm of your days are shattered into an unrecognizable crazy-quilt."[2] Many of us know this crazy quilt. There are literally over a hundred possible symptoms of grief, which is why the quilt can feel so crazy. From the more obvious—sadness, anger, guilt, anxiety, loneliness, numbness—to the physical—fatigue, low energy, tightness in chest/throat, changes in appetite—to the mental—confusion, inability to concentrate, poor memory—to experiences of hearing or seeing the deceased. Symptoms may come and go and last far longer than we wish they would, especially if we don't acknowledge and work through them.

Grief, unfelt, becomes a stalker. It may be immediate and demanding or subtle and creeping. Either way, it *will* eventually conquer its prey, so there's really no point in trying to run. Better to turn and face grief, feel it, express it. There are almost as many styles of expressing grief as there are symptoms. Whereas one may express anger, another may be sad and tearful, while still another may be distant and numb. This can be particularly tough for families. Couples may have a hard time understanding one another's grief process—one partner wishing to talk about the loss over and over, and the other wishing to forget it. Grieving parents may find it hard to live up to their previous level of parenting and responsibility, leaving siblings lost and alone without the grief-stricken parent's guidance. As one person turns to the other hoping to talk, cry, or share emotions, they may be distraught to find the other is unavailable. As Anne Morrow Lindbergh aptly writes, "...even for those in the same grief. Grief can't be shared. Everyone carries it alone, his own burden, his own way."[3] This is, perhaps why grief feels so isolating. It can feel as if no one understands the burden we bear, even our own family.

In the field of mental health, the focus of grief work has traditionally been on individual healing. But that's a mistake. My experiences have taught me that grief is not meant to be an individual process. Families who fail to turn together in grief will eventually fall apart. Families who engage in the work of grief together heal, not only as individuals, but as a whole.

It's tough. I've been a daughter, sister, wife, and mother in grief, and I've felt the short and long-term consequences. After my sister, Miki, died, the unspoken message was not to talk about it. When one of us brought up a memory, "Remember when Miki...," it wasn't like we were punished, but it felt awkward. We sensed it was too painful for Mom and Dad, so we ended up keeping things to ourselves more often than not. As a consequence, all of my siblings have said Miki's death was a profound turning point in their lives—not just because of losing our dear sister, but because it changed our family dynamics forever. Seeing how losing Miki affected my mother and father, especially, is what drove me through my hardest days of grief after Shannon died. I needed to do it differently. I knew the consequences if I failed, and I needed to be there as a wife and mother, no matter what grief had in store for me.

Miki's death profoundly changed me, too. Looking back, I can see how different it was than when

Shannon died. It didn't directly impact my life in the same way, and I was still young and inexperienced with grief, which made it simpler at the time. Still, an epiphany happened to me when she died. *I know death now.* I was eighteen years old, yet, felt suddenly grown up and ready to accept the responsibility that came with that knowledge.

Not long after Miki died, my college roommate's grandmother died. Her mother called while she was still at school, and left the message with our other roommate. "What should we do?" she asked me. "I don't want to have to tell her that her grandmother died."

"I'll tell her," I said. It felt like a mantle settling on my shoulders, and as soon as she came home, I sat her down and said the words. I felt nervous and sorry for her loss, yet somehow capable. She cried. I was there for her. It was the beginning of helping many through their dance with death.

We all need someone to help us through, you know. A friend. A colleague. A counselor. A family member. Isn't it interesting how our burdens can knit us together? Like a piece of thread—once so easily broken—becomes unbreakable when intricately woven, so the fabric of connection bonds us. Time and time again we feel each other's pain, we share each other's broken souls. Together, we knit a beautiful fabric that strengthens us. We find, like the fabric, that we are strong and we are inseparable.

Monday, March 17

It's Saint Patty's Day today. I forgot to wear green and got pinched by the kids. I actually didn't mind—it's fun for them. But the voice in my head said, *See, you're not on top of anything.* When did I become so mean?

At ten this morning, I sat in Dr. Hale's waiting

room, pretending to read a magazine, while listening in on Tre and Braxton's pre-teen conversation about skateboarding, music, and friends. Just when they were about to get to something that might have interested me, Dr. Hale called us back.

I'd been looking forward to the session with Tre and Braxton today, hoping to gain insight into their worlds instead of feeling shut out by the boy code of keeping every emotion to themself. Steadily attending my own sessions, we've also been rotating sessions for each of the four boys. I need to make sure they are adjusting well, to make sure they aren't as overcome by this grief as I have been. It was good to hear them open up a little, and I was actually surprised by how insightful and well spoken their comments were.

"I'm doing okay," said Tre. "Everything's good. We're getting along better at home," he said, looking at Braxton. "School is good. Friends are pretty good."

"*Pretty* good?" Dr. Hale asked, just as I was about to.

"Yeah. I don't like how a couple kids treat me at school. Kind of two-faced. But my good friends get me, so that's good. Other kids just don't understand. *Their* parents haven't died. It's not, like, a normal thing for eleven year-olds to be going through, and all. So, if I start feeling too down, I just try to talk about it with my mom, instead," he said, looking at me. "That way I can still have fun with my friends."

"I feel okay," said Braxton. "I guess it's been good that we've been able to come here and talk about it. I feel like I don't think about Rob and Shannon dying as much anymore, like I feel better. And, yeah, we're all getting along well at home. It's good to have them as our brousins." He gave Tre a punch on the shoulder, and they both smiled.

"Brousins?" Dr. Hale asked.

Tre, Braxton, and I chuckled. "Yeah. That's

what we call each other," Braxton said. "We were cousins. Now we're, like, brothers. We're brousins." They fist-bumped each other and chuckled again.

After just twenty minutes, they had nothing left to say. It was clear. They are doing fine. I'm starting to think the boys don't need counseling at all. *I'm* the one who needs it, not only to help me, but to help me help *them* when their rocky times decide to appear. Children grow up with grief, I know. It's not as linear a process as it is for adults, and I need to be ready for them when grief comes. The boys happily agreed to move to the waiting room and let me take the remaining thirty minutes for myself.

I started with last night's dream. "It's as real to me now as it was last night," I said. "I'm in Shannon's old house. Tre is there, young, only six or so, and Rob is there, hanging out with his buddies. They're all sitting on the sofa, telling jokes and laughing. I am across from them, seated, feeling like an outsider. I see that Tre is bleeding down the side of his face, which seriously concerns me, but he just stands there like nothing is wrong. When he turns to the side, I see where the blood is coming from. There is a dagger in his head. I gasp and reach forward, trying to figure out what I should do, when Rob notices the dagger. He grabs it, pulls it out, tosses it on the coffee table, says, 'See—no big deal!' as both he and Tre return to laughing and talking with his friends. Panicked and shocked, I start wiping up all the blood. I feel horrified by this mess I am cleaning up. They just ignore me and keep laughing."

"This mess I am cleaning up," I repeated.

Dr. Hale nodded. "You are still cleaning up their mess," he said. "It feels scary and bloody, and you feel like no one notices."

"Yes," I replied. "I *hate* that I have to clean up the mess they created and dumped on me."

"Yes," he said. "And the predominant emotion

I've been hearing in your voice lately, and today, is anger."

At first, I was defensive. "I've felt resentment and frustration, yes, but anger?" I wasn't so sure. *Aren't frustration and resentment just other forms of anger, though?* Yes. I had to admit it: "I guess I *am* angry." Angry at Mom, Dad, the kids, the Cutlers, everyone and everything. Angry at myself for feeling so angry. But the bulk of my anger is toward Shannon. Intended or not, she took her own life, and I feel angry about that, despite the deep sadness.

I couldn't say any of this out loud today and didn't. It was Dr. Hale who spoke the words I couldn't quite say, "She dumped her problems on you when she died."

It's complicated. It's messy, confusing, overwhelming. As Dr. Hale said, "Death is not fully comprehensible by any human being," and I agree. It's neither sensible nor comprehendible. So, why do I keep trying to force comprehension? I'm trying to control something that cannot be controlled and to understand something that may never fully be understood.

I'm too doggone exhausted. Dr. Hale pointed out that, not only have I had months of postpartum sleep deprivation, but because of the emotional experiences I've faced—grief, sadness, shock, anger— my body is tapped out. The adrenaline-and-cortisol- quick-fake-energy I've been surviving on is simultaneously zapping any *real* energy, like being hopped up on caffeine with the crash to come later.

Still, when I'm able to cry or scream or even feel pain, I have to admit, there is something I enjoy about it. "Why would I enjoy that?" I asked Dr. Hale before I left.

"Death is living on the edge of a cliff," he said. "You can feel very alive while experiencing the sorrow." I guess it's just a relief to feel *something* after having felt nothing for so long.

Thursday, March 20

My body aches. My throat is raw and sore. My ear throbs. I'm so tired, but I cannot sleep. As soon as my head hits the pillow, I start having "flashbacks"— vivid images of Shannon. Of what happened that night. Of what she might have felt or not felt as she died. Of what she might have looked like. Sickening, vivid images. Again, I'm left aching to know what Tre and Brody saw. How scared they must have been! I can hardly breathe when I let myself think about it. It still doesn't seem real. I'm a ping-pong ball, back and forth between shock and frustration, denial and anger, guilt and sadness. I guess this is grief.

I've been focusing more on anger toward my secondary losses than on Shannon actually being dead, because it is somehow easier. I feel the anger about my loss of identity, roles, comfort, and health, but the circumstances surrounding her death are so tragic that I can't go there. Too much pain—for her, for the boys, for all of us. Too much.

So, instead, I let the smaller things feel huge. Today, it was the thought that I need to push my selfishness aside and do my very best as a Mom. This includes playing more and having fun with the kids. *Why don't I play more? I wish I would play more. My kids are too important to let myself slack.* Perhaps this is the hardest part for me of all this grief. I don't have the luxury of stopping time. I need to be there for them *now*. I need to figure this out *now*. I need to implement the how *now*. But I don't know how.

I guess the only predictable thing about grief is that, sooner or later, we will grieve. How that occurs is a unique mystery for us all. It is our own process— unpredictable.

Saturday March 22

Yesterday, I actually let OJ take Kennedy *and* Sydney to the babysitter for a few hours. I love Liz, our sitter. She's been watching Kennedy since she was one. She's already raised her two sons and is patient and easy-going with the six children she watches in her home every day. She handles them with more grace than I could dream, but something hasn't let me send Sydney to her yet. Something that said if I gave all my kids away, even for a few hours, I would be a failure.

Yesterday, I chose to believe differently. It's time *I give myself a break—a real break*, I convinced myself. I sat on the back deck in the sunlight, took a walk on the golf course, and crashed into a two and a half hour nap. Finally allowing some help has brought the R & R I didn't realize I needed until it was here.

Having time to think helped me see how hard I can be on myself. For one, I put a lot of pressure on myself to always be productive, and not just in taking care of kids and tidying. I've been trying to be creative— to write an inspired song, article, or book. I know I can do these things. I want to do these things. But now is not the time. Forcing it will not work. It only makes me feel down on myself and frustrated.

I am also desperately trying to figure out who I am now. Desperate is never good. And, does it really matter? It's not something I can necessarily "figure out" or decide upon anyway. It's a process only time can unfold. I am who I am. Period. My actions don't define me. They are a manifestation of parts of me. If I simply press on—shooting for service, bringing joy to my family and others, eventually, I will feel whole. Right?

In the mean time, I distract myself with other things. Today was spending time with Kennedy and Sydney while OJ and the boys are skiing in Telluride with my dad. A "boy's trip," they get to be free for the weekend. *Important bonding time for them.* But I feel jealous.

How I wish it could be just the wind, snow, and me, as I fly down, ride up, and fly down again and again. I'm fast on skis. But here, I'm slow. Sluggish.

So, I threw myself into the girls. We went to an Easter egg hunt, painted our nails, and played hide-n-go-seek. We watched *The Little Mermaid*. It was Kennedy's first time, and she was in love. She's been dressed like a mermaid ever since, singing "Part of Your World" with false vibrato—such a girl! I gave Kennedy a haircut, and we played with Sydney. I even stole a short nap. For a little while, I was able to just *be* instead of trying so hard to just be *better*.

Monday, March 24

I arrived on time at the statue at Foxglen Park, to pick up Brody from school. His older brothers each had after-school activities to attend, and, being in first grade, he didn't want to ride the bus home alone. I didn't mind today—it was a good excuse to get me out of the chilly house and into the sun, and to get Kennedy and Syd out for a ride, too.

Brody hopped in the car, in the middle seat, and cooed at Sydney, making her smile. He loves that little baby, and he even seems to like his four year-old sister, Kennedy, who was playing with her dolls, in the back seat.

"How was school?" I asked, glancing at him in the rearview mirror. *He's so dang cute,* I thought. He is. With olive skin, big brown eyes, and barely-curling shaggy dark hair, there's something about Brody that just makes you want to hug him.

"Good," he said. Brody is definitely a child of few words. That's why I was surprised when he said, "I have a secret."

"You do, huh?" I asked, looking back to him in the mirror as I drove up the hill toward home. He nodded his head, pursing his lips and looking serious.

This obviously wasn't a lighthearted secret. "Well, can you tell me?"

"Nope," he said. "I won't tell anyone." He was looking down now, shaking his head.

Gratefully, I could feel what he was saying. "Well, is your secret that your mom and dad died?" I asked.

"Mmm-hmm," he said, nodding and looking up at me in the mirror, innocently.

"Okay," I said. This was the first time he'd really tried to talk about it at all. Even when I'd asked him to talk, he had always shrugged it off. This was him reaching out. "Well, I'll tell you what. I know your secret. And Dad knows. And your teachers at school know, and so do your teachers at church. And all of your grandparents and aunts and uncles know. And all of your brothers and sisters." He was nodding and raising his eyebrows, listening. "So, if you ever want to talk about it, you just come to any of us. I'm happy to talk with you about it any time, honey."

"Okay," he said.

"Do you want to talk now?" I asked, teary-eyed for all that sweet little boy had been through.

"No," he replied, and turned back to play with Sydney. "No one will ever know my secret," he said to her, light-heartedly, making her laugh. *A shot to my heart.*

Just as suddenly as it appeared, the moment was over. But I was grateful he reached out. Even if it was only to taunt me with, "I have a secret." I am grateful he now knows he can safely share his secrets with me.

Friday, April 11

Our first vacation to Disneyland as a family of eight. Well, seven, actually, since Sydney is home with Mom and Dad. It sure makes things easier, but since I'm still breastfeeding, I have to pump. For those who haven't had the privilege of pumping, it is basically the nursing mother's best option for ensuring her breasts do not explode from milk overflow while she is without the baby as her natural "pump."

OJ hurried us out the door this morning, as I put my pump back in its sleek, black leather carrying case, grabbed it, and headed out. In true OJ style, he had found a smokin' deal on tickets for the park, which involved meeting a mysterious man at McDonald's this morning, and again, at dark, at a pre-arranged point near Cinderella's castle. Such intrigue. Disneyland never felt so dangerous!

We made the exchange, got the "goods," and entered the happiest place on earth very happy to have saved nearly three hundred dollars. The boys were loving the scary rides, and Kennedy was loving Ariel, saying, "Wow, mom, a real mermaid! She's *so* lovely." Sometime around mid-day, I needed to relieve my aching bosom, so, excusing myself, I braved the trek, via foot, tram, and escalator, back to our Yukon parked in the full garage. I brought Kennedy with me since it was the time of day when all the once-excited children start crashing into a hopeless grumpy mess that requires a nap intervention. I hooked her up with Dora on the DVD player and hooked myself up to the "Pump-in-Style" with its handy car-charger. It's the same pump I've had since Braxton was a little pumpkin.

I sat in the dark parking lot at Disneyland, blankie draped just so, eyes peeled, ready to hide at a moment's notice should any unsuspecting pair of Mickey ears hobble my way. Before I knew it, both bottles from the bag were full. I hadn't planned on what to do with so much milk. I dumped one out the window so I could continue to pump until I was comfortable again, but it was heartbreaking to see the fruit of all this labor, laden with nutrients and immune-enhancing magic, floating on the gummy surface of a parking garage. So, as I finished, I packed the milk in ice and saved it. For what? I'm not exactly sure.

One power nap and hour-long pump session later, and Kennedy and I returned to our happy day. Several hours and head-bobbing, sleepy children later, we were back in our car, heading toward the siren call of sleep at our hotel. I knew I would have to dump the rest of the milk. We didn't have a fridge, and there was no way it was going to last two more days until we returned to Sydney. There was no other option.

"Shame to let this go to waste. It's so good for you," I told OJ and the kids, as I fearlessly gulped one down. "I have two more. Anyone brave enough to try?"

Various sounds of disgust were uttered from the back, but it was Braxton who asked, "What will you give me?"

"A dollar," I said.

It was full-blown Fear Factor in the backseat now as the other boys planted doubts and Braxton talked himself up for the big gulp. A countdown was decided, and then there was no time left. "Five, four, three, two, one." Gulp! A pause for his reaction.

"Actually, it's not so bad. It's kinda sweet," he said, having succeeded the challenge and earned his dollar.

"Yeah, but that came out of Mom! Eew!" the other boys were cackling, completely grossed out.

"You drank that same milk for months when you were a baby," I reassured him. "And it will make you stronger. So, way to go Braxton!" I cheered. But even *I* was cracking up on the inside.

We needed this—time together, to laugh, to have fun. A break from reality. These are the moments we'll remember someday—not just the thrill of the rides, but the thrill of chugging breast milk, Fear Factor style, on the way home.

Thursday, April 17

Well, I've done it. I just let my mother have it. She called to see if she and Dad could borrow some money or use the line of credit on our house, and I said "No." I said a lot more than just "No," though. Usually it's Dad who asks to borrow money, so I'm pretty sure Mom never saw my reaction coming.

I didn't see it coming either. The timing of her call was not good. I'd just come from a powerful counseling session in which I did empty chair work. I imagined Shannon, sitting in the empty chair across from me, and it was my job to talk to her and tell her how I've been feeling.

I stared at the chair. "I do not want to talk to you," were the only words I could eventually manage.

Dr. Hale moved from behind me to my side. "May I touch your shoulder and speak for you?" he asked. I told him he could. Dr. Hale has a way of calmness, almost slowness about him that I lack. He takes his time. He thinks things through and speaks carefully, a sharp contrast to my hurried speech. His way helps me breathe and slow down, too. Laying his hand on my shoulder, he paused, and then said, "Shannon, I miss you very much. But it's hard for me to talk to you because I am angry. I feel like you dumped all your problems on me when you died."

She really did! Taking care of her children, cleaning up her financial mess, cleaning up her house, dealing with her in-laws, dealing with her enmeshment with my parents—you name it! I was flooded with the truth, and it poured out like a stream through my eyes and nose. But my mouth needed a minute before it could speak.

I accepted a tissue from Dr. Hale. "Yes. I am angry," I finally said. "And I hate that I feel this way." Shaking my head, I let it hang, feeling defeated, as I wiped the tears from my blurred eyes. "It was your birthday on Sunday. And it completely ticked me off that our family and your friends were 'celebrating' you. Because I don't feel like celebrating."

The last words *sounded* angry. I'd been feeling it, but today I heard it. I was angry at Shannon, not just angry at myself for feeling so angry. Anger is not *me*. It's not who I want to be or what I believe is good. But, it *is* how I feel. It underlies why I am so confused and hard on myself. It fuels my desperation to feel happy and to be happy—because everyone expects me to be strong, smart, and happy, and to clean up all their messes!

As all this ran through my mind while I sat like a puddle, Dr. Hale touched my shoulder again. "I'm tired of cleaning up other people's messes!" he said, his calmness replaced by force. It hit me like a punch to my gut. I *am* tired of it. So tired of it.

Then, just moments after I leave therapy, Mom calls with yet another mess to clean up. This continues over and over, on and on, year after year! In that moment, I was done with parenting my parents. I was done with being nice about it. I was so tired of being dumped on, by everyone!

"No. Mom, no. I'm sorry, but I'm done with having to take care of everyone's problems," I said, talking slowly and firmly, trying to hold it together, but failing. "It never ends. It's always something." I couldn't stop myself, and I know I hurt her feelings. I can't pretend everything's fine any longer, even if some feelings are hurt. I needed to set this boundary. I needed them—everyone—to know I could not do it anymore. I needed to finally say the word, "No."

Of course, I felt terrible when Mom hung up on me, crying. I wish I could have said no in a loving way, but I hadn't. I sat at a traffic light and screamed out loud, like a crazy person, hitting the steering wheel in attempt to let out some of the intensity. Then, I broke down, lay my head on the steering wheel, and started thinking through the phone call before the light turned green. Fortunately, I could see that I hadn't been *mean* to Mom. Just completely straightforward, telling her how I feel. She couldn't take it. I felt bad hurting her, and I still do, but I'm not able to let them hurt *me* over and over like that anymore! A big part of the problem has been me not wanting to hurt them, so I suck it up, time and again. No longer. I am done. I can't be that daughter any more. I have too much on my own plate to be that daughter any longer.

The last thing Dr. Hale told me before I left today was, "Just let the anger come when it's there."

"I don't know how to deal with anger," I had just admitted. "I'm afraid if I let it out it will attack and take over, and I'll hurt everyone I care about."

"You won't allow yourself to truly hurt those you love," he said. "That's not who you are."

Well, the anger has come, and I have let it out. Mom is hurting. I hurt, too. But he's right. We're not permanently hurt. I know this situation will be resolved, eventually. But for now, I can't talk to her. I need to calm down, and I really need to sleep.

Friday, April 18

I didn't sleep yesterday. Couldn't sleep this morning either; I awoke in the black night flooded with anxiety. Anxiety is a ghost, haunting me most days, yet in the busyness of the get-all-the-kids-out-the-door mornings, I don't usually pay attention. Today, however, OJ took Sydney with him to drop Kennedy and the boys off, and I had time to sit in silence. The longer I sat, the higher the anxiety rose within until it literally felt like I was going to choke.

I tried to listen and hear my thoughts. They ranged from frustration about my parents to worry about my kids, to un-thought things about Shannon I had to quickly put back, to things I'm "supposed" to get done. I tried to acknowledge, then stop them, then took a bath to distract myself. That just made me realize how tired I was. So, I tried to take a nap, but the anxiety wouldn't let me sleep. It's like a pounding heart beat reminding me of all my fears. I began to wonder what internal damage all that cortisol was doing and if it would affect Sydney through the breast-milk. I forced myself up and out for a quick, hard jog, to force it out of me. And came back only after a pleading prayer: *Father in Heaven, please forgive this anger and tension in me. Please show me how to release this anxiety. Please enable me with the strength to do what I have been called to do.*

OJ is now gone to work and then to play golf, the kids are at school, and Sydney is asleep for the moment. And here I am again, trying to piece things apart and back together. Even though I thought I was not angry with Mom and Dad, the truth is, I'm furious. It's even more painful because I know they think I'm being mean and irrational when I tell them their money issues are the result of their years of overspending. They think *I'm* crazy.

What else is new? I've always felt like the crazy one in my family, or at least, since Miki died. Mixed messages can do that, I know. Hearing, "Everything is fine," while seeing sadness, isolation, and depression can definitely make you feel crazy. We never talk openly, so I'm always trying to guess what everyone feels. It's exhausting, and I know I'm often wrong. But I also know, sometimes, I'm right. Sometimes, Mom really isn't "sick"; she's sad. And sometimes, they really *are* upset with me, even if they won't say it.

Today is no different. Neither one of them has called. I thought, since Mom hung up on me yesterday, she might call to work things out, or that Dad might call to smooth it over. Instead, I'm sure they both think I am cruel to the core to say such things when they are having a hard time, too. Or, maybe I just think that of myself.

Or maybe both. The way I see it, they opened it up by asking for money again. And I *needed* to be honest with them—finally. I wish we were the type of family that tackled problems head on, that opened up and said what needed to be said. That's how I am in every other aspect of my life. But in my family, I can't be that way. I've tried so many times, but it always backfires.

I'm not ready to attempt to call them. Not yet. I need space from them. No wonder I always want to be alone or do things on my own. As long as I've been an adult, it's the only way I have known with my parents. I don't even know what to say right now. I just don't know.

Wednesday, April 23

I knew I'd have trouble sleeping after book club. It's nearly midnight, but my brain is flooded with ideas that reaffirm just how small my understanding and how large my potential.

Seven friends met at my house to discuss C.S. Lewis' *Mere Christianity*. I led the discussion, which went on far longer than the allotted two hours. Earlier this afternoon, I almost cancelled. I've been such a mess lately it seemed too much, hosting tonight, being responsible for intelligent discussion. But I know me. I know I have to force myself into social situations when I least feel like it. I know I'm always grateful, afterward, when I do, and tonight was no exception. Such stimulating conversation with women I admire and respect! My brain was wide awake for the first time in months.

One concept, in particular, stuck with me and keeps repeating in my mind:

> "...God is forcing (us) on, or up, to a higher level: putting (us) into situations where (we) will have to be very much braver, or more patient, or more loving, than (we) ever dreamed of being

before. It seems to us all unnecessary: but that is because we have not yet had the slightest notion of the tremendous thing He means to make of us...You thought you were going to be made into a decent little cottage: but He is building a palace. He intends to come and live in it Himself."[4]

How did he know I've been feeling like a little cottage? Is it possible I'm being built into a palace instead? I've certainly had to be much more patient, brave, and loving than I ever dreamed.

Tonight made me want to do even better—to understand and fix what's been going on with me. It made me want to *be* better. So, after everyone left, I opened one of my old textbooks on grief and loss, searching for words to describe me lately. *"Angry sadness," a "craziness" but I'm not "crazy."* That's me, all right. All over the place. I'm doing all I can—writing, talking, exercising, crying, praying. I'm going to counseling, trying to recognize my mistakes, seek forgiveness, look for positives, enjoy each moment with my children, and help them feel loved. I'm working to keep my family and home inching forward, desperate to ensure all is well. I'm trying to see the perspective of others—my parents, OJ, the kids, the Cutlers, other family members, and friends—and be understanding of their approach to me. I'm reading scriptures and other good books. I watch positive television or none at all. When I write it all down, I see how hard I am trying—to *feel happy*, and *be grateful* for where I am. Lewis' quote helps me feel grateful for what these experiences are making of me. But "happy" is not in the cards right now. Yes, I can feel grateful and not-quite-happy at the same time.

A few nights ago, my little a cappella group—or, the group I *used* to participate in, before all this happened—had the opportunity to sing "Come Thou

Fount of Every Blessing" for a packed audience at the church. A hymn penned in the 1700s by a twenty-two year-old named Robert Robinson, it is profoundly beautiful to me—moving. "Prone to wander…Lord, I feel it! Prone to leave the one I love. Take my heart, oh, take and seal it. Seal it for thy courts above."[5] Never have I sung with such emotion. *I certainly am "prone to wander," especially lately.* In that moment, those words were written for me.

This is just one way God speaks to me—through music. I somehow felt my heart was "sealed," and I felt connected again, *normal.* Dressed in a black chiffon dress I not only love, but that actually fit me, I felt pretty again, with curled hair and heels. But more so, I was with OJ, with*out* children, being Christi and nothing more. I could feel a *spark* of happy inside me again, a little seed of hope that I will heal. Hope that I can feel joy again, even if it's not quite here yet.

I planted that hopeful seed—felt a spark of it in book club—but don't know where it is right now. I keep digging, but all I seem to find is that I'm again planted in grief, drained, and trying to understand why this has to be so hard. As one grief expert wrote, the "term 'grief work' is an apt one, for grief requires the expenditure of both physical and emotional energy. It is not less strenuous or arduous a task than digging a ditch."[6] I'm beginning to believe it.

THIRTEEN
Build Bridges

"The I in illness is isolation, and the crucial letters in wellness are we."
~Author Unknown[1]

I am an introvert. It's taken years to understand this about myself. As a teenager, I behaved like an extrovert, always planning activities for my friends and me. When we weren't asked out on dates as much we would have liked, we started asking guys out instead. The self-proclaimed "Queens of Creative Dating," my BFFs and I asked different boys out on new adventures every weekend—including candlelit dinners on mountain tops and canals, board games in airports, rides on gondolas with Italian Opera-singers, scavenger hunts on playgrounds at parks, and to top it off, a lovely rendition of "Can't Help Lovin' That Man," sung in three-part harmony—by us, of course. I was always busy and always wanted to be around other people. I thought sitting home, quietly reading was "boring," and even once told my intelligent, wonderful, book-loving friend, "Don't just *read* about life. *Live* it!" Ah, the folly of youth.

College brought social interaction to a new level. I pledged a social club and continued my creative dating spree, edging toward my goal of dating one hundred different guys before I got married. By now, they were asking *me* out more, which was great. But I felt like, if I had no plans on a Friday or Saturday night, something was terribly wrong.

Flash forward to my years as a mother, and you see an entirely new side of me emerge: the introvert. I've probably always been an introvert, but the insecurity of youth had its hold on me, surrounding myself with others seemed to tell me I was loved. Now, as a mother and wife of an extrovert husband, I don't need activity to feel loved. In fact, most weeks I feel so "loved," I might just be squeezed to pieces! The more I am needed, the more I need myself, and thus, the years of the introvert were born.

I crave alone time. It's a basic need. Too much time together drains me, and I feel tired, over-stimulated, and not like myself. Give me some time alone, however, and I come alive—pondering, creating, engaging. As soon as I've had my quiet fill, I immediately want to be with others again. That's when I decide to host a luncheon or take the kids on a trip or initiate a "girl's night out." Yes, at heart, I am an introvert, yet the extrovert in me lives on. Who knows? As my children grow, move away, and need me less, I just may see my extrovert emerge anew.

Introvert or extrovert, there are times when all of us need connection, and times when we all need solitude. There are many times when we need another to lift, teach, amuse, and love us, and plenty of moments when we need to lift, teach, amuse, and love ourselves.

There's a difference, though, between *solitude* and *isolation*. Solitude is time *alone* with a *purpose*—to rejuvenate, relax, and rest. Isolation is *purposefully* being all *alone*—pushing away, withdrawing, internalizing. Solitude says, "I need a break from everyone and everything right now, but I will return, and I'll be even better." Isolation says, "I don't need anything nor anyone. I'm relying only on myself."

In our dark times it is easy to feel better off alone and isolate. Our suffering is personal, and no one shares it in the same way, so, why even bother? But, I can tell you—we *do* need others, whether we feel like it or not. The day we don't need anyone else is the day we die, because it is the day we say no to love. It's no wonder isolation leads to loneliness, illness, failure, even death. We need connection to survive. As poet Mark Nepo writes, "The question to put to our daily lives, then, is: In love, in friendship, in seeking to learn and grow, in trying to understand ourselves…When pressed by life, do I bridge or isolate? Do I reconnect the web of life and listen to its wisdom? Or do I make an island of every confusion as I try to solve its pain?"[2]

Making islands of ourselves only causes more pain. Instead, we must get out and build bridges. Not dozens of quick, flimsy bridges, but rather, a few solid, sturdy ones. Of course, bridge building may be easier for some than others; for some, building solitude is the challenge, not the other way around. Introverts and extroverts alike will benefit from shunning isolation and seeking to build a balance between connection and solitude.

Especially me. I need to be alone, yes. *And* I need to connect. Those dark times when I want to crawl into a hole and hide are the times I most need to reach out a hand, let my heart thaw a little, and love someone. Or, to just let *someone* love *me*.

Wednesday, May 14

It's my first Mother-of-Six Mother's Day, full of hand-made cards, bookmarks, poems, and coupons good for hugs, help, and housework. I slept in. The boys brought me sliced fruit, yogurt, and toast in bed. We attended an inspiring church meeting, and OJ took care of the meals and cleaning—or making the kids clean, at least—for the remainder of the day.

OJ's gift surprised me. A white gold pendant with eight little diamonds, one for each of us, I was probably more shocked than I should have been. After forgetting to buy me a birthday gift and giving me size four jeans for Christmas, when I was one month postpartum, I was shocked. "Wow! Way to go, dear. I love it. You totally redeemed yourself," I said.

He just nodded, bowed, and casually said, "That's what I do."

Perhaps the best part of the day was the perfect mix of time alone—for a concentrated nap—and time together—windows and doors open, basking in the sixty-five-degree weather, a welcome change from the cold of winter. While the girls played dress up and danced for us, OJ and I read, and the boys climbed pine trees. At one point, hearing voices just out my bedroom window, I looked to see nine year-old Colton, swinging from the lofty pine branches to the second story balcony! Oh, they make me nervous, but, oh, I love that they do. It was one of my favorite Mother's Days of all time.

I could hardly believe it, then, when I awoke two days later to, not just blankets, but down comforters of snow! Just when I thought I was melting into spring, another reminder that winter remains. Yesterday felt like trying to rescue myself from a deep, dark well, pulling and pulling on the rope, but never seeing the light of day. I held on until OJ walked through the door from work. I kissed him hello, handed him Sydney, and hid myself in my closet, sobbing on the floor, not wanting to leak my despair onto anyone else. OJ found me, sat beside me, scooped me out of my puddle and into his arms, and listened as I blabbed on about who knows what. All I know is I was full of lots of things, and it was startling how quickly and intensely it came on. I felt really…crazy.

Sydney turned six months today, and we have come a long way in six months, haven't we? Yet something in me remains. What is this black hole?

Friday, May 16

OJ dragged me on a date today—golfing, at Forest Highlands.

Forest Highlands is ranked one of the top golf courses in Arizona, and it's easy to see why. Nestled among the largest Ponderosa Pine forest in the country, the sweeping views of the San Francisco Peaks and warm pine-scented breezes could make anyone feel like they're on cloud nine. But as OJ and I arrived for our golf date this morning, even the incredible beauty didn't inspire me.

When OJ told me he'd planned this time together, doing the thing he loves best in the world—second only to me and the kids, of course—I wasn't sure it was a good idea. Leaving Sydney is still hard for me, and playing a sport where your only competition is yourself didn't seem like the best choice for my critical mind. But I love OJ, and he was trying. So, I met him half way. I put on my golfiest clothes—a collared shirt and knee-length shorts—feeling hopeful, but was brought to tears when OJ innocently handed me Shannon's golf shoes and memories began to flood.

I pulled it together. We arrived at the driving range, and OJ set up my clubs. I watched him whack the heck out of a little ball with his driver, shooting it almost to the end of the range! The golf attendants went, "Whoa," and said, "Nice shot." Everyone knows OJ out there, and everyone knows he's good. *No wonder he loves it so much*, I thought. *He really is amazing at this.*

I, however, stunk. Whatever it was I was aiming for was lucky, because I would hit anything but that! *I should be easier on myself*, I thought. *I haven't played golf in over a year and I've only played maybe five times ever!* Still, by hole two, I was so frustrated I wanted to throw my club into the water and scream. The word that kept repeating in my mind was *loser*. I was embarrassed I was playing so poorly, and felt trapped between wanting to please OJ and run away and hide. Frustration became tears, and I turned my face from OJ, slinking under my sunglasses and visor, in the golf cart.

OJ noticed, warmed me with his arms, and whispered, "We can quit, honey. It's okay. I wanted to help you feel better, not worse."

I let myself feel his love and kept quiet, because I feared I'd hurt him no matter what I said. Instead, I left his embrace and walked among the wildflowers, letting the tears drip. I prayed. I pleaded with Heavenly Father, *please help me enjoy this time with OJ—even if only for his sake.* I really wanted to be able to have a nice day with him. Didn't he need it as much as I? Didn't we deserve it? I hit the next ball, took a moment to breathe in my favorite smell—sun-stroked pine needles—put on a smile, and gave OJ a long hug and a kiss. He really does love me. *I really do love him.*

Before I knew it, I was enjoying myself. I even hit a legit bogey—one over par, for the golf illiterate. As we played nine holes, we laughed, we held hands, we applauded each other. We enjoyed the beautiful course, expansive blue sky, and snow-capped mountain views. Best of all, it was almost impossible to think of anything besides hitting that cunning little ball as well as I could. Not only a break from my routine, it was a break from winter.

It wasn't until I slid into bed tonight and started writing that I recognized how my prayers were answered today. Yet another way God speaks to me: He changes how I feel.

Saturday, May 17

Today was…strange. I spent the morning watching Kennedy and Sydney because OJ and the boys had been at the father-son campout since last night. I was trying to get some much-needed housework done, but cleaning while watching the girls is like writing on a chalkboard while someone's erasing. By noon, frustration had set in. It didn't help that Sydney wouldn't nap, and by the time the boys arrived home, I was irritable. They were dumping filthy, smoke-soaked items all over the kitchen, and I snapped. "Seriously, boys? Who do you think I am, your maid? Get this out of here now!" Then, I felt guilty. This happens often. I get frustrated and act grumpy with my family, then my criticizer chimes in: *See—some mother you are!*

OJ, seeing I was at an edge, intervened—taking Sydney and trying to talk it out with me, suggesting all sorts of "fun" things I could do. But I couldn't open my mouth. I knew what would happen. I'd complain and say sour things that would make us all pucker, and then I'd get really frustrated because I didn't actually know *what* I was feeling nor *how* to feel better.

So, I did something else. I kept working. I organized the desk area, Kennedy's bedroom, our bathroom shelves, and part of the office. Then, I did a little laundry and played with Kennedy while OJ napped with Sydney on his chest. (I love that.) Kennedy and I baked banana bread—one gluten-free, for OJ, and one for the rest of us.

By then it was 4:30, and I was tempted to shut myself in my room, sleep, and watch junky TV all night, but Kennedy was begging to go to Forest Highlands and "golf with Daddy." Since I was still keeping my mouth shut, I let OJ load us *all* in the car, and head to the driving range. I wasn't sure this would be a good idea, especially for me. But, once more, I was wrong. We ended up staying nearly two hours, the kids hitting balls—Kennedy in her princess dress—laughing, and encouraging each other. Even Sydney was kicking and smiling as she rolled around in the grass.

Interesting what happens when I don't get in my own way. What started rough ended up a nice, normal Saturday. Just the way it should be.

Saturday, May 24

I continue to struggle. It's probably no big shocker to the on-looker. But, to me, it's a hard truth.

Somehow, I always thought I was stronger. Perhaps that's a major part of my problem. I've had this "identity" all framed for myself in which I was strong, loving, helpful, positive, talented, good. Lately, that's all been shattered. Not to say I'm bad, just to say I'm not as good as I thought.

I'm weaker. I *do* have self-sabotaging tendencies. Lately, they express themselves through dark chocolate and Haagen Dazs Caramel Cone—yum! I *do* get frustrated easily. I get overwhelmed. I let things slip by because I'm just too worn out. I feel weak. I can see *some* good too, but it stands in stark contrast to these other things, and they tend to overshadow all else.

I feel scattered. All over the place. Unable to focus. My mind doesn't work. Again, I can't see any "big picture." I'm forgetful. I don't feel intelligent, like I used to. This makes me have trouble trusting myself. I'm exhausted and I feel like every time I'm about to get some good rest, someone or something—usually some*one*—wakes me up. It's relentless! Constantly, "Mom! Mom! Mom!" and lately, it's been too overwhelming because I've had no break! OJ has been working with his Dad outside for two days—they're building a roof over our deck, and I am grateful, really I am—but he was golfing the day before that, so it's been a lot of give and no rest.

"I'm bored," I said to OJ earlier, listless.

"Aagh!" I said to myself this afternoon, frustrated.

Three times I began to cry—no, four—but the tears wouldn't come. I feel like I need to tone myself up, emotionally and physically. I need to stoop eating junk at night and exercise harder. I need to figure out what's going on with me, emotionally, and tone it up, too.

"I need time alone. I need it!" I said this evening, to OJ. I don't know why I need it so much. Others don't seem to need it like I do, but when I don't have time alone, I start to feel like a pressure cooker, ready to explode. I'm irritable. I don't want to be around anyone.

I feel antisocial. I feel so low and down on myself, like I can't handle anything, and like I'm just not able to be the nice, loving, thoughtful, talented, compassionate person I thought I once was. I don't feel this anymore. I miss that person. She feels gone.

So, basically, it's two sides of me at battle. One says, "Let's get on with life. Feel good. Look good. Be happy!" The other says, "I'm too tired! Overwhelmed! Bored! Frustrated! It's too much and too hard. I'm too weak. I can't do it."

Well, I know that's not true. I can do anything, but clearly, part of me doesn't want to yet, so I am stuck. I'm half glass-empty, and half glass-full. But I'm one hundred percent tired.

Sunday, May 25

I played my part today. I fed and dressed the kids, dolled myself up, went to church, tried to smile and ask others, "How are you?" I came home, helped the kids change clothes, made and ate lunch with the family, let OJ help me clean the dishes, tried to be patient and kind, and put Sydney down for a nap. It's exhausting being who I think I am.

I finally broke away for a two-hour nap. The kind of nap where I'm so deep in dreams it's hard to wake. *I've just arrived at the hotel for the Postpartum Support International conference, thinking, "Wow! I'm finally here in Houston. I should get up to my hotel room and relax." But I keep getting in the wrong elevator or finding the wrong door. I realize I don't have my key and need to find the front desk, so I head back to the elevator, on the main floor, and start walking around. My eyes are swollen shut. I can see only blurry images—people passing by, happy to be there, and even people giving me hugs, happy to see me. I'm asking, "Can someone please help me? My eyes are swollen shut, and I can't see." They don't seem to hear or notice there's anything wrong, and instead, keep talking to me and the others about the conference and how great it is to see each other. I am discouraged now. Why don't they see me? Why won't they help me? I just want to get to my room and take a nap. I finally fall, sobbing, on the ground near the elevator. I am pleading, "Please! Can anyone help me?" They notice me a little now, but somehow they can't, or they don't know how to help.*

Another sleepy, blurry-eyed dream where I just want to rest, but can't. A dream where no one notices anything is wrong. Clearly, my subconscious knows what's going on with me. My mind is always a few leaps behind.

Now, in an attempt to understand, I write in my journal and let the emotions take center stage— drumming up tears that won't fall, setting the scene for the drama to begin in my mind. *Why is everything so hard for me? Why am I so weak? Maybe I really am messed up. Other mothers of large families can do this way better than I can. I'm a failure. I can't handle my life. What if I just sneak out and go to a hotel alone and don't tell anyone? What if I stay here, but don't do anything except take care of Sydney—no cleaning or cooking, just watching TV, eating junk and doing nothing else? What if I give up, let myself completely break down, and be really crazy?* Worse, though, I admit, the actual words I sling at myself are *total loser*, much of the time. When did I become so insecure?

My inner psychologist tries to get me under control, gently parenting, "You're not going to do any of these things. And you're not crazy." That "Dr. Hibbert" part likes to keep reminding me of things I already know but forget, like the fact that I can be dramatic, especially when I'm hormonal or too tired, and how I tend toward all-or-nothing thinking. Not that I *want* to be all-or-nothing. Just that I *tend* to be. "Sometimes it feels like it would be easier to just be 'crazy,'" she says, "because it would mean you're off the hook. No responsibility for your actions. But, you know, in this moment, it's a conscious choice." *I know. I know.* There's always a point at which crazy is a choice. Once I let myself pass that point, the choice is made, and so are the consequences. Dr. Hibbert reminds me that these thoughts are just my way of trying to escape. They're my coping tool. I am not likely to act on any of them. A tiny hug from myself, she tries to remind me everything will be okay.

I wish someone else were hugging me and telling me it will be okay. I wish I had other characters in this drama, not just my alter ego—or, my "superego" as Freud would say. I'm working on accepting what *is*, but, like an impressionist trying to complete a work of art with her nose to the canvas, I have no perspective. I wish someone could give me perspective—tell me exactly what I'm feeling, what I need to do, what the big picture is. I know no one can do that.

I also know I haven't invited anyone in. I take responsibility for that. I let myself seem "fine" when I'm in public. I *am* "fine" when I'm in public. That doesn't mean I don't have my hard times at home, or even that "fine" is good enough. I wish others would notice the redness of my eyes, the dark circles around them, my sighing, the energy it takes to smile.

Maybe this is a second doctoral program: advanced learning about life, death, marriage, mothering, family, faith, patience, prayer. My degree will be "Doctor of Life," and I will be in good company. So many of us earn our "Doctor of Life" degrees.

Monday, May 26

Yesterday ended in a sobbing meltdown. We were supposed to have a family dinner at our friends, Scott and Cyndy's, house, but when the time approached, OJ found me in my room. Finally, the tears had come, but they wouldn't stop. I encouraged him to take the kids and go without me; I would follow when I could pull myself together. But I couldn't pull myself together. So, I ended up calling and having to excuse myself from dinner.

"I'm sorry," I told my friend, Cyndy. I could barely speak. "I just…"

"It's okay," she said, hearing my tears. Cyndy is, admittedly, not comfortable with emotional situations. I felt extra sorry and embarrassed to have to share my mess with her, but she was kind. I hung up and cried harder. It poured out for over an hour. Then, I lay on the floor in the front room and stared out the window for another hour.

By the time they got home, I was done, exhausted. OJ tucked me in, and I slept ten hours and still had a hard time getting up today—no energy, eyes stinging, head pounding. OJ was supposed to have gone golfing, but for the first time in as long as I can remember, he cancelled. I was back in bed by nine a.m., feeling like I was going to throw up. Physically ill. There seemed no way out of the dismal place I was in, so I made myself pray. I literally forced myself to my knees. I felt unworthy to pray. Unworthy to ask for help. But I did. *Father, I don't know what to do. I'm so lost. I need thee more than ever.* Somehow, I was able to fall asleep and wake up to a fresh start. Lighter. Not *better,* but able to make myself get up and try.

I know I need to make some changes. I can't afford to keep losing it like this. My family can't afford it. I came up with my top five needs, in order of importance: 1) Sleep. 2) Exercise—more often and more intensely, to get this post-baby body back into shape. 3) Nutrition—more consistent healthy intake, less emotional eating. 4) Time—to ponder and do the things I love. Time to rest. Read. Write. Play piano or guitar. I haven't been listening to or playing music, a sure sign of unhealthiness. I need music in my life. 5) Fun—getting out with OJ and friends. Laughing with the kids. Doing kind things for myself. I also need to find a way to prevent the emotional stuffing I've been doing. It's not good.

I painted my toenails bright red tonight, a sure sign things are looking up. I always tell OJ he can tell my state of mental health by my toenails. The more overgrown and under-painted they are, the bigger the problem. If I've actually taken the time to groom them, I'm probably doing pretty well. OJ knows this, and, on more than one occasion, has shown up with a bottle of nail polish and clippers, offering to do the job himself. He painted my toes pearly-pink when I was in labor with Sydney, so I would have something pretty to look at and be reminded all was well. I guess he figures it must work the other way, too. If my toes look terrific, then mental health must not be far behind. Or, at least, that's what he hopes. It seems to work, not just because my toes look appealing, but because I feel loved.

Looking at my bright red toenails now reminds me of that love, and I feel grateful. I may not have perspective, but at least I am gaining experience. One day, I will step back and see the completed masterpiece. Then, I will know I never really needed perspective, for the Master Artist knew the plan all along.

Wednesday, May 28

As I jogged this morning—okay, who am I kidding—as I walked, with interspersed *moments* of jogging, I prayed, realizing I've been trying to do too much on my own again. I pray every day—for strength, comfort, peace, forgiveness—but how easily I forget to pray for specific help. It's one of my great weaknesses, that of always trying to do things on my own. It wasn't until this morning that I prayed, specifically. *Please help me understand how to make this new family and new me work.*

As soon as my foot crossed the threshold of the front door, the phone was ringing. First, Cynthia, my friend from grad school, called, during her commute to work. She's done this every several weeks for the past few months. We catch up on grad school acquaintances and work projects, and I commiserate about the terrible LA traffic in which she's stuck, but mostly, she's checking up on me. Although I don't want to be a burden, I'm grateful she is.

Today, she validated the difficult psychological and emotional processes I'm experiencing. "Loss, grief, postpartum, family stress, trauma—you need to let others help you emotionally," she reminded me. "You need support. It's too much for you to do on your own." I nodded and took it in.

Minutes after we hung up, the phone rang again. This time, it was Emily, my dear friend since freshmen year of BYU and fellow mother of several young children. "Just calling to see how you're doing," she said. I tried to explain the emotional rollercoaster I've been on. "You need help with the kids so you can take care of yourself," she said. "I've been struggling with doing the same thing. Ever since I found more help with my kids, it's been a huge relief for me. I know it would be for you, too. Let yourself get a babysitter or housecleaning help more often. Then, focus on the things you really need, like sleep, exercise, and time alone." She was right. I do need more help with the kids. I try to do it all myself, but why? I won't be a failure if I let help in.

Then, Leonore—whom I met when we lived in Phoenix, right after Kennedy was born, immediately clicked with, and never stopped clicking—called. She's just so easy-going and real. I love that about her. We can say exactly what we feel, and neither of us ever feels judged. We laugh whenever we talk. I mean belly-aching laugh, and I love it. She reminded me I can and should have fun. "I just try to laugh about things as much as I can," she said. "It helps." She's right. Lightness is not my strong point, but, oh, how I need it!

Even Mom called today. It was brief. She had a question about something for Ashley, and then I updated her on the kids' latest activities. We haven't *really* talked yet, not since I let her have it on the phone. I want to bring it up, but I can tell that's the last thing *she* wants. Mom's made a huge effort to be more involved these past weeks, calling to talk to the kids, or ask about them. She's trying, and for that, I give her credit. I didn't hear a word from her for weeks after our disagreement. I finally gave in and called Dad a few days after. He listened in his calm way and said he felt badly about it all. I told him I thought he or she would call to smooth things over. I was honest. "It hurts that you both won't talk to me," I said. He kept saying he wasn't upset, and that Mom just needed time to calm down. "It will blow over eventually," he said. I guess her phone call is a sign that it is, though I wish instead of "blowing over," we could dig in and work it out.

Four phone calls back-to-back-to-back, to-back, today? This was highly unusual phone traffic for me. I am, admittedly, not a great phone-caller or talker. It was obviously an answer to my prayer, the answer being: let help in. In order to make this family, and myself, work, I need help. I need to reach out a little more, share what I'm experiencing, and let others love me through.

Now, I'm not going to an extreme here. I know I'm not "all better" all of a sudden. But I feel like I can see myself walking uphill again. Here's me:

See—I've got a long way to go, but I'm walking, slowly, uphill. At least I'm no longer down in that pit. Sometimes I slip and fall, and I know I will, but the point is to get going again. Just deal with the issue at hand and keep moving.

That's my pep talk for today: Keep moving.

Saturday, June 7

I painted my bedroom last weekend—the most heavenly shade of blue. It matches the huge sky outside my window on a sunny day. I just returned from Houston, Texas, where I spent four days attending and speaking at the Postpartum Support International (PSI)[3] conference, and found a glimmer of *me*. It's late—almost midnight—and everyone's asleep, but I had to write and say how good it feels to be home again, how much I love my blue room, and what a relief it is to feel like me again.

I've been a member of PSI since I was a first-year grad student with a three year-old and twelve month-old. I'd been doing research on postpartum depression (PPD) for a program development class I was taking, my program being a center for postpartum mothers and families. After having been through PPD with both my first boys, I'd been looking for resources I wished I'd had at the time. That's when I came upon Jane Honikman, Founder of PSI. At that time, Jane was still answering postpartum support calls in her own home. She was the first to validate for me that I really had had postpartum depression, that it was real, and that I was not alone.

"I knew I couldn't have been the only one," I told her, my eyes wet with validation. "I figured there had to be help out there, somewhere. Unfortunately, I was right; I'm not the only one. But postpartum depression is neither recognized nor treated as well as it should be, so we moms just suffer alone," I continued. "I'm so glad to meet you, Jane, and get involved in making things better." I started volunteering on the PSI California warmline, taking calls from postpartum moms in need, offering the support I wished I'd had.

When I moved back to Arizona from grad school, I decided to start a warmline here. I met up with the state coordinator, Michelle, who became a great friend, and we set up the phone line and answering machine in her living room that very day. The warmline was just a start and the beginning to fulfilling my dream of a support network for Arizona. The Arizona Postpartum Wellness Coalition[4] was officially formed one year later, and I became its Founder and President. I've been on hiatus from leading the coalition for the past several months, of course, so it was great to be invited to speak at PSI conference on "Perinatal Couples and Group Therapy," alongside some giants in the field. It reminds me I'm still a leader in postpartum mental health.

During my talk, I was able to share a little of *my* "postpartum couples" experience—the one I'm *still in*, I was reminded. I received an outpouring of support, doing the work I love again, surrounded and understood by friends I only get to see at this conference each year. They even sold out of my *Postpartum Couples* DVD[5] before the main conference began. The whole thing reaffirmed my love for connection, for helping others, and especially, for teaching. I could feel how far that world was from my real world, at home. It was a nice place to visit, and, in many ways, I felt found.

As Mom and Dad rounded the corner at the airport terminal curb tonight, with all the kids in my SUV, windows down, I could already hear the noise and excitement. The kids had been staying with "Mimi" and "Pop" while OJ was at a golf tournament until the next day, so the plan was for me to drive us the two-hours home. As they pulled up to the curb, the loudness grew. Such a contrast from where I'd been the past days. It was a "gulp!" moment as I was jolted back to reality. *These children are all mine!* I sucked in a deep breath, and I slowly opened the door.

"Mom! We missed you so much!" they said, taking turns kissing and hugging me so tightly I thought I would pop! Talking over one another, they couldn't wait to tell me all about their past few days.

Another jolt. Being with them again, it hit me just how much I was loved. *This is the world in which I belong,* I thought. *It's good to be home.* A smile crossed my face as I exhaled into their stories and was simply "Mom" again.

FOURTEEN
Breathe

*"As a man in his last breath drops all he is carrying,
each breath is a little death that can set us free."*
~Mark Nepo[1]

Funny how hard it can be to do, on purpose, the very thing we do 28,800 times a day—awake, asleep, without even trying—breathe. Yes, breathing is the sign of life. Deep, calm breathing is the sign of the *good* life.

In troubled times, we often forget to breathe. Rather than feel the pain, the fear, the heartache that is in the exhale, we confine the inhale. Most of the time, we don't even know we're doing it. I learned this back in high school. A junior, and embarrassed by my all-too-ready tears during a touching dance to a Billy Joel song at a school talent show, I noticed that if I held my breath, I wouldn't cry. That lesson may have been learned a little too well, for, somewhere in the midst of my four-year growing seasons, I went for a massage only to be told by the therapist, "You're not breathing."

"Yes, I am," I said. Clearly, I was breathing. I was alive, wasn't I?

"No, you're not. You're sucking in a breath and holding it."

Hmm. Was she right? When I paid attention, I noticed, she was. How long had I been doing that and what kind of damage had been done to my body as a result? I may not have had to feel things I didn't want to feel, but all those "things" ended up stuck in my shoulders and neck. Hence, the need for the massage.

That's when I started practicing deep, or diaphragmatic, breathing. Deep breathing is the passage through emotion, or rather, the way for emotion to pass through us. We breathe. We feel. We breathe more deeply. We heal. Engaging our breath from the belly, instead of the quick, chest-expanding breaths to which most of us are accustomed, we inhale to our toes, expand, both body and mind, and lean in to the purposeful exhale where unwanted energy is released. It can feel a bit unusual to breathe deeply at first, but when we focus on the body's sensations after deep breathing, we find we feel calm, more relaxed, and more centered. I know *I* do as I write this—another reminder of why I work on deep breathing at least a few minutes everyday.

Deep breathing is also helpful in calming explosive emotions, like anger and fear. Back in graduate school, I stumbled upon a technique I called "blowing up my balloon." When frustration set in, I imagined holding a balloon to my mouth and trying to blow it up as big as could be. When we blow up real balloons, we naturally use deep breathing, so this is a perfect little idea—one I've also taught my kids in recent years. I'd imagine my red balloon, and as I'd blow, I would feel all the negative energy flowing out through my breath, and into the balloon. Then, when the imaginary balloon was sufficiently large—and sometimes it was enormous—I would see that balloon *pop* along with all my negativity. Sometimes, I would let it be tied and float away—like when I wanted to wallow. Sometimes, it would fly out of my hands and flap around the room until it expired— like when I was feeling ridiculous. My balloon helped me calm down and get clear so I could respond in a more effective manner. To this day, if OJ sees me blowing up my imaginary balloon, he slowly backs up and retreats until the balloon has popped!

We can all choose to practice deep breathing. Then, on emotion-filled days, we'll be used to engaging the breath, allowing us to approach life with greater clarity. On other days, when we're about to kick, fight, or scream, instead, we can pull out an imaginary balloon and begin to blow. After all, balloons do have a way of making everything feel a little lighter, a little happier.

Monday, June 16

Happy Birthday, Kennedy! Actually, her birthday was yesterday, but the party was today. Yesterday was also Father's Day, OJ's brother's birthday, and my grandmother's ninety-second. A busy day, but I kept my cool. I'm pretty sure I was able to pull off making everyone feel special.

Kennedy's party was this morning, and a whirlwind—six little princesses, pink streamers, pin the crown on the princess, and pink cake. Though we live in a world of "I rented an exact replica of Cinderella's castle for my three year-old daughter's birthday, complete with the 'real' Cinderella, who did makeovers on all the girls, for only five hundred dollars," I do the minimum. After all, within two hours the house was destroyed again, all princesses had an enchanting time, Kennedy and Sydney were exhausted, and so was I. Why pay more than we have to for that?

The girls finally napping, OJ and I helped Tre and Braxton pack for their two-week trip with Grandpa Cutler to Washington, DC, and then to Scout camp in Pennsylvania. Grandpa Cutler's instructions had been clear: "I will be right on time, so make sure they are waiting outside, packed, with everything on the list." He means precisely what he says, so OJ had taken time off work to help me make sure we did exactly what he'd asked. At the appointed time—a few minutes early, even—we all sat on the curb, awaiting Grandpa's arrival. For one hour. Two hours. Waiting. Calling Grandpa Cutler. No answer. Waiting. Something was obviously up. Calling again. No answer. And again. We began to expect the worst.

The phone finally rang…three hours later. With no explanation for where he'd been, he asked to speak with the boys. OJ put them on. I ran and picked up the other extension, just in time to hear him criticizing Braxton and Tre, because they hadn't called him to report on a Scout assignment, as he had apparently asked them to do. This, he told them, was why he had decided not to pick them up.

"How can I trust you to take you on a trip like this if you can't even do one little thing I ask?" he criticized. "You're irresponsible, and I am very upset with you." He wasn't yelling, but there was no kindness in his voice. This, of course, upset the boys terribly. That, of course, upset *me*.

OJ and I took the phones from the dejected boys and tried to intervene, understand, or perhaps help Grandpa Cutler see that he should have called to tell us he wasn't coming or, at least, should have warned us he'd tasked our eleven year-old boys with a "mandatory" assignment in the first place. But he wasn't interested in our opinions.

"Don't try to protect them," he said, his voice growing angry. "They knew what I asked them to do, and they failed. They should be more responsible and trustworthy."

OJ and I looked at each other across the room, eyes wide, and put our hands up. The boys were sitting by, trying not to cry, and I was trying not to let their grandpa have it. I sucked in a long breath and pushed it back out. "If you're going to behave this way," I said in my calmest firm voice, "then I am not comfortable sending my boys, alone, with you, for two weeks."

"Fine," he quickly replied. "Then the trip is cancelled, because you won't let them go."

Well, this wasn't exactly the truth, but he hung up on me, so we shifted the focus to smoothing things over with the boys. They were hurt, especially Tre, who had been looking forward to visiting the Scout camp his father, Rob, had attended as a boy. I was trying to explain things in a way so the boys wouldn't: 1) think this was their fault, for not doing the assignment, 2) think this was my fault, for over-reacting, or 3) end up hating their grandpa. *Tricky.*

OJ and I spent the rest of the evening talking with the kids, each other, and off and on with Grandpa Cutler, trying to figure out exactly what had happened. He was apparently furious, not only about this, but about all these legal issues with Shannon's estate. It was getting late, and enough was enough. We finally told him we couldn't talk to him when he was acting like this, hung up, and tried to just get our starving family fed.

Staring into the fridge, I sighed. Not just because nothing sounded good and I didn't feel like cooking, but because this was another problem heaped on the pile we'd been working so hard to shrink. *Here we go again!* kept repeating in my mind. I wanted to fall into a heap on the floor in my room.

Thank goodness OJ pulled me back to the here and now when he called the kids to the kitchen. "We're having ice-cream sundaes for dinner," he announced, looking at me with his impish grin. He has this innocent, playful quality about him that can make any situation not just all right, but good. The kids were, of course, thrilled, and so was I. *What a perfect thing to say.* Sometimes OJ is the only one who knows the right thing for us to do. I smiled and nodded, and we began to heap up chocolate, caramel, and whipped cream.

This is exactly what we need, I thought, as we sat on the back deck eating ice cream, watched the sun set, and talked it out. Talked of disappointment and overcoming. Talked of family stress and family love. Talked of plans lost, and of all the excellent things we'll get to do now with those two extra weeks.

Tuesday, June 17

The morning started too early, after a too-late bedtime and sleepless night replaying everything that happened yesterday. Tired and grumpy, I dragged myself out of bed, my body like lead. As I washed my face, I checked my phone for messages and caught today's date. Eight months since Shannon died. *No wonder I am leaden.* As they say, "The body remembers what the mind forgets." *Couldn't the world shut down for just one little day so I could hide?*

Not today, it couldn't. Today was a "suck it up and be there for others" day. I finally got the girls to the sitter and began preparing for the party I was in charge of tonight for the women at church. Checking in with my committee members, decorating, and making lists for remaining items I needed to purchase at the grocery store, I was worn out by 9:30 a.m. But today was a "suck it up" day, so I grabbed my keys and headed to the grocery store.

As I stood, watching the cashier punch in the produce prices, a tousled man walked up, freaking out, because he'd lost his wallet. He ran from cashier to cashier, in a daze, asking if they'd found it, then out to the parking lot, searching everywhere, with dramatic arm gestures and sighs. He didn't see me, but I couldn't take my eyes off him. As I loaded groceries in the car, he came back by, and I quickly decided what I should do: ask if I could help. However, as I was about to speak, he slammed his car door, cursing, and peeled out of the parking lot. It put things in perspective. This man had seemed utterly lost—destitute, even. *I am fine. Life is fine.*

The boys and I hit the pool at Forest Highlands in the afternoon. Thanks to yesterday, they'd been sad, frustrated, and fighting all morning. Tre woke up missing his father and feeling low, because he can't go to camp, and because he's mad at his grandpa, I think. His smooth, white skin was flushed, and he pulled at his dark, skater-style hair. I had to tell Tre again, "This is not *your* fault."

"Well, we didn't do the assignment, like he asked. And he's *my* grandfather," Tre replied. He's been beating himself up over it. I've been trying to stop the beating.

Braxton was also down, and confused. "How can you and Dad just love Tre and Brody the same as all of us other kids?" he asked. I think he was feeling like it's not fair. Like life is not fair. *It's not*, I thought. Like this is all too hard. *It is*. I think he was also afraid that maybe, if we can suddenly love Tre and Brody like we love him, then that means we could also suddenly love him less.

I hugged him, feeling him want to pull away, but hugging me back. Now that he's almost twelve, I think he feels like he shouldn't need me. He does, though, and this afternoon, I know he knew it. "We love you very, very much, Braxton. You're my very first baby. I've been your mother since you were growing in my belly. I've loved you more than you know since before you even took a breath. I've only been their mother a few months now. But they are my sons, too, now, so, yes, of course, I will give them as much love as I give you." These are the things we're working through. They just keep coming.

I just keep coping—tonight, through service, which is one of the best ways I know to get out of myself. That's what I needed, to get out of *me* for a while. The Relief Society is the largest and longest-standing women's organization in the world, founded March 17, 1842, and its motto is "Charity never faileth."[2] I agree. It never doth. Planning and executing this dinner allowed me to set aside my troubles and have a little fun, getting to know the women I love and admire a little better—laughing, learning, and eating delicious food together. My goal was to see what needed to be done and do it. To be in constant motion. To be the last to leave. That's exactly what I did. And it felt great.

We really do need each other, I realized tonight. We really do.

Sunday, June 29

Our whole family has been trying to decide how to handle Grandpa Cutler's craziness. First, he cancelled the Alaska trip that he, OJ, and the four boys were supposed to be taking in a couple weeks. Via *fax*, no less. Cutler had called a few months ago and invited them to join him on his extravagant fishing trip in Alaska. OJ had been wary of being alone with him for a week, but he'd agreed, for the boys, who had really been looking forward to it. Now, he just cancelled it, out of the blue.

Then, Cutler has been making demands that are not only unnecessary, they are not in his authority to make. Among other things, he says we have to pay him for items we have that were Shannon's and hand over Shannon's wedding ring, which he originally agreed to let us keep, in our safe, for the boys. He's been really stuck on that ring. He supposedly bought the diamond in it and it is, as he says, "of the highest quality." Maybe that's why he wants it. Or maybe just because he likes control. I know, legally, we don't have to give him the ring, and he knows this, too. So, when we tell him, "Go ahead and get a court order," he never does.

Then, tonight, the Cutlers actually had the nerve to call and tell us they want Tre and Brody to stay with them for two weeks during the time they were supposed to be in Alaska. They said they want the boys with them for the one-year anniversary of Rob's death. *That* I can understand. But two weeks? When the boys are still upset with Grandpa Cutler? When they'd been hoping he'd call and apologize, but never did? We had to tell them the truth—that, unfortunately, we'd already planned a trip to Durango for our family during that time, to make up for the Alaska trip. OJ and I had been agonizing over how to handle the cancelled trip so it wouldn't ruin the boys' opinion of their grandpa for good. Instead of telling them the whole truth, we told them, "Grandpa can't go on the Alaska trip anymore, so he cancelled it. We're going to take you boys to Durango, Colorado, instead. It'll be really fun." They were disappointed about Alaska, but quickly threw themselves into plans of mountain biking and river rafting.

The Cutlers were not happy, of course, and, honestly, I felt for them—*somewhat*. So, we offered to compromise. "We will come home a day early from our trip, then," we said. "It will be the morning of Rob's anniversary day, and you're welcome to drive up and meet us, right when we get home, to take the boys for a few days." They agreed.

This back and forth with the Cutlers over trips and money and property has been taking up several hours each day. I am so done with it! I'm done with playing the peacemaker, therapist, and referee! My back aches, and so does my head, most days. I haven't had any time to myself, and I can feel the pressure building. I'm also sure it doesn't help that OJ's been in a golf tournament the past four days and Sydney's been teething. I'm back to way-too-tired.

I vented to Mom tonight. Our similar frustrations with Cutler have actually brought us together. We're on the same side again—the only benefit from this as far as I can see. We processed, and it became clear I'm more worried about the future than the present. I worry that the Cutlers might interfere with adoption or cause other problems that could hurt our family. Mostly, I worry about how their behavior might affect the kids. I should be at peace, because I don't actually believe they can harm us—just stir up trouble, and trouble we can handle. But my mind has a hard time letting it go.

As I held Sydney, tonight, I thought, *I wish I could just focus on you—just hug and cuddle and love you, my last baby.*

I feel time slipping as she grows, and my heart aches. Instead of just being with and building my family, these ridiculous problems are worrying my time away. Remember what Dr. Hibbert always says: "Worry is good for nothing." [3] True, true. Absolutely good for nothing. *Sigh...*

Sunday, July 20

I've been alone, in my room, for about two hours now—a luxurious amount of time these days. I had a desperately needed nap, because sleep has eluded me lately—two or four a.m. seems to be my norm to finally fall asleep. I've been trying to let myself read and relax. It's been too long since I've had true alone time, and these quick, stolen moments do not cut it.

Though life has felt much more normal lately, I'm not one hundred percent. *Will I ever be?* Grief seems to have lifted, but I still struggle. This morning, for instance, I was irritable and ended up yelling at everyone as we left for church. " Be quiet!" I'd had it. Too much bickering. Too much arguing with me. Too much noise! Too little listening! We enjoyed a silent ride to church at least, and I did apologize for getting so angry, once we arrived.

It seems no matter how hard I try, I end up messing up. It's true, time and again. I'm finally understanding, it's just the way it is. I keep trying. I will keep messing up. Period. Because I am human and imperfect, and I will never be perfect in this life. I guess it's kind of like cleaning the house or making my bed. It will always get messed up again, but I keep trying, and sometimes it stays clean for a while and I feel at peace. When it does get horribly messy, I can recognize the mess and make it whole again—clean again—through more hard work. It's the repentance process, basically.

Speaking of messing up, allow me to admit a vice. I am jealous of Linda Eyre, author and parenting expert. I've been reading her book, *A Joyful Mother of Children*, and I have been enlightened. As well as frustrated. I'm not like her. She seems to be a more "joyful" mother than I can manage most days. Still, she has had so much experience mothering her *nine* children, that her ideas are tremendously helpful. So, I keep reading all her books. She and her husband are world-known for their parenting books—excellent tips and tools I use daily. But my jealousy rears its green head every time she writes, "While I was working on a book…" *Oh, how I wish I were working on a book!* I dream of being an author and spend many hours writing my thoughts in these journals and notebooks of every color and size. In my heart, I know I'll write a book. Eventually. But not now. *Always, not now.* I guess, in the meantime, I should keep writing, for myself. Who knows? Maybe someday, these insights will prove useful.

I had started a book on grief—about when Miki died, and how it affected our family—a couple years ago. I'd planned to interview each family member, to get their unique perspective, to show how everyone copes differently, and how different ages view things. I worked on it for months, hours at a time, and even interviewed my sister, Leighton. But not Shannon. Now Shannon's gone, and so is that book idea. I'm hoping that, if I keep writing, one day, the new idea will appear.

What I probably most need is perspective. It's only been eight months since Sydney was born and nine since Shannon died. It's still fresh. I'm still so deep in the trenches, I can't even glimpse what country I'm fighting in. I forget how fresh it is, which can be good, because it helps me cope. As I write, I am slapped with the fact that I've really had no time to process these past months. We're still going through changes and trials. It's not complete. I can't yet see how things fit in the bigger picture.

Which I shouldn't be thinking about at all, since

my eyes are literally closing as I write. It's ten p.m., and everyone's in bed. That means *I* should be, too.

Thursday, July 31

Today was one year since Rob died. We spent the day driving home from Durango, with the boys.

We had so much fun, it was hard for us to leave. Riding the ski lift up—with the flowering Rocky Mountains as a backdrop—then mountain biking down, was pretty unbelievable. We drove to the old mining town of Silverton and enjoyed ice cream and the scenic drive. Racing down the alpine slide, hiking through the tall grass. We even took a short rafting trip down the Colorado River. The boys played mini-golf and did the bungee-trampoline, rock wall, and bounce house. We slept in, and stayed up late watching movies. The first night, we saw a Mama and two baby bears, just below our deck, rooting through the trash. Of course, OJ freaked us all out by running down to where they were to get a pic! "That is the worst idea you could possibly have!" I yelled. "Mama bears protecting their cubs will kill you!" The kids were begging him not to go. I think he just loves getting a rise out of us—such a kid himself.

We'd promised the Cutlers we'd have the boys home this morning, even though we'd never heard back about their plans. So, we forced ourselves away, back home. Driving, I wasn't sure how to approach the anniversary of Rob's death. We'd been having such a great time, finally free of all the drama, and I didn't want to ruin it, but I also didn't want the kids to think I forgot. Or to think they couldn't talk about it. So, as we drove, I said, "Your father and uncle, Rob, died one year ago today. Did you guys know that?" They said they didn't. "Maybe we could remember him by sharing some of our favorite memories," I suggested. And we did.

For over an hour, stories of Rob filled the car. Rob coaching games and telling funny jokes, and OJ's stories of when he and Rob were younger, in Scouts together, and my memories of how we used to argue over the dumbest things, because we were both so stubborn. An hour of talking about what life's been like in the past year, of all we've accomplished since then, of where we are now.

When we got home, we got Tre and Brody ready to go with their grandparents and called the Cutlers, but no answer. They did not come to see the boys. We never heard a word. I swallowed my frustration, blowing up my imaginary red balloon, so we could continue celebrating instead. *I'm going to have to deal with this, but not here. Not tonight.*

Instead, we hit golf balls into the sunset. *Deep breath, swing, smack!* It was satisfying to see them fly. We played family basketball. We swam.

On the drive home, Kennedy said, "I got the rat today."

"What?" I asked.

"I got a rat." I started to put the pieces together. At the pool, a friend's son had found a dead rat, wet and lying on the ground. Everyone had been grossed out as the pool attendant carried it away.

"How did you get the rat?" I asked, everyone listening and giggling as we drove.

"By its tail," she said, matter-of-factly. She explained how she'd found a dead rat in the drain of the baby pool as she was looking for toys, so she took it out.

"Weren't you scared?" I asked.

"No," she said. "It was dead," and shrugged her shoulders. This from the five year-old girl who screams at the sight of a fly! We were rolling with laughter.

When we got home, we laughed some more as we ate pizza and swapped stories or Rob until bedtime. "Remember when uncle Rob took us sledding," the boys said, "and he was going so fast he crashed into a pile of snow?" "He had a huge vocabulary," I said. "He was always using words none of us had ever even heard of. Like recalcitrant. It means 'unruly, or hard to handle' (Sounds like his dad). It was Rob's name when we did our 'Murder Mystery Dinner' party. Rick Alcitrant. He wore a leather jacket and looked like 'The Fonz.'"

The perfect way to set our own feelings aside and just celebrate Rob.

FIFTEEN
Feel

"FEEL: Freely Experience Emotion, with Love."[1]
~Me

Wouldn't it be nice if we could snap our fingers and change how we feel? Too bad it's usually not so easy.

Powerful emotions can make even the sanest feel on the verge of crazy. Grief, anger, sadness, pain, fear, can feel intense, out of control, and downright scary. Like caged predators, we box these emotions up and stuff them deep in an effort to prevent the frightening consequences we envision if they were ever to escape. We fear feeling powerful emotions, because we believe they will overtake us. We fear that once they are free, *we* may never be free of them again.

All emotions, powerful as they may appear, are simply that—emotions, like the clouds that float across the sky, which never stay for long. Though they appear threatening, the most they can do is rain or hail or snow for a little while. In raining, hailing, snowing, the clouds lose their power. They literally dissipate. So it is with emotions. We fear their threatening appearance and run from the rain of feelings, but only through allowing the feelings to rain, will they eventually drain and disappear.

Take anger, for instance. Anger is an interesting emotion. It can be intense, overwhelming, even frightening. Anger can consume us if we let it, turning an ordinary you or me into a big, green Hulk! An emotion of action, anger gets us to do things otherwise may not. This can be a good thing, such as the mother who stands up for her child who has been wronged, or it can be a not-so-good thing, such as the frustrated child who starts a fistfight. Anger, like any emotion, is neither "good" nor "bad." It's how we *express* our anger that gets us into trouble. *Feeling* helps us express anger in healthier ways, preventing outbursts that come from ignoring or stuffing.

I once heard someone say, "Just because your feelings are buried alive doesn't mean that they die."[2] In fact, the longer feelings are buried, the more they fester and grow, until they control us, stronger than ever. The only way to be free of painful emotions is to open up, take a breath, and feel what is in there. When anger comes, feel angry. If fear has you in its grips, focus on feeling that fear. When sadness weighs like a boulder on your heart, feel sad. Let the tears flow, the words be said, the moment be experienced.

Like a flashlight searching deep inside the soul, feeling enables us to see. We see what we are made of as we carry on. We see that the pressure loosens, just a bit, that the chest inhales just a little easier. We see that we survive. We see the emotions begin to unfasten themselves from being part of us, and it is then and only then, that we see—they never really were.

Friday, August 1

The last few times I've been to therapy, we have talked about the kids or my parents or the Cutlers. Today, I focused only on me.

I told Dr. Hale about my meltdown last weekend, the day before we left for Durango. I told him how I locked myself in my room to avoid spewing venom on the kids and OJ, only to find myself covered in that very venom and feeling lower than low. I told him of spending hours crying on the floor of my closet (yes, *again*), an endless parade of tears drawing forth what felt like endless emotion.

He led me through an exercise. "Visualize your emotions," he said. "Give each a name, a location in your body, a form, and a color."

I closed my eyes. Anger was the first to appear, the most powerful, living in my chest and shoulders.

Sadness was next, a sharp, throbbing pain in my gut. Guilt, "a gray, amorphous blob," as I called it, filled my head and seeped all over my body. Self-hatred was also in my head, shaped like an arrow, stabbing my brain. Anger popped up again, at the core of guilt and self-hatred, like a cannonball, weighing me down. But love was also there, in my arms and outer chest, as a white, radiant light.

Dr. Hale then led me through a second visualization. "Close your eyes and breathe deeply," he said. "You are a warrior princess. Your body is covered in armor. On your left arm is a heavy, round shield, and in your right hand, a sword."

I could see it. I stood at the top of a grassy hill, looking out over the tall trees, river, and meadows below. My body armor was silvery white and glimmered in the sun, but it was also scratched and dented. My armor protected *me*; my shield protected my family *and* me, and my sword stood for justice.

"Now, piece by piece, you can take the armor off," Dr. Hale said. "Lower your breastplate. Your arm and leg plates. Take off your helmet. Set them on the earth beside you. Sit down. You can set your shield down at your feet. And your sword, too. But, keep your sword and shield handy, because the war is not yet over."

He spoke of Shannon, saying that when she died, a battle began that hasn't stopped. He said, "You've had a year full of lies, deception, and dishonesty." This was true with my parents a little, but mostly with the Cutlers. It caught me off guard, and it struck a sad chord to hear that the war is not over and to know that was true, too.

It's not over. Today's session helped me feel a little less crazy and see that maybe there are good reasons why life feels hard right now. The Cutlers are still trying to put pressure and guilt on us and on Tre to do what they want. They don't seem to see what is best for him or our family, which I resent. We still have to conquer the hurdle of adoption. I pray the Cutlers aren't going to try and interfere with that. We're still healing and coping. It feels much better and easier, and it *is* better.

But it's not over. The war continues, and the warrior princess is resting up for when the battle comes again.

Thursday, August 7

Calling Shannon's doctor's office this morning, my heart was racing and my mouth was dry. I had put it off as long as I could, but I needed medical records for Tre and Brody, something we never did find in all of Shannon's "stuff." When I explained why I was calling, the receptionist said, "Oh, my goodness. I had no idea Shannon had died. What happened?"

Again, I had to figure out how to respond. "She'd been drinking too much wine and took too many acetaminophen pills," I said. It's what I usually say. "Plus one sleeping pill. She never woke up." Then, I always check in with myself. *Is that what really happened? I believe so, in my heart.* She may have died by her own hand, but I never say, *suicide.* It's such a delicate topic, for me and for everyone. Again, I received the "I'm so sorrys" and "How are the boys?" The doctor even called Mom and Dad, later this afternoon, to express his condolences. He was shocked, too. He told Dad he'd been treating Shannon for depression, and Dad called and told me.

It brings everything up again for all of us. Just like every time I meet someone new or run into someone from back in the day. "What happened?" and "How are they doing?" all over again. When I try to socialize with friends—like last night, going out for dessert in honor of a friend who is moving—I smile and participate, but really I am thinking, "They have no clue what this is like." They're talking about shopping and manicures, and it makes me want to disappear.

No one knows how hard this can be. No one even thinks to ask, because why would they? They don't know about the war. They don't know what it's like to try and love two new children the same as the ones you've chosen to have and have raised their whole lives. No one knows that.

Tonight, everything I've been damming up broke free. Little did OJ know when he agreed to go with me to get "first day of school" supplies. It burst as we pulled into the Target parking lot. I sat, weeping, as he did his best to listen. These weren't the first Target tears I had shed. It reminded me of when Kennedy was a newborn and I was postpartum, how I would grab the keys at nine p.m. and say, "I've got to get out of here!" Target therapy.

OJ bears a heavy burden. I'm like silly putty these days—ball me up and I'll roll and bounce, but as soon as I sit still, I melt into the carpet. OJ is the one who gets to scrape me up. He's one of the only ones with whom I can talk, not only because he's in this, too, but because so many of my thoughts and emotions make me feel like a horrible person and mother. I know he accepts me, no matter what. I know he gets it. Not everybody gets it.

Today, a woman from church called, a well-seasoned mother of nine whom I admire greatly. She asked her church-related question, we chatted for a few moments, and then she said, "You know we all admire you. Not many people would choose to take on what you've done. You're a great mother."

My heart warmed at her sentiment, but as I said, "Thank you," I was literally shaking my head, thinking, *No. Don't admire me! You have no idea the mistakes I'm making!*

It shames me, and I want to hide away. Tonight, I pulled it together at Target (by now I'm an expert at quickly pulling myself together), got the hundreds of dollars of school supplies, and made dinner. I got everyone to bed with hugs.

I do what I have to do. Even when I want to hide.

Thursday, August 14

"Bang!" I'd been putting on my makeup to go to counseling when I heard it, coming from the kitchen. Cautiously, I moved to the wall of windows and, sure enough, my nervous thoughts were confirmed. A pretty little blackbird, with a long, pointed beak, lay still on the deck below. Its dark eyes blinked, its body not moving a wink. *Is it dying?* The thought made me sick.

I had to leave right then or I would have missed my appointment. I am definitely no bird doctor, so, not knowing what else to do, I prayed for the bird, that it would heal and be able to fly away. *Silly, right?* With one last look at its still unmoving body, I walked out the door with visions of this poor little bird, flying happily along when, "bang!" it's life is suddenly changed, and might even end. Tears welled in my eyes. I could relate.

I told Dr. Hale about the bird, my reaction, and then about some of my own bangs—the vivid snapshots I keep re-experiencing. Aunt Christina's fateful call. OJ breaking the news as I drove. Seeing my father, siblings, and children find out Shannon had died. Having to explain it all to Tre and Brody. Visiting Shannon's house that very night, wishing to never return

I cried as Dr. Hale said, "Fear, anxiety, vivid snapshots, anger, sleep problems—these are all normal for trauma. And you have been through a lot of trauma in the past year."

He reminded me the year we've had is *not* normal. He helped me feel less guilty, less selfish, and even gave me a speech about selfishness—how it derives from the self and usually indicates a need the self has. My "self" definitely has needs right now. He gave me "permission" for self-focus, self-time, self-care, though it's hard for me to do.

Two hours later, I returned home and nervously made my way to the kitchen window. Dread filled me as I thought of what I would do if the bird had died. I closed my eyes and leaned in to the window. My eyes opened. There was no trace of the bird.

I can only assume that, after taking some time to get its bearings—to gain some strength—that bird flew away. And, I like to imagine, to even greater heights than ever before.

Saturday, August 16

Yesterday was rough. All day, tension pulled at me—hopeless, unhappy, fighting so hard. When OJ got home, all I could do was draw a hot bath and sink under the water, letting it drown everything out. He came in and sat quietly next to the tub. I sat staring at the wall for a while, then looked to his eyes, warm and ready to listen. I opened a conversation.

I told him how Kennedy had come home from preschool, earlier, singing a song she'd learned in Kindergarten, "I'm a little pizza." The pizza had great toppings—cheese, pepperoni, mushrooms. It was proud to be a pizza. But at the end of the song, the pizza accidentally fell on the floor. The last words were, "I used to be a pizza and now I'm a mess!" She sang these words, and even as I praised her singing and gave her a hug, I was crying. Trying not to let her see. Thinking, *That's me. I used to be 'a pizza' and now I'm a mess.*

Something about telling OJ this silly story cracked me wide open. I was literally naked, sobbing in the tub, but emotionally naked, too, every bit of pain gushing out through moaning, and weeping while he sat, feeling helpless, I'm sure. I sobbed and sobbed. Then, I screamed! So loudly, we both jumped.

Feeling even more ashamed, I broke into uncontrollable cries again, rolling onto my side in the tub to avoid OJ's gaze, clinging to myself in a fetal position. I heard OJ move away. I mean, what else could he do? I sobbed even harder, feeling so alone.

Everything poured out—out of my eyes, my nose, my mouth. I coughed and choked up the emotion I'd been caging for months. *Everything* emptied. For over forty minutes.

Finally, completely drained, beyond humiliated, lying still in the now-cold water, I pushed myself up to sitting and slowly lifted my head. Through burning, swollen eyes, I turned my eyes to see OJ, lying on the cold tile next to the tub. He hadn't left after all. He'd been with me the entire time. Seeing me sit up, he didn't say a word. He simply stood, lifted a fluffy towel off the hook, and held it open.

Wrapping me tightly, he picked me up and carried me to the bed, like a baby in its mother's arms. He tucked me in, kissed my forehead, and without a word, dimmed the lights and closed the door. *I'm not alone,* was my final thought as, for the first time in weeks, I closed my eyes and slept peacefully 'til dawn.

Wednesday, August 27

I've been trying to diagnose myself. I'm worried I might have Postpartum Depression again. Or perhaps I have Major Depression or Posttraumatic Stress Disorder or an Anxiety Disorder? I looked all of these up in the DSM-IV—the Diagnostic and Statistic Manual of mental disorders, used to diagnose mental illness—and I fit the criteria for all of them.

One rule of diagnosing, however, is to rule out all possibilities, to find the diagnosis that fits *best,* and, since none of these seemed to, I kept searching. I pulled out my grief book again, and my intuition was correct. My diagnosis is clear: deep, dark grief.

Of the more than one hundred possible symptoms of grief, I made a list of those I am currently experiencing:

> Feeling and behaving differently than normal, feeling unsettled and frightened about that; fear, panic or generalized anxiety, guilt, anger, exaggerated sensitivity to real or imagined slights, bitterness, sense of injustice or disillusionment, alienating others, withdrawal; inappropriate expectations of self (biggie!), sense of worthlessness, self-reproach, self-hatred; feelings of separation and deprivation, loneliness; "normal sense of anger at the deceased," anguish, sadness, yearning, depression and despair; lack of interest in things you used to love, apathy, decreased energy, dependency, hopelessness; feeling out of control, depersonalization, disorganization, lack of concentration, confused, lack of decision-making abilities; irritability, tension, loss of parts of my identity; values and beliefs that were once comforting are less so now; feeling like I'm going crazy; restlessness, inability to sleep, crying, gastrointestinal disturbances; tendency to sigh; lack of strength, physical exhaustion, feelings of emptiness, heaviness, nervousness, tension; searching for something to do; and finally, a "gut-wrenching, gnawing emptiness that needs to be filled and sharp, intense pangs of grief that cut into the heart."[3]

How is that for a list?

Ironically, it actually makes me feel *less* crazy. Seeing these words written in a book allow me to believe that I am somehow normal in my grief. I may be a mess, but at least I am a functional mess. In the words of psychoanalyst, Melanie Klein, "Suffering can be productive. We know that painful experiences of all kinds sometimes stimulate sublimations, or even bring out quite new gifts in some people, who may take to painting, writing, or other productive activities under the stress of frustrations and hardships. Others become more productive in a different way—more capable of appreciating people and things, more tolerant in their relationships to others—they become wiser."[4]

Wiser. That is my ultimate goal, always. It gives me hope that if I stick with grief work, I just may come out of this mess even more *functional* than I was before.

Wednesday, September 10

My mind is busy. Dr. Hale says my rational mind won't let my subconscious speak. He has, therefore, tasked me with taking time each day to listen and write down what my subconscious has to say. Here goes…

I am wounded. I visualize the wound and see myself, at the top of a basement staircase. On the right is a door with a window, streaming light blue. In front of me is a dark blue stairway, descending to black. I walk down and see a woman in the far corner, sitting on the stone floor. Head down, between her knees, arms folded underneath, her stringy hair is strewn about her shoulders. No movement, she looks defeated; she doesn't even lift her eyes as I move gently toward her. She is a prisoner. She is me. I need to set her free.

I think about the years of frustration, sorrow, and anger. I think about the loss of my family, the constant drama, change, and blame. This isn't just Rob and Shannon. This isn't just my postpartum losses, anger with the Cutlers, and frustration about trying to make this family work. No, I am starting to believe this is all just one huge final straw.

I see all the hard times, linked, like a chain spanning more than twenty years of my life. I'm ten, and

Papa dies. I'm fifteen, and Mom has breast cancer. I'm seventeen, and Miki has kidney cancer. I'm eighteen, and Miki dies while OJ is in Argentina for two years on a mission for our church and I am stuck, alone, in a depression or perhaps grief. I'm twenty, marrying the man I adore after two years apart, writing letters every week. I'm twenty-one, and Mom has cancer again, just after my wedding. I'm twenty-two and suffering from Postpartum Depression with my first perfect little boy. My gallbladder is removed after a year of doctor visits and tests, and a few months later, my tonsils. I'm twenty-four and depressed again with my second baby boy. Though it's a little better than before, this is no way to start off being a mother. I'm still twenty-four and starting graduate school in Los Angeles with a five month-old baby, a three year-old, and OJ starting dental school. I'm twenty-five and Grandma Hibbert dies, just before Rob gets skin cancer. I'm twenty-six and stuck in Major Depression while trying to begin my doctoral dissertation. I'm twenty-seven, pregnant with my third, and sicker than ever, trying to complete my last year of graduate school. I'm twenty-eight and graduate with my doctorate, give birth the next week, and move back to Phoenix, five days later. I have my third round of Postpartum Depression, this time with a healthy dose of anxiety thrown, for kicks. I'm twenty-nine, and we move to Flagstaff for a new job, new home, new life. I'm thirty, and my beloved grandfather is rushed to the hospital the day I see him at the temple. He dies of cancer that summer. I'm thirty-one, and OJ gets Diabetes and Celiac Disease just before Rob's cancer returns with a vengeance. I'm thirty-two, and Mom's and Dad's coping skills crumble. Never in my life had I felt as worried about or needed by my parents as I did throughout those months. I'm pregnant and sick again, and we move to a bigger home. Aunt Leslie dies of a rare brain disease. Rob dies. Shannon dies. The boys move in, and I have a baby, from three to six kids in three weeks. I'm thirty-three, trying to form a family, dealing with the Cutlers, my parents, everyone's grief and pain, all the changes and loss.

That just brings me to this year. We're not even through it yet. I can only hope this "final straw" is really the final one.

Tuesday September 18

I am angry with the Cutlers.

Grandma Cutler has started calling Brody and Tre every week. Very curtly, she asks to speak to Tre first, then Brody. "How are you?" she asks each boy, to which they answer, "Fine," and she replies, "Well good. Grandma loves you. Talk to you next week." The whole thing takes four minutes.

Then, once a week they each receive a greeting card with "I miss you! Love, Grandma" written inside. Brody, of course, loves getting mail of any kind, but the cards end up on the floor. Tre is confused by their behavior, and frankly, so am I. If the Cutlers miss the boys so badly, why don't they ask to see them or try to talk to them for real? Colton and Braxton are annoyed and hurt, and I understand why. All along, they've been calling the Cutlers "Grandma and Grandpa," now, suddenly, their "Grandma and Grandpa" won't even acknowledge them or their sisters! They didn't even send a birthday card to Braxton and he was confused and upset. After all, they'd sent one to Colton and Kennedy on their birthdays, plus a present. I had to explain to him, and the others, that I guess the Cutlers only want to be grandparents to Tre and Brody again. Thank goodness my parents and OJ's are grandparents to *all* the kids and understand how to work together to help them feel loved.

Grandpa Cutler, in his role as conservator, hasn't paid us Tre and Brody's support money for the past two months, and *he* never calls to talk to the boys. It's probably better this way, at least for Tre. Grandpa Cutler used to call fairly often, but would only ask to speak with Tre—hardly ever Brody. He'd ask about Tre's Scouting progress and grades. It almost always ended with Tre upset, sometimes in tears. Tre used to ask why his grandpa was so hard on him, why he never asked to talk to Brody, why his grandma never called. None of us had any answers then, and this new behavior doesn't make it any clearer. I don't understand them one bit. It seems so self-serving—not what their grandkids need at all. I wish we did not have to deal with them. I wish they could just be normal, loving grandparents. Or, I wish they would just choose to disappear.

But they're not. I heard from the estate attorney yesterday, they are requesting documents about the conservatorship. We have no idea what they are up to, but it's looking like it will be a while before we can move forward. I want the estate closed, adoption complete, and Grandpa Cutler out as conservator. I want to get past the first year since Shannon died and be done with it all!

I'm sorry. I just need to vent, but as soon as it's out, then the guilt sets in. *This is not who I am.* That's the worst part of all this—I can't handle the tension. It makes me feel like a crazy woman. I really do not like living in anger and fear.

Tuesday, October 7

Thank goodness for the kids. They sure know how to lighten things up.

Yesterday, eleven and a half year-old Tre was holding Sydney and said, "I know people always think *their* babies are the cutest, but Sydney is like, really the cutest baby in the *world*." The look in his eyes said it all; he was smitten.

I have to say, I agree. It's not just the way she

looks; it's her personality. Eleven months old, Sydney sure livens things up. She loves climbing up and down the stairs, dances whenever music comes on, and plays peek-a-boo with anyone who looks at her. Her favorite question is, "Whas-at?" as she points to everything around her, and she has an incredible sense of humor for a baby, always trying to make us laugh.

Kindergartener Kennedy has a boyfriend. "His name is Eric," she told me yesterday, her eyes going all dreamy, and sighing. "We sit by each other, and Mom, we just both love each other, okay!" So dramatic. So hilarious. The other day, I tried to get her ready for school and brought three outfits from which to choose. She gave an annoyed look and then, pointing to each, said, "Zero! Zero! Zero!" Boy, are we in for trouble when she hits the teen years!

Seven year-old Brody has been asking me to do everything for him—like finding his socks, putting his lunchbox in his backpack, or, tonight, like getting him a drink. He asked even though he was doing nothing and I was clearly busy, taking care of crying Sydney.

"Why do you keep asking me to do all these things?" I asked him. "You can see how busy I am with Sydney right now, and you're just sitting there."

"Well," he replied, "you never really do anything for me, anyway."

I stopped and stared, open-mouthed. "What? Who buys all your food, makes your meals, helps with homework and reading, and tucks you in?"

He thought for a moment, then nodded, and said, "I guess you have a point."

I got him the drink, just to be extra nice.

Today, he asked if he could have two cakes for his birthday, this February. When I asked why, he replied, "Because I want one to eat and one to smash in my face."

Yes, thank goodness for the kids. They aren't

easy, but they sure do add sweet spice to life. And boy, can we all use some sweetness.

Saturday, October 11

The one-year anniversary of losing Shannon is coming up. We've all been focusing on how to approach next week's date, how to handle it with the kids, how to handle it ourselves. It's been on my mind, keeping me up at night—until four a.m. last night.

Or perhaps, it was yesterday's "surprise" that kept me up. A summons, in the mail, from Cutlers, to appear in court for "grandparent visitation rights." *Surprise!* The document accused us of being "hostile" and refusing to let them see the boys. *Complete lies!* In fact, earlier yesterday morning I mailed the Cutlers some pictures of the kids and a copy of their report cards with a note, "Thought you might like to see these." I had just been getting ready to call and see if they wanted to visit with the boys when we go to Phoenix next week when I got the mail.

Needless to say, OJ and I are angry and confused about why they are doing this, and especially why they would heap this on our family. This week of all weeks! After talking it out and putting my deep breathing skills to the test, OJ and I actually called the Cutlers anyway and, saying nothing of the summons, told them they could see the boys Monday, while we are in Phoenix. It was the right thing to do. I already feel better as I try to understand, forgive, and be patient, despite what they are doing.

The other day Brody asked me, "What's your favorite thing in the whole world?" I didn't even have to think before I replied, "You guys—my kids and my husband." Looking into his big brown eyes, I asked him what his favorite thing in the world is. "My family," he said, and hugged me.

That moment. That is why I keep trying. That is

why I won't ever quit.

Friday, October 17

I've been waiting for this day since last October seventeenth. One year since Shannon died.

The kids were taken care of, thanks to OJ. He made them a pancake breakfast and drove them to school. He knew what I needed—time alone, time to show up. I went to bed not wanting to. Show up, that is. I slept from ten last night until ten this morning, zonked out, dead to the world. I don't remember the last time I slept so hard or so long.

But show up, I did. First, with a quiet morning, sitting on the back deck, watching the sun and wind on the trees. Then, by driving—I wasn't sure where. I ended up pulling off the road, just before the pine trees of Flagstaff drop into the red rocks of Sedona, into a small dirt parking lot, at the beginning of a trailhead. No one was around. It seemed to be waiting for me.

I hiked to the end of the wooded trail and found my secluded spot: a mossy boulder on the edge of a cliff that dropped into a canyon of red rock and green pine. The weather was perfect, the woods quiet, as if everything were paying respect to this day with me. I sat on the boulder, overlooking the cliff and felt...pensive, I guess. I didn't want to move or "do" anything because I didn't want to distract myself. Today, I wanted to let the defenses down.

So, I sat, journal in hand, and breathed, and let myself feel what was there. I wrote: *I want to say 'goodbye' to Shannon. But I can't. There are too many other things that still need to be said. Too many things that need to be understood. I find myself trying to make it real—trying to picture her dead body, to make myself feel the trauma, loss, terror, pain—but I can't. Right now, it's not real. I'm trying to force what I think I should feel, but I'm not feeling it. I'm just here—present. Maybe that is the best thing I can give to Shannon's memory. Showing up. Being present.*

I eventually made my way home from the rock and somehow managed a day of silence, able to honor Shannon. And myself. At dinner, it was time to honor the kids. OJ called us together, we blessed the food, and then, I brought up Shannon. The kids were so focused on school, friends, and Halloween plans, they didn't even remember today. I didn't want them to feel too sad, so I hesitated even bringing it up, but I also didn't want them to think we forgot. So, like we did back in July, to remember Rob, I shared a favorite memory of Shannon.

"Shannon and I were only sixteen months apart, so we always shared a room, growing up. We used to drive each other crazy. She would steal my clothes, and I would boss her around. But at night, we'd talk about our day, tell stories, and laugh. We definitely fought. But no one laughed together as much as we did. That's what I loved most about her. And what I miss the most."

The kids smiled and asked for more. "Shannon was a deep sleeper, and I've always been a light one. When she had intense dreams or nightmares, she'd wake me up saying crazy things. I could never quite tell if she were really awake or still asleep. Like the time when we were teenagers and she swore there was a little girl in the corner of our room, laughing at her. She was so convincing, and I kept saying, 'There's nothing there. You're dreaming. Go back to sleep.' She listened, and fell right back asleep, but I was up for hours, completely freaked out!"

The kids laughed, and they and OJ started sharing memories of their own. "One time, Shannon and I were playing air hockey at an arcade," OJ said. "She was so mad at me, because I kept scoring on her!"

"Uh," I interrupted, "she was mad because you were cheating, dear. I was there, remember?"

"I wasn't cheating," he said, emphasizing the

"cheat." "I was just using some new moves. Anyway, she *thought* I was cheating, and she was so mad, she ran out the door of the arcade. Rob had to chase after her to calm her down. I don't know why I liked to bug her so much, but it sure was funny. We had some good times."

Tre remembered going to Hawaii with his mother just the summer before. "We went on these awesome hikes, and one day, we saw Ben Affleck and Matt Damon in the ocean at the beach!" Always an animated speaker, just like Rob, Tre was sure excited tonight, gesturing his arms like crazy as he spoke.

Twelve year-old Braxton and nine year-old Colton remembered playing with Tre and Brody at their house in Cave Creek and Shannon watching them. "She was just really cool," Braxton said, his blue eyes smiling. "Yeah, she let us have the best treats and she helped us set up forts for sleepovers," Colton said, the light freckles on his tanned nose crinkling with joy.

"*I* remember Shannon," Kennedy interrupted, eagerly. "She was nice. And pretty." She shook her long blond hair when she said "pretty," then hugged me tightly, before hugging everyone else, one by one. It brought smiles to an otherwise gloomy time. Even Sydney was smiling as we remembered Shannon. It helped us remember *her*, and not just what *happened to* her. OJ and I hugged each child, and, one by one, they were excused and ran off to play. Ran off, to forget again.

I am not ready to forget. Not yet. All year, my focus has been, "Just get us through the first year, and then we'll see where we are." So, here we are. *But, where are we?* One year is gone, and now what? I'm not ready to move on; I'm not ready to leave everything behind. I'm hopeful that day will eventually come, but one year isn't enough time.

No. I was wrong. We just had to survive the first year. And now? Now, we just keep surviving. I'm hopeful, though. Hopeful, as we continue surviving, we will work our way, eventually, to thriving.

SIXTEEN
Hope

"May you have enough happiness to make you sweet, enough trials to make you strong,
enough sorrow to keep you human, enough hope to make you happy."
~Anonymous[1]

We can all use a little hope. Hope is the light that shines in the darkest winter, the one we take for granted until we find ourselves desperate in the cold. "Hope is faith holding out its hand in the dark,"[2] and in choosing to grasp that hand, we choose to live, for hope keeps us going, reminding us there is something to keep going *for*.

I'm no stranger to hopelessness. As a core component of depression, I have experienced, overcome, and helped others overcome it. Hopelessness is, in my mind, one of the worst emotions we can feel, because it leads to giving up, to quitting, to saying, "It's too hard. I can't do it." Yet, I have often witnessed, in the darkness of hopelessness, a spark. That spark may be impossibly small and may not even be noticeable at first, but when I see it, I know all is not lost. That spark is hope.

Hope is the *why* to our *how*. Viktor Frankl, psychiatrist and author of one of my favorite books, *Man's Search for Meaning,* quoted Neitzche, writing, "He who has a why to live for can bear with almost any how."[3] It's one of my favorite quotes of all time, reminding me, as long as I have a "why," hope is possible. As Frankl survived a Nazi concentration camp, he observed that "any attempt to restore a man's inner strength in the camp had first to succeed in showing him some future goal...one had to give them a why—an aim—for their lives in order to strengthen them to bear the terrible how of their existence."[4] Discovering *why* is "the aim" that strengthens us, that gives us hope. While we may not always be able to discover answers to our *questions* of "Why?"—why we are given a "terrible existence," for instance—we may always choose to discover our *statements* of why—why we carry on existing, despite the terribleness. Our *why* may be family, friends, or faith. It may be the desire to experience the future, to overcome, to know, or to grow. *Why* is simply another word for hope and the belief that a better future awaits.

As Irish poet, Oscar Wilde, said, "We are all in the gutter, though some of us are looking at the stars."[5] The next time we feel the gutter, we can take a deep breath, look up, and choose to see the stars. We can remember *why* we are choosing to see those stars, letting it inspire hope and swell within, like the promise of spring. After all, as this Eskimo Proverb inspires, "Perhaps they are not stars, but rather openings in heaven where the love of our lost ones pours through and shines down upon us to let us know they are happy."

Now *that* gives me hope.

Monday, October 27

One year since the boys came to our home, and today OJ and I were in court.

It didn't go as smoothly as I'd hoped. The Cutler's attorney is pushing for a full-day trial! It was horrible, sitting there, not able to say a word in our defense as their attorney accused us of "keeping the grandchildren from their loving grandparents," and "not even trying to work with them." *Lies!* I felt so insulted.

The big question, burning in my mind was, *why? Why are they doing this?* No phone calls. No sitting down together to talk it out. No attempts to repair relationships they have simply cut off—with us, yes, *and* the kids, including Tre and Brody. Nothing! Just court, money, time, and stress. *Too much stress.*

I can't handle all this stress. It's worse than any days of grief. Short-tempered and irritable, I go from zero to sixty any time I have to even talk about court stuff, then hate how out of control it makes me feel. I'm like an angry mama bear most of the time—on guard, looking for any slight toward my kids or my family, and taking it all personally. My worrying is through the roof. I'm not sleeping. I'm not healthy.

The only bright spot is that OJ and I are in this together, one hundred percent: a team. He tells me I'm not a terrible person for feeling the way I feel. He loves me, even if I can't hold it together as well as he can. The other day, he reassured me, "Not everyone could do this, dear, but *we can*." I remembered his words tonight as we celebrated our one-year family-of-eight anniversary with popcorn, Kit-Kats, and the latest *Indiana Jones* movie. A moment of joy, everyone safe and happy, and I took it in.

Unfortunately, the kids had gotten busted for climbing out the upstairs window, onto the roof, with five year-old Kennedy, while they were supposed to be babysitting, so they had early bedtime. After finally getting them all in bed, I went to my room and found Colton there, crying.

"What is wrong?" I asked. This was uncharacteristic of Colton, who is usually smiling. The only times he cries is when he gets in trouble. He's so self-disciplined and hard on himself, but he wasn't in trouble tonight. At least, not any more.

"I miss Shannon and Rob," he said. "They were my favorite aunt and uncle, and I'll never see them again."

Oh, honey.

His golden blond hair, longer now, in the skater style the boys loved, brushed my face as I held him tightly and whispered, "It's okay to miss them. I miss them, too." *Poor guy,* I thought. Colton has such an innocent joy about him, it hurt to see him suffering so. "We will see them again, honey, you know that, right?" His watery blue eyes looked into mine and he nodded. I pulled him back in. "Yes. We will see them again."

We can do it. I believe OJ is right. We *can.*

Friday, November 7

Another morning in court, sitting silently while our two attorneys argued over whether or not OJ and I need to be evaluated to see if we are psychologically fit as parents.

We need to be evaluated? It's almost like shared custody, how much "grandparent visitation" the Cutlers want. The boys would be forced to go with them on vacations, to visit them for several weeks each summer, and, if their grandparents win this court case, every other weekend! *Do they really expect us to drive two hours to Phoenix and back every other weekend, for grandparent visitation?* If they get their way, *every* interaction with Tre and Brody would be court-ordered: the kids would have no say at all. *And* we *need to be evaluated?*

The judge ended up ruling we need a "visitation evaluation," not quite the complete psychological battery the Cutlers were pushing for, but still infuriating. She also ordered all of us to attend court mediation. I'm hoping this will at least give us a chance to talk this out!

At one point, their lawyer said, "We acknowledge that the Cutlers are neither parents nor custodians—yet." *What? Yet?* Are they going to try and take these kids? Honestly, I would not put it past them! Talk about feeling a complete lack of control.

I'm trying to stay focused on what matters. I have worked for over a year, now, to make this mess into a unified family, and the Cutlers think they're going to swoop in and mess it back up? They can think again. I am deep breathing and praying, and I keep working on peace, love, and forgiveness, but just when I start feeling successful, BAM! Another blow. I am slammed to the floor again, as fear walks smugly back into my heart.

Saturday November 15

What a week. I'm still trying to wrap my head around it all.

Monday, OJ's Grandpa Hibbert died.

I guess you would say he died "of old age." Still, it jolted me. Another death. Another unexpected loss I should have expected if I weren't already so immersed in the land of the dead.

Monday was also the day that OJ, the four boys, and I went to family counseling and finally broke the news to the boys about court.

We'd been able to keep them out of it until now, wanting to preserve their emotions and their relationships with their grandparents, but with the Cutlers pushing for a court-mandated visit over Thanksgiving, we couldn't wait any longer. We hoped Dr. Hale could help us break the news honestly and fairly, and that's exactly what we did.

"Tre and Brody's grandparents have taken us to court because they want visitation rights with them," we said.

"But they can come visit us any time they want," Tre replied, confused.

OJ and I smiled at each other. "Yes. We know," we said. "But they don't seem to think they can."

We explained that Tre and Brody would be going on a visit over Thanksgiving, and that's why we were telling them about this now. We told them not to worry—that we were handling it, and that everything would turn out okay. We explained it in terms they could understand and we hoped would not burden them any more than necessary. Dr. Hale then stepped in and asked the boys how they were feeling.

"Grandma's always nice, but she is on Grandpa's

side, not ours," Tre observed. Then Brody added, "Yeah, and then she just goes to sleep when we visit. They sleep a lot." Braxton was not just hurt; he was angry. We were all angry and couldn't quite understand why the Cutlers have stopped being grandparents to all the kids, and why they want to start forcing Tre and Brody on visits. They were honest and open with how they were feeling, which was a relief, though it stung to see them hurting so much.

Wednesday was my own therapy session.

I'd already started to cry twice before I made it to counseling. Once, thanks to our babysitter, Liz, asking if I wanted to bring Sydney more often, now that Kennedy's in Kindergarten. And, twice, thanks to hearing Green Day's *Wake Me Up When September Ends* on the radio, which always reminds me of grief and loss. It's ridiculous, I know, but questions and songs have a way of doing that to me lately. I feel so guarded, thanks to this court stuff, that questions, especially kind ones, seem impossible to answer and push my emotions too far. Songs, especially lately, have been haunting me. The same ones, over and over, like Coldplay's *Viva La Vida*, reminding me I used to be something, and now I'm not, giving me a hope that someday I might be better than before. Or, the hardest to hear: The Fray's *How to Save a Life*. I think of Shannon dying, alone in her bed, every time I hear that song.

Even so, I felt like I had nothing to discuss today with Dr. Hale. I didn't tell him that, of course. I know, from experience, when a client says, "I have nothing to talk about," something big is usually lurking. So, instead, I said, "I'm just tired of myself. I don't want to burden anyone else with my negativity. I feel like I need to suck it up and move on."

He reframed this, speaking for me. "I'm hurting," he said. "But I don't feel I deserve others' support." *True. Hurting. Obviously, I am.*

We did another visualization, this time through "the land of the dead." As he spoke of ruins and fog where those we have lost remain, two words stuck out like knives: "Emptiness," and "Waiting." Such simple words, yet they evoked in me an almost sob-like reaction. *I do feel empty, and I do feel like I'm waiting. Holding my breath. Waiting for whatever is coming next.*

When the visualization was done, I didn't want it to be over. "I'm not ready to leave," I said.

"What still remains undone in the land of the dead?" Dr. Hale asked.

It took several moments to form an answer. "I need to actually *feel sad* for Shannon. I've barely begun to feel that," I said. "I miss her, and I have a right to miss her." Strange how it's taken me over a year to realize the right I have to miss her, as if everyone else's grief had somehow mattered more. "And I need time to recover," I added. "I can't take any more. I'm wiped out. I need to recover before I can enter the land of the living again."

When I got home, I wanted to hide in bed, but, instead, hid my sadness, because I had kids to care for, dinner to make, and a parenting class to teach that night—my last in a series of eight weekly classes. I'd loved feeling like a teacher again, loved teaching my friends and other excellent parents I'd met through church. Yes, it had been a meaningful experience for me—to feel capable and needed again. Still, I'd also felt like a hypocrite. Last week's lesson had been on anger management, of all things! Right in the midst of my own battles with anger, self-doubt, and court, with my own intense parenting struggles and failures, here I was teaching "the right thing" to do? It didn't sit well with me. Good thing they were finally coming to an end.

It was a powerful evening, sharing our feelings about being parents. I tied it all up by saying how parenting is one of our greatest opportunities to grow. How, as we model self-development, our children will follow and grow too. It was a good ending. I felt I'd done my best. Then, when I got home, OJ said something that caught me off guard. "You really are important," he said. "Look how you've inspired all those people." Whether he said it because that's what he was feeling or because he knew that's what *I* needed to feel, it didn't matter. I *felt* important. Important to OJ. That's all I needed.

Thursday was Grandpa Hibbert's funeral.

I was asked to sing "O My Father" at the gravesite, a hymn of returning Home, one I knew would bring emotion for me. That hymn had moved me to tears when I'd sung it in church a couple months before Rob had died. I hadn't been able to hold it together as I'd sung the final words, "let me come and dwell with you,"[6] thinking of Rob. My petty worries were replaced by love as twelve year-old Braxton offered, the night before, to accompany my singing with his guitar. He'd only been taking lessons for a few months, but was already better than I; he's so determined when he wants to be good at something. Kind of like me. Though we barely had time to practice, he played beautifully, and though I could have done better with my singing—softer, prettier, less emotional—he inspired me to push my fears aside, let go, and sing from the heart.

After the service, OJ's dad, Dave, gave me a warm hug. "Thank you so much for that beautiful song," he said. "My dad loved that song. It was perfect." He hugged me again, emotion in his eyes. Then, he told Braxton the same, hugging him and giving him a red Swedish fish from his stash in his pocket. Braxton smiled. A tender moment with our dear Papa Dave as we laid his dear father to rest.

OJ, the kids, and I then walked over to our family graves, steps away, right where we'd left them. Shannon. Rob. Miki. My Grandpa. And, a little past them, my Papa. We gathered around the headstones, took our moment as a family, and remembered just a little. Then, I shut it off. Detached. I let myself forget death for the rest of the day.

Friday, yesterday, was Sydney's first birthday. Unfortunately, OJ and I were gone most of the afternoon, at our three-hour court-mandated mediation session with the Cutlers. OJ's mom stayed with Sydney, and the other kids while we were at the courthouse. When we finally returned home, later that evening, we watched her open a present and make a mess of her little cake. She was too tired for much else, so we saved the other gifts for the next day, and she went to bed early. *Happy Birthday.* Oh well, at least she didn't know what she missed.

Overall, the mediation session went surprisingly well, though the first hour was not pretty. We were trying to explain our concerns to the mediator while Bill and Kay Cutler were defending themselves, cutting off every sentence, or so it felt. I was getting frustrated.

Soon, their words were making our point. Attempting to explain themselves, they called the kids "liars," "thieves," and deceitful," because they had "stolen" food at their house when they were visiting and "lied" about dripping water on the floor after getting out of the pool. The mediator was simply trying to understand—just like we've been trying to do all this time. He attempted to clarify, "You think the kids are liars and thieves?"

"Yes! I just said that," Bill replied, clearly irritated.

At one point, the mediator actually shook his head, widening and rolling his eyes. He looked at me, his expression saying, "Whew! What is this guy all about?" For the first time since this whole thing began, I felt like someone was actually sympathetic towards us. For the first time, I felt hope.

The mediator worked for the next two hours,

trying to help the Cutlers understand our perspective. "I encourage you to drop this case and go to family therapy with the kids and Christi and OJ, instead," he said. "It will lead to a much better outcome for everyone." I felt so relieved! Of course, I agreed, wholeheartedly. These issues will never be resolved in court. They are matters of the heart, and need to be talked out, worked out, gently, face-to-face. The Cutlers had a hard time agreeing, of course, but in the end, said they would do it: drop the case and go to family therapy.

As we walked out the door, the mediator stopped me by the elbow. "Oh, my," he said. "You've got your work cut out for you, dealing with that guy. He is *unbelievably* controlling! *Good luck.*" He patted me on the back. I could feel his empathy, and it meant more than he could know. *This really is hard.* I felt validated.

A crushing weight was lifted and replaced by heavenly love as I recalled the fast our church members had done for us last Sunday and the scripture I'd randomly opened to just before we'd left for mediation. "Look unto God with firmness of mind and pray unto him with exceeding faith, and he will console you in your afflictions, and he will plead your cause, and send down justice upon those who seek your destruction."[7] Consoled, I was. Justice had finally been found.

The verse went on to say, "Lift up your heads and receive the pleasing word of God, and feast upon his love; for ye may, if your minds are firm, forever." How could I not feel His love as OJ and I left that courtroom and actually hugged each Bill and Kay goodbye, whispering, "We're sorry for everything that's happened. We *love* you. The *kids* love you. We will make this work."

Yes, it was quite a ragged week. But at least it's had a soft ending.

Friday, November 21

It seems our hope was a little too hopeful. The Cutlers are not cancelling the court case.

After days of waiting, trying to get them to talk with us, and finally expecting the worst, they faxed us their "proposal." Not only were they not cancelling the case, they were pushing the limits with their demands. "Twice a month weekend visits" and "Eight weeks every summer" were among the worst. I couldn't stop myself from telling OJ I was "Done! Tired of pleasing them and playing nice and giving in and not defending ourselves!" Here we are, *faxing* back and forth with the Cutlers—because they won't talk to us on the phone—trying to counter their demands, while meeting with attorneys who are telling us what we should do now.

OJ and I are spent. Not only are we dealing with the Cutlers, but the kids have had half days all week, thanks to parent-teacher conferences, and Sydney's been sick, on top of the usual sports, Scouts, and activities. Yesterday, Colton and Tre found out they made the "All-Star" Basketball teams, while Braxton did not. I was so happy for Tre and Colton, but basketball is Braxton's sport—the thing he loves most, the thing he does best. Even I was shocked that he wasn't selected. I tried to explain to Braxton, "I know you're hurt, but there is greater competition in your grade, honey. You can't compare Tre making it with you not making it. It doesn't mean anything about *you*." But they were *both* upset. Tre, because we'd already said the boys couldn't play All-Stars this year, because there is way too much going on, *and* Braxton, because he didn't make the team.

It makes me, again, question myself as a mother. I feel badly I can't give my kids all the opportunities other parents can—to be on traveling teams or be at every activity or field trip. Those things feel important to the kids. As Kennedy complained to me just the other day, "You're the *only* parent who doesn't come and eat lunch with us!" *At the cafeteria? Regularly? People do that? Are you kidding?* I know it can't be true that I'm the only one, but I live in an area with super-parents who are super-involved in school and activities. It can leave me feeling inadequate, or even worse, make me criticize those other parents in my mind. *Don't they have anything better to do with their time?* That leaves me criticizing myself. *You're awful to think such things!*

On the outside, I guess I might seem pulled together, like I'm handling things brilliantly. I'm quieter lately, not wanting to spill fear and negativity onto others, yet I still function. I get dressed, look nice, act fine, smile, and nod and do all I've been asked to do. I could see how other people might not even know to ask if I am all right, but inside, I couldn't be more messed up.

Just this afternoon, I was literally shaking telling my friends, Kathy and Denise, about the court stuff. I'm fearful and angry and hurt, and I don't want the kids to know and worry about what's going on, so I hold it all in. But having friends there to check on me, to sit with me for an hour, I let it out. They saw the real me, dressed in sweats with a messy ponytail, I didn't even try to cover my dark circles. I shared how afraid I am that the Cutlers might try to prevent us from adopting the boys, how terrified I feel at the thought of them breaking up the family we've worked so hard to create and heal. Then, when I thought Tre overheard me talking about court and his grandparents, they saw me lose it. Tre hadn't heard, but the damage was done. I broke down. "See," I said to them, sobbing, "I can't talk about it to anyone." This stuff is harder than anything I've been through so far. It's accusations and courts and judges and feeling judged and second-guessing myself as a result. I honestly don't know *what* to think or feel most of the time.

Last night, I ended up acting a little crazy. Or at

least, *trying* to. Saying ridiculous things and pushing OJ away. He stayed with me the whole time, saying, "Honey, you're trying so hard to be mean and self-destructive, but you just can't. It's not you," in this "aren't you so cute," sort of voice. Thank goodness I have OJ to anchor me. It's definitely not good to be falling apart when we have major decisions to make and my rational abilities want to check out.

It's as if my brain has said to my emotions, "I'm worn out! I quit! *You* take over!" And my emotions are doing just that. No more protective disengagement or dissociation. Just emotions. If I were in therapy, Dr. Hale would probably make me sort them out. I will go ahead and try. Fear is in my chest, my core. Hunger, literal and figurative, is in my belly. My head aches. Disappointment and sorrow show on my face. Anxiety is making my hands twitch. Restlessness is in my toes, and heaviness is in my legs. Panic in my heart and chest comes in waves like a storm. I breathe slowly and deeply, but lack air. My eyelids are heavy. Anger pulses over me. Criticism, doubt, and negativity invade my thoughts, while my brain attempts to disconnect. A sly smile is on the face of fear, panic, and the anger pulsating; they're all in this together. Hope? Where is hope? It's somewhere in there, but being crushed by panic. Hope is my heart and panic is trying to smother it.

But tonight hope is returning, for we have a plan.

After many hours, meeting with two different attorneys, it is finally clear. Our best option is to move forward with adoption—*without telling the Cutlers*.

The plan is to make the "grandparent visitation" agreement at least manageable, then, to sign it and go along with whatever it says—while secretly completing the adoption. I had already started a "free" adoption, through the county attorney's office, and using our private attorney will be much more expensive. But it will be quicker, and we can't afford to wait. Apparently, the laws of Arizona state if the children are adopted the "grandparent visitation rights" will immediately be void. We also don't need anybody's permission to adopt because the kids have been with us since they were orphaned, and we are the legal guardians.

So, for now, we are hiding the adoption from everyone. Because if Bill Cutler found out, we feel certain he would intervene. My nerves are shot. I hate being deceitful, but it also feels reassuring to finally have a plan, to finally be able to take charge and do *something* to protect my kids. Knowing *why* we are doing this restores my hope that in a few months we may finally, legally, be a family, and we may finally, permanently, be free.

Saturday, November 22

Today is my birthday. I didn't remind anyone and told OJ and my parents not to give me anything. I just put it out of my head and attempted to immerse myself in boys' basketball games and Kennedy's dance practice.

Then, I came home, and, surprise! Mom and Dad had driven up from Phoenix, decorated my house, and driven home. They'd left streamers, hats, noisemakers, confetti, balloons, a beautiful plant, a card, a bracelet, and dark chocolates. It brought me to tears— a mixture of gratitude and sorrow. How many years had I wished for something like this from my parents? It felt ironic, though, that they'd chosen *this one* to celebrate me, because, though deeply grateful for their acknowledgement, time, and love, I did not want to celebrate today. I just couldn't.

I called to say "Thank you," but ended up sobbing and unable to speak. Eventually, I choked out, "I'm sorry. I just feel like I've lost a year of my life. I feel so low. Unworthy. I'm sorry I can't be happier and more grateful. I just can't today." They said they understood, that they loved me, and that they were proud of me. That meant something to me, even if I felt undeserving.

The kids kept asking what I was going to "do" today, and OJ kept trying to make me feel better by planning something "fun." But all I kept thinking was, *how can I turn thirty-four? What happened to thirty-three?* I didn't want fun, and the pressure was building until I feared I would pop.

I reluctantly settled on what seemed my only option: quarantine. I quarantined myself in the guest room—closed the blinds, locked the door, sank into bed with a PB&J, chips, carrots, a donut, and dark chocolate, and watched pure escape television to forget what today was *supposed* to be.

Now, it's ten p.m., and I've made it through.

Tonight, as I ponder the past year I have missed, I want to reward myself for so much hard work—for not giving up. The real surprise is that, tonight, as I write, I feel a little spark of hope, of some future joy. Dr. Hale says that's what's at the end of all this for me: joy. For now, I'll just have to trust him, as I cling to my little spark and simply move on—one-foot-in-front-of–the-other, knee-deep, through the mud.

Sunday, November 30

Mud is good for growing things, right? I sure hope so, because I am deep in it. It's official. I'm depressed.[8]

That's what Dr. Hale said on Monday, "Helplessness and Hopelessness? Sounds like depression." I should have seen it, but it's news to me, and depressing news at that. Why is this such a shock? I told OJ I feel unmotivated, lost, pessimistic, and this makes me feel like I've failed. "I thought I'd be better by now," I said. "I thought I was stronger."

I told him how grieving was so much easier than this. It had a purpose. I understood the need to grieve, and, hard as it was, there was value in the process. But this? Depression? It feels pointless.

As Dr. Hale reminded me Monday, "These are *symptoms*. They aren't *you*." A line I've told countless clients. A line I had no option but to believe. And, for the first time ever, I discussed taking an antidepressant. I know. I'm a hypocrite! I've helped so many clients understand how an antidepressant might be the missing piece that will help them get over the hump of depression, and yet deep down I've always felt that it was not for me. Mom used to always say things like, "You're depressed! You need Prozac." I think it was her way of making us the same, which only pushed me farther away from ever wanting to rely on a medication to feel better. *I don't want to be depressed like my mother has been for so long.*

Now, I'm starting to see an antidepressant as a possibility. I can't continue feeling so low when I need to be at my best. I can't afford to keep saying, "I'll feel happy when…" We just signed the visitation agreement with the Cutlers, and Tre and Brody will have to go on their first court-ordered visit for a week over Christmas break. The adoption process, we've learned, could take months, if not longer. Or worse. I know about worse. The war is not yet over. Happiness is only to be found now. I've been working on feeling well, for over a year on my own, doing everything I can think of—exercise, nutrition, writing, supplements, massage, therapy—and I've come a long way. But I want to feel happy again. I want to have fun again. I want to feel inspired and inspire others. I want to feel like myself again. It's time to stop fighting, and simply submit.

Could a little pill be the missing piece I need to help me grow?

Sunday, December 14

I'm staring at this tiny, blue antidepressant I'm supposed to start taking today. I've had the prescription for two weeks and the bottle of pills for one, continuously telling myself I don't need it. I've put it off as long as I can, and now, here I am.

I'll admit, I do not want to take it. *Must I?* I probably shouldn't allow myself to make these kinds of decisions when I'm so tired. Insomnia has been the worst part of this depression, keeping me up until the early hours. It was four this morning before I fell asleep.

I talked with Dr. Hale about it. He agreed I don't *need* an antidepressant, but understood why I might *want* to use one for a while. I've been hammered by everything. I'm weak. Then, add depression, and it just feels impossible. I told Dr. Hale, "I just want to recover!" He gently replied, "I think there is more to *un*-cover before you can *re*-cover." Unfortunately, I know he is right, but I feel more like hiding *under* my covers. Right now, *I cannot uncover any more.*

I realize I haven't really been living for far too long. I've been coping, surviving, managing, getting by—but coping is not living. I want to engage, set goals, dream, and travel again. I want to return to the land of the living. This little pill might just be the final ticket that gets me there. I want to do this for the kids, for OJ, and for me. I want me back. I looked to the pill and sighed.

It's time to leave winter and plant myself in the hope of spring.

Bottoms up!

Our family, after.

PART III:
SPRING

Year of
CHEERFULNESS

Spring is the melting, the warming, the blooming.
The hopeful shoots of green and the cleansing rain.
Spring is cheerfully stepping outside in the light
to find freezing winds, forcing retreat.
Friendly tulips one day, quarrelsome snow the next,
spring is unpredictable.
But the hope of spring encourages, whistles, beckons us
to step out and discover
the sun
is smiling down.

SEVENTEEN
Plant Yourself

"Is the spring coming?" he said. "What is it like?"...
"It is the sun shining on the rain and the rain falling on the
sunshine..."
~Frances Hodgson Burnett, The Secret Garden

I don't know about where you live, but in my hometown of Flagstaff, Arizona, the weather of spring is anyone's guess. Tired of the snow and cold of winter, I am overjoyed when the warm front of spring finally swoops in, only to feel duped a couple of days later when I wake to either another smattering of snow or a different visitor—the wind. These are strong, crazy, swirling winds we're talking about here, cold, blasting winds. It always catches me off guard. Out my window it looks clear, bright, and warm, but things, in spring, are not always as they seem.

Technically, spring begins on March twentieth or twenty-first, the Spring Equinox, and is comprised of the months of March, April and May. It is signaled by a greater presence of light, the sun rising earlier each morning and setting a little later each evening. For me, the season of spring is filled with hope for warmth, light, and beauty. But, it is also unpredictable. It is optimistic and lovely and disappointing and dreadful all in the same week. As we thaw from the wintery times of life, the spring before us can feel the same—optimistic, lovely, disappointing, dreadful. We want so badly to feel "better" to be "happy," to get "over" things of the past. And we *do*...for a day or two, or a week, but then we are blown right back into that freshly thawed and rained upon mud, again.

Like I said before, though, mud is good for growing things. Well, maybe not *mud* exactly, but dirt, soil. In fact, the darker the soil, the richer and more nutrient-dense it is. Spring is all about digging in that soil and making things grow. When I looked up the word "grow" in the dictionary here's what I found: "to spring up and develop to maturity; to increase in size by assimilation of material into the living organism; to promote the development of."[1] Now, we're obviously not just talking about plants here. No, we are talking about growing ourselves—springing up to maturity, increasing in figurative size by assimilating information, and ultimately, about promoting our personal development. Life gives us countless opportunities for growth, but far too often we fail to see them for what they really are. We see the obstacle, the opposition, the obstruction, but we fail to see the *opportunity*.

So let's see it, right now, for what it is. Because, to me, G.R.O.W. means: Grasp the Repeating Opportunities for Wisdom. *G*rasp—reach out your hand and take hold of life's lessons. They will keep Repeating until you do. See them for what they are—Opportunities to gain *W*isdom. Yes, when life throws you in the mud, plant yourself and G.R.O.W.[2]

It's okay, you know. It's okay to get blown about a little, to bloom only to find frost nipping at us, to finally feel the warming sun only to see a blanket of snow the very next sunrise, to again be thrown into the mud. That is life. That is healing. It is a process, not an outcome, and the point is to not only *go* through it but to *grow* through it. We all know the line from John Lennon, "Life is what happens while you're busy making other plans." Well, spring is what happens while we're busy dealing with winter. One day, we simply wake up and see the sun shining, the birds chirping, the warmth returning. One day, we will wake up and see how much we have grown.

Monday, January 5

I've finally settled on my goal for this year— cheerfulness, inspired by OJ. After telling him I had no idea what to focus on for my yearly theme, he said, "What I need to work on is kind of, 'Do your duty with a heart full of song,'" referencing a church hymn, *Put Your Shoulder to the Wheel.*[3]

"Yeah," I agreed. "Cheerfulness. Put on a smile and get the job done."

It feels like yesterday that I was sitting in my room, writing about my year of patience and my plans for a year of gratitude. Last year was so quick, I missed it. Ironic, considering I was feeling so much each day. I'm still shocked by how deep my grief has been, by its many layers and how slowly they have been peeled away only to reveal more. I know I'm only *beginning* to heal, and yet I want to be healed. I want to be well. Beyond that, I want to *feel* well. Happy. Joyful. So, like the thawing grounds of spring, I, too, hope to bloom this year, through cheerfulness. I imagine the red and gold tulips, pushing their way through the soil, eager to greet the warming world. This is me—eager to find warmth, eager to uncover joy.

But I'm not blooming yet. Not even close. I'm not ready to even *try* to be joyful. It's too much pressure for my fresh-from-winter self. That's why cheerfulness seems so right. There's a difference between cheerfulness and joy. Joy is a state of being, while cheerfulness is more about doing. I can *act* cheerfully even if I feel unhappy, stressed, or overwhelmed. I don't have to *feel* joyful to *be* cheerful. So, this is my goal: to smile when I want to scream, to hold my tongue when I want to complain, to laugh when I want to escape.

Acting cheerfully is my first step in thawing out. Then, perhaps someday I *will* bloom into something like a tulip, all cheery and joyful, basking in the sun.

Wednesday, January 7

Grandma Pace died, Lorri's mother and OJ's grandmother. The funeral is in six hours. We're here at

OJ's parents' house. It's 2:50 a.m., and my entire family is sleeping. I am awake.

Lying in bed, eyes open since midnight, staring at the outlines of Elmo, Winnie the Pooh, and other shadowy dolls on the shelves of the playroom, I finally decided to get up and write in this journal, to clear my tangled head. I'm trying to be cheerful, despite the fact that I'm worn out, with a sore throat that's getting worse, and supposed to be singing a difficult song in a few hours—*Come to Me*, set to Mozart's *Moonlight Sonata*.

I've been trying to *not* think about it for hours. *Perhaps I need to just allow the memories to come.* And so I do. No tears. No sorrow even. Just memories. Of my energetic, always interested in what I had to say, aunt Leslie. Of my intense, prolific, life of the party, brother-in-law. Of my "say it like it is," hard on the outside, soft on the inside, grandfather-in-law. Of my smiling, gentle, concerned, grandmother-in-law. Of my life-long companion, confidant, and... *Nope, not going there.* Too much to think about. Instead, I just let the wall back up, and feel...exhaustion. And, eventually, dreams.

Friday, January 9

It's been a long week. In fact, the only free time I've had is when I went early to the funeral, so I could practice my song. I suddenly realized I didn't have a baby hanging on me or five other screaming kids to tend to, and it felt like heaven. It's pathetic, I know, that practicing for a funeral song with a swollen throat is my definition of heaven. But, so it is. Even more heavenly, though, was that I sang my heart and voice out, and I touched people through my song. Lorri and her sister, Jeanne, both thanked me, through tears. "It was perfect," they said. "You did a great service for our mother today." Speaking of tears, I saw OJ cry for the first time. Ever. As he spoke of his grandmother and of life beyond this one, he cracked, and so did my heart, with love for him. I know it was emotion for his grandmother, but it was also for everything else. Even he feels it.

It's hard. Life as "parents of six," that is. I sometimes still have to remind myself, *you really do have six kids, you know*. It somehow justifies the hardness. Today was hard. "Meltdown madness," I'm calling it. First, Sydney's been sick most of the week—throwing up-sick, and then, coughing-sick. Although she seemed better today, she was still clingy and cranky, crying any time I set her down or if she didn't get exactly what she wanted. She has been glued to my hip. *Is this a one year-old thing or just her personality*, I've been wondering. I sure hope it's the former.

Then, Kennedy came home early from school today, faking sick, which I, of course, didn't realize until she was already home. She may not have been physically sick, but emotionally, she had meltdown after meltdown, all afternoon. By the time I miraculously got Syd to sleep, the only thing I could do to calm Kennedy was have a tea party with her. I think she'd been feeling neglected because Sydney's been sick and sucking all my attention away. I guess she just needed a little "mommy time."

Today is Tre's twelfth birthday, by the way. He had two meltdowns. First, he was upset about how his party was turning out, and didn't like the presents I bought him. You know, the usual birthday child meltdown. I think he thought he was getting something else, but honestly, I don't know what he thought. I tried my best to guess what he'd like, but I guess I missed the mark. The second meltdown was when he got frustrated with Colton, yelled at and shoved him, got in trouble when I caught him, then screamed in frustration and threw a shoe at the wall. Hard. After being sent to his room, to calm down, I went and sat on his bed and helped him talk it out.

"I just feel so much anger with my grandparents!" he said. "I don't understand why they made us all go to court and go on visits with them, and I don't know how to handle it." As he spoke, I could see it steaming out of his eyes and clenched fists. He was rocking and deep breathing, like I'd taught him, to calm himself down.

"I understand your anger," I said. "It doesn't make sense to any of us. But you can't let them get you so upset at everyone else. It only hurts you." He nodded, and we discussed, again, ways to cope with his anger. "Remember, talk it out, like you're doing now. Write it out. Scream into a pillow. Take a personal "time out" if you need it. Go do something active, like kicking a ball or shooting hoops. Take a rest and listen to music. Any of these things can be a big help. Okay?" He hugged and thanked me, and was able to calm himself down, just in time to enjoy his three-friend birthday sleepover.

Next, was Colton's turn. He was angry because Tre's friends were rude to him, trying to kick him out. Then, Brody. He fell and claimed he "broke his foot," then burst out crying because he thought Colton broke his toy. He was just way too tired. Braxton came to me for a long talk about: 1) his frustrations with his brothers, 2) his feeling that he has no close friends, and 3) his string of bad luck—he lost his brand new cell phone and had to get a huge cavity filled yesterday. Finally, I tucked OJ in bed at 9:30 because he's been miserable—coughy, achy, stuffy. I'm sick too, but a little better than he seems to be, so I am trying to at least help him get well. A stream of endless needs today, all pouring onto me.

All of this happened while buying gifts, making a cake, and preparing food for a birthday party, going grocery shopping, running to the post office and bank, finishing laundry, signing papers for adoption, and, this morning, taking a mandatory nap because I was feeling so sick, I could not stay standing. *Crazy!*

The *craziest* part, though, is not that everyone had a meltdown today. No, that's more common than I like to think. It's that *I* did *not*. I felt mostly calm, despite it all. I've definitely had my moments of feeling overwhelmed, but I haven't "lost it." At least, not yet.

It's true, I miss having "my life," and there are times I still feel the shock of, *is this really my life now?* Granted, we've just come off an extra-long winter break, thanks to three snow days, into a week with a sick, barfing baby, and a funeral, in addition to adoption proceedings. It *is* crazy, isn't it?

Yes. It just *is*.

Monday, January 12

Tonight, we finally told the kids about the adoption. It's been hard, keeping it from them these past months, but we felt it was the only way to keep them out of the stress and drama of it all—kind of like not telling them their grandparents had taken us to court. Tonight felt like the right time, since we have our first adoption home study visit on Thursday. We wanted to wait as long as possible, so when they went on visitations with their grandparents, they wouldn't have to keep our secret. But, they probably will have to before it's all said and done.

We brought all six kids into the library, our front room that's filled with built-in shelves and books. They were a little rowdy, as usual, bugging each other just like siblings do.

"Dad and I need to talk to you about something important," I said. They gave me half their attention. "We are adopting Tre and Brody into our family. Officially. We started the process with the court already, and the adoption agency will be visiting us here at home in a few days."

The response was unanimous. "Woohoo!

Finally. Real brothers!" followed by high fives and bro hugs, and hugs and lovies from the girls, too, of course.

OJ and I smiled at each other, and then I added, "We want to make sure you all feel good about it, and answer any questions you might have."

"How long will it take?" Tre asked, excitedly.

"We don't know for sure, but probably at least another month or two," I said. "We haven't told anyone yet, so we're hoping you guys can keep it a secret for a while."

"Why?" they asked, understandably.

"Are my grandparents going to try and stop it?" Tre questioned, and they all became still and looked to us.

"We don't know for sure if they would try to stop it or not," OJ said.

"But, don't worry," I added. "We don't think they *could* stop it, even if they wanted to. We just don't want to have any trouble. We've had enough trouble with courts already. We just want you to be a legal part of this family. Forever."

"That's what we want, too," Tre said, and Brody and the other kids nodded in agreement.

"We also want you guys to think about whether or not you want to change your names at all, when you're adopted."

They all looked surprised, and said, "Whoa. Cool." Then a huge grin came over Brody's face as his brown eyes lit up with excitement. "I want my name to be...Alex Hibbert!"

Where does this kid come up with these things? We all laughed, shaking our heads. Brody is such a character. "Well," I said, "you should probably keep the first name your mother and father gave you. And you should probably keep your last name, too. But you might want to add 'Hibbert' to the end. That's what I suggest, but it's up to you."

It had been tough so far, having different last names—hard for schools and sports and activities to keep track of whom the boys belonged to. I liked the idea of finally having the same name. Apparently they did, too. Just as quickly as they'd gathered to hear the news, the boys ran off, teasing each other, with Kennedy following behind.

Part of me is excited to have everything underway, but part is still nervous about having to deal with the unpredictable Cutlers. It was hard on all of us having the boys court-ordered to go on vacation with them for an entire week over this past Christmas break, having them call, again, crying to come home, and having the Cutlers act as if nothing were wrong. It feels like this is some kind of game for them, and that brings back the fear. I wonder if I'm holding back a little in how I'm embracing my new sons because of fear—fear of more games, fear of the unknown, fear this won't work.

All I can do is name the fear and then drown it out by hugging them, loving them, tucking them in. I'm replacing fear with its opposite. I'm drowning it out with love.

Tuesday, January 13

It dawned on me the other day just how selfish I am. I may *do* a lot for others, but I'm not sure I always do it with "a heart full of song." It's hard to give in and allow myself to feel charitable when I want time alone, when I want a break, when I feel my life is "*so* hard."

Dr. Hale says I am one of the most unselfish people he knows. "If you were any less selfish," he told me today, "I would be very worried, because it wouldn't be healthy." I thanked him for the complement, and, in the next moment, forgot it. As any good psychologist should, he called me on it, saying, "I don't think you believe me. I think you feel like I don't understand."

Right on the money.

He *wanted* to understand, so we discussed my view of selfishness. "Yes, I do a lot for others," I explained, "but I am selfish in the sense that I hold back. I don't fully put myself into what I do. I don't allow myself to truly give, to 'let go,' to really love."

"That's not necessarily selfishness," was his reply. "It sounds more like inauthenticity."

Hmm. It made me wonder. *Am I selfish? Am I inauthentic?* I hate thinking I'm either, but if I'm being honest, I'm sure I'm both, at times. I've already seen how I selfishly hold back. Perhaps inauthenticity pops up when I do things for others only out of a sense of duty or "rightness," instead of out of pure love? But isn't love at the core of my sense of duty? I don't know. I accept it. I'm selfish. I'm inauthentic. Whatever I call it, it's something I need to work on.

Next, we talked about the adoption. I told him my recent state of thinking—of my worries, of my fears. Talking about it today made me realize I hadn't really thought or *felt* about it until now, at least on a personal level. Adoption is the next thing to do. The *right* thing to do. Like a checklist: it needs to be done. Adoption is part of protecting the kids, completing our family, and healing. That all remains true. Today, however, I simply began to ask, "What do *I* think and feel about it?" and Dr. Hale helped me process.

"Part of me is nervous about a problem arising," I began. "But another small part is nervous for when it's complete." Strange, I know, but there it was. Our family is already forever changed, and adoption is perhaps just finalizing those changes. So, maybe, change is scary. That's what "they" say, right?

"Maybe I'm holding back with the boys because of my fears," I said. "I'm sure, in part, I am. Maybe that's why I feel so selfish." But even as I said it, I could feel love for the children, and protectiveness. I want them to find healing. I want them to be children, to grow and be healthy and happy.

Dr. Hale thought for a moment, and then spoke. "In my last session with Tre, he said, 'My life now is really great.'" He looked to me, smiled, and paused. "He *is* happy with you, Christi. You're a wonderful mother to him, to both of them."

My breath caught for a moment, before the tears began to spill. I wiped my runny nose with a tissue as I nodded and cried. "Thank you," I was barely able to say.

I felt so sad that Tre had to say such a thing, but so grateful that he did. Grateful Dr. Hale knew to share it with me. Grateful Tre is feeling happy and wants to be here with us. It was such a gift to hear that today.

Wednesday, January 14

I had just put Sydney down and was about to hit my bed for a nap, too, when the phone rang. It was Mom. She said she was calling to see how the kids have been. I told her their highs and lows and then said, "Mom, I think we need to talk about *us*."

She's been upset with me since before Christmas, when we had another blow out in my failed attempt to actually see eye-to-eye. I'd been trying to open a conversation about our lack of conversation. I'd spoken truthfully, directly, in as loving a manner as possible, saying things I knew she didn't want me to say. Explaining the frustration OJ and I feel with them because there's no real communication. Telling Mom how hard it is to work through my issues with Dad and her in my therapy, because things never seem to change. Explaining how tired I am of pretending all the time in our family, how much I hate that we ignore all the hard stuff.

"I'm telling you all of this because I hope we can change," I'd said, carefully. I felt the need to over-explain things, to try and smooth it over. "We just need to get it all out in the open so we can make sense of it."

I honestly don't know if I've *ever* felt like we could talk about our relationship with any sort of resolution or understanding. When I was a little girl, I could talk to my mom about anything, but that was kid stuff. These bigger issues have always been difficult for us. Whenever I talk with Mom, I just end up feeling like there's something wrong with me. I end up feeling confused.

"Children shouldn't tell their parents how to live," she had said, in reply.

"Well, then parents shouldn't rely on their children for their support to live," I replied. "I'm not telling you how to live anyway, Mom. I'm telling you how I *feel*. And, how I feel is *real*. It's based on real experiences."

"We're not going to change to be like you! It's arrogant for you to think we would!" She was growing angrier, and so was I, though I was yanking myself back from expressing it.

I wished she could see I didn't want her to be like me. I just wanted a healthier relationship—free of stress, free of criticisms or defensiveness—a loving relationship, focused on healing. *Was that so much to ask?* After that conversation, I started to see, perhaps it was. Our family system, at its core, had been set up, years ago, to keep Mom and Dad from having to deal with very painful feelings. That's why everyone had gone along with pretending and ignoring. That's why I felt so different in the family, because I couldn't do it. Why would they want the system to change when it was keeping them protected? When I looked at it that way, I guess I couldn't blame them.

I don't know what else we said, but she slammed the phone on me, and didn't talk to me for weeks. She almost didn't even come up to our house for Christmas. I had called to make sure she was planning to come, but she wouldn't answer. I'd left a message, "Mom, I hope you are planning to come up for Christmas. If you want to talk about anything, please call me. Anytime." She'd never called. In fact, Dad, and Ashley came without her. She drove up with Bud, late Christmas Eve. Christmas morning, she would barely look at me. She wouldn't accept the gift I gave her and ignored me most of the time. We've barely spoken since then.

Why was I surprised, then, when I asked her to talk today and she said, "I don't see the point." She sounded calm, but defeated. I didn't want her to feel defeated. I just wanted to have a conversation with my mom.

"The *point* is we need to at least try to find some understanding," I said. "We need to find a way to change our interactions for the future."

So, we talked. Labored. For ninety-five minutes. I was highly frustrated. We couldn't seem to get each other, even though we both were trying so hard. I actually had a headache from it, but near the end, we both cried. We both softened.

"I don't understand what you want me to say," Mom finally said, through tears. "I'm not good at expressing my feelings. I know you want that, but it's just so hard for me. But, I love you, Christi. No matter what, I always love you." I experienced a different side of my mom—almost childlike, a more vulnerable side, a side without walls. I don't think I've felt that from her since I was young. Even though our words were not getting through, I could *feel* her love for me. I could feel her desire to have me love her, too. It was a good thing, a deep breakthrough, even if we didn't actually come to any kind of surface understanding.

"I love you, too, Mom. Thank you for trying with me," I said, as we hung up.

We have work to do. But that's okay. We got somewhere today. Plus, I am good with hard work, especially if it helps me, or my mother, grow.

Thursday, January 15

We had our adoption home study today.

Last week, OJ and I met alone with our case worker in her retro white brick office for over two hours, answering all kinds of questions, from, "Name, age, family history?" to "What are your parenting philosophies?" It felt like a test, though I kept telling myself we weren't at risk of failing. I was wringing my hands under the table, especially when she asked, "Is there anyone you think might object to this adoption?" We almost didn't answer. We almost didn't say, "The paternal grandparents." But we did. It wouldn't be right if we weren't completely truthful. She listened carefully as we told her just a little of our history with the Cutlers and explained that we don't, by law, need their permission to adopt the boys. *Let us just be a family,* I was praying, in my mind. She, thankfully, seemed to understand and even empathize. *Sigh…. Temporary relief.*

Today, I worked to gets things clean and orderly for the home visit. Again, I felt I was being graded, this time on my ability to display a warm home environment and loving family, and to demonstrate my parenting skills, in a real-life way. Basically, I felt I needed to shine, even though I haven't been feeling very shiny, and that put me on edge even more. The visit lasted two hours, with introductions, followed by a tour of our home and each child's bedroom, and individual interviews. I was especially nervous as we all left the family room and each child was called back, one by one. What would they say about me? About OJ? I was wracking my brain for the worst possible, but could only think of, "My mom's tired all the time and gets mad when she doesn't get a break. And my dad is always golfing." It was out of my hands anyway.

After the interviews, as our caseworker prepared

to leave, I was caught off guard when she said, "You have a wonderful family. Your kids are beautiful, and you two seem like really great parents." I couldn't stop the tears from filling my eyes. I needed that little victory, that acknowledgment that I am doing okay, from someone who's qualified to say so. I needed it more than I'd realized.

Monday, February 9

Snow day. Again. After a three-week Christmas break, thanks to snow, and weeks of sick kids and more snow, I'm exhausted. My eyes burn, I've pulled something in my back, I'm still clinching my jaw all the time, and I have a cold that just won't quit. I long for a true vacation, but that, right now, is unattainable. Even a little alone time feels impossible, and snow days do not help.

Ugh! The kids just came in cheering: we have another one tomorrow.

I'm angry with the Cutlers, tired of having to fight them to protect our family. I've been mad at OJ for not helping enough. *Make a dinner, entertain some kids, do some homework, clean something!* My mind has been criticizing him all the time. I'm also frustrated with the kids, who haven't been doing their daily zones or keeping up with their work at school.

Under everything, however, I know I'm mostly concerned about doing the right thing with the adoption. After all this time, our attorney is suddenly changing his mind, counseling us to tell the Cutlers about the adoption right before the hearing. I feel for the Cutlers, but based on our history with them, I believe that is the *wrong move*. OJ and I have been praying all week to know what we should do. I'm worn out from everything—battling in this war, taking care of all this legal junk, and taking care of all of us.

I feel alone, like the snow days have snowed me

in, too. Thanks to this antidepressant I've been on for nearly two months now, I can't feel deep feelings; no tears will come, which I really hate. It's like a huge part of me is missing. I'm "better," but no longer complete. My brain tells me I need this antidepressant to cope as long as we are still at war, but once the adoption is finalized, I hope to no longer need the extra help. There's such a stigma with psychotropic medications. I've known this for years and have always believed there shouldn't be. We should feel good about using all the tools available to make us well. Taking a pill shouldn't be considered a weakness any more than going to therapy should. Yet I understand why it's such a tough choice. Sometimes, it can make me feel like I'm weak, like I can't do it on my own. So, I remind myself, "This medicine doesn't make you weak. It gives you the little lift you need to work harder and be stronger." I have long believed and told my clients this. Now, I know it.[4]

Today, in therapy, I told Dr. Hale my anger has returned. He had me lean back and close my eyes. "You've left the land of the dead," he said, "and entered the war zone."

No wonder I've been so frustrated and exhausted. As he spoke, I felt like Frodo, from *Lord of the Rings,* or something—one misfortune after another—and honestly, it was good to feel mad about it again, to let the feelings out a little. "The anger, this time, is a call to action," he said. *Yeah. I like that. But I also need to be careful not to be forced into reaction. I do not want to behave like a madwoman, say or do hurtful things, or hurt myself out of anger. That part of anger, I do not like.*

"Your antidepressant is your shield," he continued, slowly. "You need it right now, to prevent severe blows. Someday, you'll no longer need it." I liked that, too.

I opened my eyes and spoke. "I saw myself wearing shiny, strong armor now. I was feeling less like I was drafted for the war and more like I am the one with the plan: the general." *And generals are not cheerful; they are tough.*

Tough as I may be, the armor is heavy and cumbersome. He's right. It *is* shielding me—from incapacitation, and from other deep feelings that could prevent my ability to act and lead. I long for the day when I can remove the armor for good. I long for the day when, instead of battles and war, my family can finally focus on what really matters: joy, and love, and peace.

EIGHTEEN
Practice Cheerfulness

*"Sometimes your joy is the source of your smile,
but sometimes your smile can be the source of your joy."*
~Thich Nhat Hanh

Don't you just love cheery people? I do. I *really* do. You know, those people who make you smile no matter what—who laugh at everything, who always have something bright to say, no matter how dark things seem? I've admired people like that all my life, figuring they were pretty lucky to have been born with such a healthy dose of good cheer.

It seems I've always had to *work* at being cheerful. It's not that I'm an *un*happy person, just not "cheery" per se. One thing I have learned is, while there may be people out there who are naturally cheery, and good for them, if we work at it, we can *all* bring a little more cheer into the world. The Bible advises, "A merry heart doeth good like a medicine…"[1] It's true, isn't it? Isn't that why we all love being around people who are merry? Because it fills us with something good and untouchable, something that makes us whole?

Cheerfulness is a choice. Like any other talent or skill, it requires practice. If I want to play the piano, I can't expect to just sit down, pick up Mozart and "tickle the ivories." Far from it. But if I'm willing to work, to put in my thirty minutes, or more, a day, then someday I will be able to "tickle" a little Mozart. The same goes for cheerfulness, or any other personality trait. If I want to be more loving, kind, generous, assertive, I can. If I want to be a leader, a hard worker, a motivator, I *can*. All it requires is choosing to work on and improve that trait. Isn't that great news? I think it is. If it's up to me, then it's not up to anyone else. I, alone, can change and become who I want to become.

One of the best ways I've learned to change

toward cheerfulness is by examining my thinking. Most of the nearly 60,000, on average, thoughts we have each day, we don't hear—which is probably a good thing. Through practice, we can train ourselves to hear the ones that matter, to pay attention and gleam valuable nuggets of truth about how we feel, what we need, and ultimately, who we are. Our thoughts, feelings, body, and behavior are not only related, they influence each other and are also influenced by the thoughts, feelings, reactions and behaviors of our past. The good news is, once we see this cycle repeating, we have a choice. That choice is to either buy in to the vicious cycle, to ignore it, or to listen, and, like a parent, intervene when we hear something that doesn't quite make sense.

My own classic example comes from when I was in graduate school. Here I was, two small kids, my husband in dental school, attending a full-time doctoral program, working part-time as a fitness instructor, and obviously surviving on very little sleep. One day, I came home to a surprisingly empty house. OJ had picked up the boys on his way home and taken them to the park. I had two blessed hours alone. Immediately, I began cleaning, trying to remedy the bomb of Superman capes, lion's tails made of belts, Scooby-Doo bowls, and silly straws, that covered what once had been our small living room and kitchen. It wasn't until I dug into the pile of mud-stained t-shirts and loincloths to start several loads of laundry, that I noticed my body was tense, my frustration mounting higher than the pile before me, and I heard a sing-song voice within saying, *I can't handle this. I'm going to freak out!*

"Wait a minute," I said to myself, out loud. "I heard that! What exactly *can't* I handle?" It was the first time I had heard my automatic thoughts and stopped to question them. I was just doing laundry, so why was I so frustrated? After a few moments of listening, I heard my answer: *I'm exhausted. I have a quiet home. I want to take a nap, but I have to clean and do laundry.* Well, did I *have* to do the laundry right then? No. It was a choice I was making. I decided to unmake that choice and instead chose to take a nap. Sure, the house was still a mess when my family came home, but the difference was *I* was no longer a mess.

In *Hamlet*, Shakespeare writes, "There is nothing either good or bad but thinking makes it so." [2] We choose whether our thoughts continue to drag us down, in negativity, or pull us up, with cheer. I recommend becoming cheerful. Start simple. *Try* to smile. *Practice* smiling, especially in the un-smiley times. Then, work on *really* smiling—lighting up when you're around those you love. Eventually, you may not be able to stop yourself from laughing, from humming, from singing and dancing, and soon, from bringing joy to your little corner of the world.

Yes, practice a little cheerfulness. It really is good for the heart, like a medicine.

Sunday, February 15

I used to say it felt constant and continual, handling six kids and all that came with it. It was one after another after another. Now, it feels like one on top of another on top of another; now it is constant, continual, and simultaneous.

I admit, a complicating factor is my own drive for life, coming back, full force. I want to write music, and I'm helping with my Arizona Postpartum Wellness Coalition's legislation committee and trying to get us a grant. I'm also teaching an "Enhancing Marriage" class, starting Tuesday, and I'm working hard planning our next Relief Society activity for church, a play about the ten virgins. I want to do it right, and maybe I'm going over the top, but it's the final one I'm in charge of, since I have been called to work with an entirely different set of females: the eight to eleven year-old girls. I'm still going strong, and stronger each day, with my P90X workouts, still fighting to get this post-baby body back in shape. And, I just put together a proposal to speak at the Postpartum Support International conference in a few months, all while still fulfilling orders and mailing out my *Postpartum Couples* DVDs. Is that all? Maybe. But that is a lot! I'm trying to do all this stuff in between my primary responsibilities as a mother, household manager, and wife. So, even though I am feeling so much better lately and finding my drive again, the result is leaving me worn out in a whole new way.

I've been thinking, however, and I am pleased to report I feel content with my life, overall. Hard as it is, the work I am asked to do is full of *meaning*, and that makes all the difference. I am leading my family, enriching my children with love and learning, and providing a beautiful home for us. These are important, and I believe the sacrifices I am making are worth it. It also helps to have some of my own outside interests—to utilize my skills and talents in the service of others. It's part of my life's purpose.

I have realized that, even though my physical self tells me I want to rest, have time alone, relax, have fun, and so forth, my spiritual self is saying, "I want to return home completely used up! Worn out, tired, and having used every talent, gift, and strength I've been given so they don't go to waste."

Well, I feel I am doing *that* a little better, but I still need to listen to my physical self. I wouldn't want to use myself up *too* quickly.

Monday, February 23
Last night was filled with intense dreams. I haven't had dreams like these in a while, and they caught me off guard.

OJ is out of town; the house is flooding and collapsing. I am home alone, with the kids. I had tried to stop the floods, somehow knowing they were coming, but couldn't, so, now, I am running down the staircase, grabbing the kids, pushing them in front of me as water floods everything, as the roof sags and the walls fold behind me like origami. I keep trying to call OJ on my cell phone as I run, but my phone is rerouted to an operator who knows his number, but won't help me. I don't know why. The front door, below, is open and filled a quarter of the way up with water. We're almost there. I know we will be safe if we can just get outside.

I'm walking through my Dad's dental office. I need a filling and have an appointment today. As I approach the silvery dental chair on which I'm supposed to lie, I noticed it is occupied, and Dad, Mom, and Dad's assistant all stand around. They look up and watch me as I turn the bend to see who's in the chair, as if they're waiting to see my reaction. I look at them, then down at the chair. It is Shannon. She looks a little different and very still, but it is she. Everyone tells me she is alive and has been all along. Shannon just lies there, looking at me. "No! This isn't real!" I say. "It's just a dream!" Mom and Dad try to calm me, saying, "It is real. It's not a dream. We know this is hard, but it was the only way to help Shannon with her recovery." I am furious. Yelling! Saying, "I don't believe any of you! This is an awful thing to do! Why are you doing this?" Saying, "You can't do this to me! And to the kids! They're better off now!"

After I woke up and remembered the dreams, I recounted them to OJ and suddenly, began to cry. I couldn't stop. I sobbed in my bed, head covered with a blanket, curled onto my side, until I had to get myself up and the kids off to school. It was the first time since December that I have felt that grief and sadness and pain of loss. Though it's not nearly as intense as before, partly, I'm sure, because of the antidepressant, it reminds me of the true pain and sadness of our situation. Sometimes, it feels like I'm the only one who knows the truth of it all.

At the end of this morning, though, I feel strangely relieved. It's a relief to feel again, to remember how real the trauma has been. It's a relief, even if it is hard.

Wednesday, March 4

I don't just feel better, I feel really good. Joyful. I remember, just months ago believing with my whole heart I'd never feel joy again. I remember thinking perhaps I wasn't meant for joy, but I can tell you, *I am*. I am great when I'm joyful. I make others' lives better, especially my family's.

Admittedly, I'm not the best "play with the kids" kind of mom. I'm more of a "have deep conversations," "discuss the meaning of life" kind of mom, so it's hard to play dolls and color all day and love it. Still, I've been making an effort. The more cheerfully I approach my work—even doll-playing—the happier I find myself. The happier I find myself, the happier the kids. Instead of waiting to *love* getting down and playing, I simply get down and play, *with* love. Then, I seek the joy of that moment. And the next. And the next. This is helping me want to seek and notice *all* the joyful moments of motherhood. They are there, and have been all along, but too often I've missed them simply because I wasn't looking outside my own darkness and stress. Lately, I am finding so many lovely moments, so many moments filled with joy.

One of my favorite moments has become bedtime with Sydney. I say, "Wanna go night-night?" and sixteen month-old Sydney sings, "La, la, la." This is because she loves having "la-la's" before bed; she loves to hear me sing my *Lovey Lullaby*. I wrote it when she was a newborn, needing a special song to mark this last baby of mine, needing a refuge from all the hard stuff. I'll pick her up and start singing, "I la, la, lovey-lovey love you, so I'll sing a la, la, lullaby…"[3] She'll motion to her crib and I'll lay her down as I finish, "Close your eyes and let this la, la, lullaby inspire your la, la, lovely dreams."[4] She'll reach up, turn on her crib nightlight, and roll over for twelve hours. It is bliss.

There's so much to teach, so much to do, and I *want* to do it—even if it's hard. Life has new meaning for me, having lost so much has helped me appreciate what is right in front of me. You never know when another blow will hit. It has also helped me grow. I'm more settled, comfortable, and confident. I care a little less about meaningless things and a little more about those that matter most. I'm growing my relationship with God, too, relying on Him to light me up. I'm feeling creative and joyful because of that light. I want to share that light, for it is the experience of the love of God. It changes me, improves me, and I desire to continue improving. I'm enjoying this. All of it.

I told Dr. Hale I feel a huge change in me. My heart has changed. I'm not doing things for glory or fame or acknowledgement as much as I used to, which must mean I am discovering my own self-worth. I am living in the moment, looking around, and seeing who needs me. I am taking advantage of "free" time when it pops up, because it is very rare. I am trying to pace myself with my own drives and goals. I recognize the need to sacrifice right now for my family. I feel so much more comfortable in my role as mother of six, and in my own skin.

I realized, today, that I am happy with my life. I feel free. Like I have great potential, and I can finally embrace it. So many ways I could go; I can't wait to see where I end up.

Monday, March 9

Our family birthday: Today, we were granted our adoption. It only lasted about ten minutes, and it was perfect.

I arrived nervous, half-expecting the Cutlers to have shown up, but they didn't. It was only OJ, the kids, minus Sydney, whom we left with a babysitter, my good friend Cyndy, and Mom and Dad. Braxton, Colton, and Kennedy stayed outside with Cyndy while the rest of us were led into the courtroom. I took a deep breath, exhaled, and my pulse slowed. I finally believed this was actually going to happen.

The white-haired judge smiled warmly, welcoming us. His cheerful energy put us at ease, and we all smiled in return. OJ and I were able to tell the judge how much we love the boys, and the boys were able to tell how much they love all of us. "It's been great to have a place to live and all," twelve year-old Tre said. "But now, it's like we'll have a home." It filled everyone's hearts with emotion and eyes with tears.

The judge said, "It is clearly in the best interest of the children. The children clearly want to be adopted. Therefore, adoption granted." He read the kids' "new" names (no, Brody was not Alex; he was still Brody), with Hibbert at the end. Then, the judge pronounced, "with all the rights and privileges as if they'd been born into the family." That hit my heart. *As if they'd been born to me. They really are mine now.*

"Woo-hoo! Brody Hibbert!" Brody said. The other three kids came in, and we all gathered around the smiling judge for a photo, while he asked each child questions about their likes and dislikes. Joy abounded. We went for Mexican food afterwards, with Mom and Dad, had a relaxing afternoon at home, and, at the end of the day, invited all our friends over, to celebrate, with an ice cream sandwich open house. A truly great day.

I'm still a little nervous about what may come, but mostly, I feel relief. Extreme relief, like I can't exhale long or hard enough. Our attorney advised us to wait thirty days for the appeal period to be over before we break the news to Cutlers. It's going to be a long thirty days, but I know this was right. The kids feel happy and safe, and that is what matters most. We are a true family now!

Thursday, March 19

The second to last day of our Mexican Riviera cruise, and we're back at sea. Several of our family friends had invited us on this trip, months ago, and the timing couldn't have been better—to leave the weekend after the adoption. Though our little girls are home, with OJ's parents and mine, the boys have been living it up in their private interior room. They've ordered Jell-O and mac 'n' cheese at all hours of the day, and night, stayed up later than we even realized, and slept as late as we'd let them. OJ and I have been refreshed by time alone in our exterior room and time to play with the boys and our friends. It has felt like a true celebration.

I've worked hard to keep myself positive and cheerful this trip. I've definitely realized how much negativity I've allowed into my thoughts over the years, and it's just not worth it! It can be stressful to take any kind of vacation, especially when kids are along for the ride, and the lines can be long getting on a plane or a cruise ship. As we boarded the ship I was shocked to find so many grumpy people—grumpy because their rooms weren't ready yet or grumpy because the buffet wasn't open yet, or because "they only have soft serve ice cream and I'm starving!" I sat in my chair by the pool, watching these people, put on a big smile, and attempted to be as cheerful as possible, recognizing I could easily have been any one of those grumps if I hadn't been making a concerted effort to be cheerful. I was tired and hungry, too. I wished my room were ready so I could plunk down on my bed for a bit, but acting cheerfully in the midst of so much complaining showed me the ridiculousness of being in a bad mood when you're on vacation. Why leave home at all if you just take all your "baggage" with you?

I made a commitment right then and there that I

would never let myself be in a bad mood when I'm on vacation. Just when I feel tired, frustrated, stressed, I paste on a smile and find the good. I remind myself, "Hey, you're on vacation! Who cares if there's a long wait, or things aren't turning out right at first." I can choose to feel joyful, and, I have been. Let me tell you, it has been such a blast.

First stop was Cabo, where our entire party boarded the largest Catamaran I've ever seen, the "Eco Cat," and sailed to a distant cove, to snorkel in the not-as-warm-as-we'd-like Pacific. But it was the ride back to the ship that really got the party started, first with a BBQ dinner and all the sodas the boys could drink, then, with blaring Mexican club music. The entire boat was up on the huge stretched out canvas, dancing to "Yo Quiero Mueve, Mueve" (Spanish for "I Like to Move It, Move It"). The boys were doing crazy moves, like the running man, while OJ did a little of his famous "Robotto," and I tried to keep up, laughing, hysterically. The funniest was a drunk, balding, fellow passenger, in short swim trunks, who was doing hip thrusts and clearly unaware that everyone on the boat was watching and busting up! As if that weren't enough entertainment, however, the real show soon began: Humpback whales suddenly appeared and stopped all sea-craft in the area. A mother and her calf seemed to know they had an audience. They were flipping and breaching like they'd been trained at Sea World! The boys were mesmerized and got some excellent photos. It was truly spectacular, as if all of Cabo were saying, "Congratulations, Hibberts, on becoming a family!"

Next, we were off to Mazatlan. Our family snuck away, alone, to enjoy a relaxing day at the beach, complete with boogie boarding and shopping. The highlight, however, was hailing and squeezing into the funkiest little "taxi" I have ever seen! It looked like a cross between a golf cart and a hula skirt. The driver insisted it was safe, and we just went with it, since there were several other "taxis" like this, carting tourists, too. I couldn't stop laughing at how ridiculous we looked, sitting on each other's lap, holding on for dear life, and singing along to *Low*, by Flo Rida. Who would have guessed Brody knew all the words! I guess I need to monitor their music a little better.

Yesterday, Colton's tenth birthday ("Double digits!" he kept saying), we were in Puerto Vallarta. In my opinion, the best of all, with beautiful beaches and a lush, green jungle. Our family and friends went zip-lining together, through seventeen different lines on the jungle canopy. Afterward, we all agreed the best parts were gliding hundreds of feet up, over a huge canyon with a magnificent river below. I even did two lines over the canyon, upside down! It was the bomb! We finished off the day by swimming in the river and jumping off rocks. After a little shopping downtown, we boarded a local bus back to the ship. My friend, Cyndy's, son almost got hit by a crazy taxi driver as we were crossing the street from the bus! I saw the driver coming around the bend, full speed, and screamed! Luckily, he heard the scream and stopped, just as Cyndy grabbed her son out of the road. We were safe. The driver got a ticket from a cop that was parked across the street. A scary end to a fabulous day, made even more fabulous, because justice was served.

We've been to many shows—singing, dancing, circus-type, comedy, and magic. I even did my first karaoke—terrifying! I now know the rule of Karaoke: You need to be either really bad or really good. I was neither, but I went for it, singing Fiona Apple's *Criminal*. Another Karaoke lesson learned: Choose fun songs that the crowds know and will enjoy! Oh, well. Next time, I'll know better.

I know bad can happen. I know it will again, some day. So, I am fully invested in enjoying the good while I have it. I'm making the most of each day by turning my face to the sun.

Thursday, March 26

I've noticed I've been avoiding myself. I've been avoiding this journal. I have not wanted to write or think too much. It makes me wonder if feelings are starting to surface I don't want to deal with. I don't usually think I'm one who tries to run away from or escape difficult emotions, but I feel I am now. I wonder, now that adoption is over and our cruise is done, if, subconsciously, I'm saying, "Okay. It's time to finish this grief work." Or maybe, I just fear having more drama from Cutlers, whom we still have to tell about the adoption.

I hear myself say, *I just want that joy again.* I've *felt* it. It's real, and I want it. But real life is hard, and it's not always going to feel perfectly joyful. I have to work at it, always. That is true and it is a big bummer. I don't even want to think about any of this right now. So, I'm choosing not to...

Sunday, March 29

I felt off from the moment I awoke, but pulled it together only to lose it again, yelling at the kids on the way to church. I felt *awful*—like I'd "ruined everything." At least, that was the thought I heard in my head.

Luckily, I was able to tell myself I hadn't ruined everything and talk myself out of the negative thinking that usually grabs me by the neck and drags me quickly down. We arrived at sacrament meeting, and I selected seats in the back, so I wouldn't have to see people and let them see how I was feeling. I felt out of it, not wanting to be there, and definitely not feeling any kind of spiritual connection. So, I prayed. I prayed that I might feel *something*. Something to turn me around.

Being the first Sunday of the month, it was fast

and testimony meeting, when members of the congregation go forth and share their thoughts and feelings about the Gospel—their testimonies—instead of having the usual assigned speakers. Always some of my favorite meetings, I feel uplifted hearing others' stories, struggles, lessons, and inspiration. The thought came that I should share my testimony, but I pushed it away, feeling "unworthy" or something, because of my mood. So, I sat and waited, feeling my heart flood with emotion and that familiar burning that told me I simply *had* to get up and share. Time was officially up, but I had to do it. I forced myself out of my chair and looked at the floor as I walked the aisle to the front, up the stairs of the stage, and to the pulpit. There, I opened my heart for everyone to see.

I can't remember everything I said, but I know I shared some experiences of how the scriptures have answered my prayers directly, and I know I ended with, "God *does* hear us. He *does* protect us. He *loves* us. He gives us the safety and peace our families need. All *we* have to do is kneel in prayer, then open our scriptures to hear His word."

I said these things in a forceful way, almost like I had to speak these things, to release the tension in me. And it was released. And I felt free.

As I returned to my seat, embarrassment engulfed me. Perhaps, because I made us go over time or perhaps, because it was such raw emotion. I don't know. But, I felt embarrassed. *Why did you do that?* I heard in my head, but I sat with it. I let the embarrassment have its moment, then turned my back, and it snuck away. I didn't care how it felt after. I had done the right thing by speaking.

Later tonight, I talked and cried to OJ for the first time in a long time. I felt emotion, but wasn't sure what. I tried to sort it. Sadness—missing Shannon and wondering if I'm grieving again. Fear—about what's next with the Cutlers, or with my own life. *How do I proceed, now that the adoption is done?* I keep thinking. That was the last big item on our list. Now what? I guess I'm afraid of making the wrong move.

I also sensed my lack of faith. I have difficulty distinguishing between what I desire and whether it's okay to truly, one hundred percent, ask God for what I desire. Even though I believe I have mostly righteous desires, I'm sort of lowering my head, a bit fearful, as I ask for help. Sort of, "Can you do this for me? Or, if you can't—it's okay. I totally understand. No problem. Either way." I mean, I do want to live by the words, "Thy will be done." I agree with this principle, fully, but what I'm beginning to think is this: I'm so familiar with everything being changed in an instant, I'm so afraid of losing, of my life taking another major turn, that I'm afraid to desire *anything* too much. I feel unworthy to ask, fearing my own motives. In the past, I've wanted things for the wrong reasons, too many times. Now, I want to do what's right. I want to do what's right for me and for my family, according to God's will for us.

I've decided to submit one of my songs to a songwriting competition, and I've decided to start writing again, not just in my journal, but for real. Those are desires. Now that I know my weakness in faith, I'd like to experiment in faith. I will put my whole heart and soul forth as I work on these things and *show* my Heavenly Father my faith. I will let go and allow *Him* to show *me* my path. This is my desire. For, I know He will always lead me down the path of growth and learning, the path that leads back toward Him.

Thursday, April 2
How lucky are we to be in Telluride for a family ski trip? Very lucky.

As I drove the kids to this masterpiece of earth, where we met up with OJ who was already here with friends, I caught myself *smiling*. Spontaneous and genuine, it wasn't even the pasted on kind. Fancy that! Even the Cutlers seemed a distant memory. We may still have to break the news to them about the adoption, but as I drove to Telluride, they felt more like a bothersome mosquito—troublesome, annoying, wish it would leave me alone, but it's just doing what it does, and is ultimately no threat.

I feel love growing inside. I feel my heart opening. I feel forgiveness, for myself and others. I feel calmer. I feel satisfied. I see how I've been torn down so I could be rebuilt. I know I need many more renovations, and I still have much introspection to work on. I don't yet see the complete big picture, but I finally have some perspective. I do feel changed—me, but more me. More spiritual. More loving. This isn't to say I don't have my weak times. I *do*. But I can stop it so much sooner. I can change my thinking. I can remind myself of that bigger picture. I can breathe and I can live "in the now." I can let go. I can live.

I need to live. This moment is all I truly have. A little bit better each and every day. That is my goal.

Wednesday, April 8

I need to admit something—something I want to do. Here goes: I want to write and publish a book. I want to write a personal narrative that includes tips and suggestions I've learned as a psychologist. I want to be honest and real as I write, hoping others will be touched, will be able to relate, and will learn something new.

Whew, I admitted it! It's hard to admit, because I'm completely intimidated. It's also hard to make myself sit down and write, because I am afraid. Reexamining the recent past is not high on my to-do wish list. In fact, I keep hearing myself argue that I just got through all this. *I'm finally feeling better, and you want me to drag it all out again?* It does sound crazy. I keep praying and can't escape the feeling this is what I need to do right now.

I've actually been arguing with myself quite often. Today I heard myself saying, *you are lazy! Stop watching TV. Don't lie down. There's too much you need to do. You don't deserve a break!* All this, even though I was truly worn out. The good news is I can hear myself. I can change my unhealthy thoughts and push away the really unhealthy ones. I've recently avoided several unnecessary moments of anxiety by telling myself, *Quiet down in there, I'm trying to relax!* And I actually minded myself! So, when I hear myself saying, *write a book? You can't do that. You'll fail! You'll be the laughing stock!* I don't listen. Instead, I tell myself, *just you wait and see.*

Saturday, April 18

Bill Cutler called this evening. He was polite, but short, as he got to the point. "I'm calling because I have this paper here that says we have a legal right to a visit with our boys in a couple of weeks and a legal right to several weeks this summer that we need to schedule." Since the thirty-day waiting period was now over, we'd thought he would have received the official adoption notice from the court by today. Apparently, not.

"Listen," I said. "The kids love you, Bill, but they've been hurt by your decision to take us to court, to force them on visits, and also by how you've treated all of us and their other grandparents, my parents."

"It had to be done," was his no-nonsense reply. He insists he has done right and that we or the kids are the reason he has had to treat us badly. "Besides," he added, escalating, "the boys aren't mad at *us*. They're just following what you, their 'parents,' have taught them! They're brainwashed!"

Now *I* was starting to escalate, but I fought it, keeping my voice even and tempered. "That's just not true, Bill. They are hurt, and you need to lay aside your wants to do what is right for *them*."

He immediately went into defense mode, as I took a deep breath and braced myself for the truth to finally come out. "Well, I have this court document in front of me for Grandparent Visitation," he said. "So, *you* need to get down to business and schedule these visits with me, whether the kids want it or not!" He'd opened the door; it was time to walk through.

"No," I calmly stated. "No, actually I *don't* have to, Bill." Pause, silence, and inhale. "The boys…have been…adopted."

"What?" he asked, incredulously.

"We have adopted the boys, Bill, and they don't have to go on *any* visits they don't want to go on anymore," I said. "Your 'Grandparent Visitation Rights' have been terminated."

I felt at once triumphant and humbled. I had great power here and did not want to abuse it. I knew this was a terrible blow to him and would be to his wife. I knew this was one sword I needed merely to unsheathe for its power to be felt. I didn't need to wield it.

"How is that possible? You can't just adopt the boys without our permission. We're their grandparents!" he spat out in frustration.

"Actually," I replied, "we can. Both their parents are deceased, and we've been their guardians ever since. Legally, we didn't need anyone's permission."

Stunned silence again. It was I who spoke first, now that he was seemingly listening. "Listen, Bill, the boys are really happy. This is what they want, and they're doing terrific. You should call and talk to them so you can see for yourself. They *really* are happy."

He asked only a few questions, the first being, "Did they change their names?"

"Yes," I said. Then, explained how, according to their own wishes, they'd added "Hibbert."

"Well *that's* the most interesting thing I've ever heard," was his firm and sarcastic reply.

"Look, Bill, we asked the kids what they wanted. They wanted to be adopted. We asked them what they wanted their names to be. They actually both wanted to change their entire names and completely lose your last name, but we reminded them that someday they would want their dad's name, so they agreed to just add Hibbert. Again, if you and your wife will just call and talk to them, they can tell you all about it."

I suggested that everyone would be best served by having the Cutlers attend counseling with the boys and Dr. Hale. "It would be a safe place for you and the boys to discuss all that's happened and to begin to clear up any issues that have arisen as a result." He didn't seem entirely convinced. He was clearly upset, perhaps angry or in shock. Still, he agreed they would come to counseling in the next couple of weeks, and I agreed to set it up. "We want to help you repair your relationship with the boys," I said. "No more forcing them to do what the adults want. We just want them to feel safe, and we hope you will work with us so you can enjoy a healthy relationship with them."

I'm supposed to call them on Monday, to work out the counseling appointment. I hope, for the boys' sakes, they will follow through. I hope our future with the Cutlers will be more like this present moment than the past.

I was amazed at how well I handled this conversation. I'm not usually good at keeping my voice cool in the face of confrontation. I tend to get worked up the more I talk, and I'm great at winning an argument. Tonight, however, the more I spoke, the calmer I became. Tonight, I was the epitome of assertiveness.

NINETEEN
Live in the Now

"Learn from yesterday, live for today, hope for tomorrow."
~Albert Einstein

Back in graduate school, when my colleagues would say things like, "How do you do it—school, internship, homework, and two kids?" I would reply that having two kids, in some ways, made things easier. I didn't have time to stress about assignments or over-study for a test. My kids forced me to budget my time wisely. They forced me to live in the present.

We usually live anywhere *but* the present. Our minds are so focused on the past, what *has* happened, and the future, what *will* happen, that we miss the very moment that *is* happening, here and now. How many times have you been driving and suddenly gone a couple blocks and didn't even notice? Or, have you ever been at dinner with friends or family and checking your texts at the same time, completely missing part of the conversation? Or how about this one, for you parents— have you ever heard your child saying, "Mom!" or "Dad!" and realized you've tuned out the first ten pleas for attention?

We miss moments all the time. Sometimes, because we don't like what we're doing and *want* to miss it. Sometimes, because we're distracted by doing too many things at once. And, sometimes, simply because we're not practiced at noticing what is right in front of us. Some may question, "What does it matter if we miss moments? They're just *small* moments." Small as they may be, however, if you're missing moments, you're missing life.

Life happens in the moments. As Eckhart Tolle wisely wrote, "…Being one with Life is being one with Now. You then realize that you don't live your life, but life lives you. Life is the dancer, and you are the dance."[1]

Beautiful, isn't it?

When I want to become "one with life," one with "the now," I look around and, using all my senses, soak up my world. Or, I'll go for a walk and listen to the birds in the trees, feel the breeze on my skin, smell the blossoms newly formed, see the clouds shifting in the sky. Sometimes, when my mind gets stuck in the past, I imagine a wall coming up that blocks everything but what is right in front of me. I tell myself "face forward," and it reminds me to be where I am. When the good moments come, we can mindfully pay attention; they will not last long. When the not-so-good moments come, we can also mindfully pay attention. The not-so-good moments are where learning happens, and they also will not last long. In fact, we often later realize, they were better than we'd feared. Gratefully, we can seek out the blessing of each moment. Search for joy and love. Put all of who we are into what we are doing right now.

Once we learn to "live in the now," we understand why we don't want to miss the moments. The moments are where we are made. As the old saying goes, "Yesterday is history. Tomorrow is a mystery. Today is a gift—that's why it's called the present." Let's go and unwrap our present today.

Sunday, April 26

Our first attempt at a full family campout was a success, despite the crazy spring winds.

We spent some quality time together, just our little family—playing games, talking, laughing, and trying not to wake each other up as we slept in the cramped camp trailer. Several other families came along, too, so there were plenty of friends to combat any impending "I'm bored-om." But the best part, for me, was seeing the ecstasy on the kids' faces as they behaved like NASCAR pros, racing their quads, dune buggies, and go-carts through the dirt roads and forest surrounding our campsite. I love racing quads, too. I'm pretty fast, I admit. Even Sydney loved it—digging in the dirt and following Dad around while he played pit-crew. Kennedy was my shadow, riding me around on her mini-quad, coloring, helping me cook, and watching the occasional Barbie movie when we both needed a break. Naps were plentiful, and so was reading and great conversation. It was just what we needed.

Now, we're back home and cleaned up...and worn out. I must say, I've been a bit grumpier about camping today, having had a bit *too much* family togetherness. So, I'm recovering in my clean, quiet room, with the door locked. Great as it was, the one thing I've learned this weekend is the high price I'm willing to pay for *space*. Space is a hot commodity when you have six kids. It was a challenge to share cramped quarters this weekend, with neither room to turn nor place to sit. Yes, I *need* space, and coming home from camping, I am all the more grateful to be living in this house, with separate rooms and even separate levels!

I do love my family. I love the memories we created this weekend. However, I can definitely love our fine family moments even *better* when I have a little space.

Wednesday, April 29

It was a typical Wednesday—completely crazy. I've been juggling all day.

The morning started normal enough, with the *beginning* of a workout, but Sydney woke early and kept saying, "Owside!" (or something close to it). I eventually gave up and took her grocery shopping instead, dropping Kennedy at school on the way, since the boys had left her and she'd missed the bus. The rest of the morning flew by. I shopped, unloaded groceries, took Syd for a quick walk as she begged "Owside" again, finished my P90X Arms and Shoulders workout, and bounced Syd on my knee while attempting to finish a song I'd been writing for Brody's baptism, called, *Baptism Song*. Creative, isn't it?

I looked at the clock: noon. I was supposed to be at a friend's luncheon by now. Seeing as how I've isolated myself lately, I was determined to make myself go. So, I pulled my sweat-drenched hair into a new ponytail, put on fresh deodorant and clothes, changed Sydney, and sped off to the luncheon. Trying to settle in to conversation at the party, Syd was toddling around when she bonked her face on another kid's noggin, and started balling, a goose egg appearing. So, I grabbed some lunch to go, and hurried us home for her nap. So much for socialization! With only forty-five minutes until the kids got home from school, I headed to my room for *my* nap just as another friend called, asking to come and borrow some serving dishes for a wedding. I shot back up, gathered the dishes, and by the time I'd helped her load them, the kids were home.

Kennedy was begging to play with a friend, and Colton had his friend over to practice their piano recital duet. Next thing I knew, we had three extra kids over and Syd was awake again—with diarrhea. I almost forgot to pick up Braxton from school and then learned that Tre was also supposed to practice a piano duet. After hunting him down, he was angry, because apparently he hadn't learned his song yet. So, I tried to help him learn the song, before rushing the three boys out the door to piano practice. Braxton was supposed to have a basketball game, so I gathered everyone else to the car, but the phone rang just then, and it was his coach telling us the game was cancelled. Thank goodness, we hadn't left yet! *One less thing to do.* Then, "Oh, yeah! Brody!" He was at this friend's, and I totally forgot about him. So, OJ picked him up on his way home and brought the piano boys home, too, while I made dinner, and ran to the post office to mail my psychologist license renewal, at the very last minute, as usual!

At 6:15, after Syd's third poopy diaper and first bath, our Home Teachers showed up, men from church who visit once a month and share a lesson. We actually had a fifteen-minute lesson, with, *One, two, three, four, five, six,* yes, *everyone* present and listening. *Miracle!* (Counting has become my saving grace, by the way.) But Syd started crying, and as I was walking her around so I didn't disturb the lesson, she started gagging. I ran to the sink just as she barfed all over! *My streak of sick kids continues since before Christmas!* Mostly, it landed in the sink, thank goodness!

Back to the bath, this time with Kennedy, who I'm pretty sure hadn't been bathed all week. I dressed Syd in her cozy PJs and held her while she cried, ready to catch more barf if needed, until she finally fell asleep on my bed. Colton helped get Kennedy out of the bath while OJ was taking Braxton to an activity. He came home, moved sleeping Syd up to her bed, and she barfed all over again! So, he took her to the shower while I cleaned up the third round of throw-up and started another load of wash. At 8:30 we finally got Sydney feeling better and sleeping and OJ and I plunked down and got lost in *Lost* before the older boys came home and Kenny came down at 9:00, reminding me I didn't actually put her to bed!

No wonder I'm just this side of being completely crazy myself! That's the tricky part: to remain sane amidst the craziness. *Cheerfulness, right?* I'm not sure how cheerful I've been, but I am definitely learning the true definition of "Live in the now!" Hopefully, tomorrow's "now" isn't quite so...*alive*.

Saturday, May 16

When Cyndy called a couple weeks ago and mentioned her husband was going to Ireland on business and she was considering joining him, I said,

"You should definitely go. I'd sure go if I were invited."
She jumped on it. "You would? Then, come with us!"

It seemed a little crazy, flying off to Ireland in
two weeks—setting up sitters for the kids and leaving,
just like that. When I called and told Mom about it, she
offered to watch the kids for the entire time, saying,
"You've got to take an opportunity like this when it
comes." It was a done deal. We were going to Ireland.

For seven days and nights we drove the country
and saw the sights. Mostly, the sights were lush green
hills, beautiful old castles, bridges, and sheep. There
were sheep everywhere. We pulled out the map each
day, picked a route, and drove. Then we found the best
bed-n-breakfast we could find and camped for the night.
Luckily, with my "no bad moods on vacation" rule in
play, I didn't have a single bad day, jet-lagged as we
were.

Cyndy and I sat in the back of the mini-car,
crowded on all sides by our oversized luggage. We
created a list of questions as we drove, so we could get
to know the Irish culture a little better and make small
talk with the locals. Our first question, "So, what's the
deal with all the sheep?" got us a chuckle and a head
nod, like, "Yep, there are a lot of sheep." We also asked,
"Is painting your house and fences a big deal here?"
prompted by the staggering number of people we saw
painting their houses and fences. Yes, apparently they
take more pride in keeping things painted than we do,
and it was unusually sunny while we were there.

Another question, "Do you have SUVs?" got us
a blank stare. We had to explain, "Any large cars?" "Not
really," was the response. "So, are there no large families
here, then?" Another chuckle. "There are some, like the
Catholic families." *Interesting.* I love learning about other
people and ways of life.

We also kept a list of all the amazing sites we
discovered. "Old, abandoned stone cottage," "Beautiful

stone bridge," "Gorgeous abandoned castle-like structure," "Short, long stone wall, surrounded by sheep." We soon discovered these "amazing sites" were everywhere! So, we just started adding check marks. "Another old, abandoned fill-in-the-blank. Check!" "Another person painting adorable picket fence. Check!"

OJ got to golf on one of the best courses in Ireland, with rough so deep, it was nearly impossible to find a stray ball. I would know. I tried to hit a few myself! We visited the Cliffs of Moher on a rainy day that was so windy, our umbrellas blew out, and drove the Ring of Dingle, with thin roads perched on the edge of towering cliffs that dropped to the roaring ocean. We also found my new favorite chocolate caramels in the gift shop of an *actual* castle—Butlers Chocolates—and the best gas stations, with fresh fruit and home baked goodies—*delicious*! We could have eaten out of the gas stations all week, especially since, unfortunately, the rumors are true, and much of the local fare was not as flavorful as one might like.

The best things we saw were the road signs. Really, Irish road signs are as charming as the sheep on the hills—I took picture after picture of them. My favorite was near the ocean, a bright yellow sign with a picture of a car going off the cliff into the water! It seemed particularly funny. *Why would anyone need a sign to know not to drive into the ocean?* But, you know me. I can create a metaphor out of anything. I will forever use that photo in speeches with the analogy, "It might seem unnecessary to have a warning sign not to drive your car off the cliff into the ocean, but then again, how many of us could use a warning sign telling us not to drive ourselves off the edge sometimes?"

My favorite, however, was celebrating American Mother's Day (Irish Mother's Day, we learned, had been celebrated weeks before) at the most adorable bed-n-breakfast, Mallmore Country House, in our favorite town of Clifden. We'd read about it in our travel book, and just had to stay there. Luckily, we'd gotten the last two rooms the night before. After settling in, we explored a nearby abandoned stone castle by climbing over fences and through mud-bogged grasses. We went to dinner in town, shoes muddy and grass-streaked, and then returned to our adorable room with two twins, decorated in soft blue and white, with big, bay windows overlooking the rolling green yard and the lake beyond. We all met up in the fancy parlor at bedtime, in our PJs, and sipped the best black cherry herbal tea, talking and laughing until we were way too tired. In the morning, we slept in as long as we could without missing the traditional Irish breakfast—two eggs, Irish sausage and bacon, tomato, potatoes, herbal tea, brown bread, and Irish butter—personally my favorite of the Irish meals. We then spent the rest of Mother's Day exploring waterfalls and driving wherever our map and the Ireland guidebook would take us. We even ended up driving into the ocean—literally—to visit a tiny island you can only get to at low tide. You should have seen the screen of our GPS. Our little car looked like it was floating in the middle of the blue! There, we posed for pictures at an ancient cemetery, fed a donkey an apple from our car window, and when the roads became skinny, got stuck sideways trying to turn our mini-car around! We then made our way back to Galway, to enjoy an Irish Pub dinner before meeting up for our new evening herbal tea routine in our hotel room. Yes, we swiped some tea from The Mallmore.

We woke up each morning and seized each day! I think that's one lesson that's come of all this—I don't believe in waiting for the "best time" anymore. I know time is short. "I will prepare and someday my chance will come,"[2] Abraham Lincoln once said. I believe if you want the memories, the fun, the adventure, you prepare for it, and then, you take the opportunity when it comes. The best part of taking *this* opportunity was that traveling to Ireland was my first true sign that I am well. That *all* is well. That there is so much beauty and richness to life, and I am here, ready to enjoy it.

I felt so blessed to have gone to Ireland. It showed me how much we create our experiences and how many times I've created negativity in the past. I made an effort not to think about sleep or worry about any lack of it. I focused on feeling happy and acting cheerfully. I laughed and laughed. It feels like a huge weight is lifted when I can shove away the negative, focus on cheerfulness, and let love in.

I loved my trip to Ireland. And, you know what? I think *Ireland* loved *me* a little, in return. Ireland and I have a thing for each other—we're sort of dating now. Wink, wink.

Monday, May 29

I've been thinking about wanting peace and how I would probably feel greater peace if I just gave up the idea of writing and focused solely on my family—creating memories with them, loving them, and letting my own "needs" go.

That's a fine life, isn't it? Caring for my family? Many women would love that life. So, I begin to fold up my thoughts and ideas and place them in the closet of my mind, but they keep coming back. They won't leave me. They must come out. I must speak. I must write. It is the only way.

I seem to be avoiding writing at all costs—washing the dishes, doing laundry, organizing cupboards, straightening, decorating—doing anything that can seem important in the moment and distract me from this task. I sit down to finally write just as I look at the clock and mysteriously notice the kids need to be picked up from school. I wonder why, if I am filled with so many words that must be heard, why do I avoid giving them a voice?

Well, I know why I avoid it. It brings reminders of Shannon. Lately, reminders seem to be filling my world. Just now, I was putting clothes away in my closet, whittling away the growing pile of frustrating clothes discarded on the floor. *No, that doesn't look right, that's too wintery; I'll be too hot.* Something fell. It was an envelope. I picked it up and felt a jolt. Shannon's death certificate. Mom and Dad had given it to me months ago, figuring the boys' new parents should keep it. I promptly put it away. In fact, I have put all the trinkets I've kept for her boys away, together in a big flowered box, tucked neatly behind my jackets.

Sometimes, I find the envelope with the autopsy report hidden in my nightstand. *Another jolt.* I still haven't read it. When I see it, I slide it aside, feeling a steel wall pop up in my mind to block any and all thought or emotion. Even now, I can feel that wall sliding up and see myself wanting to hold it down, to access even a speck of that space and see what's really in there. The wall is strong. Stronger than I am right now.

Interrupted. Two kids just came in and they both should be in bed. It's hard to get in touch with any emotion other than frustration when I'm constantly interrupted! My heart is racing. I'm breathing heavier. *Deep breath. Inhale. Exhale. Breathe.* I need to relax when these moments come. I'm doing better, working on being more present with my kids and not allowing the illusionary emotions of guilt, suffering, and martyrdom to come in. It's a work, and it is in progress. It's a challenge to be "me"—to be the very best eternal soul I truly am—with so many interruptions.

See how easily I distracted myself away from the emotions brought up by writing?

Tonight, I was pondering success and how it seems so fickle. It's so "Me! Me! Me," like a child learning, "Mine! I want it!" Writing this book is my want, but do I *need* to succeed at writing this book? I'm not sure I need it. Then, that little voice comes and says, "Yeah, but it would be nice, wouldn't it?" I have to admit, it *would*.

This writing is going to be much harder than I thought it would be—so permanent, so open to criticism. It brings up so much. I don't *need* success as much as I need to successfully take care of myself so I don't burn out. Still, I *need* to write. *That* I know.

Wednesday, May 31

I "graduated" myself from therapy today. It was a touching final session.

We spent the first half discussing the boys' session with their Grandpa Cutler last week. Dr. Hale said the boys did great expressing their true feelings, but that it was obviously hard for their Grandpa to comprehend. The boys told me the same thing, feeling confused by the entire exchange—from Grandma Cutler not coming to the session at all, to Grandpa Cutler dropping them straight home instead of taking them to dinner after, like we'd planned. We haven't heard a word from them ever since. They never even called and talked to the boys about the adoption. It's hard to understand for us all, and not what I would wish for them or the boys. *But*—a big but here—it's been so much lighter not having that stress in our lives.

We discussed all we have been through together, all that I have learned. I was able to thank Dr. Hale for being one constant in my ever-changing world. Dr. Hale told me I've done great work, that he's enjoyed our time together, and he even offered me a job, if I ever want it. He agrees I have worked hard for a very long time, and it is time to go it alone again.

We psychologists don't often get closure. Most clients just stop coming once they feel better. I'm glad I was there for my "graduation ceremony." Like other graduations, it was really a commencement—in this case, the commencement of being well again.

Saturday, June 3

I had a dream with Shannon last night.

I am in Shannon's white closet, trying to get dressed in her clothes. But nothing fits or feels right. Shannon isn't here, through I wish she were, so she could tell me what to wear. I hear a noise, and, looking toward the doorway, I see Rob, seeming sad. I try to explain to him how much Shannon loved him. "She loved you so much, Rob. I hope you know that." He doesn't seem to hear me. He only sits on the floor and stares at the wall.

I woke up, almost in tears. I do feel like I try to "fit" in Shannon's role, as mother. I feel like I'm always trying to make sure the kids know how much their mother and father loved them. I only hope *they* will hear.

Though it's still windy, like spring, summer break is upon us, and that means changes in more than just the weather. Tre's sixth grade graduation and the kids' last day of school are both tomorrow. It's really not much of a day, more like a few hours. Then, boom! Summer break! I look forward to less managing of schedules, homework, and mornings, and to more swimming and late nights, sitting on the deck, watching the sunset. I am *not* so eager for the mess, noise, and constant-ness of six kids home for the summer.

I'm also weaning myself off the antidepressant. I've already cut the dose in half once and then again, and next, I start skipping days. With the court out of our lives and the adoption complete, I feel ready to manage on my own again, though I hope I haven't set myself up for disaster, abandoning my resources right when summer arrives. After caring for very sick kids again, all last week, and getting a nasty stomach flu myself, I am finally physically "back." But, emotionally, I am drained. Add my nervousness about summer coming and weaning off my meds, and I'm feeling a bit irritable, like there are subconscious emotions that want to rise to the surface.

I'm trying to be realistic here. To acknowledge both the positives and negatives of summer and where I am, and go with the flow. *I'm better at going with the flow now, aren't I?* I sure hope so.

TWENTY
Discover Authenticity

"Authenticity is a collection of choices that we have to make every day. It's about the choice to show up and be real. The choice to be honest. The choice to let our true selves be seen."
~*Brene Brown,* The Gifts of Imperfection[1]

Am I a perfectionist? I've often wondered. I definitely have moments when I want everything "just so." But, no, I would not say I am a perfectionist, for I do not *believe* in perfection—at least not in this life.

What is "perfect," anyway? A dictionary tells us it means "without faults."[2] The media tells us it means looking, doing, or being the very best. However, *research* tells us perfectionism has nothing to do with self-improvement *or* being our very best. Perfectionism, instead, "hampers success. In fact, it's often the path to depression, anxiety, addiction, and life-paralysis."[3]

Perfectionism not only involves trying to be without faults, which is impossible; it involves trying to be without faults according to an *external* standard. It is measuring oneself against another person or concept. It is seeking to make others think more of us, seeking to help ourselves *feel* like more. Engaging in this game only leads to a poor sense of self-worth and confusion about who we really are. Thus, the pursuit of perfection is a hopeless cause.

Instead of perfection, what if we strived for being *authentic*, for being *complete*? That's what the Greek translation of the word "perfect" actually means, according to Aristotle—"complete," "so good that nothing of the kind could be better," and "that which has attained its purpose."[4] When we seek to attain our purpose, to fulfill our *internal* standard of life and who we must become, we live authentically. We are *complete*. And, I believe in being *complete*—in discovering who I really am, striving for authenticity, and making *right* choices that help me feel whole.

I understand that "right" and "wrong" can be relative; it's a popular position these days. On a personal level, it's much less relative than most of us think. Yes, both the "right" and the "wrong" choices lead us along our path of learning and growth. Unfortunately, the wrong choices come with baggage. They detour us and create pain, not only for us, but for those we love. Each time I choose to throw anger at someone, or to sabotage myself, I make a wrong choice, and pain follows. If I ignore the voice in my head, warning me to back away from a frustrating situation or to slow down and get some rest, I choose poorly. And, yep. You guessed it: pain.

Seeking to do right, to be complete, to live authentically, is the opposite of perfection. We open our eyes to what is real instead of striving to be something that is not. The more we work on living authentically, the easier it becomes to recognize our crossroads of right and wrong, to make healthier choices, and to feel more complete. Once we know better, hard as it may be, it's even harder to *knowingly* let ourselves cause pain, especially to those we love.

So, no. I'm not a perfectionist, though it can seem that way when I'm constantly trying to do what's right. Trust me, it drives me crazy at times, holding myself accountable for so many moments of my life. Yet, it also creates a greater atmosphere of love and acceptance, for myself, and for those around me.

Living authentically—listening to the whispers and doing what's right, being true to who I really am—helps me appreciate the good *and* the bad, for I see them as opportunities to grow. The more I grow, the more *perfected* I become: she who has "attained her purpose;" feeling "so good nothing of the kind could be better;" *"complete."*

Thursday, June 8

We're leaving soon for our first family reunion on Mom's side since I was young. I can't wait to show the kids Chicago, the "windy city," where I lived when I was little and Dad was in dental school at Northwestern. OJ and I *almost* lived there to attend graduate school, if Northwestern hadn't closed their dental school months before. Flying to Chicago will be Kennedy's first time on a plane, and she is beaming with excitement. All the kids are. OJ and nineteen month-old Sydney are staying home—for an easier trip, OJ says, though I know it's also so he can golf, guilt-free. That's okay, though. It's *my* family's reunion, after all, and I'm sure we will have a great time without him, even if it means flying solo with five kids!

Strangely enough, I'm actually more nervous about spending so much time with my family than being alone with the kids. Things have been so tense with my parents these past years. I've been so immersed in raising this new family, I've barely had time to keep up with any extended family. I haven't seen Aunt Christina or my closest cousin, Hilary, since they came for Shannon's memorial, and that brings reminders of my sister again. I wonder, *what will it be like, not having Shannon at the reunion?* I wonder, *what will everyone say about how I am doing with her children?* I guess I feel a little guarded about potential criticism. I want so badly to do be doing this well. And I want everyone to treat me normally, honestly, too—not to tiptoe around or watch me too closely. I don't want to be "poor Christi" again.

Before we get to things with my side of the family, however, we have an important visit to make on OJ's side. We're stopping in Scottsdale before we head to the airport so we can visit OJ's dad, Papa Dave, in the hospital. He's had diabetes since he was thirty, just like OJ; now he has cancer. About seven years ago, he was diagnosed with a disease of the liver that the doctors said would eventually kill him. I remember Lorri and Dave sitting their five sons, two daughters, and many in-laws down, and breaking the news that our beloved father and father-in-law would not live long. We cried and mourned losing our "Papa" at that time. But he is strong and takes great care of himself, so here we are, seven years later, going through it again—this time, I fear, for real. After OJ was diagnosed with Celiac Disease and learned of the connection between Celiac and Diabetes, he suggested his dad get tested. Sure enough, Dave had been living with Celiac Disease all this time, and hadn't changed his diet. At seventy-two years old, it had done a lot of damage, internally. The doctors think it led to the liver disease that led to his cancer.

We're not ready to lose someone else. I pray he can make it. I pray my kids don't have to say goodbye to another person they love so very much, so very soon.

Thursday, June 18

Any worries I had about being with my family for our reunion were misconstrued. Our trip to Chicago was a blast.

It was great to see cousins, aunts, and uncles I haven't seen in years, and it was even better to see the kids having such a wonderful time. Even the flight there was a joy, with the boys loving every free soda, and Kennedy exclaiming, "I'm just so used to this!" an hour after we took off. We toured Sears tower, Lincoln Park Zoo, and the Magnificent Mile, where Kennedy experienced her first visit to the American Girl store. Two stories of lifelike dolls and accessories? Her eyes were as wide as I've ever seen them! An almost-six year-old's dream! We had a family talent show. Kennedy and I sang my *Lovey Lullaby*. Ten year-old Colton impressed us with Coldplay's *Clocks* on the piano, and twelve year-olds Braxton and Tre cranked out Red Hot Chili

Pepper's *Dani California,* on the guitar and drums, while my dad and brother sang, to everyone's delight. Clapping and singing in a room packed with family, my heart smiled and thumped with gratitude.

We toured the suburbs, where I lived until I was four, which brought back a few memories. I was so little, I was amazed I still have any left! It was comforting to be with Mom and Dad, to see them enjoying themselves with their siblings, kids, and grandkids, to lay aside our differences and remember how much I love them. That's what being together always seems to do: re-connect us. I was touched by the kind and supportive discussions I had as I reconnected with my cousins. I was surprised to know they often think of us, and to learn how much they admire and respect me and what I've been able to do as a mother. It overwhelmed me in a good way and pushed up emotion for Shannon, reminding me I am not alone, and that Shannon is remembered.

Now, we're home, and it's back to business as usual—cleaning, laundry, kids running everywhere, and OJ coming home late after golfing "an extra nine." I try to be an understanding wife, but it's argue season, thanks to OJ's "mistress," as I like to call golf. I'm working on the proper term for his disorder, because it has definitely reached clinical levels. I'm thinking "Obsessive-Compulsive-*Delusional*-Golf Disorder." It's long, I know, but it perfectly describes his symptoms. I'm pretty sure I could insert a number of other words into the "golf" section and it could apply to many husbands (hunting, boating, skiing, video-game playing, etc.), and thus help many families. I'm hoping I can get it in the DSM (the diagnostic manual for psychiatric disorders) some day. Then, maybe I can get him diagnosed and into treatment.

Business as usual.

Saturday, June 20

Tomorrow is Father's Day and OJ's birthday—a double whammie. This year, I opted to give him exactly what he wants: a full day of completely guilt-free "whatever." He was, therefore, gone from 8:00 a.m. until 8:30 p.m. today, golfing.

I admit that I really dislike this time of year, and not just because of golf. OJ's birthday is always near Father's Day, and that same week we have Kennedy's, Grandma's, and OJ's brother, Cory's, birthdays all on the same day. Lorri's birthday is two days later and then, Nana's birthday. I try to make it nice for everyone, but it can be a challenge. For OJ, I made a gluten-free cake with chocolate ganache, bought gifts he'll probably return, because that's what he always does, and I'm making BBQ ribs and potatoes tomorrow—a boy favorite. But, if I'm being honest, it feels pretty much like our norm around here—OJ gone all day and me home, taking care of things—only, I don't get to complain about it.

So, I'll complain to my journal instead. I'm wiped out! I see a pattern—wake up tired, try to get going, work on the house and kids, try to exercise. Try to do something fun with the kids. Lose steam early to mid-afternoon. Attempt a rest or nap, which usually fails. Force myself back to work with a vengeance. Begin to feel frustrated again, after dinner. This builds until I'm on the brink of a disastrous meltdown! Lose it as little as possible. Try to tune out with TV and junk food (I feel fatter lately). Crawl into bed around 9:30 or 10:00.

How can I pursue any of *my* goals and dreams? The only time I feel even slightly able to is when I get in bed and it's finally quiet. I want to stay awake all night in that quiet—to read or write, or just to think! But, my eyes are so heavy and burning, I end up turning out the lights and crashing to sleep, instead. Otherwise, it's a constant stream of "Mom! Mom!" all day and night.

From the second I get up—usually to kids in my face—
to the second I get in bed, after the kids finally decide to
sleep, I rarely have a moment for me. I've learned
enough to know I'm much better, creatively, after I've
had time to ponder. I'm much better all around after
I've had time to be creative. I miss feeling inspired. I
miss feeling connected and like I'm learning, I miss *me*.

The same words keep flashing in my head like a
warning sign: *Something's gotta give!* And, it *does*.

Hopefully, it's not my sanity.

Sunday, June 21

My good intentions have failed. I botched OJ's
birthday.

I held it together yesterday and tried so hard not
to give in to my frustrations this morning, but they've
been building for a while, and, by the time I had gotten
us all to and from church this afternoon, I was begging
for a nap. "I know it's your birthday," I said. "But, I'm
on an edge here. I'm sorry, but I'm desperate." OJ
kindly agreed, and I fell hard into dreams I didn't
remember.

After an hour, it was tough to pull myself back
to reality. I did so to Braxton arguing with OJ, and Tre
faking sick because he had a headache from his
sleepover the night before. OJ forced me to leave with
him and drive to Forest Highlands, finally seeing the
"Help me!" in my red eyes. We pulled into the parking
lot. I spilled it all.

"It's so overwhelming," I told him. "There are
too many kids! Too much stimulation! Too many
problems! I'm so constantly needed—by you, the house,
the kids, by everyone! I can't do it all! Something *has* to
change!" It was almost like all the emotions I'd been
feeling when I started the antidepressant back in
December were now flooding me: anger, irritability,
frustration, and, I didn't want to admit it, but sadness,

too.

I felt like a total whiner, especially since it was his birthday, but I couldn't help it. I was broken. OJ listened and held me, and he made a commitment to help me get a break. I think he knew he was part of the problem and was trying to make himself part of the solution.

It made me wonder, *Should I go back on the meds? Would it be any better with them? Should I have waited until summer is over?* I could hear Dr. Hibbert's voice again, telling me I am learning how to be me again, how it makes sense that old feelings or issues might resurface now. "Not to mention," she said, "it's intensely busy with the kids right now. It's just the way it is."

But do I need counseling again, Dr. Hibbert? I shouldn't have stopped the medication and counseling right before summer. That was a huge mistake, wasn't it? It certainly felt right at the time. I'm probably having rough days because of summer stress. I'm still struggling to parent these boys. Tre's been especially hard for me; I feel a wall with us too often. I struggle to love him better, and it can be awkward. I wish it were smooth. Yet, I don't think it was a mistake to stop counseling and medication.

It's so easy to doubt myself. I'm so easily pushed off my game. Perhaps, what I really need is to drop the game all together. That's what today was—dropping the need to be everything to everyone and instead, getting in touch with me for a while. I'm sorry it had to be on OJ's birthday, but looking back, I gave him a great weekend.

He is just fine. And now, so am I.

Thursday, June 25

OJ is golfing, but I don't mind. *Really.* Because *all* the kids are at Mom and Dad's house until Saturday! *Thank you, Mom and Dad!* As I sit and bask in the glorious stillness, I realize this is the first time we've had the house to ourselves since we inherited our new family. I'm using my time wisely—resting, reading *A New Earth,* by Eckhart Tolle, and pondering.

Last night, I prayed, *Heavenly Father, please show me my path.* Before, my path was clear: Build this family and help us heal. Now, I'm not so sure about my focus. *Help me face my frustrations and find the understanding I seek.* Today, as I read and think, I feel my prayer being answered. Some important things are becoming clear.

I had the opportunity to speak to a women's group the other night. Usually, I'm at ease speaking and know exactly what I am going to say, but this time, I was uncertain—so much so that I changed the whole talk an hour before. I ended up sharing stories of my past two years. I spoke of overcoming challenges, of becoming better through them, and of discovering joy. It felt right and seemed to be what the women needed. At least, I hope it was. I received several sincere "thank yous" and a few "I appreciate you being so reals." Mostly, though, that talk was an important beginning to my *own* understanding, the understanding I've been continuing to reflect upon today.

What am I beginning to understand, through all this reading, listening, and teaching? First, I am way over-identified with my story. *Still.* When I shared it, the other night, it was with a distinct purpose to connect and teach, and *that* felt right. But, too often, I share for the wrong purposes—to get attention or sympathy, or to make myself something other than just *me.* I know better.

I also see I'm too caught up in my "self," my "ego." Ironic how I've spent all these years studying the importance of a sense of self, yet, here I sit, knowing it doesn't matter as much as I like to believe. Sense of self is a concept—it is my *perception* of who I am. It's not who I *actually* am. Getting stuck in my sense of self, in ego, I end up over-evaluating and trying to be something

I'm not. I find myself trying to make me "right" and others "wrong." I get caught up in what kind of "mom" I am—how I'm *doing*—instead of *being me,* in my role as a mother. I am caught up in my sense of self. When I'm caught in my *sense* of self, I am out of tune with my *real* self, and also with God. Like I taught in the women's group last week: if I'm not connected to my true, eternal self, and to God, if we're not a team, then all relationships and aspects of my life are weakened.

I've been very identified with my roles: mother, wife, daughter, psychologist. It's hard not to be when they're my whole world, or seem to be. My need to cling to my roles, I am seeing, comes from a feeling of "I am not enough." I feel less than, so I try to *be* something more, to play a role—"the perfectly loving mother," for instance. Perhaps, I even try to *be* myself, although that is just another role. Eckhart Tolle's words say it best: "You are most powerful, most effective when you are completely yourself. But don't try to be yourself... If you can be absolutely comfortable with not knowing who you are, then what's left is who you are..."[5] I need to be *me* more—aware, awake, conscious, and connected. I need to be still, to disconnect from my roles, and to connect with God daily. This is knowing and embracing my self-worth, and it is essential to remembering who I am. It is essential to tapping the peace and love I desire to bring to everyone else.

This was another light bulb moment for me, today: self-esteem and humility are the same. As Tolle writes, "True self-esteem and true humility arise out of that realization. In the eyes of the ego, self-esteem and humility are contradictory. In truth, they are one and the same."[6] *How true this is!* It reminds me of my own struggle with songwriting and performing. There was a time when I felt like I was sharing my songs as a way to prove I was good enough, to show "what I've done." Soon, I became embarrassed to share, because, deep down, I knew I was doing it for the wrong reasons. For a long time, I stopped sharing completely. I was essentially *trying* to be humble by not sharing my songs, but I wasn't humble. I was just insecure.

Now, when I'm sharing songs or giving talks, I do it from a place of love. I feel more like I'm communicating and connecting with people this way, and that feels right. It's more like, "This is me. I hope you like it. I hope it helps you." Like my talk the other night; it felt real. It felt right. Yes, I did share a song, and that felt right, too, because I did it for the right reasons.

I needed this time for self-reflection. Look how much I've already discovered! *Self-esteem and humility are the same.* Isn't that how Jesus Christ lived? It's definitely how *I* want to live. Less of me means more space for God and for everyone else I love.

That is humility.

Thursday, July 2

The kids have been sick in a constant humming rotation, like a swarm of bees ready to sting me if I surface from the water. Okay, maybe that's a rude way to put it, but that's the visual I had as I sat down to write this—a constant stream of need.

This feels like a huge problem today. A burden. Some time ago, however, I learned there really are no "problems" in life, only *situations*. *I* am the one who decides to turn my situations into "problems." I am, therefore, choosing *not* to turn this into a problem, but rather to state, "I have some *situations* that need *solutions*." I've been tapping the Dr. Hibbert in me for help. Here's what we've come up with so far:

Situation #1: I get most frustrated when I'm trying to do something—writing, for instance—and the kids interrupt me. My default is to say, "Forget it! I won't even try!" and turn to novels and chocolate instead.

Solution: Imagine I will always be interrupted. I learned this from the *Don't Sweat the Small Stuff* chapter titled, "See the glass as already broken (and everything else too)." A Buddhist teaching, "the essence...is that all of life is in a constant state of change. Everything has a beginning and everything has an end... A glass is created and will eventually break."[7] If I *expect* my time to be "broken," I will feel less frustration when it actually *is*. It prevents me from continually seeing the kids as "interrupting," allowing me to focus on what they need, to be more present, and to patiently, cheerfully love them better.

Situation #2: I get triggered by the kids and OJ when I'm feeling frustrated. The kids fight; OJ tries to intervene and just gets mad and yells, causing more tension. I take it all on. I take offense. I become defensive, and it leads to unnecessary stress between us.

Solution: I'm practicing being neutral. I ask, "What if this didn't affect me at all?" and it makes a huge difference. It allows me to watch, to see when I'm being triggered, and identify what is really happening. I name it out loud, "Ego," and then, let it go. "Oh, yeah, I don't need to engage in this," I remind myself. "I can just be present. Neutral."

Situation #3: I get overcome with emotions, especially when I'm too tired, which is often. It's like the emotion *becomes* me.

Solution: When a powerful feeling appears, I take a few deep breaths and feel it. I say, "There is anger in me," or, "I have unhappiness in me," and naming the emotion somehow separates *it* from *me*. Sometimes, it even simply goes away. I'm less likely to feel I've "become" angry, depressed, etc. It's a much more peaceful way to live, and I'm much nicer to be around.

These are *all* tools that create a more peaceful way to live. When I recognize the "situations" as they come, get in touch with the reality of them, and work for a solution, I find myself feeling spontaneously free.

Thursday, July 9

We've been on vacation at our friends, Leonore's and Adam's, cabin in scenic Greer, Arizona. Basking in wildflowers, streams, and perfect weather, it's been wonderful to just have fun with our friends. We've also been basking in some much-needed R&R.

But the fun and R&R ended, temporarily, this afternoon, when Tre started a fistfight with Braxton, over a ping pong game. According to the other boys, he threw punches and his paddle, and then slammed the garage door, saying he was running away.

I had been pushing a litter of little ones, my own included, on this crazy, old, red wooden swing that's more like the Teacup ride at Disneyland than an actual swing, and met Tre stomping down the dirt road from the cabin as I was heading back. It was clear from his heavy breathing, clenched fists, and red eyes that he was not well. He wouldn't look or talk to me, and wouldn't stop walking when I asked him to.

"What's the problem?" I asked, irritated because the boys had already told me what he'd done. He knew he'd clearly been wrong, and he was not listening. But the way he looked at me, with fire in his eyes, I knew this was bigger than just a fight between brothers.

"The *problem* is that I'm here in this family!" he finally exploded, then ran to a nearby pine tree, started climbing the two by fours nailed to its rising trunk, and hoisted himself onto the towering tree house, dangling his feet from the edge.

Not wanting to provoke him, or me, further, I calmly said, "Well, when you cool down, come and get me. We need to talk."

I turned and walked back up the dirt road to the cabin—to give us both space, I told myself—to let him calm down. I only got a few steps away before stopping dead in my tracks. *What should I do?* I pleaded, looking up to the huge, clear sky—the question I ask so often when dealing with these boys. In a moment, I knew. I needed to go back. Even though I had a pile of young kids and Sydney with me, Tre needed me. Now. I asked Colton and Braxton to take the kids home, then turned with Sydney, toward the tree house.

I said a quick, silent prayer. *Father, please help me know how to handle this. Show me what he needs. Give me the words. Help me love him.* Then, quietly, I sat down at the base of the tree and waited. It only took a minute for Tre to make his way slowly down the ladder and sit near me, crying and averting his eyes.

"What's going on?" I asked, in the most loving voice I could summon.

"Well," he said, looking deep into my eyes so I could see the pain and anger, "my parents died—that's one. And now my own brothers pick on me and don't like me. That's two." There it was.

"I think number two is a result of feeling angry about number one, honey," I said, looking back into his eyes so he could see my compassion.

He nodded, slowly. "Yeah."

I moved closer to him on the pine needles that smelled like summer. I put my arms around him and held on. He leaned his head on my shoulder and wrapped his arms tightly. And let it out. *Let. It. All. Out.*

"You don't deserve any of the bad things that have happened," I told him as he sobbed and shook in my arms. "It's not your fault, honey. And, it's not fair."

I patted his hair, kissed his forehead, and Sydney kissed him, too. We hugged and cried together as Tre told me, "Sometimes it's just too hard. Because my parents died, and then I have to get used to our house and our rules."

"I know, dear. It is hard, I know."

He caught his breath. "I know I wasn't such a

great kid before," he said. "I mean, I got into trouble a lot and kinda thought it was cool to do bad stuff. So, it's just like I've got to get used to it here."

We talked about how I believe the real Tre is the one who is loving and helpful and sweet, and how the other stuff he did or does isn't really him. "It's just a way of trying to help yourself feel better. But it's not really a good idea, because it doesn't work. Right?" I said. He nodded.

I asked him to describe what he feels like inside, about his Mom and Dad.

"It's like…an emptiness…like a big hole."

So, we called it "the emptiness." We talked about grief. I explained how grief works and that it's normal to feel depressed and angry. I tried to externalize the struggles he's facing and encouraged him to know they are not who he is—they are just struggles.

Mostly, we just sat and loved each other in the stillness of the forest until he turned and, hugging me tighter, said, "I'm sorry. It's just…I'm so glad you're my real mom. Thank you," and cried even harder.

I've never held him as tightly as I did in that moment. It broke my heart and healed it all at once. "I love you so much," I said. "Dad and I both do. We love you, and we're so glad you're part of our family and so proud of you and all you've been able to do through your trials."

All the while, Sydney climbed on and off our laps, planting butterfly kisses, snuggles, and "lovies,"—a twenty month-old's way of showing us how much she cares. It made us both smile. We could feel the love. In the warm forest air, in the smell of wild grass, in the sun, in Syd's kisses, in each other's arms. This was real.

That's all we need when times are rough, isn't it? Authenticity, warmth, kisses, lovies, and the innocent heart of someone who cares.

TWENTY-ONE
Be There

"They may forget what you said, but they will never forget how you made them feel."
~Carl W. Beuchner

Too often, fear pushes us away when instinct urges us to stay with someone in need. We feel helpless, uncertain; we don't know what to say or do. Or, we may realize there really *is* nothing that can be said or done.

Some of us attempt to help by making food, watching kids, keeping busy—*doing* for the other. Others of us simply shut down, becoming helpless or falling into our own emotions, instead. Others erect walls, pretend everything is fine, or ignore the situation until things blow over. Yet while each of these may have their place in helping others, none fully connects us with those who need our love.

No matter how normal life could seem after Shannon died, whenever I shared our story, I felt odd again. I'd meet someone new. They'd ask how many kids I have. I'd say, "Six." They'd make some kind of comment like, "Wow! Haven't you ever heard of birth control?" or "Well, aren't *you* a saint!" Depending on how well I planned to get to know them, I'd either laugh it off, faking it, or actually tell them *how* I got six kids. When I did, the blank stares, dropped jaws, and tear-filled eyes would remind me, *I am odd.*

Then, the trite words of assurance would come—"Well, everyone sure looks great *now*"—or uncomfortable avoidance of me, or questions to make sure we were "okay," because everyone needed us to be "okay," so *they* could feel okay. These *really* made me feel odd. I made it easier for people, saying things like, "Yeah. It was crazy. But, everyone's doing great," and I could see the relief in their eyes. I understood why the awkwardness was there. I knew they were trying, but just didn't know how. I could handle the oddness.

Sometimes, instead of feeling awkward or odd, I felt *loved*. The "I'm so sorry," the presence, the listening, the hug, the encouragement, the respect, were all signs that *this* interaction was not about making *them* feel better. It was about loving *me*. I remember one time, at a basketball game, meeting the mother of one of Colton's teammates. All four boys played basketball at the time, and we practically lived at the gym on Saturdays, chasing Sydney, often trying to watch two games at once. One day, this mother of Colton's teammate stopped and introduced herself. She had noticed we had many children and asked, "How many do you have?" and "How do you manage?" Something in me needed to share it all that day, so I did. As I spoke, her eyes filled with tears. She listened and nodded, and before I knew it, we were both in tears. "I'm sorry I'm crying," she said, "but I'm just so sorry for all you've been through, for all the kids have had to go through." She patted my arm and gave me a hug. To this day, I can't remember her name, but I remember how she made me feel. She understood where I was. She got it. She was fully present, in that moment, and it was exactly what I needed.

Having someone just *be there* with me in the sadness, grief, and shock of it all always felt like the thing I needed most. It's what I've learned to do for others in their times of need, too. Helpful as it can be, anyone can make a meal for someone or watch kids. Don't get me wrong, all of these things I appreciated and needed at some point. But only the truly extraordinary will sit with us, feel with us, connect. And there is a big difference when they do, for connecting implies a willingness to not only reach out, but to consistently be with and *see* the other person. The people I feel closest to are those with whom I have connected. Whether they were there for me, or I was there for them, the point is, we were *there* in times of need. We may not hang out all the time, or even seem like we have much in common, but we stuck around. We kept coming back. We made a lifelong impact on one another. That's the best gift we can give anyone—to help them feel loved. To help them know they are not alone. To connect.

How do we connect? We listen. We hear. We respond. We feel. We reach out and ask, "How are you?" and wait for the honest answer. Then, we reach out again. And again. We say, "I'm so sorry. My heart is breaking with you." We look past our discomfort, or we say it out loud, "I don't know what to say or do. I just want to be here for you." We are willing to be in that space of our own discomfort or pain, because we know it's not about us. It's about loving the one we love. As we provide space for the other person's needs, they feel our love more completely. We connect. Strength and healing are in the connection.

The next time someone shares their "story," their loss, their pain, we can choose to connect—to stay with them in that space. It doesn't take much. A look, a tear, an embrace. It's being there for one another that heals us. It's being there that bonds and makes us inseparable forevermore.

Friday, July 17

We're finally here in Encinitas, California, for our annual beach vacation. We arrived at noon today, after a five a.m. wake-up call from Sydney, and spent the day boogie-boarding, settling in, and trying to have fun, even though our minds have been back in Arizona, with Papa Dave.

We left Flagstaff yesterday morning and drove to Paradise Valley, two hours south, to OJ's parents' house, where we planned to spend the afternoon and evening with our dear Bema, Lorri, and Papa Dave. He had been feeling utterly miserable from his chemotherapy treatments, so miserable, it turned out, that he'd decided just that afternoon he was done with them. We arrived as he came home from his last treatment, and Lorri told us the news.

As I got the kids settled and OJ helped his dad settle into bed, one by one, OJ's siblings and their families showed up. I don't think it was planned. The little ones gathered outside for games while the older ones gathered inside for...we weren't sure. There was a reverence in the home, even with a dozen grandkids playing basketball and swimming and another two dozen siblings, spouses, and older grandkids, wandering around. Something important was happening, though we didn't yet know what.

I felt removed, at first, tending to the children, not sure of my place as OJ and his siblings went to sit at their father's bedside. Dave and Lorri's house has always been a comfortable place for me, for all of us, a place where the kids and I have always felt loved, a place that feels like home. OJ and I actually lived there when Braxton was first born and for a few months after Colton was born, just before dental and graduate school. Oh, how Papa Dave loves babies, and oh, how he adored our baby boys! I recall Braxton's first Halloween, dressed in a black and orange onesie—Dave was humming and making him look like he was dancing and pushing this mini shopping cart they had at the time. We were all busting up! Even Shannon, and Tre and Brody, were always welcomed as part of the family. Shannon or I would bring her boys over all the time to jump on the trampoline, ride bikes, and swim. Tre and Brody have called Dave and Lorri "Bema" and "Papa" for as long as I can remember. Included by all OJ's siblings, too, they were part of the Hibbert family even before they were adopted. As I sat remembering these things, yet feeling uncertain about my role now, OJ, and then Lorri, and then his sisters, and then everyone invited me into Dave's room, saying, "You're part of this family." It was a relief, because *I am*.

The room was suddenly filled with emotion as all seven children, almost every spouse, and all of the oldest grandchildren, my four boys included, intuitively gathered in Papa's room. Again, it wasn't planned. Not a word was even spoken. It just sort of…happened. As Papa Dave sat up to speak with Lorri by his side on the bed, I began to realize what this was: his final goodbye.

He shared how he wished he'd had a chance to say goodbye to his own father, whom he'd buried just months ago, and shared his knowledge that life continues beyond this realm. He spoke of his fears of leaving his beloved wife, Lorri, of how much he loves her, how he cannot stand the thought of being without her—his "rock" and "source of strength." Their love of nearly forty-six years is a beacon of hope for all couples, and he encouraged us to love our spouses and rejoice in our families, as he has done. "I've lived a good life," he said. "I've felt blessed to have had a great family and good people in my life."

We sat, silently, for over an hour and listened as he tried to be strong, despite his body's weakness—struggling to keep his eyes open, to keep from shaking, to sit up in bed and say what needed to be said. His voice was the stalwart, stubborn, loveable patriarch we all know and love, yet his body was irony—his frail face, bone-thin shoulders, and swollen, tight, legs and feet—betraying his true strength.

Dave finished speaking, still trying to hold himself up as Lorri rubbed his back, and they both invited us to ask questions—to say whatever we wanted to say. As each of his children spoke, tears were shed, stories were shared, and attempts at laughter ended up awkward and unsuccessful. It was tender, heartbreaking, comforting, and so many other things I could never put into words.

Finally, I moved to Dave's bedside, took his hands, and, through choking tears, eventually said, "You've always been an incredible father to me. Thank you." As we embraced, I told him, "I love you," and he said the same. Not wanting to hold anything back, I couldn't help but whisper in his ear, "You are an even *more* amazing grandfather. Everyone here would agree. I feel lucky because OJ is so much like you—he admires you so much, and I feel blessed, because I'll get to have a piece of you with us always, through him. He is amazing, and I thank you for him." Then, I added, with a smile, "Even if you gave him Diabetes—it's okay."

"Oh, thank you, Christi," was his soft reply. "I love you." Something about these words—hearing him say my name and speak so lovingly, broke me, and I began to feel the loss even before it had occurred.

We left, reluctantly, this morning. "You can stay with your dad if you want, dear," I'd told OJ. But we knew there was nothing we could do and it could be weeks before he was gone, so we left for vacation at Lorri's rented beach house, where she would have been had Dave been well. OJ was quiet as we drove. "Is there anything you didn't say to your dad that you think needs to be said?" I asked.

"I wrote him a letter," he said, staring at the road. "I gave it to him before we left. It said everything." I reached out and held his hand. He turned and looked at me, then turned back to the road.

So, we're here on our vacation, and the kids are having fun. My mom and dad are here with us, which is good, in light of things. Dad took the kids to a Padres game, giving OJ and Mom time to rest, while I am having a moment sitting out here on the deck. The sound of the waves, crackling electric wires near the streetlight, and a rainbow windsock shuffling in the breeze are all that's here to distract me.

Soak it up, I hear as I sit and listen. *This is a moment, and moments change quickly.*

I love our Papa, and I love my Hibbert family. It's so hard to say goodbye, but what a gift last night was. How many people get the chance to gather with family and say everything that needs to be said? I'm so very glad we got the chance.

I wonder what I might have said if I'd have had a chance to say goodbye to Shannon?

Sunday, July 19

It is five a.m., and I am in the back seat of a small car as OJ is driving Dad and me back to Phoenix. OJ's dad, my father-in-law, died, just over an hour ago.

Now, here we are, riding the long desert road from San Diego, cloaked in stillness and our thoughts. The vibrations of the car make it difficult to write, but they soothe my tired body, and so does writing. I see OJ right there, to the front and left of me, staring straight ahead, elbow on the armrest, thumb pressed to his chin, and I wonder what he is thinking and feeling.

I was awakened shortly before the call came by a car alarm. I got out of bed, looked out my window, and it stopped. I stumbled to the bathroom, and just as I was climbing back in bed, it started again—"beep-beep-pause," "beep-beep-pause." So, I went to the front room, where OJ had fallen asleep on the couch, and peered out the open screen doors. All I could hear was the sound of the ocean waves and the light tapping of the vertical blinds, blowing in the breeze.

I went back to my room, climbed into the humid sheets, and began to pray for Sydney, asleep in the little closet in my room; for the kids, asleep down the hall; for OJ, asleep on the couch; for his family, Dave first, that he might find peace and comfort as he prepared to depart; for Lorri, that she might be blessed with extra strength, and, somehow, peace; for all the siblings, for understanding, and for comfort. I don't know how long it had been when my ears heard the bedroom door squeak, and, as my eyes opened, I saw the outline of a figure moving in the dark.

It was Mom. "Christi," she whispered.

"Yeah?"

"OJ's dad died. I think you'd better come out. He's pretty upset," she said.

I rushed to the floor of the dining room, where OJ sat, back against the wall, phone to ear, blank look, talking with his mom. Curling into his lap, I draped my arms around him. Within minutes, we had our plan: I would leave immediately with OJ and my Dad, who had to get back for work tomorrow. Mom would stay and watch the kids, then drive them back Tuesday for the funeral on Wednesday.

I felt torn as I thought of leaving the kids, whom I knew would need my comfort and love at this time. They have already experienced such loss! This is just more. But Mom reassured, "Don't worry. I will be here with them," and I know she will. She will turn it on, be the fun-loving Mimi the kids all adore, and they will be great. She, of all people, knows how to handle loss. She is the person you want in a crisis situation. This is where she shines.

So, here we are, in the silent car. OJ drives. Dad sleeps. I write. I tried to sleep, but it won't come. I'm trying not to think of losses past or fear of losses future. I'm trying to be present, here, in this moment, as my mind drifts to moments just passed—smiling with Kennedy as we jumped over waves yesterday, sitting around the thirty-inch pizza at dinner last night with my family, singing Sydney her *Lovey Lullaby* as she floated to sleep, gently holding OJ this morning, while he heard the news.

I am grateful to be where I am. I *want* to be here, heading back with OJ. I want to be of service. I *need* to be there—for OJ, for Lorri, and for whoever needs me. "Support person" is my role, and I need to play it well. *But,* I also want and *need* to be there for *me.* I want to experience this death with everyone. Somehow, it seems less my "right," because he became a father to me only fourteen years ago—like I'm peering into the private moments of a well-lit window, late at night.

I remind myself, *it's my loss, too. It's okay to want this for me as much as for anyone else.*

Tuesday, July 21

"Oh, child…don't ever discount the wonder of your tears," I recently read. "They can be healing waters and a stream of joy. Sometimes they are the best words the heart can speak."[1] My heart spoke volumes today.

Early this morning, I already had to retreat to my room, a place of refuge where I could let my sadness out in private, but OJ found me. He tried to comfort me. "I'm sorry, dear," I said. "I didn't want you to have to see this. He's your dad, I know. But I already miss him so much, too."

"Oh, honey," he said. "It's okay to be sad. You have a right to feel this loss, too." He looked me in the eye when he said that last part, so I'd know he meant it. Then, he put his strong arms around me, kissed my forehead, and held me tightly.

As we stood, embracing while I cried, Lorri and her sister, Jeanne, walked in. "I'm sorry I'm such a mess," I told them. "I'm sorry you have to see me like this. I know it's really your loss, but I just can't stop cry…" I couldn't even finish my sentence.

"Oh, sweetie. You're in good company. I've been crying all day," Lorri said, hugging me, as her tears began again.

My tears kept falling. Hard as I tried the rest of the day, I couldn't hold them back—tears for missing Dave, for missing Miki, for missing Shannon and Rob, for so many things. I cried as we viewed the body at the mortuary, and as I watched OJ and his brothers clothe their dad and place him in the casket. I cried as I watched Lorri touch the body's lips, as her own tears flowed for love lost. I cried as we all tried to make it real, and because we were in the same room where I had done my sister's hair and had tried to make *that* seem real, too. I cried at the viewing—observing the wetness on other's faces as they stared at the body, the remnant of the man they once loved. *Still* love.

I still love.

We all do.

Wednesday, July 22

At nine this morning, the entire Hibbert family was taking our seats in the front pews. We'd just had a family prayer before closing the casket, saying our final goodbyes, and filing into the chapel, like a parade, all eyes on us. I glanced behind me. The room was packed, so much so, they had to open the overflow section, which was also packed. So many people here to remember Dave, and to support the Hibberts; it touched me like a much-needed hug. I held my breath to hold back the flood.

We sang an opening hymn, which I didn't sing. It was too hard to hold back my emotions, and, since I was going to be singing a duet later, I needed to be tearless. Someone offered a prayer. I braced myself as the first of Dave's children took the podium to share memories of their dad.

Dave "Double Junior," as his dad and grandpa called him, the eldest, spoke of "Mr. Wonderful," his father's nickname, and of so many achievements. "But, his greatest," he said in broken words, "was staring death in the face." Then, Sam, third oldest, took over. Big and tough, he was emotional. He loved his dad. Craig, second oldest, was hilarious as he shared what he called "Dad-isms," like, "the red-headed stepchild," "misery's child," and other favorite phrases that always made us shake our heads and laugh. Lindsay, sixth child and the first girl, "Daddy's little girl," loved her Daddy. "He's a wonderful Papa," she said. She shared how he always had Swedish fish in his pocket for grandchildren, or *any* children, who would stand at attention and, when asked, "Who is the greatest?" would say, "You are!" and salute. Cory, fourth, reminded us "He truly was the GOAT—Greatest Of All Time," another of his many endearing nicknames, one I'd forgotten, but one I will never forget again.

Then, OJ, the fifth boy and spiritual leader, the patriarch of the family now that his dad was gone, spoke. "Dad served others," he said. "And, when you are in the service of your fellow man, you are only in the service of your God."[2] I could hear the cracks in his voice, the pain as he tried to hold off the flood. "His earthly accomplishments, varied as they were," he continued, "pale in comparison to his eternal accomplishments." And he broke. Only the second time, ever, I had seen him cry.

Finally, Amy, the "baby," thanked everyone—for coming, for the years of support, for being part of our lives. And, she thanked her dad. "He is Mr. Wonderful. He is the greatest. I love you, Dad," she ended. You could feel her great loss. I could feel my loss. All the while, I dammed up the tears that wanted to spill. For each of them. For me. For all our children. I was next, and walking to the front to sing, I held my breath, tearless.

My sister-in-law, Emilie, and I took our place and poured our souls into the perfect song to remember Papa Dave, *Well Done, Thou Good and Faithful Servant.* My voice shook a little on the higher notes, but somehow, I made it to the very last words, "Well done," before the dam began to crack and I had to cut the last note lose. I returned to my seat. OJ hugged me. And, snap! The dam broke.

I made it through a touching tribute from Dave's best friend and the closing hymn, then followed the casket outside into the hundred and ten-degree Phoenix summer. We hugged family and friends who had come to support us, and then drove to the cemetery where we melted as OJ gave a sweet dedicatory prayer at the gravesite. Then, it was done.

Back at the church for a family luncheon, Braxton pulled me aside. "I want to play a piano song," he said. "For Papa. *The Hardest Part,* by Coldplay." No one had asked him to sing or play something for Papa, he said, and he felt sad about it. I had no idea he'd wanted to share a song, but now that he was asking, I was determined to make it right for him. He asked me to sing, we practiced twice, rolled a piano into the doorway of the multipurpose room where everyone was eating lunch, and he played his little heart out for Papa as I sang about how hard it is to let go. He'd chosen the perfect song. My heart swelled with gratitude and love for being able to be a comforting part of my boy's thirteen year-old grief.

Off to Bema's. Twenty minutes to change, pack, and load the car, and we were on the road, heading back to California. It was eight p.m. by the time we ate dinner. The kids were wild, and all were spent. OJ was frustrated with the boys, so he put them to work. They complained so much they got more work. Braxton told me, "I honestly think Dad hates me." I told OJ he needed to talk with Braxton, but came out minutes later to hear OJ telling all the boys they're spoiled. I felt disappointed in all of us, and put the kids to bed, despite their arguments.

I was trying hard not to lose it. All the Zen breathing that had gotten me to this point was fading. I was so upset with OJ. I knew I shouldn't say anything, but I did, and I hate that I did. Why couldn't I just let things go—not point out to OJ how hard I've been working these past weeks? Why couldn't I have just put myself to bed and not complained about how we would manage here once the rest of his family showed up? Why did I have to complain about something that's not even a problem yet?

Why couldn't I just have loved him tonight, instead?

Friday, July 31

We drove almost all day yesterday—through LA traffic, one stop at In-N-Out, then home to Flagstaff. The family vacation was enjoyable, complete with day-long trips up and down the stairs to Grandview beach, playing with cousins of all ages, hanging out with California friends, and plenty of good eating, courtesy of Wahoo's, Pipe's, and the cinnamon buns from VG's Donuts, my personal vice. Kennedy was queen of "surfing" on the boogie board; Syd ruled the sand, getting it in places I didn't even know it could get; and the boys were kings of the waves, boogie-boarding and even learning to surf, and of the skate park, perfecting their kick-flips and ollies.

Fun was had for all, despite the high levels of cortisol flowing through each adult's brain as the Hibbert family members kept arriving: up to twenty-two people in a three-bedroom condo. Granted, eight of those were my own family, but we were all in one room, and even if it was a large room, it was rough to get any rest. The original plan had been for us to stay at Lorri's rental for a week, first with my parents, and then, with our friends, Scott and Cyndy and their kids. But, plans had changed, of course, and rightly so. It was good for Lorri. She loves the beach and her family, and she had plenty of each. We got to spend time with her and have special moments with each other as we all tried to process this loss. And no one got sunburned—just tan, as it should be.

I was observing myself all week. There were plenty of ultra-stressed moments, dealing with family personalities, my own included. There were plenty of moments I wanted to scream, "That's it!" and run away home. There were only a handful of moments I actually did act crabby or raise my voice. I stopped myself. I stayed silent. I held my tongue, and simply got to work.

On the really rough days, I grabbed a boogie-board and floated out in the ocean, eyes set on the horizon. I breathed and smiled on purpose and took in the sight of the sinking sun as I waited for the next wave. I reminded myself, *I am love. I am peace*, and I chose to believe it again. I wanted to be helpful in this space of loss, even if it had brought up my own tangled web of grief, too. I believe I was. It was good to be together. I've never felt as much a part of the Hibbert family as I did this past week.

What was the lesson from all this? I can *decide* and not feel *decided*. I can be cheerful, loving, patient, and as kind as possible, despite my circumstances. I can dig in and work, and let go, and just be *me*. In doing so this week, I received so much.

I was pondering these things, hopped up on feel-good podcasts from Steven Covey, Eckhart Tolle, and Tony Robbins at 12:30 this morning, as I pulled into our driveway. We were finally home, and everyone was anxious to get to bed. Until we realized we had no way to get into our house! We'd left the garage door opener in OJ's car, and the keys were locked inside. We banged on the door of Scott and Cyndy's house, hoping they might have a key. They were sound asleep, so we ended up calling AAA to rescue us.

I tried to remember my lesson from this week—to remain calm and make things as fun as possible—as, from 12:30 until almost 2:00 a.m., our family camped out on our driveway. Lounging in beach chairs, wrapped in blankets, some lying down on pillows, we gazed at the star-strewn sky. Flagstaff wasn't named the "World's First International Dark Sky City" for no reason; the show was glorious! The Milky Way, Big Dipper, Pluto, and Saturn were all present as we spoke of the vastness of things and the smallness of things. We laughed, we sat still, and we felt a sense of awe. Several satellites and shooting stars later, we were safe inside our home.

Stargazing with my family in the still of night, after driving all day? What could be better? It certainly could have been worse, and I was grateful cheerfulness was on my side, for we were able to make a *moment* of what could have been a *situation*.

But the best part was little Sydney, who, in the shuffle of finally getting into the house, had quietly grabbed her pink riding toy. I came outside to find her in the middle of the street, cruising down the hill in front of our house, lifting her feet, and screaming "Whee!" at 2:00 in the morning.

I called OJ to come see. We shook our heads and laughed, grateful no neighbors were awake to witness our lack of parental supervision. *If only I could be like Sydney,* I thought, as I scooped her up and hugged her off to bed.

Twenty month-olds sure know how to live from the heart.

TWENTY-TWO
Go Deep

"If you put yourself in a position where you have to stretch outside your comfort zone,
then you are forced to expand your consciousness."
~Les Brown

My last doctoral internship was in a neuropsychology program at St. Jude Medical Center in Fullerton, California. I worked in the spinal cord and brain injury units, assessing patients' brain functions and helping to rehabilitate damaged areas. It was fascinating work.

Some patients were able to describe items in great detail, but could not name a single one, a phenomenon called anomia. Others could remember everything perfectly and write it all down, but had absolutely no speech—aphasia. One patient's memory was severely damaged. He could barely speak, remember his own name, or perform any fine motor task, like writing. But, an accomplished musician, when we gave him his clarinet, he was not only able to assemble it quickly, he could play the most beautiful music. Each of these patients still possessed what they needed somewhere in their minds, but they could no longer *access* all of what they needed. This offered great insight into how much our minds can hold and how we tap only the smallest fraction of our true capabilities.

Think of the surface of the ocean, vast beyond comprehension. This represents consciousness—the mind's ability to form thoughts, ideas, and perceptions, to pay attention or monitor behavior, to conceptualize, to synthesize. The potential for conscious thought is incredible and unlimited.

Now, consider all that lies *below* the ocean's surface. This is our subconscious, immense and deep, even more vast than the surface of consciousness. Some parts see the light of day, and others are so dark and mysterious they will never be known. So, how do we make our subconscious known? And, is it even important to do so?

I often do an exercise with clients where I ask them to, first, tell me about the situation causing them distress until they can feel it in their body, and then, immediately after, to tell me the first early childhood memory that comes to mind. Without fail, the memory they choose is related to their current stressful situation and somehow sheds light on it. Dreams work the same way, dragging up subconscious material that relates to our current emotional state, teaching us from our own files of experience. When we face the darkness of our subconscious, we stretch our consciousness. We heal. We grow.

"What the mind forgets, the body remembers," the saying goes, and it's true. Emotion is absorbed by the body, deep in the cells and atoms. It burrows into our muscle fibers, and nestles into our blood. Even if we don't consciously feel it, it is there. Our memories are coded according to emotions, and similar emotions are more likely to bring up subconscious memories. We try to forget or ignore or repress painful experiences, but one day we see a commercial or an old friend, or visit a place from our past, and suddenly, our once subconscious emotions are there again, knocking on the door, desiring to be processed. Or, our subconscious speaks through physical symptoms, like muscle pain, headaches, toothaches, and panic attacks.

Many of us are more likely to run away than face our subconscious, but that is like trying to run away from a ghost sitting right on our shoulder. The best thing we can do is to acknowledge the subconscious when it comes to visit. Sit down and have a conversation. Bringing light to deeply hidden thoughts and emotions can feel scary and hard to do. It is, at first, but it is also freeing, like a massage. A nice little back rub can relieve stress, but at some point or another, we all could use a little *deep* tissue work. It hurts to have our pains massaged and worked through, but in the end, it frees us of the tension. It is the path of healing and growth.

Making conscious the hidden secrets of our subconscious may not be comfortable. But then, comfort is overrated. If we choose to grow, we choose discomfort. Growth is after all, by definition, an *un*comfortable stretching to something greater.

Sunday, August 8

It's late, and I'm writing by flashlight; the power flickered out a short while ago. This sudden shift into darkness reminds me of how I've been feeling.

Grief is a visitor in our home again. OJ's feeling it. He's tired, cranky, and seems to always be either meandering or zoning out. I feel it, too—the pain and listlessness, the deep desire to shut myself away from everything and everyone.

We had a long talk on the phone as OJ was driving home from a golf tournament in Phoenix today. We spoke of the past three years, since he was diagnosed with Diabetes and Rob got sick, and of hard times even before then—graduate school while raising two young boys, moving, having more babies and more postpartum depression for me, starting businesses, and so many family crises. It feels like there have always been crises.

I told him how sad I am to lose his dad, yet how beautiful it was that he was able to wrap things up so well, say his goodbyes, and help us find closure. OJ spoke of wanting to shut inside himself to cope, of how he knows it's better to let me in, but sometimes, it's hard to do. It made me see how much I've done the same, turning in and away from others even as I desire to be more connected. We talked of the struggle to connect with other people—friends and even family members—how it can feel like no one gets it anyway, so why even try? I didn't realize we shared that belief.

We reminded ourselves it's only been a few months since the adoption was finalized and plenty has happened in between. OJ put it in perspective. "Like my Diabetes," he said, "yes, it's easier to live with now than it was at first. But, it doesn't go away." Our losses and challenges don't go away. We just learn to live with them.

Today showed me how hard I've been trying *not* to feel, and how I've pushed emotions to the side or shoved them deep in an effort to just be happy. You know what? I *am* happy. *And* I'm sad. I'm worn out. I'm motivated. I'm so many things.

I received a touching email today from an unknown woman who was at the Postpartum Support International conference I spoke at on Thursday. It seemed ridiculous to drive to LA and back only days after we'd come home from California to give a nine-minute talk on "Postpartum Depression and Couples Therapy" as part of their first ever "Father's Panel." OJ had encouraged me to go. He knows how I need to speak, and I wanted to be there for that talk, even if the timing was not great.

The events of the past few weeks, of losing Dave and getting through, had impacted me deeply—so much so that I changed my talk, last minute, deciding instead to share the time when, naked and sobbing in the tub, I sat up to find OJ lying beside me. Sharing such a personal story opened me up to the audience. They could feel my passion when I said, "It doesn't matter so much what a father *does* or *says* to his postpartum partner. What matters is that he is *there*. Just *be* there for each other." Short as the trip was, it felt important. It gave back a part of me that has been missing. It motivated and inspired me. Apparently, it inspired others, too. The email today simply said, "My trip from New York to California was worth it just to hear your talk. Thank you."

It's all worth it if I can touch even one soul. Today, I touched OJ's soul and he touched mine. I must not hide away—from OJ, from myself, from the world. I must not ignore the whispers of light, especially when it's been feeling so dark.

Thursday, August 13
What is this?

Today, the kids are back in school, Sydney's at the babysitter, and I am alone again. I've looked forward to a day of solitude all summer. It has gotten me through many rough moments. So why is it, the moment I got home from dropping the kids off, I began to pour out tears I feared would never stop? Why do I feel so heavy, achy, and exhausted?

What *is* this? Relief? Grief? Fear? Pure physical exhaustion? Is this a "now what?" feeling? Or, a "finally, I can feel!" feeling? Or both? It feels strange. It feels unsettling. It feels like something wants to take me to the land of the dead again. Back to intense grief.

I've been there before. And, I'm never going back. I'm *here* now. Still a bit uncertain where *here* is, but, *I am here.*

Friday, August 28

Whew! Another whirlwind day! It's been that kind of week, month, and year. Between back to school meetings and supplies and kids' activities, we've been running crazy. Add in a couple sick kids and me trying to write a grant for my Coalition, and it gets a bit crazier. The epitome of crazy came yesterday when Colton ended up writhing in pain with an abscess on his bottom!

The doctor, unable to do the procedure, told me to take Colton to the ER. Of course, as soon as I told OJ, he insisted I bring Colton to his office so he could do the "surgery" himself.

"Are you sure you can do that? You're a *dentist*!" I reminded him. But OJ thinks he can do anything—and, I have to admit, he usually can—so, reluctantly, I arrived with Colton at the office, just as the last patients and staff were leaving for the day. Smiling at each one, I locked the door behind them. This was definitely something that needed to be kept secret! I headed back to OJ's desk phone, checked in at home, and returned to find poor Colton, face down, bum up, on a dental chair, the abscess sanitized and surrounded with blue bibs! (For any patients of my husband, please don't worry—he was very sanitary.)

"It's just like a dental abscess," OJ assured me. "Well, kind of."

Lucky for Colton, and for OJ, it seemed to have worked. His little dental chair surgery avoided a lengthy trip to the ER, with the bill to match, and Colton is feeling much better today.

I'm realizing that this is "normal" life. I need to expect life to be like this—a little chaotic, a very quick pace, full, unpredictable—*and* rewarding. I may not need to expect more dental chair surgeries. At least, I hope not! Being married to OJ, you never know. I should prepare to be unprepared. Expect the unexpected. Plan for plans to change. Let OJ help—even if it requires naked bums in his chair.

In this unpredictable life I need help and flexibility. My work, my passions, my solitude—when flexible—can be molded into the small spaces that life hasn't otherwise filled. This leaves me feeling more present, more rewarded by all the chaotic, quick events of each day, and less "abs(c)-ent" (Get it?) in my life.

Thursday, September 3

I dreamed of Shannon last night.

Shannon was murdered. It is years later, and, while cleaning up a pile of dirt and ash from her backyard, I find a rusty axe. I know it is linked to her death. Somehow, I find the owner of the axe and show up on his doorstep, confronting him. He admits he murdered and buried her. "But you won't be able to do anything about it," he laughs, and slams the door in my face. I am first enraged, then sorrowful, and then, strangely at peace. At least I finally know the truth.

The dream stuck with me as I woke, exercised, and got the kids up for school. It kept sneaking up on me and wanted to bring up painful memories. "Not today," I told it. But, at breakfast, it was Kennedy who brought up Shannon and Rob. We were all caught off guard when she asked, "Tre and Brody, do you know how your parents died?"

Tre was silent. After a brief hesitation, Brody answered, "Yes. Cancer."

In her adorable, six year-old, innocent way, Kennedy said, "Yeah, but your mom took the wrong medicine, and then she died."

"No," Brody said, matter-of-factly. "She took medicine, but it wasn't the wrong one. Plus, she had wine."

Death is hard enough for children to understand, let alone *this* death, which the adults were still piecing together. It was so strange to hear this six and eight year-old debate facts they barely understood like they were arguing over their favorite TV show. I corrected them. "She didn't take the wrong medicine," I said, kindly. "It was the right one. She just, accidentally, took too much."

"Yeah," Brody added, "plus she had wine."

"That's right. The medicine and the wine made her not wake up." The kids all nodded, and then switched the subject to backpacks and recess and after school plans.

It's jarring, how this pops up so easily and unexpectedly. It feels like I'm on a cliff, peacefully admiring the view, and then, *wham!* I'm shoved off and falling. In that fall I can believe Shannon is still alive and Rob is, too—like they are just away for a little while. I suppose, in actuality, they are.

But then, I hit the ground. Hard.

Tuesday, September 8

It's Miki's birthday. I did the math, twice: sixteen years since she died. She would have been twenty-four today.

I called Mom and, well, what do you say? "I just wanted you to know I remembered," is what came out. That's all I *should* say, right?

She seemed grateful for the acknowledgement, though it always feels insufficient, to me. I know she was letting herself be "depressed" today, her way of mourning, of loving Miki. I'm glad she can do that for herself. We never do fill the holes of the ones we've lost, do we?

Before we hung up the phone, Mom surprised me. "You're doing a great job handling everything," she said.

"Oh. Thank you," I stuttered out, my eyes growing moist. She doesn't always say things like that. "I'm doing my very best."

"Well, your best is far better than most people's," she said.

We hung up and I sat staring at the wall for a moment, taking it in. *I guess my mother really is proud of me. I guess she has noticed the work I've been doing, and she thinks it is good.* I guess I needed to hear that more than I'd realized.

Remembering Miki today, I felt happy. I felt grateful to know Miki lives, to know I will see her again. I imagined what she might look like right now—faithful, brilliant, and full of light, like she was as a child. And wise. I imagined we'd have a lot in common and could talk for hours. I imagined *she* would be proud of me.

I think I am proud of me, too.

Sunday, September 13

Something's trying to knock me off my rocker. I've had to work extra hard to keep my sanity.

I made myself go to church, even though—who knows why—I started crying just before we left. I worked hard to smile and reach out to others. I always seem to feel better after church. I did. For a bit.

When we got home, I changed into comfy clothes and made myself go walking with OJ, even though I didn't want to exercise. I ended up starting an argument with him, five minutes in, over nothing, really. I apologized, but it was hard to shake the disappointment in myself. So, I took an emergency nap, hoping it might help.

When I awoke, I had to find OJ. I needed to get out whatever was stirring me up inside.

"Can I just vent?" I asked him. We've been through this many times, and he knows when I ask to vent I mean I want to talk without him trying to solve or fix anything. I simply need him to listen.

"This is hard," I said, meaning, life. There it was. "And, please don't think, if I complain to you, that I'm not grateful or happy or I don't feel blessed. I do. I just think this is all very hard sometimes." *Hmm. Is that really it?* I wondered.

He nodded and sighed. "Yeah," he said. "It's hard." He hugged me, and his simple validation somehow made everything okay.

Could it be so simple? Could it be that even though we're not in a major crisis right now, it's still hard? Could it be that it's hard having three sick kids home all last week, and having twenty-five teens over for Braxton's birthday party late last night? Could it be hard not having sweets while I'm on this month-long health challenge, and keeping a routine without feeling bored? It's hard doing the very same job, day in and day out, twenty-four seven. It's hard being a mom. Could that be it? It's just hard?

A few weeks ago, a friend of mine, who had recently been faced with several major life events all at once, said, "I've learned that I can do hard things. And, I'm teaching my children that they can too." It was simple. The message stuck with me. *I can do hard things too.* Sometimes, the hard things only last for a short while. Sometimes, they last a long time. Sometimes, they get easier than they once were. But, that doesn't mean they shouldn't feel hard or we have to pretend they're *easy.*

We *can* do hard things, and, when we try, we grow stronger. It's like weight training—the more we lift, the stronger we become, until we can lift heavier loads, until even our bones, our foundation, becomes stronger. "Kites rise highest against the wind, not with it,"[1] Winston Churchill once said. So it is with us.

Let the winds blow. I will rise and soar as I cheerfully repeat, "I *can* do hard things."

Thursday, September 17

A few months ago, I was asked to be an expert witness on a court appeal case for a woman charged with child abuse ten years ago and sentenced to forty years in prison, without a possibility of parole. Today, I made time to begin reading through the court documents, medical records, and police reports—from the time of the incident, and the past ten years.

Having such an intimate look into another woman's life has been humbling. She was young, she loved her baby, and from what I am seeing, she was overtaken by some form of postpartum disorder. My heart aches for this woman, who lost everything—her boyfriend, her freedom, her baby—essentially, her life. That poor baby, too! The biggest tragedy is that this even had to happen. It could all have been prevented if they would have had someone, like me, to help.

It reminds me I have knowledge and skills that can make a difference. It pushes me to use them, to be of service, to ease others' suffering. It makes me confused again. *Do I continue to take on career responsibilities? Do I start seeing clients again? Or perhaps I buckle down and just be Mom?* One thing is for certain: I can no longer hide.

I have been hiding, you know. I'm not writing, like I'd set my goal to do, and I avoid music for some reason. Lately, I just want to veg, watch TV or read, or do mindless chores, because it's easy. I ask myself, "What if I just did what's easy from here on out?" Certainly, I've earned a little "easy" for a change? I imagine the easy life, and how *easy* it would be to only do what life gives me and not seek the higher way.

Then, I imagine after I die. Everyone would be asking, "What happened to you? You could have done so much, yet you did nothing to amplify what you were given." I don't want to live like that. It makes me very *un*-easy. I want to die used up, with nothing left to give, knowing I left it all on the playing field.

Perhaps I question my career so much not because it's the "wrong" thing to do, but because, in many ways, it's a lot harder for me than being a full-time stay-at-home mom—though that is definitely hard in its own way, too. Time is limited, and adding anything extra is tough. Yet, I feel a call to work on this appeal case and to continue running the Coalition, to continue teaching and speaking. Perhaps, I will soon be up for seeing a few private practice clients and gaining momentum with my writing. On paper it sounds like a lot, in addition to managing a home, husband, and six children!

I crave a meaningful life, but I don't want to be

so busy that I miss out on *living*. A meaningful life, it seems, isn't *meant* to be busy. Perhaps a meaningful life can be *full?* There's a difference, I believe. Perhaps I can have a full life, without being busy? Yes, I believe I can. Though, I bet it's not easy.

As OJ says, "Since when did you ever do the easy thing?" He's right. I'm not very good at easy anyway.

Saturday, October 3

I wish there were a website called, "How Am I Doin'? dot com." I could type in my health and sleep habits, attitude, parenting challenges and successes, how I spend my time, and include intentions, follow through, and a true measure of how hard I try. Am I flossing? Wearing my retainers? Cleaning my skin? Drinking enough H2O? Taking vitamins? Relaxing? And so on.

Then, it would give me a progress report, like the kids get from school. "This is your grade in each area, and these are the assignments you're missing. One hundred percent on this one," it'd say. "Es (Excellent) for effort in all areas, except these three, where you have Ss (Satisfactory) and these two NIs (Needs Improvement)."

Finally, the report would outline strategies to improve my "grades." "Definitely play more guitar, and sing more to your kids." "Eat two squares of dark chocolate each day, and take a power nap." "Laugh more, and give up those doubts." "Listen to your soul. It knows way more than that over-thinking brain of yours."

Ahh…feedback. No longer just me in my head. Wouldn't that be nice?

Sunday, October 4

OJ's been in golf tournaments since Tuesday. Today is Sunday. This means he's been gone all day, every day this week, as *if* he were at work. He's not. He then stops by for a quick sit on the couch before heading back for evening activities like the "night-glow putting" or "pitch into a kiddie pool" contests, and other manly events. Then, Saturday comes, with its usual, crazy, basketball games and kids-needing-friends-or-they-will-die-of-boredom, and where is OJ? Golfing in yet another tournament. Showing up around four p.m., worn out, and, as he put it, needing "some show time." (Translation: curling up with his blankie on the family room lounger and hitting "Deadliest Catch.")

Don't get me wrong here. I support my husband's hobby. He is a wonderful golfer. He's been Flagstaff City Champion and Forest Highland's Men's Champion and almost always places in the top three if he doesn't win. I enjoy seeing his joy as he wins tournaments and impresses the other men on the course. Yes, I support him fully.

What I do *not* support, however, is him being gone for six days in a row now, and coming home, today, to me thoughtfully asking, "What do you need, honey?" to which he replies, "I need to watch TV." He plunks down in front of CSI while I attempt to hold my sanity together after a yesterday of chasing Sydney up and down hallways of an old middle school as I attempt to watch three sons play in two gyms at either end of said school. I nurse one son's injured ankle, and manage six year-old diva daughter who is "So bored!" Then, today, got all six kids to and from church and handled whining and arguing, while making breakfast, lunch, and dinner, and never once got to plunk down to watch TV, or even just to think!

It dawned on me tonight that I've been at my "job," on the clock, for over a week now. No break. No going home or leaving the job. Meanwhile, OJ's been on a week-long vacation. That just doesn't work for me. Especially tonight, as two boys tell me at 7:30 they have projects due tomorrow, after they've enjoyed a weekend of birthday parties, basketball, and sleepovers! *Ha! The nerve!* So, I tell them, "Sorry, but you've earned a week of early bedtime. I will be removing your electronics, and you are grounded each day until all chores and homework are done." Then, I help them finish their projects and get to bed, before I stomp back to my own bed to write this out so I don't explode!

I know, I know. This is just the life of a mother. *I know.* But on days like today, the word "mother" is a four-letter word. (And the word "OJ" might be one, too!) On days like today, I long, instead, to hear the words, "Calgon, take me away!" and be whisked to a foamy tub next to the calming waves of an exotic sea, where I will sigh with relaxation. "Ahhh."

Yeah, right.

Thursday, October 15

I *felt* today. I cried and slept and didn't get dressed out of my yoga clothes. I didn't finish yoga. I didn't go to my Toastmasters meeting, and I didn't do any "work."

I did clean the house for the cleaning lady and let her in. I did make a healthy lunch and watch *Project Runway* and take an hour-long nap. I did cry as I watched the new lead singer of Journey tell his story on Oprah. I did read *The Bell Jar* and make pizza and macaroni for the kids. I did drive the carpools, tuck them in, and kiss them goodnight. I did sob in OJ's arms as the feelings swept over me so unexpectedly. I did remember Shannon and miss her and remembered our lives one year ago and two years ago and days in between, and it felt like no time had passed. Although here we are, a new family—doing well, moving on.

Yes, I felt today. It felt lost and familiar. It felt like a relief and a burden. And I feel drained.

TWENTY-THREE
Let Go

"You will find that it is necessary to let things go; simply for the reason that they are heavy.
So let them go, let go of them. I tie no weights to my ankles."
~C. JoyBell C.

I heard an excellent analogy once, listening to a talk by Dr. Wayne Dyer, comparing life to driving a speedboat. No matter how fast or slow we drive, he explained, there is always a wake behind the boat. Sometimes the wake is small, and sometimes it is mighty. But does the wake ever drive the boat? Of course, not. We do. Or we *don't*. It's up to us. We can see the wake, watch it, even revisit it, but it doesn't determine our future path. I loved this idea. It got me thinking about my "wake." It got me thinking, *the wake may not drive the boat, but it sure can make things choppy if we're driving in circles.*

Revisiting the wake *can* be helpful in the same way that if we're pulling a water-skier who has fallen we must return and pick her up. Revisiting and processing painful past events can bring comfort, healing, and peace. The trouble comes when we continue to circle. Driving in circles creates rough water that's difficult to navigate. It leads absolutely nowhere, and we get seasick in the process. The same goes for living in the past, bringing it back over and over, failing to pick up that lesson to be learned, failing to move on.

Our past, once examined and processed, must be let go. This doesn't mean we forget what we have been through. It means we no longer allow the past to make us seasick. It means learning the lessons and letting the memories of the past live within us—fondly remembering, but not hanging on. The past is no longer here. Like the wake, it is behind us.

As author Hermann Hesse once said, "Some of

us think holding on makes us strong, but sometimes it is letting go."[1] All that's here is *now*. And right now, we have a choice. We may drive in circles and remain seasick, sitting in the back of the boat as we gaze at the wake. *Or,* we may step up, courageously take the wheel, and drive again. We may look ahead and notice the sun rising in the liquid sky. We may see the beauty we were missing when our eyes looked only behind. We may finally recognize we're headed for newer and greater horizons than we ever could have imagined.

Friday, October 16

I'm tired of pain. I'm tired of negativity. I'm tired of feeling restricted. *Here I am complaining again—yuck!* I'm tired of that, too.

It's the day before "Shannon Day," and I am a pendulum, taking the familiar wide swings from one side to the other. Back and forth, back and forth before, hopefully, settling right in the middle. I don't even know if I'm meant to revisit Shannon and all that *went* when she went away. I'm surprised to find I don't want to revisit the past. The trouble is, *the past* seems to be revisiting *me*. The message I hear, loud in my head is: *This is not finished.*

I know it's not. I know each time someone speaks of her sister and my heart holds tight before it crumbles. I know when I am reminded I'm the mom of, not four, but six children, when I say, "I've adopted two," or when some little event occurs that reminds us all of what life was like before. I know.

The pendulum has not yet settled.

This is not finished.

Saturday, October 17

It matters. These past years I kept asking, "What does it matter? We're just going to die. All we take with us is our souls. So, what does it matter if I achieve something, or succeed, or even try?"

I used to believe achievement and success were important. I wanted to "be someone," to "make the world a better place," to "make a difference," to "leave a legacy." I wanted all those clichés. Then, life and death happened, and took with them any meaning in the things I used to desire. Anything outside of being with and loving my family has seemed, on some level, pointless.

Somehow, tonight, two years to the day that Shannon died, I know *it matters.* Not in the ways I used to believe. It doesn't matter if I leave behind a book or a successful psychology practice. It's great to help people and love them, but once I'm gone those tangible reminders ultimately fade. No. What matters is how *doing* those things *changes* me—how they become part of me. How I grow. On top of loving my family and being as kind and charitable to all as I possibly can be, if I choose to write a book, or serve through psychology, or create a song, I will take with me the growth that came through them. *That* goes with me into eternity. *That* matters.

It's such a relief to know.

Later tonight…

It's almost ten. Everyone is sleeping, but I'm wide-awake, because I did it. I just read the autopsy report. My pulse was quick, my breathing shallow, as I wondered, *Why did I wait so long?* I pulled it out of my bedside drawer, where it's been hiding these past months—these past years. I opened the envelope. I sucked in air, and held it.

The details gripped my heart—"sparkly toenail polish," "nose and belly rings," "green tank with white bra top and white capris." So real. So *un*real. Details like she was found on the floor. I'd always believed she was in her bed. Morbid details—how much her liver and brain weighed, and what they looked like, detailed descriptions of internal organs—information gleaned only about bodies no longer living. *They took apart my sister.*

Describing her arriving in a "body bag," with a "tag around her ankle and rigor mortis not fully set in," was *too* real. I turned the report over on the table and sat on the edge of my bed for a few moments, to wipe my eyes, to catch my breath.

I have to do this, I said in my head, *for Shannon. For me. For the kids. I have to know as much of what happened as I can.* I was searching once more, this time, for answers. I reached out, turned the papers over, and began to read again. Skimming medical details that didn't mean anything to me. Scanning for the end, the final decision. The final words: "Cause of death: accidental overdose."

I know those words aren't real, I thought, as I brought my hand to my mouth and shook my head. *I know Mom doctored them with the help of her friend.* Had I thought I might find something different, something new? *As much as I share her desire to protect the kids, I also desire honesty.* Hadn't I expected these words? *Don't we all have a right to know the truth?*

I wasn't angry. Only sad. Sad for everyone still here, and for Shannon and Rob, no longer here. Sad for whatever happened that night to make her drink too much and take those pills and never wake up. Sad imagining how sad she must have been once she realized, from the other side, what she had done.

Had it simply said, "suicide?" I guess I'd wanted this report to tell me the truth, to explain exactly what had happened. No amount of taking my sister's body apart could explain what I knew deep inside my heart: Suicide or not, she did not die on purpose. A cry for help? Maybe. A drunken mistake? Probably. The Shannon I knew, and still loved, would never leave her boys parentless on purpose. *Never. That I know.*

I touched the report once more, then slowly

slipped it back into the envelope, walked to my closet, and hid it with the other reminders of Shannon in the flowered box behind my jackets. I returned to my bed, alone, turned out the lights, and let go.

Someday the boys will ask and I will explain the honest truth—or, at least, as many pieces of the truth, as I can. Because, the truth *matters*. The truth heals. "And ye shall know the truth, and the truth shall make you free."[2]

Monday, October 26

Friday, OJ and I drove to Las Vegas, checked in to our hotel, dressed in our most rock-n-roll outfits, including leather pants for me, met up with our friends, Jim and Tracey, and headed to the U2 concert at UNLV, laughing the whole way. The energy in the stadium was undeniable as the Black-Eyed Peas opened the night, with *I Gotta Feeling*, and became irresistible as Bono belted out, *Pride (In the Name of Love)*. OJ and I were singing and cuddling and smiling and laughing. It even got me dancing again. I'd forgotten how much I love music. Who better than my all-time favorite, U2, and the dynamic Black-Eyed Peas to remind me?

After a midnight buffet, a long, solid sleep, and a late checkout from our hotel, I sat in my car, writing in my journal, with the windows down and the sun on my shoulder. OJ was playing golf with his buddy, and I was enjoying the crisp, clear day. As I sat there writing and waiting for OJ to meet me to begin our four-hour drive, something else became clear. I did *not* want to go home. When OJ and I met back up an hour later, he felt the same. So, we called Lorri, who, being the amazing Bema she is, agreed to stay with the kids an extra day, and we checked ourselves back in to an even better hotel.

We swam in the pool, read, and napped. OJ was wiped out, but I was still pumped! I had to have more music! So, I bought a last-minute ticket to see Rob

Thomas, the lead singer of Matchbox Twenty, a band I love, with One Republic, in concert that night. I made sure OJ was cool with staying behind—he was relieved, actually—and headed to the Rio, all by myself. Brilliantly navigating the late night Las Vegas traffic, I found the theatre, picked up my ticket from will call, and made my way to the front row balcony. It was easy to get lost in the songs that would become a forever part of me— Thomas' *Little Wonders* and *Someday*, and One Republic's *Stop and Stare*, to name a few. The singers' passion and intensity partnered with the truth of the lyrics and beauty of the music, springing me back up, re-awakening my own love and passion for music. I felt alive. I felt at peace. I felt like me again.

Today, we drove home, and what was the first thing I did after hugging and kissing the kids? I picked up my guitar, practiced voice, and got out my songwriting book. As I wrote fresh lyrics, I stared at the pale walls of our house, craving color again. Yes, color. I've always been energized by color, yet I've lived in this house with neutral walls for over two and a half years. I remember breastfeeding Sydney, staring at those walls, wishing they were more lively, but fearing any more change. I needed comfort more than color at that time, I suppose. Now, I was picking paint colors to bring my home in line with my newfound inner spark. Amazing as it seemed even to me, I could actually feel a spark. I still feel it.

I finally see how much music, creativity, beauty, and fun matter. I can no longer participate in the lie that these good things aren't important. They are. I am trekking up the gorgeous, snow-topped peaks of life, stick in hand, smile on my face. And, doggone it, I am going to enjoy the view! It will take a while to reach the top, but for now I really am embracing and loving the climb.

(Here's me--not to scale)   (This is more accurate!)

Wednesday, November 4

I'm crying. Again. It's like crying is trying to scare hiccups out of me. It's catching me off guard so often.

It's settled heavily that Shannon was the best friend I've ever had in my whole life, besides OJ. We grew up together. We shared bedrooms and friends and laughs and secrets. We fought and screamed and yelled and cried and made up and helped each other and grew together. We knew each other, and also knew we'd support and sustain each other, no matter what. We were supposed to grow old together.

I never realized, until now, how much I loved Shannon—not just as my sister—as my truest friend. I never realized how much I'd miss her. Each time I hear someone speak of her sister—going on a trip together, talking out a problem, venting about another family member, I think, *Must be nice for you. My sister died. And, I miss her and what should have been all over again.

I wish we could go to Jamaica, like we did when our kids were little and I was offered a job teaching aerobics at a resort for a week. Just the two of us, leading water aerobics at the pool or Pilates on the beach, learning to scuba-dive and reggae dance, sleeping in, and reading in hammocks as the sun sank in the turquoise water. I wish I could hug her, hear her infectious laugh, and just sit on my bed, telling her everything. She's the one I want to talk to about all this. Ironic. She understood and loved me; she wanted the best for me. It's taken too long to see how much I love her still, and how huge the hole is she left behind.

I read, in one of my grief and loss books, about writing a goodbye letter, but I'm just not ready. Still. After two years! I've been harboring Shannon in me like a private treasure, not willing to let go, not wanting to believe, to know she is gone. I can see now how I waited to read the autopsy report and how I've avoided pictures of her, or her journals. Or, how I've told myself it was "okay" that she died, because "we had a complex relationship," thus allowing myself to experience the anger but not the *sorrow* of losing her.

I've allowed myself to help *others* grieve Shannon, to make sure *they* are okay, especially the kids. I've told myself I had less right to miss her than they did, or than Mom, or Dad, or Ashley, Bud, or Leighton, or even her close friends. But now I see: it was a lie. A lie of protection to keep the pain away. A lie of sympathy, to help me do the work I was asked to do— to function, to build this family.

Now, we're finally out of crisis mode, yet we gear up for, hopefully, the final battle with the Cutlers next week for conservatorship. With holidays approaching, holidays that, for the past two years, have been duties rather than holy occasions to be celebrated, no wonder I'm being caught off guard by tears, exhaustion, and confusion. No wonder I want to isolate. No wonder I want to hide. No wonder I want to run away from this pain through work. It's just a huge hole—sad, empty, and lonely.

It's time to get honest with myself, to dive into that hole. *But am I ready? I still don't feel ready.* It's time to grieve this loss completely, to finally set Shannon—and *me*—free.

Saturday, November 21

Last year, Dr. Hale made me promise to celebrate my birthday once the "war" was over. I think I finally kept that promise. My "Black and White Charity (have-a) Ball," tonight, was fabulous!

I spent all week decorating and setting up our house, planning the menu, and organizing auction items, a great distraction from real life and from the fact that Sunday would be my birthday. Tonight, it all came together. Complete with black and white food, fifty people in black and white dress, and a silent auction, we raised fourteen hundred dollars for The Arizona Postpartum Wellness Coalition—money we desperately need to keep our postpartum warmline and brochures up and running.

I hadn't told anyone this was my way of throwing a birthday party, my way of celebrating the end of the "war." Years ago, tired of birthday disappointments, I decided to take matters into my own hands and do something new every year for my birthday. I went to the opera, skydiving, to see a band I'd never seen in concert, or, when life was too busy, I just *learned* something new. A year before Shannon died, I added, "Do something for someone else" to my birthday rules, and donated my birthday money to the Make-a Wish foundation, which I've loved ever since Miki was granted a wish. Just months before she died, we went to Disneyworld.

But the past years, I've just been in survival mode. I guess that's something new—surviving major loss, depression, and grief—but it's certainly not fun. I haven't felt like celebrating at all. Honestly, this year, though I know I needed it, part of me still felt undeserving, especially of having others celebrate *me*. But OJ announced, in the middle of the ball, that my birthday was tomorrow. He surprised me, and everyone else, with a beautiful birthday cake, with thirty-five candles. I smiled, my eyes wet, and made a wish before them out. My wish, however, had already come true: I felt like "me" again. I felt loved. Even better, I felt *deserving* of celebration and love. I soaked it up.

My favorite part of tonight, though, was the entertainment—Colton, Braxton, Tre, and me, playing in our band, "The Mama's Boys." Catchy, isn't it? I sure thought so, although their response was, "Mom! That's so embarrassing!" Well, embarrassing can be fun, and it sure was tonight. Dad came, with Ashley, and played in the band with us, too. Mom was "sick," of course. I'd prepared myself for it, even though hours before she'd still insisted she would be there. I admit, I wanted her there, to celebrate with us. To celebrate with *me*. At least it was the only disappointment of the night.

We played seven songs, including a little Beatles and Coldplay, Braxton and Tre collaborated on a song they wrote, which was amazing, and even Colton played a little of Journey's *Don't Stop Believin'* to get the crowd going. I shared two of my originals, with the boys and dad playing along—*Opportunity* ("Did I miss an opportunity? Did I miss a chance for love?"),[3] and my newest song, *You've Got an Angel*.

"I wrote this for the kids," I told the audience, "to remind them they are never alone." It felt like the biggest success of my life to sing: "That's right. Life's not fair. Sometimes the load you're asked to carry seems too heavy to bear. Ooh, and I know that sometimes it seems there's not a soul in sight. But if you look a little deeper, then you'll begin to see the light. 'Cause, you've got an angel..."[4] I sang, and felt the truth of the words, feeling triumphant for a moment. It was a true celebration that we had made it through the "war," through so many wars.

The grand finale was, *I'm Yours*, by Jason Mraz, with Dad on guitar and backup vocals, Braxton on lead guitar, Tre on the drums, and me, on guitar and lead vocals. The room was filled to the brim, everyone singing along. That's what I will remember as my thirty-fifth birthday gift—the beautiful moment of sharing a song with those I love, of seeing the smiles and feeling the love for our family. I felt whole.

Now, as everyone sleeps and I write, I'm emotional just thinking of it. I feel gratitude, for all the people who came to support me, for OJ's efforts to make this birthday one of my best, for the passage of time, and for the chance to grow through it all. I feel blessed to be where I am right now: awake, appreciative, alive, and, heading up to Kennedy's room to be The Tooth Fairy, before I finally sink into bed.

Wednesday, November 25

We're supposed to be going to court next week for, fingers crossed, the final stint. This time, we are asking for conservatorship, so we can manage the boys' inheritance without any outside interference.

Today, we learned that the Cutlers are trying to "make a deal" with us. Their attorney contacted OJ, stating, "They agree to give you conservatorship if you agree to grandparent visitation." OJ called and told me.

"They already *have* grandparent visitation rights if they would just pick up the phone and call the kids!" I said, a little too forcefully. "But they've chosen not to do that. And we *won't* agree to any court-mandated visits anymore. We won't. EVER." Then, I added, "Besides, visitation has nothing to do with conservatorship!" OJ agreed, of course, and said he'd relay the message to the attorney for me. "Thank you," I said. "Really, thank you. I can't handle it. It's too much. I'm tired of all the anger and pain and heartache. I have nothing left to give."

It immediately brought up my defenses, reminding me of last year, of being "at war" and feeling under attack. Tonight, as I knelt in prayer, seeking forgiveness for my own anger and resentment, seeking peace, all I could feel was pity for the Cutlers, for what they've lost and how they don't see their hand in it. Again, I felt empathy for how hard it must be for them. I've always been able to find that perspective, even with them, and, hard as it is to feel, it comforts me. *I'm not this terrible person who hates and acts out in anger. I feel. Deep down, I really do care.*

Still, as much as I empathize and wish things were different, I know that their happiness can't come at the cost of the boys' or our family's. We have this defense for a reason. Though it's hard, I still know we are doing the right thing.

Saturday, November 28

I lost it today. I mean, really blew it. Completely flipped out. Screamed and yelled at OJ because he "cleaned out the attic" in a way that was "*so* not helpful." I know. It sounds just as crazy as I was.

Feeling tense this morning, I decided to tackle the jungle that is our attic, implementing my long thought-out plan for untangling the mess, as a way to distract me from my inner demons. Knowing I was not well and seeing me get to work, OJ tried to be helpful by jumping in, and taking over.

"Please don't help me," I said, irritated. "I've worked so long on a plan for this space, and I know exactly how I want it. I really don't need you in here." I guess he didn't believe me. He kept working, doing it his way—adding more furniture and creating less space, and adding more *mess*, as far as I could tell, too.

So, I flipped. I tried not to, believe me. I walked away several times, took a bath, and finally just left it altogether and made everyone lunch. I listened as Dr. Hibbert whispered, "Listen to yourself, thinking all these catastrophizing, all-or-nothing things. You have a choice to change this, you know. You know better than to give in to the negativity." Or, at least, I listened at first. After a while, I was hearing things like, *What if I don't want to control my thoughts! I'm tired of having to always do the right thing! I'm sick of "Dr. Hibbert!"*

Proud of what he'd done, OJ called me to the

attic to show it off. It was exactly how I *didn't* want it. I could hear the thoughts boiling inside. "Don't go there," Dr. Hibbert said. *Shut up, Dr. Hibbert!* I replied. Then, when OJ admitted he'd found one of his Christmas gifts I'd hidden in the process of his "help," I lost it.

"If you would just listen to me, you wouldn't have ruined everything! I was just trying to feel better, to get some work done. But, no! You had to take it over and ignore everything I said! And now, look at me! I'm acting like a crazy person! Is this what you want? For me to be crazy? Because it sure feels like it! Stop *trying* to help me and just *help* me!" Somewhere inside, I knew he was trying to be helpful, but I was way past empathizing. It was like being right back in last year—feeling completely hopeless and lost, and alone, and hating myself for how I was behaving. I spent the next hour sobbing on the floor of my closet, a sign on my door that said, "Quarantine. Do NOT come in!" I couldn't handle the thought of poisoning anyone with my negativity. I spent the rest of the day trying to put me back together.

Why did I lose it so badly? Well, for one, when I looked at the calendar it just so happens I'm pre-menstrual. I know people like to joke about it, but over the years my PMS has become chartable just by watching my moods. It's no laughing matter. Trust me! I don't even know it's hormones until after I've lost it and beaten myself up about it. I check the calendar and, yep, it's that time of the month. Strangely, once I realize hormones are the culprit, I feel relieved. *At least there's a reason for my insanity,* I tell myself. That's what happened tonight.

Second, it's not just hormones. It feels like a mix of slag floating in me—frustration, and hurt, and anger with the Cutlers about this court stuff I wish we didn't have to do—and emotional residue from last year—feeling out of control, no one to turn to, alone, and scared. I have not fully dealt with these emotions yet. I can finally see just how much I've avoided in order to cope and get by. Now, it's all here again, or *still* here—feelings about Shannon, Rob, my mom, my dad, my family, my life, and what's been lost.

It seems superficial, this holding on, this inability to just get over these losses. I *want* to be able to do that, but it doesn't work that way. I'm also seeing how hard holidays can be. Too much brought up, too much brought back, and although I've known holidays are a hard time for people who've had trauma or loss, this is my first real experience with it. Even last year was too foggy, because we were in the midst of craziness still.

There's just so much to understand. I'm humbled again. I see my weakness. I'm not always as strong as I think.

Thursday, December 3

Well, it's done! After so much stress, what a simple hearing and what a relief.

It only took ten minutes once we were finally called into the courtroom. The Cutlers weren't even there, but their attorney was—with a signed document consenting to our appointment as conservators. The judge had no misgivings. "It makes sense since you are their parents," he said. We now have the documentation making it legal and proof that we are done with court!

I felt peace today. Just calm and peaceful, again knowing that all is in God's hands—that there is no need to fret and there never was. God will always make it work.

Sunday, December 13

I've been at the *Evolution of Psychotherapy* conference since Tuesday, when I overcame strep throat, a blizzard, and two cancelled flights to take matters into my own hands, making the eight-hour, icy drive from Flagstaff to Orange County, California. Now, I'm suddenly back home after a whirlwind day of driving—listening to podcasts, crying to OJ, pulling over for a power nap, and seeing five rainbows (that must be a sign, right?)—and singing *O Holy Night* in a trio for our big Christmas music program at church tonight. Whew! What a day.

This week has been good for me, exhausting and exhilarating all at once. The conference was incredible. Days of hearing from the leaders in the field of psychology was bound to motivate me. There were other benefits, too. For one, having time on my own for several days allowed me to think, feel, process, and get spiritually connected and in touch with my soul again. I also had the opportunity to share a room with Julie, my dear friend I never actually see. We met a few years ago at a conference where Julie was performing one of her songs. She's a well-known LDS singer-songwriter, and, I came to learn, a therapist, too. I was speaking on postpartum mental health. I asked about her music, wishing I could perform like she did, and she asked me about my doctorate, wishing she could have hers, too. We spoke only five minutes, exchanged numbers, and, living in separate states, became friends through phone calls. Sharing a room at this conference was only the second time we'd met in real life. Julie's friends were at the conference, as well, so I got to be social and observe myself in new situations. I was observing myself all week. It brought some valuable insights.

Julie and I also had some great, open discussions where we shared what we see in each another. Two therapists, together for several days, with little sleep, sharing insights at one o'clock this morning? Let's just say it was honest and emotional. And I loved it. Julie pointed out how much I try to minimize what I've been through, not only with others, but with myself. It helped me see that I fear placing the burden of my experiences on others. I feel responsible to clean it up after sharing, because it can be too much. I also fear going back to grief. So, instead, I focus on others' experiences and emotions. This has helped me develop greater listening, empathy, and charity. Julie said I was very present and focused on what matters, but I know it also distracts me from continuing to heal.

Being around so many new people this week helped me see that I *have* become more cheerful. I am good at connecting with others and helping them feel good. I have joy with me, which is incredible, and I share that joy. Still, I think I've equated joy with being "over it" or "fine," and that's why I feel so shocked when suddenly I don't feel fine. Talking with Julie about it this morning made that clear. Sobbing to OJ about it this afternoon made it clearer: I'm still wounded. I miss my sister, and I can no longer hide or neglect it. It feels good to actually bleed and not just Band-Aid the wounds.

It's coming to the close of another year and hopefully to the close of this crazy chapter of my life. What better time to reflect on where I am? I may be wounded, but I'm also grateful, hopeful, and even joyful. I'm thirty-five years old and finally feel like a real adult—settled a bit, but unsettled, too. And that's okay. I love being a mother and delight in my children. I love OJ and how he loves me. I love that I've been given gifts that allow me to help people, to make a difference. I feel I've proven myself professionally, and as a mom, wife, and daughter, already, and I'm more internally settled than ever before. Much more comfortable in my own skin. Comfortable being me.

I really like me. I like who I am becoming. I've got a vision for my life, and I'm on track with it. I know my focus: family, humility, charity, patience, gratitude, cheerfulness, joy, love. Faith, meaning, wisdom, inspiration, and yes, even peace.

I may be a little banged up. The hardest days may be yet to come, though I hope that's not the case. *It can't possibly be the case, can it?* The point is: I'm doing it. I am doing the work. And I *love* who I am being.

My favorite photo of Shannon (age 3),
and me (age 4 ½).

PART IV:
SUMMER

Year of
JOY

Summer is the vibrant dawn of a green day.
It is kisses from the sun,
and laughter in the rain.
Summer is the wonder—
the spontaneous bliss of shiny souls
emerging and taking center stage.
Summer is the time to fly—diving, swooping, rising—
the unfurling of dusty wings
as hearts sing
and soar.

TWENTY-FOUR
Submit

"Then a woman said, "Speak to us of Joy and Sorrow."
And he answered:
Your joy is your sorrow unmasked.
And the selfsame well from which your laughter rises was
oftentimes filled with your tears.
And how else can it be?
The deeper that sorrow carves into your being, the more joy you can
contain."
~Khalil Gibran, The Prophet

Summer is the time to shine, with longer days and sunny evenings that inspire us to get out and make things happen. But as a mother, I usually feel conflicted when summer rolls around. I welcome an end to the countless activities—homework, early mornings, and running-kids-about-crazy-pace of the school year. By the end of May, my mind and body are just shy of admission to the mental hospital. Yet it's always a jolt to suddenly find myself in the schedule-*less* void of summer, with children of all ages running *me* about. Though the *idea* of summer is lovely, for me, the transition's always tough.

Over the years I've worked at getting the hang of the summer shift. First, I acknowledge summer for the dramatic change it is. I remind myself that I'm still recovering from the mayhem. I slow down my work schedule, set up summer "laws," and hold a family meeting to get us all on the same page. I acknowledge my fears, worries, and insecurities. As hard as it is, I expose them so they will no longer hold me back, and I remind myself that only *I* stand in my way of a shining summer.

The same goes for experiencing joy. Only we stand in our way. It's there, you know. Deep within. Joy is always there, part of our very soul. Think of a baby, of children. They live, unfettered by life. They smile spontaneously and often. Young children are the definition of joy. Yet over time, they too become unhappy, and unsure joy even exists. Yes, life comes along, and stresses on us, and traumatizes us, and our joy eventually gets so covered up, many of us don't even believe it's there.

Now, I'm not just talking about *happiness*. Happiness is great and all, but it's just an emotion, like sadness or pain or excitement. It's fun while it lasts, but doesn't usually last—for most of us, anyway. No, I'm talking about joy, which, unlike happiness, is a state of being. We can be faced with challenges, situations, and life stress and still *be* joyful. Even when we don't *feel* happy, we can *be* full of joy. Khalil Gibran is right. Our sorrows only make our joy that much more incredible.

How do we uncover and rediscover our joy? Again, we can learn a lesson from summer. Since I don't always feel happy about summer setting in, I have learned to first, accept where I am. Then, to *submit*. I allow myself to *do* less and *be* with my family more. I travel, take the kids to the pool, take naps with the windows open, listen and watch as the birds sing and soar, and make an effort to witness every sunset with OJ by my side. I sing, write songs, and re-connect with *me* again. And I read. I read all summer long because: 1) I love learning, and 2) it is one activity I can do and not feel frustrated when I'm interrupted, because with six children at home all day, that is about the only thing I can count on—interruption.

That's my approach to summer—to first acknowledge what's holding me back, then, to let it go. Once I finally submit, I ease into summer like a sundress. The same goes for joy. As we acknowledge what blocks our joy, as we focus on healing our wounds, embracing our past, and letting things go, we soon discover the wonder of the joy within. We begin to feel like summer as we evolve into a being of joy.

When the summers of life come, we have a choice—to fight the summer moments through fear and clinging to how things used to be, or to acknowledge what's holding us back and let it go. If there's one thing I've learned, it's that we must embrace the summer moments while they are here, gaining strength from all we've been through and preparing for what is to come. We must, likewise, acknowledge joy once we find it. For the only *sure* thing is that every summer will fade. There will always be another fall.

Wednesday, January 6

I started therapy with Dr. Hale again, hoping to figure out why I'm having such a hard time. I can't sleep, and the nightmares have returned. Something is trying to speak to me.

But I can't go there. My heart keeps closing off. I avoid writing, talking, reaching out, and anything that can become too emotional. I just want to feel happy—to forget.

Even more, I want to be whole again. I've avoided this pain long enough. So, there I was today, on the leather sofa in Dr. Hale's office, hoping he could help me let myself remember.

"Close your eyes and imagine we're in a submarine," Dr. Hale said. "I am driving, and you are the passenger." He described the scene of the water's surface, with debris floating, as if there had been a shipwreck. "But we are comfortable as we submerge ourselves," he reassured me, and painted a picture of colorful fish and coral that reminded me of scuba diving.

"Now we're going to go a little deeper and see what the wreckage looks like below." Suddenly fearful, I was surprised by the words in my head: *I do not want to do this! I want to stay with the light and the pretty fish and the coral.* But I said nothing as he described descending into the darkness of the ocean floor where the shipwreck lay.

We landed on the bottom as he told of strange-looking creatures lurking about—some with sharp teeth—swimming in and out of the ship's ruins. "But we have a light," he said, "and as we shine it, the creatures recede. They don't like the light." I liked this metaphor.

"Protected by the thick Plexiglas and steel of our submarine, we are safe. We can look around. We're just here to observe what's down here," he said. In silence, we stayed on the black ocean floor, and breathing deeply, I took a good look at the remains.

It must have only been a few moments, though it felt much longer, before Dr. Hale started the submarine's ascent. We slowly resurfaced. I opened my eyes, and he calmly asked, "What did you see?"

"I saw a ship in pieces, with seaweed growing and treasures rusted. The pieces were all about. The pieces were many things," I said. "Shannon was a huge one. And Rob. And Papa Dave. And the deaths of so many loved ones in the past few years. And fear of who is next. And losses related to those deaths—my identity, life as I knew and expected it, the family I had loved and desired. And a normal childhood experience for our kids. And a peaceful last birth experience for me. And all the times people say, 'You're so strong,' because I don't feel that. And this new identity, which resembles the old one, but is so different. I'm so different." My soliloquy was followed by building emotion on my part and a respectful silence on his.

"But there were other pieces," I slowly added. "I could also see how much I have grown. And I could feel grateful." My eyes searched his. He nodded and smiled. "I've worked so hard—to do better, to be better, to build a family and a home and a new me—to build a new ship and let it set sail," I said, doing a terrible job of holding back my tears. "But, I am exhausted." That's when the sobs broke through. That's when I finally let the pile of emotion pour out. Dr. Hale sat with me, the patient observer of my troubles and supporter of my growth.

In just forty-five minutes I was walking out the door, but not before Dr. Hale acknowledged the work I had done. "You did great today," he said. Then added, " Just promise me one thing."

"Sure," I said.

"Promise you'll go home and take a nap. You *are* exhausted. You need rest."

I don't have to be told twice to take a nap. So, I promised. And I did.

Sunday, January 10

Why do I keep returning to Dr. Hale's office, even though I always feel wrecked for days after? Why do I keep letting him guide me down and back up, despite my reflex to run away? Because my wounds need healing. Hard as it is, I know I must do this work.

I'm learning that emotional healing really isn't so different from physical healing. With a physical wound, like a cut or a broken bone, the body immediately begins to heal itself. It may require medical intervention, but the wound heals with time. However, if the wound becomes infected, the process is a little more involved. A closed, infected wound needs to be reopened, drained, cleaned, and bandaged in order to prevent further infection; time alone won't help. While it doesn't sound very appealing to have a wound re-opened, the small amount of pain in doing so is far worth it in the long run.

The same goes for emotional wounds, like mine—wounds that are closed too quickly, that are not fully cleansed right away. They become "infected," leading to increased pain and suffering down the road. The best way to heal these wounds is to re-open them and go deep.

That's the hard part, though—going deep.

Though I know, intellectually, the benefit, the reality is it hurts in a way I can't explain. I resist, wanting to forget, to just move on, but I know that's not how it works. Dr. Hibbert keeps reminding me, "Going deep is a crucial element of healing, especially for those who have suffered trauma." *Trauma?* It sounds so—*traumatic.* Yet, that's how Dr. Hale sees it, and that's how the psychologist in me obviously sees what I have been through, too. When I get honest, I know they're right.

I have to push myself deeper, cleansing as I face the darkness, just like I do for my clients. I go at their pace. Back off when it becomes too much, and make sure I let them resurface in time to bandage the wound before they step out my door.

I will reexamine, re-clean, and re-bandage myself again and again. As many times as it takes for this wound to heal.

Monday, January 11

In an effort to get out of my isolating pattern and re-connect with the world, I invited Cyndy to lunch today. It's strange how I have to force myself to do something like going to lunch. Intellectually, I know I'll love it once I'm there, but physically, it's hard to make myself leave home these days. Talking to my good friend, I hoped, might bring a little sunshine to my muddled mind and give me fresh perspective.

We took our seats at the new Greek restaurant, placed our orders, and I asked Cyndy how she'd been doing. We discussed the usual things—her kids and husband, work, church, friends, and family. It felt good to listen to her and get out of my own head for a while.

"So, how are *you* doing?" she asked. I also started with the usual—my kids and husband, work, church, friends, and family. Then, I took a risk. I unleashed everything I hadn't been telling her or anyone—how crazy and oppressed I'd been feeling, what I was wishing

I could do, my dreams, my aspirations. We'd been to Ireland together, after all. We were bonded for life. I didn't realize how uncomfortable Cyndy was with what I was dumping on her as I continued. "I just feel like there's so much I want to do, you know? I want to write a book and speak around the country and write and share my songs, and sometimes, I just feel this passion and drive I can't ignore. It's so frustrating, because I can't do any of it now. I'm a mom of six and I need to be there for my kids. And I've really been l struggling to feel whole again, too. I'm still so heavy with grief after all this time. I feel stuck. I want to be better, but I'm not yet. You know what I mean?"

"Wow," Cyndy widened her eyes and took a deep breath. "You make me feel lazy."

I laughed. "Well, I'm not trying to make you feel lazy. You're definitely not lazy. I'm just trying to get some of this stuff out of me, to get some perspective. Aggh. I'm sorry. I didn't mean to dump." I shook my head, starting to wonder if, perhaps, I *was* crazy to have all these passions and especially to express them to other people. I didn't want to make her uncomfortable. I just wanted to feel connected to someone again.

"You don't seem that way at all, though" Cyndy said, smiling at my head-shaking. "I mean, you don't seem like you're struggling. You're a good show. I mean, you *put on* a good show."

"No, you're right," I said, giggling. I had suddenly found my perspective. "That's exactly it. I am a good show. I am." She was right on the money—better at this "emotional stuff" than she thinks. She laughed and so did I. "Yes. That is exactly the way to describe me. I look all pulled together. Look at me. My clothes are nice and my hair's all curled. I'm smiling and even laughing! I'm a psychologist who helps people when they feel like a mess, and I'm a mother of six. I totally appear to be the do-it-all woman, don't I? Yes, I am a good show. Because that's what it is—a show. Inside, *I* am the one who's a mess."

Cyndy smiled and leaned forward, trying to reassure me. "Well, you don't seem like a mess. And you do make me feel lazy. You do far more than most people, that's for sure." She paused and looked me as I started laughing again. We were both amused by this conversation. "I like your show," she said. "It's fun to watch." We both laughed some more.

We finished lunch and I went home smiling at my folly. *I am a good show. Yes I am. It's helped me cope all this time. It's helped me get by.* But shows aren't real. It was an eye-opener today to see how hard I've been working to keep the good show going for everyone else and for myself.

It's time to get real. I have to let go of the need to be *something* and just be me. If I happen to be a "good show" to some, so be it, but I can't live my life based on what others want to see. I have to be true to who I really am—to my family, my values, and my good little desires. No more "good show." Time to turn the TV off, tune in to my soul, and be the true me. It takes way too much effort to be anything but real.

Tuesday, January 12

We did "empty chair" work in therapy again today. I sat in Dr. Hale's chair, staring at the folding chair in front of me, tear-choked, and tried to speak to Shannon.

"I think I'll speak to Miki first, instead," I said. I could see her golden curls, bright eyes, and dancing smile, and I felt the depth of how I still miss her. "I miss you, Miki," I said. "Even more, I miss the possibility of our relationship that was lost when you died sixteen years ago." I remembered her energy, her vitality, her courage. I thought of how she inspired our entire town with her battle through cancer, and how, at such a young age, she seemed to "get it." Now, as I imagined her in the empty chair, though I still saw her eight year-old body, her warmth and wisdom made her seem older than I. "You are an inspiration to me, Miki," I said. "I look up to your courage and ability to fulfill your life's mission," I said. " I hope I can do the same." I calmly wiped my running nose. "I love you."

Miki vanished. Shannon appeared. Or, at least, she was supposed to. I couldn't see her like I could Miki. I kept trying to look at the chair only to turn away instead. I couldn't speak. I just sat there sobbing and shrugging my shoulders.

"May I speak for you?" asked Dr. Hale, who was standing to the side. I nodded. He moved behind my chair and, touching me on the shoulder, said the words I could not say: "I miss you… And I've been angry with all you've left for me. It's been really hard on me. It's been hard on all of us." He paused and looked down at my wet face as I looked up behind me and nodded again. Looking me in the eye, he slowly said, "And I feel someday you will thank me for what I am trying to do." I kept nodding and shaking my head, opening and closing my eyes, tissue in hand, wiping my face, blowing my nose. For several long minutes.

Finally, I opened my mouth, prying the words up off the ground. "And," I finally said, "I love you." It wasn't that I didn't want to say the words. It's just that my body wouldn't let me at first; the pain was too great. But I did it. I broke through and said what needed to be said.

We had ten minutes to put me back together at the end of the session, and I feared it might be impossible. My eyes were sore and I felt a pull to want to cry more, but I resisted. I thanked Dr. Hale. I made it to my car. I headed home, ready to hide for the rest of the day. Turning left, halfway home, a police car pulled up behind me and turned on its siren. *This can't be happening,* I thought, and pulled over.

I blew air up toward my eyes and blinked them, trying to erase the tears and puffiness, but it was no use. The cop came to my window. "You crossed a double yellow line back there, when entering the left turn lane," he said.

Are you kidding me? I didn't even know I'd done it. It had literally been a few feet if I had. "I'm sorry if I did that," I said, trying to stop from crying more. "I didn't know I'd done that. It's kind of a rough day." I blinked back tears. He looked empathetic and said he'd be back in a minute. I sat in my car, my head about to explode from the frustration of it, trying to breathe myself through and not make a scene.

You know what? He gave me a ticket. "Sorry," he said. "You can go to traffic school, though."

"Yeah," I said. "Okay. Have a great day," and carefully drove away.

Sometimes we're just not meant to catch a break, I guess. I went home, turned on the TV, wrapped up in a blanket, and let myself escape from my labors for a time.

Saturday, January 16

I looked OJ in the eye and said the words today: "I need help. I *need* a break." It's one lesson I've learned well. If I don't ask, it won't happen.

Luckily, OJ is a good one. He's all for me getting a break, at least in theory, and happily agreed to be in charge for the day. "Do what you want," he said. "Don't worry about us." I grabbed my purse and headed for the one place all frazzled moms go to decompress—Target.

Before I even reached the freeway, I already had three phone calls from kids. "Where are you?" "When are you getting home?" "I'm hungry!"

"Tell Dad!" I told them as kindly as I could muster, then turned off my phone.

After an hour of picking up what I needed and too much of what I wanted, I made my way home only to find OJ, painting the "dungeon." It is what we affectionately call the unfinished part of the basement. *No wonder the kids have been calling me!* There had been seven voicemails when I'd finally checked my phone.

"Great, he's painting the dungeon," I said out loud to myself, "but why *now?*"

"Why now?" I asked him, calmly, yet with a hint of irritation.

He attempted to reassure me. "Just ignore everything," he said, again. "*But…*could you pick up some more paint?"

Being the sucker I am, I was off to Home Depot, this, after "picking up" shotgun shells for him earlier at Wal-Mart. *Some "break" this is!*

It was lunchtime when I returned, and the kids were attacking me. "Dad's been painting *all day!*" "He won't even make us lunch!" "We're *starving!*"

Just then, "Dad" walked into the kitchen. "You didn't make them lunch?" I asked.

"Sorry," he said, "I've been painting," and kissed me on the cheek. "But, I've gotta go," he added. Apparently, it was *conveniently* time for him to leave to shoot guns with his church buddies. It wasn't even something he did—shoot guns—but all the other guys were going, so he was too.

I held it together. I made lunch, finally got Sydney down for a nap, and agreed to let Brody and Kennedy have friends over. *I really am a sucker!* I had just settled onto my bed to take a little break when I heard OJ pull up. Meeting him in the family room, I asked, "How was it, dear?" with a hint of sarcasm. (Okay, maybe *more* than a hint.)

"It was pretty great!" gave me a kiss, and sat down on the couch with chips and salsa to watch the Cardinal's game.

Seriously? This *is being in charge?* Final straw. Breaking point reached. "Uggh!" I sighed, loudly, and stormed out of the room.

Fleeing to my only place of refuge in times like these, I went to the tub. I could see this was all OJ's fault. My mind took off. *All he does is think of himself! Can't he give me just a few hours of one day? Is that too much to ask?* But luckily, my rational brain started kicking in. *It's not all his fault,* it said. *He was trying to help by doing the painting, for you, and he already had his shooting gig planned. You didn't expect him to miss his activity, so why are you so disappointed he left?* I am the one who asks him to take care of home projects all the time, so I was grateful he was tackling one. But today, I needed him to take care of me.

Finally recognizing something was wrong, OJ followed me, and apologized.

"Do you even know what you're apologizing for?" I asked.

"I think because you wanted a break, but didn't really get one. Right?" He does try.

We spent an hour talking—trying to understand him, me, and this whole situation. It wasn't *all* his fault. I know I seem "fine" on the outside, but I've been feeling on edge since counseling started again. Sometimes, I want to quit so I can go back to just feeling well, but that would be equivalent to learning I have cancer and then hoping if I ignore it I will be cured. I vented all this out to OJ. He listened. I forgave him.

Not exactly a day off, but then, did I really expect it would be? Although I didn't get the day I *wanted*—*Who needs more stuff from Target anyway?*—perhaps I did get what I *needed*: a little love and understanding to buoy me up for whatever rough waves lie ahead.

Sunday, January 17

I finally have my theme for this year: Joy. I can't say why it's been so difficult to choose this time, other than 1) I'm reluctant to give up "cheerfulness," and 2) I've been feeling so uncertain about what's next for me.

As I've prayed and pondered this coming year, it's dawned on me that, although cheerfulness has opened the door to *some* of the sunshine of joy, I have yet to truly understand and embrace joy's full light. I admit it feels ironic to choose "joy" when I've been struggling to *feel* joy these past few weeks. Between keeping up with kids and therapy, I'm barely getting by. Perhaps it's a sign that I'm on the right track. After all, I know these yanking emotions are not only blocking my joy; they're primarily a result of what I've been unearthing. Perhaps the unearthing is exactly what I need if I want to cultivate joy, and perhaps the focus of joy is exactly what I need to carry me through the unearthing.

I don't yet *know* joy. I *want* to know it, and I'm *ready* to know it. So, here's my chance—to overcome these dark times, re-discover my own light, and let it shine again, perhaps even more brightly. Here's to The Year of Joy. I feel a light coming on just thinking about it.

TWENTY-FIVE
Time + Work = Healing

"Many of the great achievements of the world were accomplished by tired and discouraged men who kept on working."
~Anonymous

They say, "Time heals all wounds." In a way, it's true. Time brings perspective, understanding, even clarity—if we let it. I would argue it's not *time* that heals, but rather, the *work* we do *in* that time.

I once heard a great analogy for this; I can't remember where. If I were running late for work and discovered my car had a flat tire, would I say, "Oh, my tire is flat. Well, I will just sit here and wait for it to heal." Hopefully not. Giving the tire time does not repair the flat. Time may help me find another way to get where I'm headed—someone may stop and offer a ride, or I may decide to get some exercise by taking a bike—but the tire won't "heal" until I fix it.

The same goes for us. Sure, things might change over time. We may move on, or think we have. Healing usually doesn't happen spontaneously. We have to work at it.

It certainly helps if we not only seek healing, but we are willing to change and grow through it too. The truth is, we probably won't be the same after we're healed, and why would we want to be when we could instead improve? "Healing does not mean going back to the way things were before, but rather allowing what *is* now to move us closer to God."[lxxiii] That sounds nice, doesn't it? Why is it so hard, then, to actively *seek* emotional healing and growth? Perhaps another analogy will help.

A former client of mine told me this true story several years ago. I will call him Mario. Mario was from Columbia. When he was young, he and his family caravanned with several other families from their home to a distant village. They were well into their journey through the thick jungles when they came to what should have been a bridge spanning a large river. It was just after the rainy season and the land had been hit hard. When the families arrived, they were stunned to find the river had swollen so greatly, the bridge had washed away. I can hear Mario's accent: "The river was *roaring*. The earth *shook*. It was so powerful, it was like…*the voice of God*." Knowing there was no safe way to cross the wild river and no other way to reach their destination, the families prepared to return home.

Just then Mario noticed one of the men in their group tying a rope around his waist. The other men and women were pleading with the man while Mario and the children stood by, but it was useless. The man was determined to cross the river. Knowing there was nothing else to do, the other men helped secure his rope, then formed a line, holding tightly, to anchor him as he dove in. Mario watched the man swirl and paddle, going under for periods of time, then gasping for air. Minutes passed, and he seemed to be getting nowhere. He was shoved under time and again. The men held tight as he fought his way up for breath, bearing scratches and blood from the rocks below. This went on for over twenty minutes, the man never giving up his battle for the shore. Miraculously, the man made it to his goal—torn, wounded, but seemingly energized as he climbed the muddy bank, untied the rope, and ran off down the road.

Mario paused as he finished his tale, emotion in his voice. "Do you know *why* he did that?" he asked, sincerely.

Mesmerized, I replied, "No, *why*?"

"Because his wife had just given birth to his first son and he *had* to get to them."

So it is with healing. If we stand at the roaring

river's edge yet can see the greater purpose—the love, the light, the joy—that awaits, it's worth the battle to get across. We might, and probably will, get beat up and bloodied along the way. We might feel like we're drowning. If we anchor ourselves with good people—people who love us, people who help us—and God, we will find ourselves, one day, safely on the other side.

"Our sorrows and wounds are healed only when we touch them with compassion."[lxxiv] Let's have a little compassion for ourselves. Let's fasten the ropes firmly, dive in, and let the compassion of others hold us tight. The reward is worth the fight.

Monday, January 18

I'm in a clean, modern apartment, sparsely furnished, with huge windows and no ceiling, set on a pier, overlooking the ocean. Shannon is here, and I'm holding a baby. It is peaceful in this room—calm and full of love. Without warning, the entire room begins to shift off the edge of the pier until it tips sideways into the ocean. The walls, furniture, and floors fall, and I am surprised to be falling with them, like I expected Shannon to fall, but not me. I know before we hit the water that we won't all survive. The water is cold and debris is dragging me under. I break free and frantically search below. I find the baby and am able to pull her with me as I kick upward. Then, I see Shannon, panic on her face, sinking down into the blackness. I can no longer breathe. I know I can't save her. I kick my feet to the surface and…

I wake up, breathless.

Tuesday, January 19

"What is going on with me?" I asked this morning, first in prayer, then in my session with Dr. Hale. After recounting my recent nightmares and the meltdown on my "day off," he recommended we revisit that little devil, anger.

"I want you to be angry at everyone and everything today," he encouraged. "Just let it out." I obeyed.

I expressed ridiculous anger for things out of everyone's control and resentful anger for things that should have been controlled. Anger toward Shannon— for dying, for not being able to choose health and life. Anger toward Rob and Shannon—for their parenting and for not dealing better with Rob's parents, leaving us to clean up their messes. Anger toward the Cutlers—for hating us for doing our duty the best we know how, for throwing away what could have been love for the kids *and* them. Anger toward Mom and Dad—for having so many problems all these years and making it seem like their problems are more important than mine, for not being able to show me how much I know they care. Selfish anger toward Lorri—for feeling like I can no longer turn to her as my support person, for how she needs me more, now that Dave is gone, for needing me when I need myself. And anger for *all* the people who need me—my kids and OJ included. I expressed anger toward myself—for losing my identity, and my temper too often, for struggling so much to find my way, for feeling so alone.

These are the things I said today, and you know what? It was easy to do. They flew out of me and vanished in the air. They didn't stick to Dr. Hale like they sometimes stick to OJ. I could finally see how this emotional roller coaster has been fueled by anger.

"I don't know what to do with the anger," I said. "So, it comes out against people I love—OJ and the kids mostly. And against me, too. But this helps—to just set it free."

Then, I made a harder confession. It's one I haven't admitted to anyone but OJ and, even then, it took months to verbalize. It's the thing I have most feared. The thing I would never expose. Until today. "I struggle in loving Tre and Brody," I admitted. "It makes me feel like a demon. I should love them like I love my other kids. I'm deeply angry with *myself*. I feel like a failure—like I should be able to do better."

I sighed and folded my arms across my chest, looking down, to avoid his eyes. "I've noticed that Tre and Brody have bonded with you to a high degree," Dr. Hale gently replied. I lifted my face and saw his sincerity. "It's taking time for *you* to bond with *them*." *Bonding?* "You're worried it won't happen. That seems completely normal to me."

I nodded, tears welling. *Bonding. That's what this is, isn't it?* Every parent and child must bond, not just newborns. Bonding takes time. *It's not that I don't love Tre and Brody. No, not at all. It's just that we need more time to bond.* I sighed, still nodding and looking at Dr. Hale. *What a relief,* I thought as I smiled.

Letting the anger dissipate in that office felt like scrubbing out my heart so it could heal. "Don't hold to anger, hurt or pain. They steal your energy and keep you from love."[lxxv] Yes, they do. So I am working on letting them go.

Wednesday, January 27

Yesterday was a rough day. School was cancelled again, after a snow *week* while OJ was skiing with his buddies in Telluride. *He's much better at getting his needs and wants met than I am*, I thought. Most men seem to be. I, however, had been losing it with the kids all weekend, and now that OJ was home was barely holding it together.

"It's too much!" I vented to him in our locked bedroom, my voice clearly portraying the tension I felt. "I can't handle all this! I'm done!"

OJ tried to empathize. "It's been a very stressful week, dear," he reminded me. "You haven't had much sleep. You're *way* too tired. You know you always feel worse when it's late and you're tired. Go to bed."

Somewhere within, I knew he was right. I

wanted to listen, to stop the escalation, to let whatever I was feeling go. But I didn't listen. I couldn't stop myself. The spiral had begun, and I was simply along for the ride. I let the anger turn, focusing on my weakness, and then let it explode out in sobs. "This is how it *is* now, *isn't* it? Why am I given these kids if I can't handle it?" My voice rose in frustration, tears mingling with dramatic body gestures and pacing. "I'm such a failure!" I said. "I *hate* myself!"

I had no idea, until this morning, that six year-old Kennedy had been listening at the door.

"Mommy, I heard you and Daddy talking last night," she told me, a little tear forming in her eye. "You said, 'I hate myself!' and it scared me."

What kind of mother lets her child hear her say such things? I chastised myself. This was just more proof of the terrible mother I am.

Of course, I didn't tell Kennedy that. I took a long, deep breath, and pulled her tight, taking a moment to think. "Do you know how, when you make a wrong choice and treat someone poorly and you feel badly, because you know you chose the wrong thing to do?" She nodded a little. "Like, if you were mean to your friend one day, because you were too tired, but later you realized you were wrong?" A bigger nod.

"Well, I was feeling that way yesterday. I was mad at myself for choosing wrongly." She seemed to follow, so I added, "But everything looks much better after a good night of sleep. I feel much better today. I don't *hate* myself. I just hated how I *acted*."

Kennedy looked me in the eye and gave it a little thought. "Yeah," she finally said, "maybe you just lost your talent for being nice to us."

"Yep," I said, smiling at the innocent way she hit the nail on the head. "For a few days, I did. But don't worry," I added, looking her in the eye. "I'm going to get it back." She smiled my favorite smile. I hugged her, and we both laughed.

It was a reality check. I'm tired of that self-loathing thing. A small part of me still believes "I'm not good enough," and probably always has. I know how these things work—we learn how to embrace our self-worth through interactions with our parents, teachers, friends, and family. Somewhere along the way, we pick up lies, like "I'm weak," or "I'm unworthy," or "I'm just not good enough." Small as it may be, that part of us can have a loud voice sometimes, too loud for our own good. I know better than to listen to that voice, but it can still be a struggle.

Now Kennedy has heard the voice. I hope it doesn't become *her* voice. I need to say goodbye to the indulgence of self-loathing. Yes, it is an indulgence. It's a lot easier to just feel down on myself than to actually do something about how I feel. I need to get myself figured out before it is too late.

Thursday, January 28

I'm at a hotel in Prescott, Arizona, because OJ forced me to come, because I couldn't seem to force *myself* even though we both know I need time away, alone, to—to what? I'm not exactly sure. To rest, relax, *revive*? Yes, and I sense, even more.

Whenever I leave, it takes a while to let go. First, to let go of the fear and guilt of leaving. It's not that I fear the kids or OJ will suffer without me. No, it's more like *I'm* afraid to suffer without *them,* especially this time. I am afraid to obtain the one thing I most desire—peace and quiet. I'm afraid that in the quiet I will not find peace.

Second, to let go so I can recover. I'm like a frozen computer. I've been allowing myself and others to just keep typing. I punish myself by rejecting love—my form of self-destructive behavior—and it gets to a point where I don't even realize the martyr I've become.

I get why OJ can be so frustrated by me. I beg for help then push it away once it's there. He says, "What can I get you for dinner, dear? I want to help." I say, "I don't know. It's too late now. Nothing sounds good. Don't try to help me. I'll just eat cereal." Then, I point out all his mistakes and blame him for how I feel, but I'm the one ignoring the bright yellow road signs warning, "Cliff ahead! Turn back! Sheer drop!" I'm the one not willing to accept the olive branch, not willing to let him love me, not willing to give myself a break.

So, like a frozen computer, the only solution is to turn off for a while, to unplug before rebooting. I started by spending several hours vegging out with random TV and eating mindlessly, the easiest way to distract myself from too-scary feelings. Then, I took a hot bath and attempted to read for a while. Finally, I forced myself to sit still. I closed my eyes, took several slow, deep breaths, and observed the pictures in my head.

I saw myself lifted up, like a hot-air balloon, over the heaviness of the earth, the heaviness that has been my overburdened heart and mind. I floated above Prescott, in a brown wicker basket, watching the sunset on the rolling hills. I saw the thoughts coming heavily like dark birds, trying to land, but I didn't engage. Instead, I simply noticed them and one-by-one, they flew away. In that moment, I was light. In that moment, I felt free. I recognized how heavy the earth had been. I resisted coming back down.

Eventually, I let the balloon descend. Returning to the heaviness, I realized my recent troubles were not merely the result of being too tired or unable to handle six kids on a snow week. Though the snow didn't help, my troubles ran much deeper. As the balloon landed, I was reminded of the conversation I had the other day with my dear older and wiser friend, Carole. "It's clear you are in a lot of pain," she had said. It hadn't stood out at the time. It sure stood out now.

Can it be? Am I still in pain? I've tried everything: ignoring the pain, being patient, cheerful, and grateful about it, grieving it, therapy for it, talking about it, writing, singing, and teaching about it. I just may have failed to do the one thing that will actually help: *experience* it. Sure, I've allowed myself to experience the pain in small doses, here and there—caught off-guard by a tearful commercial, a song about losing or loving, a book about sisters. I've allowed myself to go even deeper in the safety of the therapeutic relationship, confident my psychologist guide would not let me drown. Perhaps, though, I am not as confident in *me*.

Tonight, in the safety of solitude, I can finally say, "I am in pain." It's vast as an ocean and as deep. It moves like the waves and swells and fades, and sometimes the waters are calm and still, the sun glistening off the surface. Ahh—those are the memories, the good memories. Sometimes, I think I'm merely going for a swim through the memories, when it suddenly turns, like a terrible storm, catching me in a tsunami of sorrow, until I'm hurled under, ripped and torn, then washed up on the shore. Sometimes, it stops my breath, tension crushing my gut.

Yes, the familiar physical reminder of loss has returned. Loss I want to forget. Loss I will never forget.

Friday, January 29

"What is the *loving* thing to do?" A former therapist of mine once asked me this, and it's been at the forefront of my mind. I've been trying to do the loving thing today, first, by putting the Do Not Disturb sign on my hotel room door and allowing myself to sleep in, and then by gently getting dressed in comfortable, plain clothes, no makeup, my hair combed into a low ponytail, and going to get a massage.

My back, neck, and shoulders were hard as a

rock. "Wow," the therapist, Karen, said, as she started working into them. I laughed and said, "I get that a lot." It wasn't funny, just another reminder I've neglected my body, and other things, for far too long. They're connected, you know—the knots in my body and the knots in my mind. In fact, massage reminds me of therapy. Both locate the painful spots, apply gentle pressure, and work until the knots release. I've been going deep in therapy. Today's massage was the same. I love deep pressure on my back and shoulders—it hurts in a way that relaxes me, knowing my body's being healed. Karen was strong and got the job done. Boy, were there moments of toe-curling pain! Internally, the pain was there, too.

Not long ago, I was lying on Shannon's massage table. Every massage I've had since she died has reminded me of her. She was always the one who worked out my knots and took care of me. I remembered the last massage she'd given me, in her own home on the blue massage table I now had in the attic of *my* home, collecting dust. Her hands were strong as she found the balls of tension and released them. I was lying on my side, just a few months pregnant with Sydney. *Just a few months before she died.*

Yes, every massage has reminded me of her, but today was different. Today, I let the reminders come. Face down, staring at the floor, I imagined those toes were Shannon's, the music was Shannon's. I let myself imagine Karen's hands were Shannon's, healing me. Taking care of me. It was as if she were there, saying, "I love you. I miss you. I am so grateful for your choice to raise my sons. I want to strengthen and support *you*."

I let her. In that moment, as Karen's hands performed this service for me, I realized how much I had shut Shannon out. Tears stacked behind my closed lids thinking of it. *So sad it's taken so long to see.* My nose was dripping and I held my breath so Karen wouldn't hear my sobs. She worked to release the knots in my back; I let myself release the knots of grief.

Now I'm back in my hotel room, emotionally exhausted, but writing. The loving thing for me right now involves allowing myself to *feel*, to miss Shannon. I can hardly believe how much the memories hurt, months and years later. I've been telling myself it's been too long and that I've already grieved. But this has been a lie. Today I see, it no longer matters whether I believe too much time has passed or whether anyone else understands or whether I even understand. It never has mattered. What matters is that I acknowledge and allow the pain to have its presence in my life. In so doing, I allow the craziness to stop and peace to enter.

It's as if I've been shutting Shannon out of my heart. I can see her, cold and hungry, nowhere to turn, sleeping on my doorstep. I've been ignoring her knocking for over two years. But no more. I want her in my heart. I want to take care of her. I want to allow her to take care of me. We need each other. Though she is my pain, I need her. I'm not fighting anymore. I'm just letting it be. Like the massage—breathe deeply. In. Out. In, out. It begins to loosen. The intensity begins to fade. And then, release.

Later tonight...

I feel different. Something has, not so much shifted as, settled. Shannon has a place in me. As OJ reminded me, earlier today, I'm working on forgiveness, aren't I? Forgiving Shannon and the past, allowing her to become part of my present and future. Allowing her to fuel me and heal me and nurture me, to be my partner in mothering.

I can tell I've changed, because I wrote to her tonight. I finally see, although the stories I write are in first person, I have been writing to Shannon all along. The only ear I have been writing for has been hers. It's as if this book is finally being born. It now has a purpose. It will lead me through forgiveness, and it will heal us all.

As my last full day of quiet draws to a close, I feel stronger. I feel at peace. No wonder I was afraid to come here and be alone. I couldn't see just how far and hard I was willing to run to avoid my sorrow. But now, I've stopped running. Now, I sit in my hotel room at the computer desk and type. I am a writer, aren't I? *I* know I am. I don't need anyone else to know it. Not yet. So, now, I write...

For Shannon:

Today was the first day I could speak to you. Sure, we'd spoken in therapy, you in the "empty chair," me struggling to pour out my heart, holding back the darkest truths. But tonight, I can finally say what's been with me for so long.

This afternoon I found myself on the flat warm table of a massage therapy school as a strong woman named Karen worked out the physical knots and I attempted to work out the emotional. That's when you appeared. I remembered your hands firmly and gently working out the knots of my muscles. I remembered my one and only session of acupuncture, shortly after Kennedy was born, and how you took such care of me, nurturing my postpartum body until I felt so much better. I slept like a rock that night. I remembered all the times you'd call just to see how I was doing, to check in on the kids. As I was brought back to Karen releasing the tension in my shoulders, I remembered she had been you not so long ago.

And what was different today is...I allowed myself to remember. I imagined Karen's hands were yours and you were taking care of me as I have so desperately needed, yet fearfully refused. Yes, you were with me. So long you've been knocking and I've been terrified to hear, but as I opened the door today, there you were, patiently sleeping on my doorstep—cold, shivering and hungry, but so full of gratitude and love. So ready to care for me so I can take care of our children.

I'm no longer trying to keep you away. I've invited you in and you are once more, as you always have been, living in my soul. You are nurturing me again. My heart aches for the time we have been apart, yet heals each time I reticently admit...I miss you. And I always will.

TWENTY-SIX
Do It

"There's doubt in trying.
Just do it or stop thinking."
~Toba Beta, Master of Stupidity[1]

We've all been taught that trying is a good thing, haven't we? We're told to "just give it a try," then "try harder," and "try, try again." Trying *is* a good thing. How else would we overcome our fears and taste the sweetness of success if we never gave it a try?

Webster's dictionary defines "try" as "to make an effort at, attempt; endeavor, connotes experimentation, testing or proving something."[2] Trying thus implies not only an effort to *do* something, but also a *hesitancy* on our part. "I will try, but I am not sure about it. I am fearful. I am not sure about me." This is where trying can turn into our nemesis. We try to be happy, try to be better—we try to overcome worries, fears, and emotions. "Surely trying is better than *not* trying?" most people would say. But I say, "Not always. Sometimes, the problem *is* the trying."

Sometimes we're trying so hard we fail to actually *do* what we are "trying" to do. I once heard one of my favorite authors and philosophers, C. Terry Warner, speak on this very subject. He told of a mother and son who couldn't see eye to eye; they didn't understand each other. As he witnessed their trying efforts to love one another, he said to the mother, "Stop *trying* to love him, and just *love* him." Stunned by this simple wisdom, the mother got the message, loud and clear. She had been trying so hard to figure out *how* to love him, she had failed to *love* him. She embraced her son, and weeping, whispered, "I love you."[3]

The same is true of each of us from time to time. I am *trying* so hard to feel better, I end up with a list of to-do's that completely undermines the possibility of actually *feeling* better. I am trying so hard to be a good mom, wife, daughter, I end up missing the moments when I can just *be* the mom, wife, or daughter. I am trying so hard to be happy, I miss the beauty and love in me that create happiness with ease.

Sometimes it's better *not* to try. Sometimes, the best way is to simply *do*. Simply let go. Simply feel it. Simply love. Simply experience life.

Simple, isn't it?

Wednesday, February 20

After waking early, exercising, getting the kids out, and seeing a couple for therapy at my office, I arrived at Dr. Hale's office for my own therapy. *Would it disturb my clients to know I am also a client right now?* I wondered, half-laughing at the irony as I walked through the door.

"I'm not sure what to talk about today," I said, knowing full well that when clients tell *me* they have nothing to say we usually end up having our most powerful sessions.

"Okay. I'd like you to lie down on the couch, then," was Dr. Hale's reply. Despite the stereotype, I'd never actually done this, though I'd had clients who'd asked to do so. It was a nice change of pace. He handed me a blanket, which I tucked into the maroon leather couch around me. This was his way of saying he was taking care of me today, and I welcomed it. I closed my eyes and focused on breathing while he sat in his rocking chair and walked me through my life.

He said that Mom and Dad died emotionally when Miki died. I've never heard that before, but it felt true. He said I'm desperate for someone to take care of me. And he's right. Like OJ recently alluded to, I'm more needy than I've realized. He spoke of the "role of responsibility," how I've played it well, and how it's also been my curse. "You can continue to play it well," he

said. "But you don't need to always play that role."
Then, he acknowledged the intense work I've been
doing this month. "You've been working *very* hard," he
said. "It's time to slow down a little. Pace yourself, and
back off from deep-sea diving for a while. It's time to
resurface and lie on the shore."

I could feel the truth of his words, and the
sadness. "I'm depressed," I admitted.

He rephrased it. "No, you're not depressed.
You've just been through so much. You're completely
worn out." I could feel it. *Completely worn out. Yes.*

Forty-five minutes later, I was off the couch and
out the door, headed home to take care of everyone else,
but before I committed to take "an internal vacation," as
Dr. Hale put it. Walking through the snow to my car, I
exhaled deeply, and, like a hug, gave myself the rest of
the month of February, the month of love, to love
myself just a little better.

Sunday, February 14

I'm staying on my internal vacation while
enjoying a little external vacation as a family. We're in
Phoenix, spending the day with Lorri.

The Phoenix winter, as expected, is perfection—
so warm and summery, it's rejuvenating. I feel better
here. I just returned from a gentle walk around the block
where I realized how much pressure I put on myself
almost all the time. Walking, for instance, hasn't been
just walking for I don't know how long. Instead, it's
meditating, praying, practicing gratitude, song-writing,
exercising, even trash-collecting, since I decided a few
months ago I could be perfect in not littering and thus
took it upon myself to pick up all trash I see! I know. It's
insane! My standards have been way too high, so I am
letting them go. It was a joy to just calmly walk today.

Yesterday, Lorri and I went to a women's
conference and had the opportunity to hear M.

Catherine Thomas speak. A religious scholar, professor, and author, I'd never heard her before, but let me say, she was remarkable, with light absolutely streaming out of her. That light found its way quickly to my heart as she spoke of bridging the gap between *trying* so hard to do what is right and actually *doing* it.

She spoke of self-evaluation and the need to "stop evaluating and simply come" to God. It's not about trying harder; it's about loving, about letting myself "feast on love," as she said. She spoke of our "self," our false self, who we think we are and need to be. I've been on the lookout for my "self" for quite some time, my "ego," as we call it in psychology. She called it a "mortal overlay," a term borrowed from a fellow professor that refers to the body and the mind and all the things we create our identity to be. Her message: stop identifying with the mortal overlay and speak from my soul.

She didn't stop with merely telling us what to do. She led us through the most powerful meditation I have ever experienced. I could actually *feel* my spirit. I comprehended, even for a moment, that it truly has no beginning and no end. When I focused, I could expand my spirit even bigger than my body, allowing me to experience just how vast each soul truly is. Meditation— I'd been trying to do it for so long, yet she converted me in a five-minute experience. I was hooked.[4]

Now, I wish I could tell M. Catherine Thomas how, in sharing her knowledge with us, she touched me deeply and gave me exactly what I needed. The Buddhist proverb is absolutely true: "When the pupil is ready, the teacher will appear."[5]

Wednesday, February 17

I've been engaging in my new and improved spiritual practice every day—meditating to get in touch with my soul and with God, feeling my spirit grow and stretch, and connecting with the many pure, transcendent qualities at my core. It is a whole new way of being for me.

I've always exercised, read scriptures, and prayed to start each day. But now, after exercise, I do the spirit meditation I experienced the other day. I pray. I sit still and listen. I read scriptures, and the answers come flooding in. Then, I get to work and seek to maintain that connection all day long, checking in periodically through breathing, prayer, and pondering. It's not easy—I'm having to get up an hour earlier to fit it all in—but it's worth it. I feel like a new woman.

I'm learning how to allow my weaknesses to teach and propel me instead of holding me back. I still make daily mistakes. I put up walls, push others away, betray my intentions to love and serve others. I engage in negative thinking and feel frustrated, criticize myself and others, and so many other things! Yet something is different. I'm *seeing* these things, for one. Perhaps more than I used to or perhaps merely in a different way. I see them as ways to grow and not proof of my own inadequacy. I seek forgiveness as soon as I catch my mistakes, then let my repentance burn up guilt or self-criticism in its process. I love myself better, and thus love others better, too.

I never would have guessed I needed a spiritual adjustment. I thought it was an emotional, mental, physical shift that was needed. But, beneath all these, my spirit is ready for a new level of understanding and connection, too. My hope is, the more comfortable I become with the spiritual realm, the more I will remain there, keeping it a focus of my daily life. As M. Catherine Thomas writes, "In the sky of your mind, you are the sun!"[6] I want to shine like the sun. I create my world, and I am working to create joy.

Monday, February 22

I'm living in an apartment with Braxton and Tre. I'm outside in the courtyard, helping someone, on a sunny day, when I see the boys climbing the metal stairs, waving hello. As they open the apartment door, I hear a gun go off. I see blood fly as I run to the apartment to find Braxton and Tre lying just inside. They have been shot.

I lock the doors, try to secure the house, and tell them to stay low as I begin to examine their wounds. Two women break in the window and one pulls a gun. Somehow, I know I am stronger, so I wrestle it away and pin her down, knocking the other, smaller one, down and out with a kick. I've got the gun now, and I'm desperately trying to call 911, but there are no land lines in our house and each cell I try either won't dial or keeps leading me to random numbers.

At first, I think I'm dialing wrong, because my hands are shaking and I'm so scared about the boys. The woman I'm pinning down is laughing. "You're not leaving here or calling anyway," she says. I realize they've tapped all phones and locked us in. I can neither call out nor leave. I look over at the boys. They seem like they're not injured at all, but I know they need to get to the emergency room. I keep searching for a way.

Next thing I know, it has been a week. We are still prisoners, and I am still trying to find a way out or call for help. There's a party in my apartment that my captors have put on, and everyone is dressed up, sharing drinks, relaxed and chatting. I see a guy I know from across the room. It's our attorney. I know he can help. I pull him aside and tell him all that's happened. He seems to be polite and listening. I know he wants to help me, but I quickly realize he can't help, because he is in on it, too. Everyone is in on it.

I woke up panicked, anxious and afraid, and dragged myself out of bed to find the kids making Top Ramen for breakfast on yet another snow day.

It is going to be a very long day.

Thursday, February 25

OJ was in a dune buggy with his buddies somewhere in the California sand, the kids were in school for the first time in a week, and I spent the morning in therapy, discussing hypotheses for why I've been so up and down.

Just when I start feeling better, things always seem to take a turn for the worse. My list of potential diagnoses was long: Depression? Seasonal Affective Disorder? Pre-Menstrual Syndrome? Pre-Menstrual Dysphoric Disorder? Grief? Burnout? I'd been researching and presented them to Dr. Hale today.

He disagreed with all of them. "The only diagnosis I've ever written down for you," he said, "is Adjustment Disorder, with Depressed and Anxious Mood." I know that diagnosis well—the least harmful one we psychologists most often give, since everyone is always adjusting to something. "I've seen *times* of depression and anxiety in you," he continued. "But never long enough to qualify for a diagnosis. And never with the extreme hopelessness characteristic of depression." He reminded me that I have a stressful life, between kids, husband, home, work, parents, more legal issues with the Cutlers, *yes, more!* and so on. "Also," he gently said, "grief is still there. It comes and goes, as it should, but it is still there."

I shared with him my nightmare from Monday, and it was clear his assessment was right. "In the dream," he said, "the boys have been injured, and because of that, you end up trapped, trying to help the boys and 'free' all of you, especially yourself. But you seem powerless to escape. Everyone is telling you, 'Relax. Forget it. It's not an emergency; you're fine.' But you're relentless and angry that they give you this message. Even the women sent to 'trap' you, the ones you initially fought and beat, don't have to fight back or even *try* to keep you prisoner. You're somehow so easy to overpower. You're defeated already."

Defeated. That's what's holding me back. I receive all kinds of messages that everything is "okay," but it's not always so. I relate to being a prisoner, not just of my circumstances, but of myself. I defeat myself. "This is how I am now," "This is how it is," "I'm crazy now," "I'm not a good mother, person," and so on. Yet I never give up. As Dr. Hale pointed out, "Even though the kids are the 'reason' you're a prisoner in your dream, you are working hard to free all of you out of love for them."

I do love them. I love me, too. That's why I work so hard. Dr Hale tells me I'm doing more than enough to try and be better. Between exercise, therapy, spiritually seeking, going to the doctor yesterday to check my hormone levels, and doing my best to sleep, eat, and keep up with life's demands, I am doing plenty. Maybe even too much.

I'm beginning to understand how all this *trying* is getting in my way of actually *being* well. Perhaps, if I stop trying for a while I will, hopefully, finally heal.

TWENTY-SEVEN
Forgive

"To understand everything is to forgive everything."
~The Buddha

At the core of every trauma is a spiritual wound. That's what I have learned—not just from my own experience, but from those I help in therapy. It may be easier to see or feel the physical, emotional, or mental wounds, but trauma also impacts the delicate spirit, whether we sense the impact or not.

When a wound exists, it must be healed, though it is not always easy to know where to begin. Some may outwardly question God, faith, or the meaning of life, but for many there will be no obvious spiritual symptoms. Instead, most of us will work for months to heal the pain and grief of trauma and finally start seeing progress in the physical, mental, and emotional realms. But something will still feel "off." We won't be able to put our finger on it. It may feel like we really haven't made any progress or like we're sliding back again. That's not what it is.

I'm not a spiritual advisor, but I can tell when a spirit has been broken. I know a few things that can help. For one, seeing the spiritual wound, and being willing to ask, "Is it possible there's a spiritual wound in me?" Once we open ourselves to the possibility, we begin to discover clues to the truth. We begin to sense the spirit's needs, and we can begin to address them. That's another way to help the spirit—listening and addressing what comes up. This may involve seeking guidance from religious or spiritual advisors, searching scriptures or good books, kneeling in prayer, or simply sitting still. Then, we can accept what we find. We can also accept that our spiritual hurt has nothing to do with how "good" we are or how much we love God or how spiritually in-tune we are. It is simply the result of the trauma we have endured.

One of the most common spiritual needs I see, when we've been wounded, is the need to forgive. When we've been hurt by others, by life, or by ourselves, forgiveness is essential to healing. Some of us turn our backs on our need to forgive, convincing ourselves it's not important. Others openly hold a grudge, not able to work through and let it go. Many of us hold on to hurt as a badge of honor, feeling we've somehow earned the right to never forgive. Sadly, some of us *are* able to forgive everyone except ourselves.

The fact is, most of us have forgiveness wrong. We think we must forgive the other person for *their* sake. As Mark Twain said, "Forgiveness is the fragrance the violet sheds on the heel that has crushed it."[1] The violet shares its fragrance even though it has been hurt. What a gift it is to the heel that has crushed it! But the true glory of this statement is what the violet gains. Though crushed, it still expresses love. That is the core of forgiveness. We must forgive others, show love and mercy even to those who have hurt us, for our *own* sake.

When we fail to let go of what has been done to us, to forgive and move on, we cause ourselves greater pain. Imagine I've injured my elbow. It's hurting, causing me pain. Do I beat it up more, yell at it, tell it how much it has hurt me? After all, it *is* hurting. Don't I have a right to hurt it right back? This sounds ridiculous because hurting our elbow more only hurts us. Don't we do this with others all the time? We hold onto anger, heartache, and pain, refusing to let it go, refusing to ever forget what has been done to us. In hurting our partners, parents, friends, even strangers, we only hurt ourselves more.

Instead, like we would with our own elbow, we must find a way to nurture those who have made us feel injured. We must find a way to forgive them, to love them when they, and we, need it most. Don't get me wrong. This doesn't mean we let them hurt us more. It simply means we stop hurting ourselves.[2] The same goes with self-forgiveness. We only hurt ourselves when we fail to let it go.

As author Lewis B. Smedes once said, "To forgive is to set a prisoner free and discover that prisoner was you."[3] If we want to heal, emotionally and spiritually, forgiveness is the way. Forgiveness cleanses, wipes the past clean. It opens us to what matters and what we really need. It heals our hearts, and that is what spiritual healing is all about: seeking the parts that have closed in pain and gently nurturing them back open. Open, to receive earthly and divine love and help. Open, to receive and live life again.

Sunday, February 28

It felt like the moment Shannon died, God gave me a sharp turn in life. I was moving along brilliantly when the wheel was jerked ninety degrees.

At some point, I started trying to turn back, find the old path, and carry on. I have been questioning—lost, confused, and hard on myself—but today I finally understood. That path is dead and gone, and it is okay.

Things are not and never will be the same and neither will I, but a fresh new path awaits. Though it may be tough to stay the course when it's so rough and unfamiliar, I will keep moving forward, for I am beginning to understand I am on the path to joy. Today, as I pondered and questioned what I needed to do to *feel* that joy more in my life, I sat still, listened carefully, and suddenly knew the answer. *No* answer was the answer. *You're doing fine,* was what I felt, and I let myself believe it. *Simple. Life can be so much simpler, yet so much richer.*

Tonight, at the dinner table, nine year-old Brody was asking all kinds of random questions. "Why do we have fingers?" "Why is there snow?" "What color is the most in the universe?" He fired them off, all in a row, barely taking a moment to breathe. The rest of us laughed as we tried to formulate answers. It was hard to keep up. "If the sun exploded, would Jupiter be hit?" "What country do they speak sign language in?" Joy filled the room, bubbling up from each of us.

My new path *is* the path of joy. Joy resides in me and in the simple things—in dinners and conversations and questions and laughter. Brody also helped me realize something else tonight, something I once knew but had forgotten. It's not always *answers* that we need anyway. Sometimes, it's better *questions*.

Friday, March 5

Another rough week. After ups and downs, including more court stuff related to how Bill Cutler settled Shannon's estate by blowing a huge chunk of the boys' inheritance, anger came back—to OJ *and* me—as we prepared to file an objection. Just when we start feeling well again as a family, something always shows up to remind us of the crazy situation we're still in. At least, instead of stewing in it, we used our anger to fuel us forward. It again started the downslide of emotion and building frustration for me, until last night when, desperate for something that could help, I started reading and came upon an idea that opened me to the truth.

I was reading, in M. Catherine Thomas' book, *Light in the Wilderness*, about the word "atonement" and how it really means "at-one-ment." I was reading how we are *always* "at-one-ing" with something. I already believed that we are always either moving toward growth and goodness or slipping away. This made it even clearer: I am seeking to "*at*-one" or *be* one with *something* at all times.[4]

As I thought about this, I turned my attention to my body and began to sense an underlying darkness in me, a layer I had not noticed before. How long had it been there? Was this grief? Or pain? Or, *what?* All I knew was that it was in me, and I did not want it there. The more I focused on the darkness, the more I could feel it trying to at-one *me* with depression and despair—a resurgence of my familiar internal war. That's what caught my attention as I read on—"It is a spiritual *war*fare."[5]

That's what this is. In addition to the emotional, intellectual, and physical warfare, I am engaged in a spiritual *war, too.* I could not deny it, yet it shocked me. All this time I had continued my spiritual practices, even increased them. I hadn't felt angry with God, as far as I could tell. I had felt spiritually strong, faithful, diligent. And I *had* been. But that had nothing to do with this spiritual war. Hadn't I learned this about war these past years? One can be faithful, yet the war rages on.

I never understood, until that moment, just how hurt my spirit might be, how much the trauma I had experienced had cut to the core. It had been fighting, for sure. But it was time to let the fighting end.

I knelt in prayer and said out loud, "Heavenly Father, please remove this darkness from me. Please help me do what I must to be full of light, full of love, to finally heal." I kept my head bowed into my hands on the bed as I finished my prayer and sighed, and then felt a little crazy as I suddenly lifted my head and yelled: "You will not turn me! So, just leave me alone!" Crazy as it felt, I said what needed to be said. Whatever was at war with me needed to know the war was over. The darkness could not win. In telling the darkness it could not win, *I* had won already.

I felt myself strengthen, sensing something important had just taken place. I knelt in a prayer of gratitude, then stood and looked around my quiet room. Yes, something had changed. I sat down and began to read again. "...do what you can do a step at a time. Seek to understand the principles of healing from the scriptures and through prayer. Help others. Forgive..."[6]

The key to spiritual healing: Forgive. Not just the Cutlers or Shannon or my parents. In that moment, I surrendered forgiveness to God for the turn my life was given. I prayed for forgiveness in return—for holding on to hurt and anger, for not seeing until today how I could truly let it go. As I rose from my prayer in that quiet, love-filled moment, I began to understand. In seeking forgiveness for my mistakes, I had unknowingly begun to forgive myself.

Thursday, March 10

"Are you able to accept anger as part of your life?" Dr. Hale asked in our session this morning.

That didn't even compute with me. "I can't *accept* anger," I told him. "I work to *overcome* anger." This was one of the rare times when we were not seeing eye-to-eye.

"You are great at courageously feeling and facing other big emotions," Dr. Hale pointed out, "including trauma and horror. But if you have one blind spot, it's anger." I didn't want him to be right, but I knew he was. *How could I not have seen before that anger is just another emotion, like joy or sorrow, enthusiasm, or pain? How could I have helped so many others recognize this, yet be so blind myself?*

"I guess you're right," I said. "I've been working on allowing a space for grief in my life, and I guess anger can work the same way."

Anytime I had not been able to keep anger at bay, I had felt like a failure—weak and wrong. In my mind, *feeling* anger equaled poor behavior, meanness, or being a "bad" person. That just wasn't true. I'd had good reasons to feel angry. I wasn't weak for feeling that emotion, and I certainly wasn't a bad person.

Dr. Hale pulled it all together. "It seems, for you, that when anger is there, depression follows."

Yes! Anger has been tough, because it's contradictory to

who I want to be, to who I believe I am. This explains why I've been in a spiritual warfare. Anger and depression are definitely war for the spirit.

"You used the word 'oppressive' to describe your feelings these past months," Dr. Hale continued.

Yep. Unacknowledged and unprocessed anger can sure feel oppressive, especially when I turn it on myself. I nodded.

"Oppressive is an 'other plane' kind of term—describing a more spiritual level of emotion," he said.

The anger is both a cause and part of this spiritual wound. "Yes," I said. "That's exactly what it is. I've only recently discovered my spiritual wounds. And I've only recently felt them beginning to heal. Perhaps, because I haven't allowed myself to feel anger as an emotion I've unknowingly allowed it to oppress me, to keep hurting me on a deep level."

He nodded. "It's time to accept anger as part of your life. And to realize you are a wonderful person, whether you feel angry or not."

A breakthrough day. Anger is an emotion like any other. Like sadness or grief, I can just feel it and let it go. "Yes, I believe I *can* accept anger as a part of my life," I concluded.

I'm finally getting it, and it feels good.

Saturday, March 12

Did you know that for Christmas I spent several days sewing ten twin-sized, colorful, minky blankets for all the kids, OJ, Dad, my brother, Bud, and Lorri? I did. It's a tradition I started. Every other year I've made OJ and the kids a new blanket. A few years back, I made one for Mom and for my sisters, Ashley, Leighton, and Shannon. This past Christmas, I was finally making one for everyone else on my list. I wanted to make myself one too; I even had the fabric laid out, ready to sew, but I ran out of time and put the fabric away, figuring it didn't really matter if I had a blanket. What mattered was I'd completed the gifts for everyone else. What mattered was they knew I loved them. As they opened their gifts Christmas Day, I could see by the looks on their faces—they knew.

Today, I made my blanket. It's the softest, furry yellow on one side and smooth, dotted cream on the other. It's all clean and fluffy at the foot of my bed. OJ took the kids to Phoenix for the weekend, and having this time to care for myself was exactly what I needed.

I had a moment on my jog this morning. As I crossed the bridge over the pond, almost home, I felt prompted to stop at the water's edge. I heard the pond ripples gently lap, the flap of a goose's wings and swish of his landing. I then closed my eyes, inhaled deeply, and listened. I could see how I had been blocking love because I hadn't felt worthy of it. I'd blocked love from OJ, from the kids, from friends, family, from myself, and especially from God. Just like I'd done with Shannon, I'd locked the door on so many others who'd been ready to nurture me.

It was an unexpected turning point, that moment at the pond. My instinct was to criticize myself for mistakes. Instead of beating myself up, I immediately let go of the need to self-criticize and decided to forgive. "I love you, Christi," was what I felt, what I heard. But it wasn't a message from *me*. It came from the wind and the trees and the water, not a voice as much as a knowing. I could feel God's love for me, powerful and true. My heart was full, and I gently whispered, "I know you do," and cried.

That great love inspired me to come straight home and love myself by beginning to sew my blanket. As I sewed, I thought of the blanket I made for Shannon years ago—hot pink polka dot minky on one side and a soft, bright orange stripe on the other. She had loved it. It had been high up on Sydney's closet shelf after she died, a gift from the aunt she would never know. I pulled it off the shelf a few months ago. It was well-used and loved now, rocking Sydney to sleep. I thought of Rob, how I'd never made him a blanket and wish I could now. I let myself miss them both. I thought of the kids and how the blankets I've made wrap them in warmth and comfort when I cannot be there. I thought of OJ, of all we've been through, and how *he* is *my* warmth and comfort. I thought of me, of all I've experienced, of all I've withheld from myself because I could not let go and forgive. I thought, *I really have done the best I can.* Today, I believed it was true.

Soon my blanket was complete. I smiled, wrapped myself tightly, and took a nap. *This blanket is me, loving myself, beginning to really let love in.*

Saturday, March 20

"I'm excited again!" I'm excited about writing, about learning, about teaching. I'm excited about spending time with the kids, OJ, and friends, and about traveling again! I feel passionate again. I am loving my family, and I am loving myself. I am showing up in my life, and it feels terrific.

I traveled to Phoenix for a voice lesson with John yesterday. I've still been going, off and on over the years, when I've had the energy and time, but it had been a while, and singing yesterday, I felt uncertain of what might come out. What came out, however, was beautiful. "You're working with a new voice," John said, surprised and happy for me. "After years of blending your upper and lower registers, your voice is finally balanced," he said. "It is full and rich. I can tell you've been working hard."

I had been working hard, practicing to old lessons on my digital recorder, driving kids around town, in moments alone, or whenever I could find the space. It had paid off. John explained, now that my voice was "right," I could put the power back in and it would not fail me. We practiced. It worked. The power was there. "You can just let go and sing," he said.

So it is with life. I've been making it right, through these years of hard work, blending and balancing the "upper" and "lower" parts of me. Now, the power can come in. I'm excited again! I can finally let go and sing! I can finally let go and love. I can finally let love return to me.

TWENTY-EIGHT
Receive Love

"Being deeply loved by someone gives you strength,
while loving someone deeply gives you courage."
~Lao Tzu

It's been said, "It is better to give than to receive." The idea originated in the Bible. While I am not one to disagree with the wisdom of the Bible, I have to admit, I no longer believe this is true—at least not in the traditional sense.

It is better to give than to *take,* but *receiving* is not the same as *taking.* Taking implies selfish motives, withholding, and lack of love. Receiving is lovingly *accepting* that which has already been given, and receiving love—from others and from oneself—is the key to giving even more.

It's taken me a long time to understand this. I *believe* in giving. I'm a helper by nature, and that's why I chose to become a mother and a psychologist. I believe in loving others in the ways they need to be loved. But that requires *receiving* love, too. Think about it this way. If someone I care deeply for gave me a gift, wrapped beautifully and topped with an elegant bow, and I said, "Thank you so *very* much," and then hid it away on a shelf somewhere, did I really receive the gift? No. I was given a gift, but did not receive it. The same goes for love. If I refuse love or insist, "No, *I* am the one doing the loving around here," then I'm refusing my loved one the opportunity to love, too. That's not very loving.

Yes, receiving love is as important as giving love, and, yes, it is also the key to giving greater love. It's impossible to give, give, give, and still have anything left. Believe me, I know. I get myself into trouble over and over because I forget to slow down and *receive* a little more. It is a cycle, after all—give, receive, give, and receive. I thought of this once as I watched the ocean waves. They ebb and flow in a constant, calming pattern. What would happen if the waves never ebbed? They would flow and flow, creating floods and tsunamis, destroying all in their path, and eventually, running dry. The cycle of the ocean is and must be complete. So must the cycle of loving. Receiving completes and reenergizes the cycle of love. When I focus on receiving what is there for me, I am more full of love, more complete. Then, I give even more.

Receiving love is also the key to self-love. So many of life's struggles come from failing to receive love from our spouses, children, family, friends, and especially from our Higher Power. Underlying these struggles is almost always the same core issue—a failure to love oneself. When we block or ignore the love we are given, it can become a habit. Soon, we've forgotten that innate ability we once had to just let love in. We forget *how* to love ourselves, how to be gentle and kind, and we forget how to let *God* love us—how to feel and acknowledge our innate worth and potential. Learning self-love is the gateway to truly loving others, for it's hard to give something we have not yet received. Receiving is what it's all about.

That brings us full circle. In order to give love, we must receive love; as we receive love, we learn to love ourselves; and as we love ourselves, we have so much more love to give. It is okay to receive love. In fact, I'd say there are plenty of times when it's actually *better* to receive than to *give*.

Tuesday, March 30

I "graduated" from therapy today—just like last year, except *that* was Kindergarten and *this* is elementary school graduation.

"I feel…different," I told Dr. Hale. "On a new path, with a new way of being. I'm beginning to trust who I really am."

"Who *are* you?" he asked, a question that, before today, would have puzzled and overwhelmed me.

"I'm just me," I replied. "All the things I do, or how I act, those are merely skills or talents, strengths or weaknesses. They're not *me*. I can use them to help others and myself, but really, I'm just this calm, loving, even joyful presence, and when I remember to tap into that presence, then I can act from who I really am."

He smiled warmly and nodded. I shrugged and smiled, too. I recalled all we'd been through together, and I was flooded with gratitude for all Dr. Hale had done for me. In, fact, sitting there, I realized that he was the only person, myself included, from whom I had *never* blocked love. Though I knew we'd meet again, especially professionally, I felt immensely grateful for his willingness to guide me through my darkest days and sadness at the idea of walking out that door.

"It's like your old life is closed and now you're opening a new chapter," he said, as we shook hands and prepared to part.

"Yes," I agreed. "It feels like that story has ended. I've got a lot of life ahead of me, and I'm ready to start living. Thank you." And that was that.

You know what they say about endings, right? It's just a *beginning* in disguise. "What we call the beginning is often the end. To make an end is to make a beginning. The end is where we start from."[1] Here's to getting started. Here's to my beginning.

Friday, April 23

I was caught off-guard this morning when Mom called and asked if I had "a few minutes to talk." If she calls, it's only for small talk, so I was nervous right away.

I was right to be nervous. We ended up in a two hour conversation of talking, listening, trying to understand, defending, explaining, cautiously speaking, feeling crazy, frustrated, and finally, spent. We covered a lot of ground, starting with Mom stating, "I am so hurt by you and what you did."

"What did I *do*?" I asked. I had no idea. We'd barely interacted in months.

"Un-inviting us for Christmas," she sobbed. She explained how hurt Dad and Ashley were, how it hurt her so much that she recently started losing her hair from the stress of it. "It's the biggest hurt of my life," she said.

Well, I was completely shocked. It's true I changed our usual Christmas routine last December. Feeling so overwhelmed by everything that had happened these years, by always trying to do what everyone else needed me to do, I finally got up the courage to admit to myself what I really wanted for the holidays: peace, quiet, and my own little family.

Weeks before Christmas, I kindly explained this to Mom, to Dad, to Ashley and Bud, and also to Lorri and OJ's whole family. We had arranged to spend the days leading up to Christmas with our families in Phoenix. We had Christmas Eve dinner with Mom and Dad. I knew Mom was upset by it. I told her I knew it would be hard for her—ours are her only grandchildren—and I encouraged her to please talk to me, but she didn't bring it up again.

I took a deep breath, listened, and tried to understand. "I hear what you are saying, Mom. You needed us, and you felt I was shutting you out of your family." I could hear the hurt in her voice, and I *did* understand why she would feel hurt—that's why I'd asked her to talk to me about it back in December. "*And,*" I continued, "I think I did the right thing—for my family." That's it. The right thing for my family and for me hurt those I care about.

I said what was in my heart, even if she might not have liked it, because we needed to get to the truth. *There has been enough pretending*, I thought. *I can't pretend anymore.* "It's been hard being in a 'parent' role with you and Dad," I said, "always having to take care of you since you first got cancer when I was a teenager. And then, when Miki died. You've missed a lot because of your grief, pain and depression over the years, and it has affected our relationship. We're distant, because of it." This was the first time I'd ever said it out loud, and it brought with it increasing emotion.

"I hurt and *I* miss Shannon too, Mom," I said, as the flood began, breaking my words. "I've just been trying to understand…what has happened…to our family."

It took her a few moments to gather herself, so distraught were we both. "I know," she finally breathed out. "Me, too."

We began to actually talk—about the present and the past and things of the future. She apologized for something she said years ago I thought she'd forgotten. She apologized for hurting me. I apologized for hurting her. Two hours later, we were both completely drained, but we ended on a hopeful note.

"I don't care about the past, Mom," I said. "We can't change it. We just have to find a way to communicate and hope we can do better in the future. Let's start fresh, Mom. I really do love you."

"I love you, too."

Monday, May 31

We just returned from our Memorial Day campout, complete with late nights, early mornings, great conversation with friends, overeating, and throwing up-Sydney. Kennedy was so fast on her quad I couldn't catch her, dressed in her sunflower dress, pink sandals, and baby goggles, with a mane of crazy hair flying out of her hot pink helmet! The boys stayed in their own tent and, in true teen and pre-teen form, slept in later than anyone. Braxton kept saying, "I'm a 'gangsta' now," wearing his pants all saggy with a green ski hat, black shades, and his iPod in his ears nonstop. He called his braces "grills" and did a "gangsta dance," which looked like a backward "running man." He's been in full teenager mode for a while now—moody and confrontational—so I loved seeing him let loose.

"You're definitely *not* a gangsta," I teased him. "I'm pretty sure you're a *poser*."

He smiled and danced again. "This is how gangstas dance, mom. Get with it."

OJ and I just laughed and rolled our eyes. I love when we can be silly together, and we all had a blast! However, if I have to take any more vacations, I just might collapse.

Now that we're home and cleaned up, my thoughts are turned to summer. How did I miss that there are only two days left of school? Why haven't I figured out a summer plan yet? I'm somewhere in between anticipating more time with the kids as a *good* thing—a time to create memories and have fun—and being completely panicked. I know how this works by now. Without a plan, I am doomed!

I know I'm sounding dramatic, but our campout was good at pointing out one of my biggest flaws: short-temperedness. I'm working on it. I try to be honest with myself about how I'm feeling and ask for help before it becomes too late. I try to forgive myself when it does get too late. I'm getting better, but it is still, unfortunately, a work in progress. I keep hearing myself bark at the kids, "Come on, you guys! You know better!" Or, chanting away to OJ about "all I'm doing," and how I "never get to have fun!" I guess it comes with the territory, which I remind myself, is still peopled with six children, including two teenagers, and just to spice it up, a feisty two year-old and a saucy almost-seven year-old. It's a recipe for a mommy meltdown! And summer's only going to compound things.

Wish me luck—wish us all luck. I love life! I even love summer. Probably because it hasn't started yet.

Wednesday, June 2

I need to be reminded of what loving myself *is* and is *not,* so I am going to make a list...

Loving Myself Is *Not*:
Refusing Help
Failing to connect with OJ
Too much sugar, chocolate,
or junk food
Too much escape television
Constant distraction and
noise
Pushing away love
Helping others every time
they need me
Looking for validation from
external sources
Isolating
Self-focus all the time
Other-focus all the time
Unrealistic expectations
Forcing myself on when I
need a break

Loving Myself *Is:*
A massage, a warm bath
Exercise, a walk on a lovely
day
Reading a book I enjoy
Learning
Good sleep, a nap
A little dark chocolate each
day
Fun with my kids
Time alone with OJ
Quiet time—to ponder,
pray, and re-connect
Helping others as I am able
Expressing my soul through
my talents
Opening my heart to the
kids, OJ and others
Recognizing my efforts, big
and small
Gently working on my
weaknesses
Taking a break; then
carrying on

I feel more loved already.

Tuesday, June 15

Today is Kennedy's birthday. We had a birthday breakfast with streamers, a birthday party, and tonight, a small sleepover. She is as excited as any seven year-old girl would be, smiling all toothless and adorable. I am excited that she's so excited.

I am *also* smiling. I've had a few ups and downs with summer, mostly related to my menstrual cycle, thank goodness, but I'm doing okay. I submitted two songs for a songwriting competition next month—completely intimidating—but it's time for me to get out there, do what I love, and let myself shine.

I'm still seeing clients a few hours a week. I've been busy working on the grant our Arizona Postpartum Wellness Coalition received—"Operation Education," where we set up a perinatal mood disorders curriculum that can travel around our state. I also just found out our court date is set for June thirtieth, when we get to state our objections to the judge and hope he can do something about Shannon's estate money being blown. I've been working hard on that postpartum legal case I mentioned a while ago, reading page upon page of police reports, preparing to write my report.

Add all that together and my smile becomes a little fake as I hear the voice of criticism in my head—saying I shouldn't have the kids watching so much TV, that I didn't brush Syd's teeth last night, and that I got mad they were eating cake and gummy bears at eleven a.m. when the kitchen was supposed to be "closed" and zones weren't done. I am lovingly telling that critical voice in my head to shut it. I'm reminding myself that, even if I'm not perfect in how I manage my kids, I am loving them. That is my key to summer sanity: focus on the loving and let the rest go.

I wish I had more time to write, but I'm running

out the door again to drive kids hither and yon. Yes, I could use more time alone. Yes, it's hard feeling like I'm constantly waiting for whoever needs me next. But instead of griping about it, I gave myself a fancy title— "Lady-in-Waiting." Not as grand as "Princess" or "Queen," of course, but fitting. I may be the Queen the rest of the year, but I'm the Lady-in-Waiting during the summer. When the next little prince or princess summons me I'll say, "Yes, Lord or Lady, you rang?" Then, smiling, I'll obey.

TWENTY-NINE
Obey the Whispers

*"I know that truth is waiting if I slow my mind and feel—
for thinking cannot tell me what is real."
~Lyrics from my song,* Surrender

Most people don't seem to like that word—*obey*. I admit, I haven't always been so keen on it, either. Too often thinking I know best, my attitude has been, "I'll obey—*if* it works for *me*." But when we're talking about obeying something bigger than the "little me," about obeying our soul's voice, Higher Power, or God, I can tell you that obeying works…*always*. When we listen and obey the whispers, we will never be led astray.

There are some principles that are time-tested to be true, and when we live according to those principles, we experience an increase of joy. Obeying the whispers is one of these. Call it your conscience, a guardian angel, the voice of God, the spirit, your intuition—it's like a radio wave continually broadcasting, which you can only hear if you sit and tune in. It is up to each of us to listen for this guidance and up to each of us to choose to obey.

This may seem like a pretty non-psychological topic, but it's true in a psychological sense, too. For years, I've been teaching people to tune in to their true voice, to listen to their conscience, hear those whispers, and obey. Doing so prevents harm, gets us out of addictions, into our goals, and *over* all the lies we tell ourselves about who we are and who we are not. I'm not talking about obeying the whims of man. I'm talking about Truth in its purest form. Why *wouldn't* we want to obey?

Over the years, I have learned that obeying the whispers is the way to peace and joy. We spend so much time and energy trying to do it on our own, do it our way, that we miss the very voice whispering exactly what we need. By submitting, humbling ourselves, and actively listening to those whispers, we receive answers, and by obeying those promptings we receive an ease and certainty about life.

As one author so aptly put it: "Knock, ask, listen, receive, obey."[1] It really is the simplest and most fulfilling way to live.

Wednesday, June 16

Just when I feel I'm getting the hang of things, I'm thrown for another loop.

Yesterday, after a good, busy little summer day and watching the very touching finale of *Lost*, I heard a ruckus downstairs. Running to the boys' area in the basement to see what it was, I found Tre and Colton physically fighting. Two friends were sleeping over, and all six boys were down there, the four watching the two throw punches at each other! A "game of hide-n-seek gone wrong," they called it. Four stood, laughing and cheering, while two beat each other up. They may not have had any wounds I could see, but all six looked guilty, and they didn't argue when I firmly, loudly said, "Get to bed."

As usual, Colton was immediately humbled and harder on himself than I could ever have been. Braxton was trying to play it cool, but knew he was in trouble, too. "You should know better than to just stand by and let them hurt each other, egging them on," I told him. He had to agree. Brody disappeared—I didn't even notice until later he'd snuck off quietly to bed. Tre, ever verbal, just like Rob, expounded his defense, escalating his emotions until he ended up breaking down. This is a regular occurrence.

But tonight, I wasn't buying his excuses of what Colton or any of the other kids had done. I'd caught him, red-fisted, when he knew there was absolutely no hitting in this house. He knew he was wrong, even if he couldn't admit it. I wish it weren't always a fight with Tre, but it is, and I had a sense of why. I have long felt the anger beneath his behaviors and attempts to be okay. "What is going on with you, Tre?" I asked.

"It's just," he hesitated, "I remember walking in on my mom that morning, and I thought she'd be okay. And then, at Mimi's house, I heard she was dead, and I just wished I could die, too." I'm never prepared for these moments, and even if I were, what could I possibly say?

"I know, honey. I'm so sorry," was all I could muster, and I pulled him close while he cried on my shoulder.

"I'm just so glad I have second parents," he finally said.

"Me, too. I love you, honey."

"Me, too."

It's heavy and deep. I know the day will come when he asks, "Did she do it on purpose? Was she trying to leave me?" and I'll have to say, "Her only mistake was drinking that night. That's her mistake." She'd never leave those boys on purpose. I know that. Someday, when they're ready, I'll make sure they know that, too.

This isn't just parenting. It's trauma and grief and healing. And it is hard. But I'm so grateful he has us. I'm so grateful that we have him. I really do love those boys. Really.

Friday, June 25

Quiet time. The kids are at Mom and Dad's and then Lorri's house for the weekend—bonus points for the grandparents. OJ's in a golf tournament, and I am blissfully alone. I'm lying on the couch with the doors open to the cool summer air, breathing in the gentle monsoon afternoon. All day a word has been whispering to me: *Submit.* Submit—not just to this quiet space, but submit to the way life is.

Yesterday, OJ and I got in a heated argument, because *I* think I need more help and *he* thinks he's more helpful than he is—a classic couple's quarrel, I know. He is wonderful in so many ways, but I'm feeling the pinch of summer and he's been playing in more golf tournaments than ever. I want him to be happy. These tournaments make him happy, and he's so good and usually wins. Still, I need help at home, so it's hard to see golf as anything but his mistress most of the time. It's our constant tug-of-war. Over the years, I've tried every way to work it out—ignoring it, talking about it, nagging, arguing, begging. Yet, here we were again. Thank goodness yesterday I heard, "submit," and did. I let go of the rope. I submitted. I accepted that this was where we were, and it was a relief. We ended up having a *real* conversation, and I finally felt hopeful that we're in this summer madness together.

The same goes for me personally. I need to submit. "Let go and let God," as they say. I don't need a "to-do" list. I don't need to know if I'm doing everything I need to do. I just need to listen, to accept summer and where I am and what *is*.

I'm submitting. Knocking. Asking. Listening. Receiving. Obeying. And right now, napping.

Friday, July 2

For whatever reason, I awoke primed with fire and ready to spatter it all over. I've admittedly been a little on edge for the past couple days, but after a late night with Kennedy's sleepover friend crying for her mom and an early morning with Braxton's eyes stinging in pain, I feared I might fall off the edge today. I took Sydney for a walk and tried to "make a good day," to "suck it up"—and I did, for a while.

Then, I saw OJ, who had slept in, after ten hours of sleep, and felt my fire intensify. "I've got the fire in me today," I said, a friendly warning. He heard me and tried to spell out the ways he would be helpful today, including starting the built-in shelves we've been wanting in our bedroom, but I was definitely in no mood to help. I knew from experience my job today was simply to cope.

OJ started on the bookshelves while I, with great anxiety and guilt, took Sydney to the babysitter. Even though all the kids were home, I knew I needed a break from at least our spunky two year-old and calmed myself by repeating this fact in my head. I then hit the grocery store and, almost two hours later, returned home to find OJ, still "getting ready" for his project. *Deep breath.*

Okay. I'll just do a little housework then, I thought, but as I tried to go into the bedroom to get the laundry, OJ barred the door. "Do not come in!" he said, but it was too late. I'd already seen the ripped up carpet, cords flying like snakes from the walls, and the floorboards removed! He explained he needed to do some electrical work before he could start building the shelves. "Electrical work?" I asked. "Since when do you do electrical work?" I was having flashbacks to Colton's bum abscess surgery in the dental chair.

It soon became obvious that Braxton's eyes were not getting better, so we ended up at the eye doctor, the pharmacy, and then Little Caesar's to pick up pizza for the "starving" kids waiting at home. I walked in the door, threw down a couple slices of cheese to calm my grumbling tummy, and bravely made my way to the bedroom. Just as I'd feared—OJ's chaos continued. Now the saws and drills were sprawled out at the foot of our bed and large holes were cut into the wall, just for kicks. It had been four hours and no sign of a shelf.

Luckily, I heard that word in my mind again— *submit.* Almost simultaneously, I thought, *I should just go to the pool with the kids.* So, I did, and they were happy. I lay in the sunshine and attempted to read and relax a little, but Kennedy's sleepover friend was not a strong swimmer and needed attention and Kennedy was begging me to play with them. *Submit.* So, I played "mermaids" and floated Kennedy around the pool and forgot about reading or napping, feeling like a good mom for a while.

We headed home, and on the way I called and asked OJ to pick up Sydney, and Braxton's eye drops, so I wouldn't have to make a third trip to that side of town. I also hoped to squeeze in a quick break, knowing once precious Syd got home I would become her pet for the evening. Finally showered and dark chocolate in hand, I lay down on my bed, ready to veg out with a quick *Top Chef*, and guess what? The TV was out, thanks to OJ's "project" which was now going on six hours long.

OJ returned, feeling like the good guy, since he'd run my errands as I'd asked. "Sorry, hon," he said, handing me Syd, kissing me on the cheek, and heading back to the bedroom. "I've got to go finish my project." So, I got the kids playing together in front of a movie and sat on the couch with them, trying not to lose it. An hour later, even though OJ had gotten the electrical done and the room mostly put back together, it had been over seven and a-half hours and there were no shelves. He walked over to me and cluelessly asked, "What are you doin' for dinner?" *That's it!*

"*You* do whatever you want," I said, as composed as possible. "*You* are in charge! *I* am taking a night!" I walked to my room, and then yelled, "What happened to shelves?" before slamming the door. Quarantine time.

I knew he was disappointed and frustrated because he thought he was doing me a favor, and I was frustrated because I was doing him a favor, and I'm always doing him favors and he doesn't get it! After three hours, mostly alone, watching my two-star movie with chocolate, I was finally humbled, and no longer on the defense. Feeling defeated, disappointed and beaten up by myself, I heard a thought, *why don't you go check the calendar.*

Just as suspected, I was premenstrual. *Hormones. Again. Why does it always come as such a shock?* Perhaps I should watch my calendar a little more closely. Get a little more sleep. Try to avoid major stress during that week. Or just plan to quarantine. First, postpartum depression—several times. Now PMS. All I can say is…watch out, perimenopausal me. Watch out. *Ugh!* It's not gonna be pretty!

Saturday, July 3

Everything looks better after a good night's sleep—*and* a healthy dose of estrogen to re-regulate my brain. That's one of the most important things I've ever learned—that estrogen is a precursor to the neurotransmitters of the brain that make me feel well. When estrogen drops, like it does in the premenstrual week, so do my neurotransmitters. There is a very real reason I feel completely crazy several days each month![2]

After reminding myself of these important facts last night, I went to bed early, and feeling better this morning, OJ and I finally worked things out. Tears, hugs, "Sorrys," and we were ready for a family-focused day. We spent the morning and early afternoon at the Forest Highlands pool. Surrounded by vibrant green pine trees, the blue of the sky mirrored the blue of the water and brought a feeling of radiance and relaxation. Sydney has become a water monkey, jumping off the side of the pool like a bomb's exploding behind her, then crawling along the wall singing, "Monkey dance, monkey dance." Kennedy was decked out in goggles, swimming laps across the pool like a pro. OJ created a highly entertaining game for the boys and him I like to call "try to jump over Dad without getting flipped!" Everyone at the pool was rolling with laughter watching

OJ act like a ninja, flipping the boys right and left as they tried to dive over his head! We finished it off with cookies and snow cones for lunch, then headed home for a quick rest, and closed the day with a family bike ride to the park for a church party complete with barbecuing and playing football. A perfect summer day.

Tonight, I finally started my period. It's no coincidence I felt so much more "normal" today and no coincidence that tonight I'm thinking, "Get interested in others again. Get out of your box." In fact, there's a study from the 1930s in which researchers found women tend to focus more inward during the premenstrual week, needing more self-care and personal attention, and tend to focus more outward when estrogen starts building again, at the beginning of a new cycle.[3] That's me, to a T, and tonight, I want to focus outward again. I remember fondly my year of cheerfulness—how it pushed me to reach out to others more, to listen, to show love, to actively seek those who needed a little cheer. The truth is I haven't had that focus for a while. It's time to refocus, to reconnect.

I just read these words by Marianne Williamson, "And what is the light we see, when our minds are reconciled to Truth? We see not only that we are one with others, but also that all of us carry seeds of the divine."[4] I love helping others find their divine, for that is how I find mine. It's time to reach out again. Today, I started with my husband and family, but I can do more. "What matters is that you reconnect with love *now*, that your mind be healed of its insanity *now*, that you forgive yourself and others *now*."[5] Now. Yes. When it comes to loving, healing, and forgiving, there is absolutely no time to waste.

Friday, July 16
I drove all day and arrived in Utah at my charming hotel suite at 7:30 p.m. Tomorrow is the music

workshop I've been looking forward to for weeks. Going to this workshop is my attempt to start living life again. I'm not sure what to expect. I both believe in my musical talents and question them. I think I'm feeling intimidated, because this isn't just me singing to a room full of people in the middle of a seminar I'm giving. This is me in a room full of other talented singer/songwriters who are actively pursuing this as a career!

My brain says "that's silly," and I know it is. I'm the only one criticizing me—at least for now. I've worked my way through the layers of loss, pain, and grief of my past. Now I need to focus on what I *desire*— on creativity, connection, being inspired, and inspiring others. I love that word, "inspired." It means "in-spirited." I am in the spirit when I am inspired.

For too long I've been afraid to desire anything. It's as if, when life took its turn, I threw my hands up and said, "Okay! You take the wheel then!" And now I'm afraid to take it back. I've been afraid to desire anything because obviously God has His plan for me, and who am I to desire any differently? But I've been wrong. I know now. It's okay, and even good, to desire. It's part of the master plan for me—I will receive according as I desire. Not always, I know, but I'm still the one in the driver's seat and it's time I put my hands back on the wheel.

It's time to let go of the past—of doubt, of fear, of worry and thinking too much. It's time to submit to where I am and where I'm headed, to dream and desire, then get out there and finally believe.

Saturday, July 17

I'm getting out of my box. Today's music workshop was very interesting, learning about songwriting, producing music, making demos, being a vocalist, and all kinds of things I realize I have no clue about. Not only did I get great advice and tips, especially for better songwriting, I got motivation, and a little dose of reality, too.

No, I did not win anything in the songwriting competition. My song critiques were very honest, though constructive. *Isn't that what I asked for?* First, I apparently broke several "rules" of songwriting, which, to be fair, I only learned about in class today. As I heard the rules I knew I'd be in trouble! *Oh, well!* Then, I had to laugh because, as I listened to the critique for my song, *Overnight*, which I wrote about becoming a mother, the evaluator seemed hesitant. She said, "Uh, I'm confused about this song. You're talking about having a baby. It's sad and hard, but there are moments of goodness and love." She paused, and then added, "It's almost like you're writing about postpartum depression or something." *Duh!* Why did I submit that song? It *was* originally written about postpartum depression—for my video, *Postpartum Couples*—but I ended up not using it in the video, and now I only sing it at postpartum conferences and workshops where it is very well-received, I might add. I shook my head and laughed out loud. "Well, at least she got what it was about!" Hearing others' critiques is hard, especially when my songs are so personal. But I want it. I *need* honest feedback. It challenges me. It pushes me. And then…I grow.

One of the speakers today asked us to envision our perfect plan of how things would look for our music in the future. When I closed my eyes, I saw me as a full-time Mom, writing a book that is published and touches people. I'm asked to speak about the book, and as I speak, I share a song or two. As I share songs, people are touched. And someday, my kids are involved in music with me, too, an important part of our family as we grow. Such a clear image I saw! It was the first time someone's asked me to dream in quite a while, and I was grateful.

I also took away the fact that I don't have to

wait to work on singing, writing, songwriting, piano, guitar, and speaking. I may not be in a place right now where I can go out and share these talents, but if I work on them, when the opportunity finally comes, I will be ready.

Here's to being ready!

Sunday, July 18

I dressed up, got in my car this morning, and drove until I found an LDS church building with people walking in. I love listening to people from other places, and today was especially touching. In Relief Society, our women's class, a woman who'd been badly burned in a plane crash just two years ago spoke. Her adorable face and body had been scarred. Yet here she was today, speaking of faith, of family, of motherhood and the healing power of God, of love, and the beauty of life. I later learned her name was Stephanie Nielson, well-known writer of the "NieNie Dialogues" blog. [6] Her message today was a turning point for me. I wrote her an email when I got back to my hotel room, thanking her for her brief comments and for reminding me not to take a single thing for granted. It brought everything into clear focus.

Now, I'm sitting on the grounds of the Provo temple, quietly gazing at its unique circular structure and golden tipped steeple, and pondering how I got here. Here, in this peaceful place under the gaze of the impressive Wasatch mountains, here at the workshop yesterday, and right here, with time alone to think and to listen. Here, going to that particular building today. I finally get it. I've listened to the whispers, and now I'm beginning to see the perfect design of it all.

It's like Sydney, trying to put together the more challenging twenty-plus piece puzzles. She loves puzzles, but once she gets the idea that a piece goes a certain way or in a certain place, she gets stuck on it. She pushes and tries to force it in. I'll sit by, trying to guide her, and whisper, "Turn it around," or "No, not there." Sometimes she's still enough to hear me and will follow my guidance and direction. Many times, however, her effort is so all-consuming she doesn't seem to hear me at all.

That's me. Trying so hard. Giving it my all. Great, pure intentions. Desiring to do it "right." But pushing so hard, I don't hear the guidance. "Not there," "Turn it around," "Try another piece."

Tonight, I hear it. Tonight, I commit. I'm ready to obey the whispers, to give my all, to do whatever it takes. I will listen, and I will hear. Then, I can stand back and see the puzzle from a much more skilled and advantaged perspective—the eternal perspective. He whispers what to do. He always whispers. And I am listening.

THIRTY
Flourish

"Turn your face to the sun
and the shadows fall far, far behind.
Like a curtain opens up inside
and I'm dancing again
upon the stage of life."
~*Lyrics from my song,* Face to the Sun

Some time in the midst of grief and my year of Cheerfulness, I came across a page in a magazine with a photo of a sunny, tropical beach and the words: "Turn your face to the sun and the shadows will fall behind you."[1] Apparently, it's a Maori proverb. It was exactly what I needed to hear. I tore it out of the magazine and tucked it into the corner of my bathroom mirror. Those words picked me up on many a stumbling day, reminding me I can always choose the sunny option.

Although I spent an entire year staring at and even working on that phrase, it was some time before I understood its full meaning. It's more than choosing to smile instead of frowning or looking for the silver lining, though surely these are desirable practices. Turning one's face to the sun means actively *seeking* the very best of life. My primary training as a psychologist was on how to help people *overcome* their struggles—to help them feel "better." Through my own overcoming, I have discovered, at least for me, it's not good enough to just "feel better." I want to be my very best. Psychologist Martin Seligman once said, "We can clear a rose garden, but at some point we're going to have to plant a rose."[2] We can overcome our problems, but at some point, we're going to have to work on becoming who we are meant to be. We don't have to *settle* for just "better"; we can *seek* to be even "better than better."

The field of Positive Psychology calls this flourishing. What a great word, don't you think? When I hear "flourishing," my mind is swept to a garden with trees tall and shady as the afternoon, flowers dressed and dancing in radiant colors, leaves and bushes green as summer, and that little something extra that tells you the best is yet to come. *That* is flourishing—"to grow luxuriantly," to "thrive," "to prosper."[3]

Wouldn't we all love to flourish? Imagine being able to say, "I'm not just *better*, or even *well;* I am *flourishing!*" To me, it is a worthy goal. It reminds me that no matter my circumstances—whether I'm rich, poor, young, old, burdened with trials, or living carefree—I can overcome, become, *and* flourish! In fact, the way I see it, if we're choosing to grow, then at any given point we are all either overcoming some*thing*, becoming some*one*, or flourishing some*where*. We all have the power to grow "luxuriantly," to surpass our own expectations of what life has had to offer all along, to find that wink within.

I know there is a grander, simpler, masterful *something* out there for each and every one of us. There is a path of flourishing. The trick, however, is to make sure we don't stop our journey before we discover it. When we tap into that something—that path—when we continue to work, turning our face to the sun, we will flourish. It's what's waiting at the end of each seasonal cycle of growth—just like summer. That's what turning our face to the sun really means: living with purpose and intent, seeking the light in all things, allowing ourselves to flourish like summer, and letting the sun do what it does best—warm us up and help us grow.

"When life comes 'round and knocks you in the head,
stand up, plant your feet, and then
look up.
There are miles of sun ahead."[4]

Tuesday, August 10

It feels great to smile spontaneously. I'm finally getting the hang of joy. I'm not always "happy;" I still feel grumpy sometimes, especially when I'm tired. I still get moody thanks to hormones, and I make plenty of mistakes, like slipping into old habits of laziness, selfishness, or rejecting love. But...I'm also getting better. I'm *less* tired, *less* moody, and *less* grumpy than I've ever been. I work hard to remain open—to freely give and receive love—and I overcome laziness more often than not.

I still, and always will, have countless areas that need improvement. Yet they no longer overwhelm me; they simply motivate me to keep improving. For instance, I tend to be too serious. It makes sense. My life *has* been pretty serious for a while, but it's time to let go a little. I dream of being the kind of person who is fun and full of life, who inspires and uplifts anyone within my reach. So, I'm starting with laughter, which is not only healing, but also a sign I'm not taking myself too seriously. I smile on purpose and laugh as often as I can. I'm intentionally setting my focus on the things that matter and seeking daily connection and truth.

Today, I laughed out loud, and almost cried, when I saw all six kids squeezed into two and a half year-old Sydney's small, plastic playhouse, outside on the back deck. She has loved that little house, playing in there for hours. Today, she ran around the house, inviting everyone, "You wan come to my house? I'm habin' a party!" One-by-one, the kids showed up and rang her little doorbell. "Oh, hello!" she said. "Please do come in." First, Tre. Then, Kennedy. Then, Colton and Brody, and finally, Braxton. All squeezed into the four-by-three foot playhouse! As Sydney served them "tea" (water) and "cake" (Nilla wafers), they drank with their pinkies up, giggling as they praised her party-throwing and cooking skills. I watched through the open window, full of gratitude and wonder.

I'm finally learning to embrace the wise saying, "Come what may and love it."[5] I *do* love it. I love it *all*. Come what may.

Thursday, September 9

It's been a long time since I've written. School's in motion again, and so am I. With more kids at more schools with different schedules—preschool, elementary, junior high, and high school—and me trying to do my thing more, let's just say life is full, but so far I'm keeping up.

I guess I've taken the concept of flourishing to heart. I've rediscovered my passion for teaching and have been putting together several seminars that are all happening within a few weeks. Saturday was "Women's Emotional Health Across the Lifespan," and then next Friday, I teach "Perinatal Mood Disorders: Advanced Clinical Skills." The day after, it's "Train the Trainer" for my coalition's "Operation Education" program, and the next Wednesday I'm off to Utah to teach "Grief, Loss and the Family" and a half-day "Women's Emotional Health." I have my two-hour "Perinatal Mood Disorders: Assessment and Treatment" teleconference a week after that. Add in my regular work—clients, postpartum support group, coalition, and the Personal Growth Group I just started—and believe me, I am stretched. I'm even supposed to drive to Phoenix tomorrow for a four-minute spot on a talk show about men's postpartum depression. Yes, they get it too![6] It seems crazy since it's a four-hour drive, round-trip, but I am looking forward to a day off, to shop, have lunch, and just be me for a while.

Even though I'm busy right now, I feel a deep sense of meaning in what I do. Finally, I am putting the lessons from my personal life to good use, helping others grow, too. I feel I am fulfilling my life's purpose, not just in my career activities, but also as a mother and wife. I feel alive and kicking again and that means more joy for everyone. I delight in my children. I laugh more with OJ. I'm looking for joy, embracing joy, and sharing it. I'm appreciating the smaller, more meaningful moments, like not-quite three year-old Sydney telling me, "Nice pants," as I came home from work today, or Braxton still putting up with a hug from his mom now that he's fourteen and in full teenager mode. Like nine year-old Brody and eleven year-Colton "working out" together, and seven year-old Kennedy whispering, "I love you more than all the stars in all the universe." Like thirteen year-old Tre coming in to kiss me goodnight. I know better than to become too busy to take these moments for granted. If there's anything I have learned, it is that.

I'm also kinder to myself. I finally feel comfortable in my own skin. I've learned to see the good in me, to ignore the voice that tries to tell me I am weak, to embrace my weaknesses and see them as areas for future growth. Maybe that is the true key here: I really do feel comfortable with who I am, and that makes me comfortable not just in my body, but in my mind and soul. I feel my worth as a soul. Deeply. I truly love myself. *That* is my definition of joy—receiving the great love God has for me, allowing that love to fill me to the brim and spontaneously spill onto everyone I meet. I feel calmer. Less pressured. Less worried. *How did this occur?* Could it be I really am growing? Could it be this summery year has finally allowed me to bloom, and I have blossomed into the most amazing creature: *me*?

The other day I met someone new who asked what had happened when Tre and Brody came to live with us. Again, I told the story. "Oh, so you're their aunt?" the person asked. It jolted me to hear it. "I guess, technically, I am," I said, feeling protective and put on the spot. "But really," I added, "I am their mother."

Yes, it is fall again, and as I sit here bundled up and reflecting, I can see just how far I have come. I think back to three years ago, when I was merely coping—when any little thing felt so impossible. Today, things feel possible. I am changed. I really am growing. That is the truest joy to me.

Wednesday, October 13

Sunday will be three years since Shannon died. Three years. It sounds so long, yet feels so short.

This morning I woke with a start and a tear falling from my eye. My dreams are reminding me, again, of my fall. Last night's dream was so vivid. I wonder what it means?

It's my birthday. I'm dressed up, in my car, and heading to a birthday dinner where I'll meet OJ and my family and friends.

I'm in a hospital just like the one where Miki was sick when she had cancer, and I walk into a large, furnished living room with high ceilings, where Mom is apparently living. I'm here to take her to the party, but she's in the back room, not yet ready. I'm waiting for her, looking around, remembering she's lived in this hospital a long time, and trying to remember why she lives here.

My kids walk in. I hug them, and, just then, the ground starts rumbling. It's an earthquake. In fact, it's three earthquakes, one right after the other. Mom tells us to take shelter in the open, main area of the apartment, since the hospital doors and frames are old and unstable. I'm terrified of the earthquakes—scared for the kids and me, but Mom keeps doing her hair and make-up. She doesn't seem scared and acts like this is normal.

When the earthquakes are finally over and we are all safe, I ask, "Isn't it strange to have three earthquakes in like, three minutes?" No one replies. I start to feel like I should probably stay at the hospital a while to make sure everything is okay instead of going to my birthday dinner. I remember needing to stay and take care of Miki in this hospital, before. I wonder where

Miki is and think I should find her in the hospital and go take
care of her instead of going to my party.

I notice people gathering outside the French doors of
Mom's apartment, on the lawn. I walk to the doors and open
them. The group is growing, complete with friends and family, but
mostly with people I don't know. They've set up long tables and a
buffet and are loading up plates and sitting together, chatting. I
know they are here to celebrate my birthday, but I didn't want a
big gathering like this. They don't even seem to see me, let alone
ask what I want.

Dazed and disappointed, I walk outside, sit at a table,
and watch everyone eat with their families, enjoying themselves and
laughing. OJ sits down next to me, starts eating, and looks at me
expectantly. "So?" he asks, implying, "What do you think of your
party?" I just look at him, shrug, and start to cry.

When I awoke, it was hard to shake off the
anxiety and sadness. That's why I had to write. Writing
helps. I can already see the meaning of the dream much
more clearly. The three earthquakes represent three
years, and even though it may seem like "no big deal" to
anyone else, they are scary and real to me. During the
earthquakes, we had to seek shelter from the "open
space," instead of the old, unstable door frames—being
open was the only way to survive. The earthquakes
happened in a hospital, a place where people go to heal,
and specifically, the hospital where Miki had been ill.
Mom was living in that hospital, not yet ready to "move
on." I was helping her come to "the party." I was
visiting, hoping to quickly leave, feeling like I should stay
and even help others, but wanting to celebrate and enjoy
my loved ones instead. Clearly, I was conflicted. Even
when a party gathered "for me," I felt removed and
wasn't even seen. Everyone said they were there for me,
but it didn't feel that way, and it wasn't what I wanted. I
wanted something special and meaningful and not a big
gathering of people that didn't even notice.

I *am* conflicted. Life carries on around me and I

am moving on with it. Yet I don't always know how I fit into that life. Though I am changed, I can still feel odd, especially around others. For instance, we will be on a houseboat at Lake Powell with friends for the three-year anniversary, this Sunday. That's probably another reason why, in my dream, I was so concerned about being around others after the three earthquakes. No one remembers like I do and I don't want to just join their "party" and forget. Remembering is part of my healing. And my joy.

Just the other day I was reminded of Shannon when I saw Brody sitting on the floor with his knees together and his legs flat out to the sides on the ground, like an "M." Shannon sat just like that when we were little girls, and it made me feel like part of her was here. Or Tre, ever trying to please me, to make sure I know he loves me; he's just like his mother that way. I tell him that and we smile, *and* we work on it, not wanting him to feel the need to please like Shannon did. It reminds me how much she loved me and how good she was at showing her love. Strange how remembering Shannon can bring me joy now, but it does.

Yes, remembering is part of my healing and my joy, so I guess I don't need to worry about forgetting. Both my subconscious and conscious won't let me forget. The dream makes clearer my fears and concerns, yes. It also makes clear my strengths—that not only will I survive another "earthquake" this year, but that I will celebrate, in my own way.

Saturday, October 16

We arrived at Powell yesterday with our friends from dental school, Mike and Natalie, and our friends from home, Scott and Cyndy, and then enjoyed a day of relaxing conversation while navigating our floating house to the spot everyone deemed best. By the time everything was anchored, the sun was setting and we were feasting on a barbeque dinner. It felt good to be around friends again, to laugh and reconnect. But I opted out of the late-night bonfire on the beach because I'd been feeling tired and…oh, uncertain, I guess, about being here this weekend, surrounded by people, when I probably needed to be alone. Trying to sleep in my stateroom, alone I *was* as I heard OJ telling jokes and making everyone laugh, always the life of the party, while I was isolating and close to tears. I told myself it was just the fatigue, that I'd feel better in the morning, and then let myself fall asleep. The night was long as the boat next to ours stayed up partying, though. I barely slept at all.

Today was a new day, and a gorgeous one at that. I awoke early, walked out the open door, and was so inspired by the rising coral cliffs reflecting off the glassy water, I grabbed my walking shoes and OJ and headed for a hike. Exploring at dawn with the man I adore, honoring the reverence my surroundings seemed to show, the day was off to a great start.

Then, surprise. We were hiking in silence, when the noise started in my mind. First, a little anxious, then tense, then irritable, soon I was fighting internally, not wanting to do anything *externally* but mimic the calm of OJ and the world around us. We hiked to the tip of a cliff and stood still, watching the sun creep over the towering sandstone across the lake.

OJ sat on a rock, taking it all in, but my mind was making it hard for me to do the same. *I'm too tired. I can't take another night of those people partying. We need to move our boat. But no one else will want to do that. Why can't I just sleep easily like everyone else? They're going to think I'm such a whiner. Why is it so hard for me to be in groups? Why am I thinking about all this right now? This view is incredible. I'm going to make this a good day, no matter what.*

I looked at OJ, leaning back on a rock, soaking up the sun. His eyes were closed, and he was smiling. I didn't want to ruin his morning, but I had to say something. "We need to move our boat. I can't take another sleepless night." His smile faded, but his eyes stayed closed.

"I don't want to discuss this right now," he said. "It's chill."

It is *chill,* I thought, *but* I *am not.* That's when the surprise *really* hit—I began to cry. I sat with my hands in my head and felt so—what? I had no idea. I couldn't understand what all this was, and I definitely couldn't explain it to OJ when he asked. I couldn't tell him what to do. I couldn't even talk. "Can you please give me some time alone?" I finally asked. "I can't do this with you here. I'm sorry." So, he left.

Confused and alone, I cried harder. I stood and made myself hike up the hills to my right, trying to work things out and slow the tears. Finally, I made it to the top of the cliff and moved to the very edge, fifty feet above the water. Peering over and gazing at the majestic view before me, I did all I could think to do—pray. *Why am I feeling like this?* I asked. *Please help me through this. Please help me understand.* Then, I sat and listened.

Before long, the facts became clear. First, I *was* way too tired, and that always clouds my emotions. It makes me feel like the sun has completely disappeared. *You know better, though,* I reminded myself. *The sun is always there.* Second, I wanted OJ. I'd wanted him to be with me last night instead of going to the bonfire and being the social butterfly. I'd pushed him away today because of it, but I still wanted him with me. *You know better,* I reminded myself. *It's just as important to receive love as to give.* Third, I did need to be alone, yet felt confined to being social, not wanting to disappoint OJ or my friends. Because, fourth, *You know what this has to do with. It has to do with Shannon and it has to do with you.*

Tomorrow would be three years since Shannon died and there was more going on in me than I wanted to show. *I'm supposed to be here, having "fun" with my friends,* I thought. I wanted that fun, that connection, that pleasure, but the truth was I could see my scars most clearly when they were set against the ease of other people. I could feel all the years of emotion, of anger, sorrow, grief, pain, and fear. I could also feel the love. Love for Shannon, love for Rob. Love for my children and for OJ. And love for me. Yes, I wanted this year to be about remembering Shannon and to be about love.

As I sat on the ledge and watched the sun, now full over the lake, the only sound was the gentle lap of the water. I matched its stillness, slowing my breath, feeling, and letting it out. The frustration started lifting. I was getting beneath it to the good stuff.

That's when I heard what sounded like a huge fish struggling along the water's edge. It was loud and crashing. As I looked down to examine its source, I was surprised. It wasn't a fish at all, but waves pummeling the shore. It seemed so out of place, these waves in the midst of a tranquil morning. *Where did they come from?*

Then I remembered the boat that had passed several minutes before. The boat was long gone, but the waves continued to pound the shore. Almost simultaneously, I recognized this was me. Waves suddenly crashing, with no apparent cause. Waves that, once crashed, had settled on the shore. It made me wonder what my boats had been and how long the waves would last this time. It also gave me hope. Hope that perhaps my waves were finally settling. Hope that, this year, I might be the one driving the boat, leaving the waves behind.

I took a deep breath, smiled at the sun, and, filled with a new determination, set off to find OJ who was already moving our boat to a better spot. It was going to be a good day after all. We were both going to make it so.

Sunday, October 17

I call every October seventeenth "Shannon Day." It's just after sunrise and I've wandered from camp, needing to start this day right, to do it my way.

Sitting in the morning shade of the red and pink striped cliffs as the sun crawls up and into the sky, my journal and pen are in hand. I watch the smooth water and imposing clouds in the distance. The clouds can come as they may. It's okay. The sun is still here. That's how I feel inside. I can remember the pain, yet see through the dark little clouds to the sunny core—to hope, joy, healing, and love. I can finally accept the clouds and let them come and rain when they need to. The rain helps things grow, even in times of summer. I crave growth. So, let it rain.

A crow was just flying, high over my head. In the silence of my thoughts on paper, the sound of his flapping wings was startling and unmistakable. I set my writing aside, leaned back, and watched as he worked. He began to propel himself higher and higher. Circling and flapping, it seemed like such an effort and I wondered, *Is it worth it?*

As I was explaining to OJ, and probably to myself, last night, it's not like I think, "I have to be sad because today is the day Shannon died." I actually resist, not wanting to feel sad at all, but this whole time of year seems to carry the past on the wind, and I'm not certain why it still surprises me. *Surely after three years, it shouldn't hurt anymore,* I tell myself. I tell myself a lot of things, and it still does. As I know, *what I resist persists.* I'd better follow my lesson from summer and just *submit.*

So, I am, and as I submit I feel—nervous, uncertain of what I *do* feel and what I *should* feel and what I should or shouldn't *do.* I also feel calm. At peace. Ready to move on. *Maybe I can enjoy today, even though it's Shannon Day.* I feel grateful for so much good in my life and in the world, for my family and the spirit that whispers, for lessons learned and yet to be learned, for opportunities to come and those already taken. I am grateful for a life of meaning—for hope and joy and love—on all days and especially today.

I miss Shannon. We've been through a lot together these past three years. Yet I'm also ready to forgive us both, to let go of the hard stuff and move on. I'm sad for how we've had to experience her death—for the trauma seared into my brain and heart and the holes that still ache when they are meant to. *And* I'm grateful that they still ache. *"The deeper that sorrow carves into your being, the more joy you can contain."*

Looking back up at the crow, just now, he suddenly seemed to hang in the air. *Goodbye, Shannon,* I unexpectedly whispered, a smile embracing me as tears wet my eyes. The crow let go and dipped and dove and carved the sky as I watched in awe. *Hello, Shannon,* I unexpectedly felt, welcoming her home, where she belongs, to my heart. The crow continued to soar. In a moment of bliss, I shared his flight. He was free. I was free.

As he almost hit the water, he beautifully swooped, then began to flap. He'll have more work to do now, to climb again, but I'll bet next time he'll flap even higher. One day, perhaps he'll reach the stars, his soaring even more exquisite—full of peace, light, and all things good. I'm reminded of a poem I once read…

> *"A crow is said to fly in a straight line from point of departure to destination, but that is not what I see. Crows fly in sweeping circular arcs across the apron of the sky, using all the available space from horizon to horizon before settling on the top-swaying branch of the tallest tree. You may think crows caw, that their voices are harsh. But I tell you a crow can whisper to its mate across a density of pines, and its voice is comfortable and reassuring. A crow is mighty in its passion, voracious in its appetite, and fearless in its flight. So I aspire to live as*

the crow flies and stretch my soul to meet the sky."[8]

I am finally ready to let myself fly. Ready to "stretch *my* soul to meet the sky." Ready for joy. Ready to love. Ready to flourish and grow. *Luxuriantly.*

EPILOGUE
Love

"What we obtain too cheap we esteem too lightly.
It is dearness only that gives life its value."
~*Thomas Payne*

Although mine is a story of growing, it really is a story of love. Love for children, new and old, love for husband and family. Love for God and life, for what *is* and what is to come, and ultimately, love for my sister and myself.

My year of Love followed my years of Patience, Gratitude, Cheerfulness, and Joy. It was the perfect final lesson to complete my seasons of growth. In fact, it wasn't until my year of Love that I began to find the perspective for which I'd so desperately been searching all those years. The pieces of my puzzling seasons had finally been placed, and I could now see the bigger picture: that my four years' themes *were* the path of growth. Patience, gratitude, cheerfulness, and joy led me to overcome, become, and eventually, flourish. Yet there was one missing piece to this path for how to grow, even though it had been there all along: Love.

Love is the underlying, unifying factor in all seasons of life. It is through love we grow the most. Love is patience through fall, gratitude through winter, cheerfulness in spring, and joy in summer. Love is the reason for patience, the measure of gratitude, the hope of cheerfulness, and the seed of joy. Love gives us the "why" and shows us the "how." It is the source from which all good things spring. Love is everything.

At its core, love is really about growth—growth of our spirit and mind and heart, growth, both body and soul. Growth is really about love. When hard times come our way, we can *go* through them, or we can choose to *grow* through them, and when we choose to grow, we do so out of love. When we help others grow, we reach our most loving potential. My favorite definition of love explains what I mean. "I define love thus: The will to extend one's self for the purpose of nurturing one's own or another's spiritual growth."[1] As we nurture and love our family, neighbors, world, and self, we grow, together, in love.

We need each other. We can only grow as high as our roots go deep, and our roots are our family, our faith, our friends. Our roots are made of love, without which we would topple at the first sign of wind. But loved, we are strong and able to withstand anything. Love comes from God and nature and light, and fills us, if we let it, like a well that never runs dry. As we receive this love, we become so full of love it pours out of our eyes and mouth and arms, filling those around us, too. Love cannot be kept, but must be given and received again—a continuous cycle that, when complete, generates greater and higher love. Yes, choosing to grow is choosing to love.

Looking back through my seasons of growth, I now see I learned the most about love. I understand love now. I know love. I know better than to ever take love for granted again. I not only made it through my seasons of growth, but my family and I grew through them; we grew in love. The seasons continue to come and go, as seasons do, and I continue to seek the lesson from whatever season I am in and to help my family do the same. I now know each cycle of seasons can be distinct—different in intensity, meaning, and purpose. Fall isn't always forced upon us. It can be a new opportunity, a *choice* to grow. Winter, instead of darkness and depression, can be a time of purposeful reflection. Spring can be more about warmth and blooming than unpredictable wind and snow. Summer can be a time of pure pleasure and fun, enjoying the blessed moments with those we love. We can't stop the growing seasons any more than a child can stop their physical growth, but we can appreciate the season we're in and choose to grow through it.

I would say it's ironic that this part of my story ended at Lake Powell, yet here I sit at the same lake, writing this epilogue. But it's not ironic; like everything else, there is a reason, there is a purpose. Being here with my family, three years later, has shown me who I am today. Patiently nurturing each child, filled with gratitude for all we have endured and succeeded, I am cheerfully embracing this opportunity to be here together. I am full of joy. I see my family's joy and peace, how the kids behave like normal siblings—shoving each other into the lake, daring one another, arguing, teasing. Just like Shannon and I used to do. As OJ drives the ski boat in zigzags, trying to dump the boys off the tube into the water, the other kids laugh and cheer. And so do I. Life continues. And so do we. Both OJ's and my families continue to be a source of strength and love for us. Sadly, the Cutlers have chosen not to be part of our lives. Our story may come back to haunt us from time to time, and we may still have our struggles, but mostly, we're just a family. That's all I have ever wanted: to be a normal family, made through love.

Yes, this is a story of growth, but also a story of love, as all stories are. Love lost, love gained, love learned or forsaken—there's only one thing that matters as we choose to grow. Love. At the start, I asked, "What will *your* choice be?" Whatever kind of mud life has thrown you into—whether the loss of a relationship, loved one, or career, life-altering medical, mental health, or financial struggles, or even daily hardships that never seem to quit, choose to plant yourself and grow. Choosing to grow *is* choosing love. No matter what season of growth you are in, choose love, my friends. Every time.

Our family, 2013. (Photo by Mechelle Felsted.)

Notes and References

Chapter 1
[1] Eccles. 31:1,3 (King James Version).
[2] Karen Kaiser Clark, *Life is Change, Growth is Optional* (CEP Publications, 1998).

Chapter 2
[1] Christina G. Hibbert, *Live Strong,* song lyrics, in memory of Rob, 2007.
[2] Ibid.

Chapter 3
[1] Stuart K. Hine, *How Great Thou Art*, Hymns of The Church of Jesus Christ of Latter-Day Saints (Salt Lake City: The Church of Jesus Christ of Latter Day Saints, 1985), 86.

Chapter 4
[1] Lowrie M. Hofford and Harrison Millard, *Abide with Me; Tis Eventide*, Hymns of The Church of Jesus Christ of Latter-Day Saints (Salt Lake City: The Church of Jesus Christ of Latter Day Saints, 1985), 165.
[2] Ibid.
[3] Luke 22:42, (KJV).
[4] Christina G. Hibbert, *Her Smile*, song lyrics, in memory of Shannon, 2007.

Chapter 6
[1] *Microsoft Encarta Dictionary,* s.v. "paradox."
[2] For more on the baby blues and postpartum depression, visit my series, "Postpartum Depression Treatment," on my website: www.DrChristinaHibbert.com.

Chapter 8
[1] Judith Orloff, *Emotional Freedom: Liberate Yourself from Negative Emotions and Transform Your Life* (New York: Three Rivers Press, 2009), 38.
[2] Victor Frankl, *Man's Search For Meaning: An Introduction to Logotherapy, 4th ed.* (Boston: Beacon, 1992), 166.
[3] Ibid.

Chapter 9
[1] Frankl, *Man's Search For Meaning*, 104.

2 Elizabeth Gilbert, *Eat, Pray, Love* (New York: Penguin Press, 2006), 171.
3 Gilbert, *Eat, Pray, Love*, 155.
4 Gilbert, *Eat, Pray, Love*, .156.

Chapter 10
1 Thornton Wilder, http://www.goodreads.com/author/quotes/44061.Thornton_Wilder (accessed October 2013).

Chapter 11
1 Orloff, *Emotional Freedom*, 76.
2 3 Nephi 22:13 (*The Book of Mormon: Another Testament of Jesus Christ*).
3 F. Scott Fitzgerald, http://www.goodreads.com/quotes/2368-show-me-a-hero-and-i-ll-write-you-a-tragedy (accessed October 2013).
4 For more on "Thought Records" and how to use them, visit my post, "Thought Management, Part 2," on my blog: http://www.drchristinahibbert.com/thought-management-part-2-how-to-change-your-thinking-and-your-life-using-a-thought-record-video/.

Chapter 12
1 For more on grief and loss, visit my series, "Dealing with Grief," on my website: www.DrChristinaHibbert.com.
2 Judith Bernstein, *When the Bough Breaks: Forever After the Death of a Son or Daughter* (Kansas City: Andrews McMeel Publishing, LLC, 1997), 5.
3 Anne Morrow Lindbergh as quoted in Bernstein, *When the Bough Breaks: Forever After the Death of a Son or Daughter,* 101.
4 C.S. Lewis, *Mere Christianity* (San Francisco: Harper Collins, 2001), 174.
5 Robert Robinson, *Come Thou Fount of Every Blessing,* Arranged by Mack Willberg (Oxford: Oxford University Press, 2013).
6 Therese Rando, *Grief, Dying, & Death: Clinical Interventions for Caregivers* (Champaign, IL: Research Press, 1984), 20.

Chapter 13
1 As quoted in *Mimi Guarneri, The Heart Speaks: A Cardiologist Reveals the Secret Language of Healing* (New York: Touchstone Publishing, 2007).
2 Mark Nepo, *The Book of Awakening: Having the Life You Want by Being Present in the Life You Have* (San Francisco: Conari Press, 2000), 22.

[3] For more information about Postpartum Support International, please visit www.postpartum.net.

[4] For more information about The Arizona Postpartum Wellness Coalition, please visit www.azpostpartum.org.

[5] For information on my Postpartum Couples DVD, please visit www.postpartumcouples.com.

Chapter 14

[1] Mark Nepo, *The Exquisite Risk: Daring to Live an Authentic Life* (New York: Harmony Books, 2005), 7.

[2] To learn more about The Relief Society of The Church of Jesus Christ of Latter-Day Saints, please visit http://mormon.org/faq/relief-society.

[3] For more on overcoming worry, visit my post, "The Worry Tree," on my blog: http://www.drchristinahibbert.com/the-key-to-worry-free-the-worry-tree/.

Chapter 15

[1] For more on how to FEEL, visit my post, "FEEL: How to Cope with Powerful Emotions": http://www.drchristinahibbert.com/feel-how-to-cope-with-powerful-emotions-video/.

[2] Iyanla Vanzant, interview by Oprah Winfrey (How She Lost Her Marriage, Her House, Her Fortune: Iyanla Vanzant, Part 2), *The Oprah Winfrey Show*, Own Network, February 23, 2011.

[3] Rando, *Grief, Dying and Death: Clinical Interventions for Caregivers*, 15-40.

[4] Melanie Klein, as quoted in Bernstein, *When the Bough Breaks: Forever After the Death of a Son or Daughter*, 82.

Chapter 16

[1] Anonymous, www.thinkexist.com (accessed June, 2011).

[2] George Iles, http://www.goodreads.com/quotes/562997-hope-is-faith-holding-out-its-hand-in-the-dark (accessed October 29, 2013).

[3] Friedrich Neitzche as quoted in Frankl, *Man's Search for Meaning*, 97.

[4] Frankl, *Man's Search for Meaning*, 97-98.

[5] Oscar Wilde, http://www.goodreads.com/quotes/25-we-are-all-in-the-gutter-but-some-of-us (accessed October 29, 2013).

[6] Eliza R. Snow and James McGranahan, *O My Father,* Hymns of The Church of Jesus Christ of Latter-Day Saints (Salt Lake City: The Church of Jesus Christ of Latter Day Saints, 1985), 292.

[7] Jacob 3:1-2 (*The Book of Mormon*).

[8] For more on women and depression, visit my article, "Women & Depression: Facts, Understanding, & Seeking Help," on my website: http://www.drchristinahibbert.com/education/womens-mental-health/women-depression/.

Chapter 17
[1] *Webster's New World Dictionary,* 3rd College Ed., s.v. "grow."
[2] For more on growing, visit my post, "GROW," on my blog: http://www.drchristinahibbert.com/g-r-o-w/.
[3] Will L. Thompson, *Put Your Shoulder to the Wheel,* Hymns of The Church of Jesus Christ of Latter-Day Saints (Salt Lake City: The Church of Jesus Christ of Latter Day Saints, 1985), 252.
[4] For more on depression and medication, visit my post, "Antidepressant? Or Not?: 12 Facts on Depression and Medication," on my blog: http://www.drchristinahibbert.com/antidepressant-or-not-12-facts-depression-medication/.

Chapter 18
[1] Proverbs 17:22 (KJV).
[2] Hamlet, ed. Wilbur L. Cross and Tucker Brooke (New York: Barnes & Noble by arrangement with Yale University Press, 2005) 2.2.259-260. References are to act, scene and line.
[3] Christina G. Hibbert, *Lovey Lullaby,* song lyrics, 2007.
[4] Ibid.

Chapter 19
[1] Eckhart Tolle, *A New Earth: Awakening to Your Life's Purpose* (New York: Dutton/Penguin Group, 2005), 115.
[2] Abraham Lincoln, http://www.goodreads.com/quotes/25634-i-will-prepare-and-some-day-my-chance-will-come (accessed October 29, 2013).

Chapter 20
[1] Brené Brown, *The Gifts of Imperfection: Let Go of Who You Think You're Supposed to Be and Embrace Who You Are* (Center City, Minn: Hazeldon, 2010), 4.
[2] *Webster's New World Dictionary,* 3rd College Ed., s.v. "perfect."
[3] Brown, *The Gifts of Imperfection,* 56.
[4] *Wikipedia,* s.v. *Perfection,* from *Delta of the Metaphysics,* http://en.wikipedia.org/wiki/Perfection (accessed October 30, 2013).
[5] Tolle, *A New Earth: Awakening to Your Life's Purpose,* 108-109.
[6] Ibid, 109.

[7] Richard Carlson, *Don't Sweat the Small Stuff—And It's All Small Stuff: Simple Ways to Keep the Little Things from Taking Over Your Life* (New York: Hyperion, 1997), 131.

Chapter 21
[1] William Paul Young, *The Shack, Where Tragedy Confronts Eternity: A Novel* (Newbury Park, CA: Windblown Media, 2011), 230.
[2] Mosiah 2:17 (*The Book of Mormon*).

Chapter 22
[1] Winston Churchill, http://www.goodreads.com/quotes/11419-kites-rise-highest-against-the-wind-not-with-it (accessed October 31, 2013).

Chapter 23
[1] Hermann Hesse, http://www.goodreads.com/quotes/168037-some-of-us-think-holding-on-makes-us-strong-but (accessed October 29, 2013).
[2] John 8:32 (KJV).
[3] Christina G. Hibbert, *Opportunity*, song lyrics, 2002.
[4] Christina G. Hibbert, *You've Got an Angel,* song lyrics, 2009.

Chapter 25
[lxxiii] Ram Dass, http://thehappymindbook.com/2192, *Healing Quotes*, (accessed February 19, 2012).
[lxxiv] Jack Kornfield, *Buddha's Little Instruction Book* (New York: Bantam Books, 1994), 31.
[lxxv] Leo Buscaglia, http://www.goodreads.com/quotes/109527-don-t-hold-to-anger-hurt-or-pain-they-steal-your (accessed September 9, 2013).

Chapter 26
[1] Toba Beta, *Master of Stupidity,* www.goodreads.com (accessed September 9, 2013).
[2] *Webster's New World Dictionary,* 3rd College Ed., s.v. "try."
[3] C. Terry Warner, *For the Power is in Them: Finding Peace in Tribulation,* lecture (Association of Mormon Counselors and Psychotherapists, Salt Lake City, UT, October, 2009).
[4] M. Catherine Thomas, lecture (Peoria North Stake Women's Conference Address, Peoria, AZ, February, 2010).
[5] Buddhist teaching, http://www.goodreads.com/quotes/33922-when-the-student-is-ready-the-teacher-will-appear (accessed October 31, 2013).

[6] M. Catherine Thomas, *Light in the Wilderness: Explorations in the Spiritual Life* (Orem; Amalphi Publishing, 2008), 93.

Chapter 27
[1] Mark Twain, http://www.goodreads.com/quotes/1708-forgiveness-is-the-fragrance-that-the-violet-sheds-on-the (accessed October 31, 2013).
[2] This idea was adapted from James Ferrell, *The Peacegiver: How Christ Offers to Heal Our Hearts and Homes* (Salt Lake City: Deseret Book, 2004).
[3] Lewis B. Smedes, http://www.brainyquote.com/quotes/authors/l/lewis_b_smedes.html (accessed September 26, 2013).
[4] Thomas, *Light in the Wilderness,* 173-4.
[5] Thomas, *Light in the Wilderness,* quoting Brigham Young, 188.
[6] Thomas, *Light in the Wilderness,* quoting Richard G. Scott, 193.

Chapter 28
[1] T.S. Eliot, http://www.brainyquote.com/quotes/quotes/t/tseliot101421.html (accessed February 10, 2012).

Chapter 29
[1] John M. Pontius, *Following the Light of Christ Into His Presence* (Springville, UT: Cedar Fort, 2011), 99.
[2] For more on the menstrual cycle and mood, visit my "Women's Emotions" series, on my blog: http://www.drchristinahibbert.com/womens-emotions-part-3-the-menstrual-cycle-mood/.
[3] As found in Christiane Northrup, *The Wisdom of Menopause: Creating Physical and Emotional Health and Healing During The Change* (New York, NY: Bantam Books, 2001).
[4] Deepok Chopra, Debbie Ford, & Marianne Williamson, *The Shadow Effect: Illuminating the Power of Your True Self* (New York, NY: HarperOne, 2011), 174.
[5] Ibid, 174.
[6] Visit Stephanie Nielson's beautiful blog at http://nieniedialogues.blogspot.com.

Chapter 30
[1] Maori Proverb, http://tinybuddha.com/wisdom-quotes/turn-your-face-toward-the-sun-and-the-shadows-will-fall-behind-you/ (accessed October 31, 2013).

[2] Martin Seligman, *Positive Psychology and Positive Interventions*, lecture (Evolution of Psychology Conference Address, Anaheim, CA, December, 2010).

[3] *Merriam-Webster Online*, s.v. "flourishing," http://www.merriam-webster.com/dictionary/flourishing?show=0&t=1383280529 (accessed October 31, 2013).

[4] Christina G. Hibbert, *Face to the Sun*, song lyrics, 2011.

[5] Elder Joseph B. Wirthlin, *Come What May and Love It* (Church of Jesus Christ of Latter-Day Saints General Conference Address, October 2008).

[6] For more on men and postpartum depression, visit my post, "Postpartum Depression and Men: The Facts on Paternal Postnatal Depression": http://www.drchristinahibbert.com/postpartum-depression-men-the-facts-on-paternal-postnatal-depression/.

[7] Khalil Gibran, http://thinkexist.com/quotation/the_deeper_that_sorrow_carves_into_your_being_the/339174.html (accessed October 31, 2013).

[8] Elizabeth Tarbox, *I Aspire to Live as the Crow Flies,* from *Evening Tide: Meditations,* (Boston, MA: Skinner House Publications, 2011). Reprinted with permission from Sarah Tarbox.

Epilogue

[1] M. Scott Peck, *The Road Less Traveled: A New Psychology of Love, Traditional Values, and Spiritual Growth* (New York, NY: Touchstone, 1979), 81.

Acknowledgements

I set out to write this book to heal myself. I had no idea how well my plan would work, nor how this book would bring me together with those I love and heal my relationships, too. People often said to me, "I don't know how you do it." Truth was, I wasn't sure how I was doing it half the time, either. But I did know one thing: I couldn't do it alone. My Heavenly Father inspired, whispered, and let me to those who could help me best. I can't express how grateful I am for God's wisdom, mercy, and unending love. We all need a village, and no time is that more true than in raising children and publishing a book. To all who have been my village, I thank you...

First and foremost, to my children, without whom I would have no great stories to share. Someday you'll understand why I wrote this book. I hope it helps you heal as much as it's helped me. It may not be easy keeping up with six active children, but you have been patient and helpful as I have been immersed in this work. I am grateful to still feel like a stay-at-home mom, even while pursuing my dreams, and love nothing in the world better than each of you. Now, go pursue yours!

To my family—my mother and father, sisters, Ashley and Leighton, and brother, Bud. Thank you for supporting my decision to share this story that, while mine, is yours, too. Our family has been through so much, and it's time for healing. We may not always see eye-to-eye, but I know you love me dearly. I love you each, too. How grateful I am for a family who not only supports me, but who loves and cares for my own family, too. We *all* love each of you.

To Jen Peterson, my first editor. Your encouragement gave me the audacity to dare, and your hours of listening and editing, and words of support, kept me going when times got rough. Without you, this book would not be. Thank you.

To Lorri—for the years of friendship and love, and for being a second mother to me. Our late-night phone sessions improved my writing and warmed my heart. And to dear Dave, for showing OJ how to be a loving father and husband, and for loving me. Together, you two were there through the rough times, and Lorri, you continue to be. I am grateful, and I love you both.

To the rest of my Hibbert family, for supporting our family through our toughest years, for believing in me and in us, and letting me share part of your story, too. I am a true Hibbert, and what a ride it is!

To Dave Eaton, my web marketing and branding specialist, for so much... Without you, I would never have had the guts to publish this book, nor would I have a successful website and my next book contract. I can't thank you enough.

To Becky Bagley, for stepping in as my editor these past months. For elevating my story and writing, for pulling the deeper details and truths out of me. It's been such a joy to rekindle our almost thirty-year friendship over this book. You are one of my greatest cheerleaders, and truly deserve your nickname, "Becky-the-Bomb!" (And thank you for my nickname, too.) ~MD, Madame Dynamo

To Denise Vitola. I thank you for your inspired editing. Your suggestions saved me from "but" and "and" embarrassment, and elevated my writing to a new level. This book is much cleaner and clearer because of you.

To Kristin McGuire Call, for your inspired cover, logo, and website designs. For really "getting" me, and for your patience as we worked to get it just right. It *is* just right. All of it.

To Joani Plenty, book campaign manager and social media strategist extraordinaire! For your "bahaha" texts, for keeping me motivated, and for always pulling through with some "Wow!" moment when I needed it most.

To Anna LaBenz, for making me look so good, and for the years of inspiring one another. To Jen Strand, for doing the deed I did not want to do—creating my notes and references section! You saved me on that one! And to Rachelle Ayala, for formatting my print book. The stress you removed from me, and your skill in doing so, saved me, too.

To Liz Pinney, who cared for my little girls, and Maritza and Lucy Vasquez, who have cared for my home. Without each of you, I would have been in the loony bin! And to those who donated spaces to me, to clear my mind and write—because with six kids, it's hard to do at home! To The Fletcher Family, Lorri Hibbert, and OJ's friend I've never even met, Grayson, thank you.

To Julie de Azevedo Hanks—for your friendship and calls of support, and for being my social media guru, helping me start my website, blog, and brand with a crash course at your home! Now, *that* is friendship.

To the early readers of the book—Jen Peterson, Carole Sheehan, Emily Davis, Jen Strand, and Benta Simms—for your patience, encouragement, and gentle guidance. And to all those who inspired and encouraged me early on, in other ways—Kris Palouda, Jennifer de la Fuente, Natalie Allen, and Jared Stewart, especially.

For feedback, criticism, and advice that shaped this memoir into a true story, I thank Jane Dystel and Miriam Goderich. It's tough to be told what's wrong with a project so dear to my heart, but your words encouraged me to make the tough choices and find my voice.

For the love, support, and feedback of so many friends—Jen Peterson, Natalie Allen, Elisa All, Leonore Driggs, Cyndy Mickelson, Emily Davis, Lynette Austin, and the book clubs who reviewed all or part of my book before its completion and provided critical feedback—Leonore's and Tracey's Book Club, Becky's Book Club, and the Walnut Canyon Ward book club. I can't thank you each enough!

To Wendy Millstine and New Harbinger, for believing in me enough to publish my next book while encouraging me to move forward with this one. Knowing I am now part of the New Harbinger family gave me the courage I needed to complete this great task! And thank you to Melissa Foster, for your e-course and formatting services, and everyone in the World Literary Café Facebook group, who answered endless questions and pointed me in the right direction.

And to all who have supported my husband, kids, and me over the years, I thank you. Though I may not have mentioned you in the book, I have not forgotten your acts of kindness, words of comfort, and warm embraces.

Finally, and most importantly, to OJ. You're right, dear. I could never have done this without you. Your words of encouragement, your help with the kids, the times when you shoved me out the door for days or a week to go write—I know you did all of these things because you love me. What a blessing it is to know I am so loved. *You* are my greatest blessing. Who can believe the path we have already travelled, and who knows what the future will bring? All I can say is I am deeply grateful to get to travel this path with you. I everything you.

About the Author

Dr. Christina Hibbert is a clinical psychologist and expert on women's mental health, perinatal mood disorders, grief and loss, motherhood, parenting, self-esteem/self-worth, and personal growth. Dr. Hibbert is the Founder of the Arizona Postpartum Wellness Coalition, the producer of the internationally-sold DVD, *Postpartum Couples,* a contributor for 30Second Mom, and Creator of the popular blog, *The Psychologist, The Mom, & Me.* A dynamic speaker, Dr. Hibbert is also a singer-songwriter and often uses original songs in her speaking engagements. Mostly, though, "Christi" is a wife and mother, and lives with her husband and six children in Flagstaff, AZ. Look for Dr. Hibbert's upcoming book with New Harbinger Publications on the topic of self-esteem after a breakup, to be released in Spring 2015.

Learn more about Dr. Christina Hibbert's blog, speaking schedule, newsletter, and companion materials for *This is How We Grow,* and join her free, online, *"This is How We Grow* Personal Growth Group" by visiting her website: **www.DrChristinaHibbert.com.**

Connect with Dr. Hibbert!
Facebook Pages: Facebook.com/drchibbert
Facebook.com/thisishowwegrow
Twitter: @DrCHibbert
Pinterest: Pinterest.com/drchibbert
Instagram: @drchristi_hibbert

Made in the USA
San Bernardino, CA
26 April 2014